Difference without Domination

Difference without Domination

PURSUING JUSTICE
IN DIVERSE DEMOCRACIES

Edited by Danielle Allen and Rohini Somanathan

The University of Chicago Press CHICAGO AND LONDON

The University of Chicago Press, Chicago 60637
The University of Chicago Press, Ltd., London
© 2020 by The University of Chicago
All rights reserved. No part of this book may be used or
reproduced in any manner whatsoever without written
permission, except in the case of brief quotations in critical
articles and reviews. For more information, contact the
University of Chicago Press, 1427 E. 60th St., Chicago, IL 60637.
Published 2020

29 28 27 26 25 24 23 22 21 20   1 2 3 4 5

ISBN-13: 978-0-226-68119-1 (cloth)
ISBN-13: 978-0-226-68122-1 (paper)
ISBN-13: 978-0-226-68136-8 (e-book)
DOI: https://doi.org/10.7208
/chicago/9780226681368.001.0001

Library of Congress Cataloging-in-Publication Data

Names: Allen, Danielle S. 1971– editor. |
Somanathan, Rohini, editor.
Title: Difference without domination : pursuing
justice in diverse democracies / edited by
Danielle Allen and Rohini Somanathan.
Description: Chicago ; London : The University of Chicago
Press, 2020. | Includes bibliographical references and index.
Identifiers: LCCN 2019052058 | ISBN 9780226681191
(cloth) | ISBN 9780226681221 (paperback) |
ISBN 9780226681368 (ebook)
Subjects: LCSH: Equality. | Democracy. |
Justice. | Cultural pluralism.
Classification: LCC JC575 .D49 2020 | DDC 320.01/1—dc23
LC record available at https://lccn.loc.gov/2019052058

Contents

Introduction

Danielle Allen and Rohini Somanathan

1. Diversity, Justice, and Democracy

All around the world democracy looks broken. In the United States one in every one hundred adults is in prison, and the country houses nearly 25 percent of the world's incarcerated individuals, despite having only 5 percent of the world's population.[1] More than half of those prisoners are African American and Latino, although these groups constitute only about a quarter of the population; reductions in access to the vote for populations with high percentages of convicted felons swing elections.[2] In India, the world's largest and most diverse democracy, communal violence often precedes elections, and political incentives have incited rather than prevented it.[3] Debates on immigration and asylum in the welfare states of the European Union are polarizing those electorates.[4]

In addition to issues of political and racial equality, the links between democracy and prosperity are under strain. Although the United States is the wealthiest country in the world, 20 percent of its children live in poverty. The percentage of children living in poverty declined in the postwar period but has been rising since the mid-1970s. In the three years following the recession of 2007, the share of children in poverty increased from 18 percent to 22 percent. An estimated 9 percent now live in "extreme poverty," at incomes less than half of the poverty line.[5] Meanwhile most income gains have accrued to the top income earners. Since 1979 the share of the top percentile of workers increased from 8 percent to 18 percent in the United States and from 6 percent to 15 percent in the United Kingdom.[6]

There has been a similar rise in inequality in many other countries. In Brazil, South Africa, and India, the top 10 percent of earners receive over 50 percent of total income, and between 1980 and 2016, the global top 1 percent has captured twice as much growth as the bottom 50 percent.[7] In India, the world's largest and most diverse democracy, the state fails to deliver basic goods of nutrition and education to a substantial portion of the population. Nondemocratic China is seen as more successful in delivery of health care to its population.[8]

As economist Thomas Piketty points out, in the wealthy developed democracies of the Northern Hemisphere during the twentieth century, war, not peace, brought economic egalitarianism. In contrast to the impact of the world wars, the post-Vietnam era of relative peace has brought historically extreme degrees of inequality in income and wealth.[9] Many of these inequalities are, in Charles Tilly's terms, "durable" and "categorical."[10] Across types of inequality—political, social, and economic—disparities commonly track ethnic, racial, religious, or other social divides. The phenomena of inequality, social fragmentation, and social hierarchy intersect persistently.

In this book we seek to understand the relations among social diversity, justice, and democracy and to clarify how social diversity should inform our thinking about both justice and democracy. Among kinds of social diversity discussed in this volume, race has special prominence. This contrasts powerfully with a landmark volume that wrestled with similar theoretical problems two decades ago. Seyla Benhabib's 1996 edited volume *Democracy and Difference: Contesting the Boundaries of the Political* only glancingly engages with the theme of racial difference and inequality. Between 1996 and the present, the continued growth in mass incarceration in the United States and its racialization have made the problem of racial domination once again inescapable. The problem of the US carceral state highlights the tight entanglement of political, social, and economic forms of inequality.

Here we should offer some definitions. By "the social" we refer, roughly, to civil society—the domain of the family, of churches and universities and other associational organizations and institutions, of the media and producers of culture, of neighborhoods and residential patterns. We take the political realm to consist of the formal institutions of the state, from its highest level of national legislatures and executive bodies to city councils and school boards and local water districts; the political realm also involves those forms of organization—from lobbyists to activists—that are deployed to pull the levers of the state decision-making apparatus. Finally, the economic realm comprises firms and profit-seeking entities but also the various mechanisms of distribution, including the family and the state and public services and infrastructure like transportation systems. These definitions of the social, political, and economic should make abundantly clear how fully entangled and mutually constituting we take these three categories to be. Among our goals has been to build a new paradigm for analyzing the interactive effects among them. We believe that this volume's focus on the entanglements of political, social, and economic realms offers analytical tools that should be widely applicable, well beyond the US state of exception. That said, given the exceptional nature of penality in the United States and its exemplary status as a contemporary problem with democracy and justice, the US carceral state exerts something of a gravitational force on the work in this volume. While most of the chapters rely on examples from the United States, we bring in comparative cases from India, Germany, and Cameroon and have challenged ourselves to construct a conceptual architecture that may be of use to those pursuing similar questions in other geographic and political contexts. The comparative threads work in support of this goal.

In this introduction we review the conceptual framework for the volume and the working method that produced it, as well as pointing to some shared conclusions that emerged from our collaborative work. Importantly, a basic feature of our working methodology involved iterative collaboration between scholars doing normative work, which entails exploring questions of justice and ethics and how we *ought* to treat each other, and scholars doing positive work, which entails using empirical and modeling methodologies to offer descriptions of the world as it is. Positive efforts to describe and explain injustice or inequality depend on preexisting frameworks for thinking about justice. A political scientist who wishes to study inequality can begin to do so only if she already has some preconception about which inequalities matter—and that preconception flows from implicit normative views about justice—and about where deviations from random distributions in social patterns strike us as *wrong*. Precisely because they implicitly depend on underlying normative conceptions, the positive analyses of social sciences can throw into relief problems and inconsistencies within those normative frameworks for thinking about justice. They can force normative questions to the surface. If political philosophers and ethicists are available to spot the normative questions that emerge from social science, an effort to revisit normative theory will then ensue. This can generate new ideals and thereby redirect the gaze of the social scientist to the salience of social phenomena that had previously been overlooked. In other words, the effort to revisit normative theory can put positive work on a new footing. A beautiful articulation of how positive and normative work complement each other and can iteratively improve one another can be found in *Educational Goods: Values, Evidence and Decision-Making*, cowritten by two philosophers and two economists.[11]

Like their volume, our volume consists of normative work that stretches in new directions because of engagement with positive social science. It also includes examples of positive social science where scholars revise their own methodological approaches to reflect the fact that their undergirding normative frameworks are changing. In this regard, the volume presents the bases for new and complementary paradigms for both normative and positive engagements with issues of injustice and inequality, but it also provides examples of the transition that scholars experience as they work themselves out of one way of looking at things and into another. At the core of this volume's work is a normative effort to reground conceptions of justice in an ideal of non-domination and political equality. Then flowing from the normative reorientation are redefinitions of key concepts often used also by those in the positive social sciences. The key concepts that have shifted over the course of our work together are ideas of justice, statistical mirroring, identity, and groups as the building blocks of social organization. Ultimately, as we argue in the volume's conclusion, these changed definitions aggregate to a new concept of integration.

2. Key Conceptual Shifts

a. Justice

Contemporary political philosophy has populated the landscape of scholarship with a handful of alternative conceptions of justice. Among the most prominent are liberalism, communitarianism, and deliberative democracy, represented respectively by the work of John Rawls in *A Theory of Justice*, Charles Taylor in *Multiculturalism*, and Jürgen Habermas in *The Theory of Communicative Action*. Those who think of justice in a Rawlsian vein are wont to rely for reference on his difference principle, which requires that economic inequalities "are to be to the greatest benefit of the least advantaged members of society." A Rawlsian picture of justice tends to incline scholars to initiate their study of social phenomena by focusing on the distribution of material goods. Taylor's arguments in *Multiculturalism* place the focus not on the distribution of material goods but instead on the value of recognition of our identities. A focus on a communitarian picture of justice is more likely to lead people to attend to processes of identity formation and identity harms such as stigma. Finally, Habermas offers a conception of justice that depends on maximizing the participation of citizens in deliberative decision-making contexts characterized by acceptably rational forms of discourse. This vision leads to a focus on political communication and public opinion and instances where political processes fail to achieve legitimacy in accord with standards laid out on the deliberative model.

In the opening chapters of this volume, Danielle Allen (chapter 2) and Melvin Rogers (chapter 3) both embrace instead an ideal of justice that rests on the principle of nondomination. Rogers defines the principle of nondomination by drawing on the work of Philip Pettit. He writes,

> To be a citizen comes with a distinct kind of power—a power to hold at bay those who would privately or publicly have you at their arbitrary mercy. In the absence of said power, one is under a condition of domination.
>
> To be dominated, Pettit tells us, involves a relationship in which one person has "(1) the capacity to interfere; (2) on an arbitrary basis; (3) in certain choices that the other is in a position to make."[12] What is significant here is that dominating parties need not use their power; they need only have the capacity to deploy their power over you if they so choose. This is really what it means to be at the arbitrary mercy of another—you never know when the dominating party will act. As defined by Cicero, a figure from whom Pettit draws intellectual energy, "freedom ... is not a matter of having a just master, but of having none at all."[13]

For Allen, the ideal of nondomination provides the core of a theory of justice that starts by repudiating the liberal habit of separating basic rights into positive and negative liberties. Positive liberties are those involved in the freedom to participate in political life; negative liberties are those securing freedom from interference (e.g., freedom of religion, expression, personal property). Counter a main line of liberalism and following Amartya Sen, Allen insists on the nonseparability of these two categories of rights and, as a corollary, on the nonsacrificeability of positive to negative liberties. The result is a framework for a theory of justice that prioritizes democracy and political equality and that seeks to measure injustice by looking for failures of empowerment and instances of domination. The view generates a new principle, "difference without domination," for guiding policy analysis.

Allen's argument aligns in many ways with Rogers's recovery of the treatment of nondomination in the works of several important nineteenth-century African American intellectuals and with his reconstitution of an African American tradition of republicanism, in his essay in this volume "Race, Domination, and Republicanism." While in the mid-nineteenth century white Anglo American liberal theorists were turning away from republicanism to utilitarianism, black American theorists continued to advance the understanding of republicanism with a particular focus on what would be required to bring about a transformation in the domineering habits of white citizens. In other words, already in the nineteenth century social and political thinkers sought to answer the question, How is it possible to transform basic habits of interaction so that dyadic interactions don't aggregate to patterns of structural domination? In the nineteenth century a part of the answer lay in mass communication—rhetorical and literary—and Rogers traces the interesting and inspiring examples of African American thinkers like David Walker and Frederick Douglass, who also sought to generate such social transformation. His argument is historical and also serves to flesh out the conception of justice rooted in the ideal of nondomination. As Ajume Wingo's chapter makes clear, the ideal of nondomination is also closely linked to a concept of dignity. These ideals—nondomination and dignity—provide the normative foundation for this volume's work. Now we turn to the quantitative and its intersection with the normative.

b. Statistical Mirroring: From Answer to a Question to Invitation to Inquiry

A mathematical fantasy has guided our thinking about social difference, equality of opportunity, and justice over the last half century. This fantasy goes by the name *statistical mirroring* or *proportional representation*. This is the fantasy that just social arrangements would be characterized by a distribution of people, across institutions, organizations, and political bodies, in strict proportion to their distribution across the population. If, for instance, Latinx Americans constitute 15 percent of the American population, we should expect to see every church, school, school board, and political assembly in the country consist of a membership that is 15 percent Latinx. Over thirty countries currently have quotas for minorities in houses of parliament, and many have extended these to the spheres of employment and education.[14] India has half of all jobs in government and seats in public universities set aside for disadvantaged minorities. Brazil has recently introduced quotas in universities for students of Afro descent. Even in countries without explicit quotas, proportional representation is viewed as a benchmark against which to measure the fairness of allocations. As Heather Gerken argues in her chapter, this consigns members of minority groups to being in the position of *never* wielding majoritarian political power in any particular organization or institution. In other words, the very fantasy that is meant to capture a core element of justice instead works to ensure a certain kind of *injustice*.

This is not the only problem with the concept of statistical mirroring. Consider the challenge of thinking about representation in situations where there is a large number of recognized minority groups, as in India, where hundreds of castes and tribes have been aggregated into two large blocs for purposes of affirmative action. Heterogeneity in circumstance and opportunity within these aggregates has made representation a contentious and often explosive issue. The math of proportional mirroring forces us into artificial and even sometimes inaccurate accounts of circumstance and need.

Another problem is that statistical mirroring, in cases where it is justified, requires a law of large numbers for it to be meaningful. Take, as an example, the Supreme Court with its nine justices. With only nine justices on the court, it is literally impossible for the court's membership to reflect the demographics of the national population. Asian Americans make up about 5 percent of the US population; that would translate into about half a Supreme Court justice. This problem replicates itself across the organizations of civil society where the top leadership groups usually consist of small numbers. Representation of particular groups in bodies of this kind is necessarily lumpy, and to the degree that we desire a statistically mirroring representation of groups across these positions, we desire an impossibility. With fantasies of this kind, we necessarily build frustration into our efforts to pursue democracy and justice. The question, then, is how better to conceptualize our goals.

These problems arising from how mathematical fantasies shape our common language for thinking about diversity, justice, and democracy are brought out in the chapters by Sethi and Somanathan. These writers help us see that instead of using the idea of statistical mirroring as a target or ideal for our efforts, we should use it as a diagnostic. A distribution of people in institutions and organizations roughly in proportion to their distribution in the population could be expected to result from random processes when all begin from an equal starting point. When we see a nonrandom distribution of people in organizations and institutions, this is a starting point for an inquiry. We have a reason to ask, What nonrandom process has led to this result? But the mere fact that a nonrandom process has led to a nonmirroring result does not in itself delegitimize that result. One first has to know whether that nonrandom process is itself legitimate or illegitimate.

For instance, among the social processes that affect macro outcomes and the overall distributions are the choices that particular individuals and specific associational groupings make about where and how to focus their energies and efforts. Danielle is a lover of poetry. Imagine that she came from an island where everyone was a lover of poetry. Rohini, in contrast, comes from an island where everyone is a lover of math. Imagine that children from Danielle's island and Rohini's island end up in school together, and imagine that the school gives out prizes in both poetry and math. We would expect an overrepresentation, so to speak, of children from Danielle's island on the poetry prize list and of children from Rohini's island on the math prize list. Presuming that these divergent interests emerge from legitimate causes, we would not consider these distributions illegitimate. In this volume, to distinguish between illegitimate and legitimate social and institutional processes, we draw on our opening normative frameworks and employ a principle of nondomination. Legitimate social processes are those that, even if they lead to disparate outcomes, are free of domination.

When we come upon cases where the distribution of people in organizations and institutions and where allocations of social power and opportunities do not mirror population distributions, we need to identify the causes of those nonmirroring distributions and make a judgment about whether those processes reflect domination. Let us make this concrete with an example. We might compare the overrepresentation of African Americans and Latinos in American jails and prisons, on the one hand, with the underrepresentation of incarcerated women in the criminal justice system. The latter gender disparity in incarceration does not cause us great concern. This is a reflection of our tacit acceptance of the idea that the fact that men are imprisoned at a higher rate than women flows from legitimate processes—men are more likely to commit acts of violence, and the disproportion flows from that. When we turn to the situation with African American and Latino inmates, however, the matter is rather different. Here the evidence is clear: for the same crimes, African Americans and Latinos are arrested and convicted at higher rates and sentenced to longer terms than whites. Factors other than a greater proclivity to criminality are at work. Disparities in surveillance, conviction, and sentencing are indicators of illegitimate practices of domination.

In both cases—the gender disparity on the one hand and the racial and ethnic disparity on the other—the statistical divergence from a mirroring outcome should be understood not as announcing a fact of injustice but rather as presenting an invitation to inquiry. Some outcomes that lack statistical mirroring may indeed turn out to be instances of injustice; others may not. Where we identify causes of nonmirroring that flow from practices and processes of domination, then the appropriate mode of response is not to adjust the outcomes artificially but to reform the processes that led to them. Most of the papers in this volume turn away from the pursuit of equality of outcome to a focus on social and institutional equality—processes and practices for the distribution of opportunity that are characterized by nondomination. Across this volume, the authors of these chapters express a shared concern to secure egalitarian social relationships and institutional practices.

c. Identity: From Fixed to Fluid and Intersectional

We have shifted, then, from thinking of statistical mirroring as an ideal outcome to treating it as a diagnostic for identifying processes that should be scrutinized for impairment by domination. This shift is linked to two more conceptual adjustments, one about identity and the other about groups.

First for identity. The papers in this volume represent a broad and, by this point, well-documented shift in the social sciences from considering identity as given and rigid to recognizing it as fluid, hybrid, and intersectional.[15] Alongside many other influential scholars, Homi Bhabha, for instance, made the case that cultural life is characterized by hybridity, or a constant evolution in how each of us represents our identity, fashioning that identity, as we do, in contexts of contestation, out of whatever materials are to hand, which may themselves have disparate historical and cultural sources.[16] Judith Butler introduced ideas about the performativity of identity and about how people transform their identities as they transform their own performances. Bhabha's and Butler's arguments have been extended through the work of feminists like Iris Young and Kimberlé Crenshaw, who argue for the importance of "seriality" and "intersectionality" to the identity of any given individual.[17] Let us take one of us as an example. Danielle happens to be a black, mixed-race professional woman who is a mother of two and also a lover of poetry. Each of these roles comes into greater salience in different contexts. When someone invokes the responsibilities of mothers, she stands as one in a long series of mothers who have been called to attention by social and cultural cues. This is true of all her roles, which we might also say (modifying Young's terminology) that she inhabits serially, one after another, in an unending sequence that is unpredictable in its ordering. Additionally, the intersections of these different roles can be complicated: her identities as a professional and as a mother are often in conflict with each other; her identity as an economically successful white-collar worker can conflict with her relational ties to African Americans living in poverty and trapped in conditions of domination.

Fluid and intersectional identities complicate the use of statistical mirroring as an ideal or target for policy because they make it harder to ascertain the meaning of particular patterns of outcome. Imagine a private high school in which 12 percent of the students are African American but most of those, like most of the nonblack students in the school, come from upper-income families. Which kind of statistical mirroring is relevant and should provoke diagnosis? Mirroring that is pegged to the distribution of racial groups or mirroring pegged to the distribution of socioeconomic groups? Is such a school meeting a standard of social equality? Or should it be scrutinizing its admissions processes for impairment through domination that results in reduced opportunity for people from lower socioeconomic backgrounds?

d. Groups: From Given to Emergent

Importantly, if one accepts the fluidity, hybridity, and intersectionality of identity, and the changing contextual salience of the various components of a person's identity, then the concept of a social group with fixed boundaries can no longer be the central object of social scientific analysis. A body of national legislators may be viewed, for instance, through the lens of the members' gender and sexual identities, and the groupings may fall out one way, while if it is considered alternatively in terms of socioeconomic status or ethnicity, the groupings and alliances of interest may line up another way. The groupings that have a meaningful impact on the political process shift and adjust over time, and those adjustments may even result from active political and social cultivation. The same is true for national populations. Where and how groups form through alliances around particular interest positions and where and how marriage markets develop and generate kinship networks are contingent matters, emergent from a variety of social practices.[18]

To recognize that social groupings are endogenous, not exogenous, sociopolitical phenomena does not require a full redirection to methodological individualism and to a starting-point assumption that the individual is the only relevant unit of analysis. Scholars can instead focus on relationality—where and how different kinds of social ties form. The foundations for such study have been laid down in network theory, starting with the foundational work of Mark Granovetter and dramatically extended more recently by scholars like Matthew Jackson. The work of sociologists and political scientists who have focused on social capital and on bonding, bridging, and linking ties is also relevant here, as is the work of neoinstitutionalists, who scrutinize the emergence and solidification of institutions in part by looking at how they entrench social ties, as in the work of John Padgett on the Medicis, banking, and Florentine politics. Similarly, historians like William Sewell and political scientists like Victoria Hattam and Joseph Lowndes have traced how alliances and solidarities adjust around linguistic shifts that tie to evolving patterns of interest identification and formation.[19]

A focus on where and how social ties form, on where and how they are deployed by political actors, and on where and how they provide the context for the formation of the identities of individuals orients social scientific scholarship toward the meso level of human experience, the practices that mediate between the micro level of individual action and the macro level of structural phenomena and aggregate and emergent patterns. Across the chapters of this volume, readers will find articles that probe the question of how macro structural patterns of social life emerge from interactions at the micro level. This focus on associational life and interactional practices — again, on the meso level of human experience — permits identification of the causal chains that give macro social outcomes group-based patterning. This paradigm shift is captured by Glenn Loury's mantra in his chapter, "Relations before Transactions."

e. Summary of Conceptual Shifts

In sum, the scholars in this volume treat identity as fluid, and patterned group experience as emergent from social, institutional, economic, and political processes. As we examine social outcomes, we seek aberrations from statistical mirroring as diagnostics. Where we see such aberrations, we consider them invitations to inquiry. The invitation is more specifically a call to take up a mode of inquiry that focuses on identifying the processes by which one set of preexisting social conditions, characterized by specific forms of group patterning, is converted into subsequent forms of patterned social relations. At the heart of the inquiry is an effort to determine when such processes are impaired by domination and, when they are so impaired, to find techniques for repairing them. Those techniques of repair might be formal policies, they might be rhetorical and pedagogic strategies, and they might be transformations in a battery of informal social practices.

Taken together, these key conceptual shifts — in the ideas of justice, statistical mirroring, identity, and the meaning of social groups — in fact amount to a paradigm change for thinking about the relations among diversity, justice, and democracy. To see the import of this, however, we also need to bring to the surface the paradigm that has historically framed work in the social sciences in this area and to specify more completely the new paradigm that we propose as a substitute.

3. Paradigm Change: From the Age of
Revolution to the Age of Diversity

As the authors of these chapters worked with one another to develop and assimilate conceptual shifts in our use of the ideas of justice, statistical mirroring, relationality, identity, and group-based patterns in human social life, we were initially surprised to discover that across our disciplines we were all wrestling with the same problems. Then we realized that this was so because our disciplines share an inheritance from the late eighteenth century, the age of reason and its age of revolution. Yet our current sociopolitical challenges flow from the extraordinary demographic transformations since the Industrial Revolution. Can the older conceptual structure serve us adequately?

Over the course of the twentieth century alone, both human populations and their incomes per capita quadrupled and the world saw extraordinary rates of human migration. The combined result is human communities that are as dense and socially heterogeneous as the world has ever seen. The human project of living together now has new contours, despite the ancient expectation that there could be nothing new under the sun. Yet core elements of our conceptual apparatus for understanding democracy and justice, liberty and equality, generally still date to the late eighteenth-century age of revolution. Ideas of rights and constitutionalism took center stage with the American, French, and Haitian Revolutions, when political decision-making was, on the whole, the province of socially homogenous groups, when the focus of political justice was political equality, not social justice, and when the emphasis was on political rights, not social rights. The deep entrenchment across our disciplines of the view that statistical mirroring is the outcome we should aspire to in our political institutions and social life is owed to one of the most important inventions of the seventeenth and eighteenth centuries: the concept of representation.[20] For better or worse, a signal invention of the age of revolution was representative democracy. The conceptual architecture that supports it also governs significant swathes of the social sciences.

The ancient world had seen cases of direct democracy, as in Greece, where entire citizenries in independent city-states assembled to make political decisions. Antiquity had also seen cases of republican mixed constitutionalism, as in Rome, where different social orders—the people and aristocrats—each had a mode of participating in the government. The early modern era gave rise to republican forms of government, where democratically organized groups of aristocrats were at the helm, as in the Italian city-states. But the age of revolution, building on the work of early modern philosophers like Thomas Hobbes and others, for the first time built political institutions in which the whole "people" was understood to participate in mass politics well beyond the scale of a city-state via the mechanism of representation. Ellen Wu explores this history more thoroughly in her chapter, but it is worth calling out a few important details here.

As American, French, and Haitian revolutionaries sought new rights and liberties, they laid the foundation for citizens to exercise those rights as political equals, bearing a vote, and expressing their political empowerment through the selection of representatives. A new normative framework for thinking about politics — one that prioritized liberty and political equality — rested on this concept of representation.[21] Operationalizing the new concept required measurement, and the age of revolution famously gave rise not merely to the concept and practice of representation but also to the discipline of demography, inspired by the work of new census takers. The ancient Romans had relied on a census every five years to establish tax rolls, but thereafter census taking had not been a routine part of political administration. The age of revolution revived it.[22]

The United States, in order to make its new scheme of representative democracy viable, inscribed a requirement for a decennial census in the Constitution of 1789. The first census was conducted by federal marshals in 1790. The United Kingdom and France followed suit in 1801 with their first routine census-taking efforts. Over the course of the nineteenth century, statistical bureaus were set up in many countries across the world and in their colonies. While the imperializing nations used their domestic census to achieve political representation in their domestic institutions, they deployed the instrument in their colonies to understand and govern foreign populations. In its colonial use the census was an instrument for forming and administering ethnic, racial, and caste groups, as Somanathan argues in this volume and as other scholars have argued more generally.[23] In the United States, where enslaved populations were included in the census in order to increase the representation of enslavers within political institutions, the census simultaneously served the purposes of political representation and racial administration.[24]

With regard to political representation in the US case, the census numbers were used to achieve statistical mirroring, by geography, in the US House of Representatives. Each state was to have a proportional representation, in relation to its population, in this legislative body. This goal of proportional geographic representation was introduced as a necessary instrument for the achievement of political equality and fairness for the population of white families. Yet the use of a principle of statistical mirroring to structure a governance institution was contested even at the time. In the US case this is most obvious in the form of the different plan for constituting the US Senate. There each state, regardless of the size of its population, received equal representation in the form of two senators. As organized by the Constitution, the Senate bore no burden to achieve statistical mirroring of the underlying population.

The analytical dynamic of the late eighteenth-century historical moment is clear. An effort to determine the nature of institutions that could count as providing (racially homogeneous) citizens of a democratic polity with political equality led to a dispute over precisely how representation should work. This led to multiple alternatives for understanding the links among fairness, representation, and institutional form. One particular set of linkages — the notion that the people themselves should be represented, and that they should be represented via statistical mirroring of the geographic pattern of their distribution — led to a discipline of measurement that is with us today. Importantly, that discipline of measurement arose because of the development of a normative commitment. The argument of those who defended proportional representation in the Constitutional Convention was that proportionality in relation to the population made representation legitimate.[25] Thus the political traditions that emerged from the age of revolution anchored a normative view that justice in democracies should be defined by statistical mirroring.

As the age of revolution gave way to the Industrial Revolution in the nineteenth century and to decolonization in the twentieth, political agendas changed across the globe. Rather than focusing almost exclusively on political rights, the mid-nineteenth-century European revolutionaries, the Russian Revolution revolutionaries, and those fighting the decolonization struggles across Southeast Asia and Africa expanded the agenda to include social and economic rights. The Indian equivalent of the Declaration of Independence, the Purna Swaraj of 1930, begins, "We believe that it is the inalienable right of the Indian people, as of any other people, to have freedom and to enjoy the fruits of their toil and have the necessities of life, so that they may have full opportunities of growth." This declaration charged Britain with having "ruined India economically, politically, culturally, and spiritually" and sought a path toward securing freedom from those four disasters. The document anticipated Franklin Roosevelt's 1941 commitment of his administration to the "Four Freedoms" — freedom of speech, freedom of worship, freedom from want, and freedom from fear. These four freedoms, in the Rooseveltian formulation, in turn informed the 1948 Universal Declaration of Human Rights.[26] The cumulative effect of this ongoing development of rights language was a progressive redescription of the rights agenda to embrace political, social, and economic questions simultaneously.[27]

With this progressive redescription of the rights agenda in hand, the newly democratizing states of the twentieth century and the postwar democracies of Europe set out to make good on these commitments, constructing welfare states to do so. As they built welfare states, they faced the same conceptual problem faced by the emerging states during the age of revolution: how to measure that which they were committed to delivering. The late eighteenth-century administrations had initiated measurement of their populations in order to deliver up statistically mirroring forms of political representation. The twentieth-century states now had to answer the question of how to define targets in the social and economic realms. Very often the goal of achieving statistical mirroring in the distribution of goods was extended from political representation to the social and economic realms.[28] We would know that we had achieved protection of the four freedoms when members of any given national population were distributed throughout the spectrum of roles and opportunities in proportion to their presence in the population. The age of revolution had established a paradigm in which the goal of political organization was the achievement of statistical mirroring of the population in whatever area of administration was under consideration. As our gathering of scholars worked together, we came to the realization that this intellectual paradigm was what we were continually bumping up against and stumbling on in our efforts to understand the relations among democracy, justice, and diversity in contemporary conditions.

As we have explained above, we eventually shifted, as a group, from a normative or prescriptive use of the concept of statistical mirroring to a diagnostic use of the idea. That shift was also linked to a shift to a focus on identity as fluid, hybrid, and intersectional, and on groups as emergent. We realized that the concept of statistical mirroring, and cases that are aberrations from statistical mirroring, could be used to identify social phenomena where what we began to call the *hydraulics of inequality* might be at work. We would use failures of social outcomes to display statistical mirroring as an invitation to ask about the processes that had led to that outcome, seeking to sort out legitimate from illegitimate nonmirroring results. And we would seek to establish a standard for social processes that would make it possible to bring justice, democracy, and diversity into harmony with one another.

Rather than adopting proportional representation of preexisting social groups as a central goal for democratic policy, we would seek to construct a new conceptual paradigm around the protection of human dignity in the associational and institutional practices that result in the distribution of political power and economic and social goods. This would require developing tools of positive social science that can analyze the hydraulics of inequality—assess how it emerges and determine when inequality flows from the impairment of relationality by domination. This would also require the tools of normative political philosophy and ethics to set a standard for modes of relationality from which domination is absent. With such positive and normative tools in hand, it might be possible to begin explaining how in our remarkably heterogeneous mass democracies we might harmonize diversity, justice, and democracy, and achieve difference without domination, a world with lumpy group-based social patterning but where those patterns do not link up to hierarchies of oppression and inequality.

We are, in other words, proposing two methodological innovations for the various disciplines represented in this book. We are urging a turn toward a focus on relationality, dignity, and nondomination, in both positive and normative work. And we are suggesting that both positive and normative scholars need to rethink the concept of representation and the question of precisely what it means to try to measure equalities and inequalities of specific kinds. Our book is structured in support of this argument.

4. Structure of Volume: Understanding the Hydraulics of Inequality and the Pursuit of Human Dignity

We begin, in part 1, with the chapters by Allen (chapter 1) and Rogers (chapter 2) that lay out the normative framework and that are already described above. Then we turn, in part 2, to efforts to shift the focus in analyses of inequality to relationality, dignity, and nondomination. In chapter 3, economist Rajiv Sethi takes us into the world of positive social science with "Crime and Punishment in a Divided Society." The core insight developed in this chapter is that stereotypes can help generate harmful social equilibria capable of explaining disparities in criminality, sentencing, and incarceration. In other words, dyadic interactions in social relations, and not merely in economic transactions, can establish macro sociopolitical phenomena. In addition to elucidating many phenomena of the current situation with crime and punishment in the United States, the chapter beautifully shows how a failure to understand the relational texture at the micro or meso level hampers our ability to understand the sources of aggregate social patterns and effects.

Chapter 4 is "The Psychology of Implicit Intergroup Bias and the

Prospect of Change," by Calvin Lai and Mahzarin Banaji, both of whom are social psychologists. Their expertise is in the relational. They ask us to focus in particular on one specific problem in human relationality: implicit bias. They consider implicit biases to be group-based attitudes and stereotypes that operate without conscious awareness or control. Implicit biases can operate in opposition to one's own conscious values and principles. So their question is, How can we fix this relational issue? Their motivation for asking this is the expectation that a fix at the relational level should redound to improvements at the larger-scale societal level. But is this true? They suggest some changes in institutional and work environments that have the potential to reduce implicit bias. For example, blinding and the use of objective criteria for student and employee selection have been shown to significantly increase decisions favoring women and members of minorities. Lai and Banaji also provide evidence that changing the nature of the stimuli received by the brain can reduce measured bias. Experimental subjects exhibit less bias when they are exposed to stereotype-defying information. But these changes are often not very durable. These authors' argument ultimately suggests that it will be difficult to improve a society's relational texture, and interactions at the micro level, without simultaneously doing away with the sorts of problematic and inegalitarian equilibria at the macro level that Sethi describes.

Ajume Wingo in "Human Dignity and Modern Democracies" (chapter 5) perhaps most directly undertakes to redescribe the core features of democracy via relational rather than distributive questions. Drawing on the comparative case of Cameroon, he explores the tensions intrinsic to efforts to provide egalitarian satisfaction of people's desire for standing, self-respect, and dignity, a desire that paradoxically brings with it a certain craving for preeminence. The question he asks is whether an effort to provide universal dignity is perhaps a contradiction in terms. For him, the problems in attempting to measure forms of equality that aren't about material goods are not merely challenges to be overcome. They may indicate that it's not possible to think about social relationality, and the human aspiration to dignity, in comprehensively egalitarian terms. In the end he leaves open the questions whether universal human dignity is the right ideal in the normative realm and whether efforts to achieve it are amenable to the measurement necessary for policymaking.

Finally, in chapter 6, "Relations before Transactions: Forty Years of Thinking about Persisting Racial Inequality in the United States," economist Glenn Loury explicitly articulates the paradigm change that undergirds the work in this first section—the shift of focus from transactions to relations. Loury is building on his early dissertation work in which he first invented the concept of "social capital," and here he seeks to spell out the fuller implications of recognizing that there are features of human development that cannot be rendered in transactional form. The argument is that no economist, or any other social scientist, can hope to understand human phenomena if she limits her analysis to transactions. As Loury sees it, the relevant shift from focusing on transactions to focusing on relations itself has normative implications. It should generate a duty of care to all of the most unfortunate among us, even those stigmatized as "other" than ourselves. Loury's essay is finally a personal plea for that shift of gaze from transactions to relations.

The chapters of part 2 highlight how much more we have yet to learn about relationality and about how interactions at the micro level aggregate into macro patterns. Next, in part 3, we explore the limits of statistical mirroring and lay out new approaches to representation, measurement, and membership. The chapters of part 3 focus on how our inherited versions of the concept of representation misfire in contemporary conditions of social heterogeneity, the diversity of individual experiences and groups, and the pluralism evident in our associational landscapes.

In "Overrepresentation: Asian Americans and the Conundrums of Statistical Mirroring" (chapter 7), Ellen Wu studies the history of affirmative action from the point of view of Asian American experience and takes us right to the heart of the paradoxes and problems involved in the use of a concept of representation as requiring statistical mirroring. She provides a detailed and nuanced historical account of how Asian Americans negotiated a collective political identity in the period from the 1960s to the present as their positioning in relation to affirmative action programs evolved. Wu's paper underscores the nontransferability of the concept of representation to contexts beyond political institutions.

In chapter 8, "Second-Order Diversity: An Exploration of Decentralization's Egalitarian Possibilities," we see Heather Gerken reconceptualizing the concept of representation within political institutions. She proposes an approach to cultivating political equality that rests on the multiplicity and variety of decision-making spheres within a federal system. Rather than considering equality to depend on statistical mirroring within every institution, she is more concerned that each citizen and each distinct group of citizens all have a real chance to make decisions that matter. Political equality is a relational good, on her account, but it also has important material consequences. She sees a relational theory of democratic justice as closely connected to a distributive theory of justice. Whereas Wu detailed the nontransferability of the concept of representation to contexts beyond political institutions, Gerken subtly transforms the concept of representation as it applies to political domains, shifting it away from its eighteenth-century version.

In chapter 9, "Contributing to a Society of Equals: Affirmative Action beyond the 'Distributive Paradigm,'" Urs Lindner adopts the "relational turn" in an effort to understand and make a case for affirmative action in Germany. He outlines the history of the development of German affirmative action and then lays out a justification for that policy paradigm that rests not on a theory of justice requiring a particular distribution of material resources but on a theory of justice focused on relational goods like self-respect and standing.

In chapter 10, "The Measurement and Mismeasurement of Social Difference," Rohini Somanathan provides a comparative perspective on the collection of social data, focusing on the role played by the state in shaping particular group identities. She shows that group affiliations depend on the incentives provided by state redistributive policy. She also investigates the topic of affirmative action, this time in India, and lays out the analytical problems built into the effort to run this program for social equality in India on the basis of a statistical mirroring conception of representation.

Then, in the volume's most provocative essay, "Immigration, Membership, and Justice: On the Right to Bring Others into the Polity" (chapter 11), Claudio López-Guerra stretches to its fullest extent our capacity to think about the relational bases of democratic politics. He asks us to reconsider whether the birth family should indeed be the basic building block of the polity. He asks us to imagine a policy in which polities are grown by allocating a right to each citizen to select some number of new people to introduce to the society. These new people might be birth children, but they also just might be friends, or acquaintances, or even perfect strangers from other countries whom one simply wishes to sponsor as new citizens. The argument is surprising and serves a truly valuable purpose in requiring readers to revisit the question of why the birth family is the basis of our social orders.

Finally, in a brief conclusion, we seek to sum up the paradigm change that we hope to have effected.

5. Conclusion: Difference without Domination

This is not a conventional edited volume—the product, for instance, of a single conference at which participants arrived with completed papers and then edited them modestly for publication. This project emerged, first, out of the identification of a grand challenge too big for any single scholar or discipline to address and, second, from the constitution of a team of scholars, with diverse expertise, to address it. From chapter to chapter in the volume you will note different citational styles. Some chapters use in-text author-date references; this is the style of the sciences and social sciences, where research findings change rapidly and citations are used to track the development of lines of analysis. Other chapters use chapter endnotes; these are the chapters from humanistic disciplines where the original text of the cited material matters and where enabling readers to find the cited passages is critical. These diverse citation styles reflect the varying intellectual tools that we believe are necessary for tackling any grand challenge — intellectual tools that permit us to achieve positive descriptions of our contemporary social world and intellectual tools that permit us to trace the architecture of normative and jurisprudential arguments over time, and to modify those for present purposes.

Contributors met three times over the course of eighteen months for extended conversations running through multiple days. We began, at our first meeting, by formulating questions together. We used our second meeting to present drafts of papers developed in response to our initial conversations and to reflect directly on the three themes that had emerged from our initial conversation. We reconsidered our essays and revised. We used our third meeting, then, for synthetic discussion — to trace the points of convergence and dissonance within our essays and to come to a clearer understanding of their theoretical implications. And we continued our conversations in cyberspace.

In its merger of the empirical and the interpretive, of the positive and the normative, this volume exemplifies a working method that we think is important for the future of the social sciences generally. As empirical scholars develop their descriptive accounts, they inevitably do so with reference at the very least to implicit ideals. The questions of what "works" or of "how" something "works" cannot escape reference to our aspirations. Good work in the social sciences, then, will be self-conscious about the role of ideals in directing the critical gaze of the empirical scholar. Good work will make implicit aspirations and ideals explicit. But then scholars must also be self-conscious about the source of those ideals and critical with regard to their caliber. These ideals are most valuable when they develop closely bound to direct analysis of their consequences for lived human relations and material social relations. The work of building and assessing ideals itself requires delving into social realities.[29] In short, in this volume we have employed a two-step analytic method, which we recommend as a way forward for other hard questions in the social sciences. Importantly, this two-step analytic method is perhaps best practiced as a collective endeavor. Such teamwork is what we have sought to achieve.

Lastly, we should note that for all the talk of equality in the volume, we scarcely address issues of economic inequality, class, and socioeconomic diversity. The same is true for issues of gender and sexuality. This is not so much an oversight as a necessary result of having identified two other important problems—the question of how to pull the relational into positive and normative intellectual paradigms, and the question of whether the concept of representation can be retooled for our age or must be abandoned. These two problems merit attention, we believe, and we simply could not allocate equal attention to all facets of inequality and domination. We invite others to pick up where we have left off—to join the team.

Acknowledgments

We wish to thank the Institute for Advanced Study in Princeton, NJ, where this project was first conceived and initial steps toward it were taken. We also thank the staff and fellows at the Edmond J. Safra Center for Ethics at Harvard University during the years 2015–18, in particular, and we thank the Ford Foundation for its generous support of this work.

Notes

1. Travis, Western, and Redburn, *Growth of Incarceration in the United States.*

2. Travis, Western, and Redburn, *Growth of Incarceration in the United States;* Learman and Weaver, *Arresting Citizenship.*

3. Wilkinson, *Votes and Violence;* Iyer and Shrivastava, "Religious Riots and Electoral Politics in India"; Ghassem-Fachandi, *Pogrom in Gujarat;* Sajjad, "Understanding the Dynamic of Communal Riots against Muslims in Muzaffarnagar and Shamli Districts."

4. Hansen and Randeria, "Tensions of Refugee Politics in Europe"; Dustmann et al., "On the Economics and Politics of Refugee Migration."

5. Pascoe et al., "Mediators and Adverse Effects of Child Poverty in the United States."

6. Bell and Reenen, "Extreme Wage Inequality."

7. Assoud, Chancel, and Morgan, "Extreme Inequality"; Alvaredo et al., "Elephant Curve of Global Inequality and Growth."

8. Steele, "Valuing the Welfare State"; Singh and vom Hau, " Ethnic Diversity and Public Goods Provision"; Singh and vom Hau, "Ethnicity in Time"; Singh, *How Solidarity Works for Welfare;* Alesina, Baqir, and Easterly, "Public Goods and Ethnic Divisions"; Alesina et al., "Fractionalization."

9. Piketty, *Capital in the Twenty-First Century.*

10. Tilly, *Durable Inequality.*

11. The two philosophers are Adam Swift and Harry Brighouse; the economists are Helen Ladd and Susanna Loeb.

12. Pettit, *Republicanism*, 52.

13. Cf. Pettit, *Republicanism*; Pettit, *On the People's Terms*; Pettit, *Just Freedom*.

14. Krook and O'Brien, "Politics of Group Representation."

15. Bhabha, *Location of Culture*; Bhabha, "Cultural Diversity and Cultural Differences"; Young, "Gender as Seriality."

16. Bhabha, *Location of Culture*; Bhabha, "Cultural Diversity and Cultural Differences."

17. Young, "Gender as Seriality"; Crenshaw, "Demarginalizing the Intersection of Race and Sex."

18. Alexander and Christia, "Context Modularity of Human Altruism"; and Singh and vom Hau, "Ethnicity in Time." See also Michael Hanchard's important 2018 book *The Spectre of Race: How Discrimination Haunts Western Democracy* on the centrality of racial categories to the administrative practices of liberal states; Hanchard argues that liberal regimes ought often to be viewed as structures of population management.

19. Hattam and Lowndes, "Ground beneath Our Feet."

20. Pitkin, *Concept of Representation*; Manin, *Principles of Representative Government*.

21. For one detailed account of this approach, see Allen, *Our Declaration*.

22. See Stigler, *History of Statistics*; Daston, *Classical Probability in the Enlightenment*; Kruger, Daston, and Hidelberger, *Probabilistic Revolution*; Anderson, *American Census*; Levitan, *Cultural History of the British Census*; Schor, *Counting Americans*; Foucault, *Discipline and Punish*.

23. See also Hanchard, *Spectre of Race*.

24. On racial administration, see Hanchard, *Spectre of Race*.

25. For instance, James Wilson was a key figure making such an argument in the context of the United States. See Ewald, "James Wilson and the Drafting of the Constitution."

26. Glendon, *World Made New*.

27. Moyn, *Last Utopia*.

28. This is the significance of the concepts of "underrepresentation" and "overrepresentation" that are used in the analysis of the distribution of all kinds of goods from jobs to seats in colleges to wealth and income and health outcomes.

29. Swift et al., *Educational Goods*.

Works Cited

Alesina, Alberto, A. Devleeschauwer, W. Easterly, S. Kurlat, and R. Wacziarg. "Fractionalization." *Journal of Economic Growth* 9, no. 2 (2003): 155–94.

Alesina, Alberto, R. Baqir, and W. Easterly. "Public Goods and Ethnic Divisions." *Quarterly Journal of Economics* 114, no. 4 (1999): 1243–84.

Alexander, Marcus, and Fotini Christia. "Context Modularity of Human Altruism." *Science* 334, no. 6061 (December 9, 2011): 1392–94.

Allen, Danielle. *Our Declaration*. New York: W. W. Norton, 2014.

Alvaredo, F., L. Chancel, T. Piketty, E. Saez, and G. Zucman. "The Elephant Curve of Global Inequality and Growth." *AEA Papers and Proceedings* 108, no. 3 (2018): 103–8.

Anderson, Margo J. *The American Census: A Social History*. New Haven, CT: Yale University Press, 1992.

Assouad, L., L. Chancel, and M. Morgan. "Extreme Inequality: Evidence from Brazil,

India, the Middle East, and South Africa." *AEA Papers and Proceedings* 108, no. 3 (2018): 119–23.

Bell, B., and J. Reenen. "Extreme Wage Inequality: Pay at the Very Top." *American Economic Review* 103, no. 3 (2013): 153–57.

Bhabha, Homi K. "Cultural Diversity and Cultural Differences." In *Atlas of Transformation* (2011). http://monumenttotransformation.org/atlas-of-transformation/html/c /cultural-diversity/cultural-diversity-and-cultural-differences-homi-k-bhabha.html (accessed January 21, 2015).

Bhabha, Homi. *The Location of Culture.* New York: Routledge, 1994.

Crenshaw, Kimberlé. "Demarginalizing the Intersection of Race and Sex: A Black Feminist Critique of Antidiscrimination Doctrine, Feminist Theory and Antiracist Policies." *University of Chicago Legal Forum* 1989, no. 1 (1989): 139–67.

Daston, Lorraine. *Classical Probability in the Enlightenment.* Princeton, NJ: Princeton University Press, 1988.

Dustmann, Christian, Francesco Fasani, Tommaso Frattini, Luigi Minale, and Uta Schönberg. "On the Economics and Politics of Refugee Migration." *Economic Policy* 32, no. 91 (2017): 497–55.

Ewald, William. "James Wilson and the Drafting of the Constitution." *Journal of Constitutional Law* 10, no. 5 (2008): 901–1009.

Foucault, Michel. *Discipline and Punish.* Translated by Alan Sheridan. London: Penguin Books, 1991.

Ghassem-Fachandi, Parvis. *Pogrom in Gujarat: Hindu Nationalism and Anti-Muslim Violence in India.* Princeton, NJ: Princeton University Press, 2012.

Glendon, Mary Ann. *A World Made New: Eleanor Roosevelt and the Universal Declaration of Human Rights.* New York: Random House, 2001.

Hanchard, Michael. *The Spectre of Race: How Discrimination Haunts Western Democracy.* Princeton, NJ: Princeton University Press, 2018.

Hansen, R., and S. Randeria. "Tensions of Refugee Politics in Europe." *Science* 353, no. 6303 (September 2, 2016): 994–95.

Hattam, Victoria, and Joseph Lowndes. "The Ground beneath Our Feet: Language, Culture, and Political Change." In *Formative Acts: American Politics in the Making,* edited by Stephen Skowronek and Matthew Glassman, 199–219. Philadelphia: University of Pennsylvania Press, 2008.

Iyer, Syria, and Anand Shrivastava. "Religious Riots and Electoral Politics in India." *Journal of Development Economics* 131C (2018): 104–22.

Krook, Mona Lena, and Diana Z. O'Brien. "The Politics of Group Representation: Quotas for Women and Minorities Worldwide." *Comparative Politics* 42, no. 3 (2010): 253–72.

Kruger, Lorenz, Lorraine Daston, and Michael Hidelberger, eds. *The Probabilistic Revolution.* Cambridge, MA: MIT Press, 1987.

Learman, Amy, and Vesla Weaver. *Arresting Citizenship: The Democratic Consequences of American Crime Control.* Chicago: University of Chicago Press, 2014.

Levitan, Kathrin. *A Cultural History of the British Census: Envisioning the Multitude in Nineteenth Century Authors.* New York: Palgrave Macmillan, 2011.

Manin, Bernard. *The Principles of Representative Government.* Cambridge: Cambridge University Press, 1997.

Moyn, Samuel. *The Last Utopia: Human Rights in History.* Cambridge, MA: Belknap, 2012.

Pascoe, J., D. Wood, J. Duffee, and A. Kuo. "Mediators and Adverse Effects of Child Poverty in the United States." *Pediatrics* 137, no. 4 (2016): e3–e5.

Pettit, Philip. *Just Freedom: A Moral Compass for A Complex World.* New York: W. W. Norton, 2014.

Pettit, Philip. *On the People's Terms: A Republican Theory and Model of Democracy.* New York: Cambridge University Press, 2012.

Pettit, Philip. *Republicanism: A Theory of Freedom and Government.* New York: Oxford University Press, 1997.

Piketty, Thomas. *Capital in the Twenty-First Century.* Cambridge, MA: Harvard University Press, 2014.

Pitkin, Hanna. *The Concept of Representation.* Berkeley: University of California Press, 1972.

Sajjad Hasan. "Understanding the Dynamic of Communal Riots against Muslims in Muzaffarnagar and Shamli Districts, Uttar Pradesh, India." In *State of the World's Minorities and Indigenous Peoples Report 2014,* 121–24. London: Minority Rights Group International, 2014.

Schor, Paul. *Counting Americans: How the US Census Classified the Nation.* Translated by Lys Ann Weiss. New York: Oxford University Press, 2017.

Singh, Prerna. *How Solidarity Works for Welfare: Subnationalism and Social Development in India.* Cambridge: Cambridge University Press, 2016.

Singh, Prerna, and Matthias vom Hau. "Ethnicity in Time: Politics, History, and the Relationship between Ethnic Diversity and Public Goods Provision." *Comparative Political Studies* 49, no. 10 (2016): 1303–40.

Singh, Prerna, and Matthias vom Hau, eds. "Ethnic Diversity and Public Goods Provision." Special issue, *Comparative Political Studies* 49, no. 10 (September 2016).

Steele, L. G. "Valuing the Welfare State: A Cross-National Analysis of Attitudes about Income Inequality and Redistribution in 91 Countries with Case Analyses of Brazil, China, France, and the United States." PhD diss., Princeton University, 2013.

Stigler, Steven. *The History of Statistics: The Measurement of Uncertainty before 1900.* Cambridge, MA: Belknap, 1986.

Swift, Adam, Harry Brighouse, Helen Ladd, and Susanna Loeb. *Educational Goods: Values, Evidence, and Decision-Making.* Chicago: University of Chicago Press, 2018.

Tilly, Charles. *Durable Inequality.* Berkeley: University of California Press, 1999.

Travis, Jeremy, Bruce Western, and Steve Redburn, eds. *The Growth of Incarceration in the United States: Exploring Causes and Consequences.* Washington, DC: National Academies Press, 2014.

Wilkinson, Steven L. *Votes and Violence.* Cambridge: Cambridge University Press, 2004.

Young, Iris M. "Gender as Seriality: Thinking about Women as a Social Collective." *Signs* 19, no. 3 (1994): 713–38.

PART 1

Difference without Domination

1

A New Theory of Justice

DIFFERENCE WITHOUT DOMINATION

Danielle Allen

1. Introduction

The modern experiment with democratic government is nearly 250 years old, yet we struggle even now to understand the ideals that are its basis, the institutional structures that are most likely to achieve the best approximation of those ideals, and the ethical obligations that fall upon democratic citizens in their role as citizens. To some extent, our struggle reflects the fact that the ground beneath our feet is constantly shifting as demographic realities undergo transformation.

The ancient Greek philosopher Aristotle recognized that the question of which institutions and norms can operationalize, or achieve the best approximation of, a definition of justice depends on underlying demographic facts: the balance of rich and poor in a city; the relative proportion of agricultural, trading, and leisure classes; the degree of education of the citizenry; and so on. His view and approach, in other words, are the antithesis of much contemporary political philosophy, which has sought to construct theories of justice that often stay in the abstract, sheering away from any definite demographic pattern or realities. Aristotle does argue for two core, noncontextually specific principles of justice — a principle of proportional equality (as in, for instance, the rule that the most talented should occupy the highest office) and a principle of arithmetic equality (as in, for instance, the one person / one vote rule). Nonetheless, he also teaches his readers how to think through the diversity of institutional mechanisms available to realize those principles, or some combination of them, in varying demographic circumstances.

In our own time it is worth both reconsidering the basic ideals of democracy and rebuilding our capacity to see the diverse array of institutional forms that can be used to realize them, given specific demographic facts on the ground. I take up the latter project of institutional inventiveness elsewhere.[1] In this essay I pursue the former project of reconsidering the basic ideals of democracy. This essay, in arguing for the primacy of political equality within any viable account of justice, provides a foundation for those other inquiries. The most significant contribution of this essay will be to articulate a principle—difference without domination—that, I argue, should take up residence alongside the other principles that since John Rawls have commonly been taken to define democratic liberalism: equal basic rights and liberties, fair equality of opportunity, the fair value of political liberty, and the difference principle, which requires that economic inequalities "are to be to the greatest benefit of the least advantaged members of society." Rawls intended the difference principle to apply to the social as well as to the economic domain. In this paper I argue that "difference without domination" should replace the "difference principle" in the social realm and should, if not replace it, at least supplement it in the economic realm. "Difference without domination" is a more strenuously egalitarian principle than the Rawlsian "difference principle."

2. Political Equality as a Multivalent Human Good: A Fresh Start for a Theory of Justice

Why start an argument about the meaning of justice by asserting that justice must include political equality or democracy? There are two possible answers. Either one thinks that participating in democracy is in itself good for human beings or else one thinks that only by participating in a democracy can human beings secure the elements of justice. The value of democracy may, in other words, be either intrinsic, deriving from what it itself is, or instrumental, deriving from the outcomes that it secures.[2] As an example of the latter, Amartya Sen has famously argued that the adoption of democratic political institutions ensures that a society will not endure famines.[3]

For the last two centuries, political philosophers in the West (in contrast, for instance, to scholars working on Chinese traditions of meritocracy) have argued that democracy has an undeniable instrumental value—in securing conditions for the exercise of personal autonomy, and possibly in securing various aspects of material well-being. They have also argued that it *may* have intrinsic value. It *may* be necessary for the full flourishing of human beings.

For Rawls, for instance, liberal democracy is good because it secures the autonomy that individuals need if they are to choose their own comprehensive conceptions of the good and to be able to select from among possible ways of life that which they believe is best.[4] This is an instrumental conception. But Rawls also attributed some elements of intrinsic value to political equality. It is, he argued, an element of self-respect, because our self-respect depends on the regard that others have for us. To be a political equal to others is to be held in an appropriate esteem and therefore to have the conditions for self-respect.[5] While one may object to this abject other-dependent conception of self-respect, it does serve to characterize political equality as having at least some intrinsic value.[6]

That said, Rawls's conception of the intrinsic human good that attached to political equality was minimalist. He did not recognize all the possible elements of this human good, as comes out in his argument with Jürgen Habermas.[7] Rawls generally tried to argue that his liberalism avoided imposing any particular conception of the good on the citizens of a liberal regime, but on this point he was being coy. His theory of justice did rest on the idea that autonomy is in itself good for people and that they ought to be given space to exercise it. It also incorporated a minimal view about the human good inherent in democratic equality. Yet Rawls objected to views that made more extensive claims about the inherent good of democratic equality, for instance Habermas's argument that democracy is valuable in itself because political participation is necessary to full human flourishing and not merely to self-respect. Rawls rejected the idea that "civic humanism is true: that is, the activity in which human beings achieve their fullest realization, their greatest good, is in the activities of political life."[8] Some people, he argued—for instance, a George Washington or Abraham Lincoln—may develop such a conception of the good for themselves. They may need the activities of a political life to achieve their full flourishing. But we ought not to impose that conception of the good on everyone else.

It's worth spelling out the content of this argument between Rawls and Habermas. Rawls's attribution to the concept of political equality of only one of its intrinsic values led him, I think, to make the wrong judgments about what to choose when circumstances seem to force a trade between political equality and other aspects of justice. By tracking the underlying argument between Rawls and Habermas and some of its history within the tradition of political thought, we will be able to see that political equality is a multivalent human good. It has more than one element of intrinsic value. I concur with Rawls that a theory of justice should begin by prioritizing the basic liberties,[9] but I think such a theory of justice requires a more careful construction of the list of basic liberties, and the relations among them, than Rawls in fact achieved. This will seem like a small difference, yet it is the sort of difference involved in turning a battleship. After many miles, the ship will end up in a very different place by virtue of having altered its starting point only slightly.

3. The Ancients vs. the Moderns on Political
Equality as a Human Good

The relevant argument between Rawls and Habermas unfolded on terrain that historians of philosophy identify as the battle between the liberties of the ancients and those of the moderns, a contrast anchored by a famous early nineteenth-century essay by Benjamin Constant with roughly that title.[10] The ancients, Constant argued, prioritized their political rights, their right to participate in the government and to take ownership over collective decisions. The moderns, in contrast, he argued at the dawn of the industrial revolution, had discovered commerce and mostly wanted to be left alone. They wanted to be protected in their property rights and rights to thought, expression, association, and contract so that they could pursue their commercial ventures, tend to their affairs, and get rich. For the moderns, Constant argued, politics had only instrumental value; it served to protect the intrinsically valuable activity of crafting the kind of life made possible by moneymaking.

Constant's argument was influentially amplified by Isaiah Berlin, who renamed the liberties of the ancients "positive liberties"; they involved a positive right, the freedom *to* participate in government. The modern liberties became, in his lexicon, the "negative liberties"; they involved freedom *from* interference, the right not to be bothered. These latter rights are the ones — thanks also to the work of Immanuel Kant and John Stuart Mill — that are understood to make the exercise of autonomy possible and to provide each individual the chance to develop and implement a conception of the good life, with minimal interference from others.

Rawls's list of the basic liberties is an amalgam of the two categories of rights. In this regard he does indeed appear to embrace political equality and to put the liberties of the ancients and those of the moderns on an equal footing. Yet there is a structure within his list, a point about Rawls's argument that has generally gone unobserved. This structure reflects the fact that for Rawls the negative liberties, the basic liberties that operate in the service of personal autonomy, are intrinsically valuable to a fully flourishing human life. In contrast, for him only one element of intrinsic value attaches to political liberty or equality — its status as an instantiation of the experience of being respected by others. The instrumental value of political liberty in securing conditions for the enactment of autonomy is more to the fore in his argument.

Running below the surface of Rawls's theory of justice, then, is an implicit argument that the ideal of equal autonomy (resting on the negative liberties) is a better starting point for a theory of justice—and the pursuit of justice—than the ideal of political equality (resting on the positive liberties). The consequences of this prioritization come out most pointedly when Rawls argues, in the revised edition of *A Theory of Justice*, that while "historical situations" and "historical limitations" (his phrases) may sometimes justify lesser political liberty, they can never justify "the loss of liberty of conscience and the rights defining the integrity of the person" (sec. 39). The "various liberties are not all on a par," he writes. While the political liberties would never be sacrificed in an ahistorical well-ordered society, less political liberty for some may be justified in some nonideal historical circumstances, yet even in those nonideal circumstances the negative liberties require absolute protection.

I use the contrast between the ideal and nonideal states here mainly to capture Rawls's own reference to specific "historical situations." A distinction between ideal and nonideal theory is, however, misleading. Even in nonideal circumstances we choose a direction for the application of our energies and efforts. That which we seek to protect absolutely, even in nonideal circumstances, in fact provides the content of our most fundamental ideals; it is that which we insist on using to shape the world willy-nilly. Within Rawls's list of prioritized basic liberties, only the negative liberties had this status.[11]

Rawls continues, "Under conditions that cannot be changed at present, there may be no way to institute the effective exercise of these freedoms [political liberties]; but if possible the more central ones should be realized first" (sec. 39). Rawls's use of the phrase "more central ones" for the negative liberties concedes the point. It's a throwaway comment, and the concept of centrality is not explicitly worked out in his argument. Yet it establishes a clear prioritization within the list of basic liberties. Among the basic liberties, some turn out to be "more central"—that is, more basic—than others. Although Rawls never offers an explicit definition of the more central freedoms, in his argument these are clearly the rights supporting personal, not public, autonomy, the rights of the moderns, not of the ancients.[12]

This is a tiny moment in Rawls's vast corpus, but I take it to be a significant mistake. If one establishes the positive and negative liberties, political equality and autonomy-securing rights, as genuinely co-original and coequal, in nonideal conditions neither set will be clearly more sacrificeable than the other, and the theory of justice—a theory that should guide us from specific nonideal situations toward improved situations—will change dramatically.

4. Rawls's Mistake

Despite what I have just laid out, Rawls believed, and argued, that in his theory of justice he had consistently treated the liberties of the ancients and those of the moderns as co-original and coequal. In *Political Liberalism* he writes, "The ancient and the modern liberties are co-original and of equal weight with neither given pride of place over the other. The liberties of both public and private autonomy are given side by side and unranked in the first principle of justice. These liberties are co-original for the further reason that both kinds of liberty are rooted in one or both of the two moral powers, respectively in the capacity for a sense of justice and the capacity for a conception of the good" (413). Yet when push came to shove, in nonideal circumstances, Rawls in fact came to prioritize the liberties of the moderns over those of the ancients. This is because he believed that the exercise of personal or private autonomy is universally an intrinsic good necessary for full human flourishing, while he conceived of the exercise of public autonomy as primarily of instrumental value to all in securing the conditions for the exercise of personal autonomy. In his argument, the exercise of public autonomy or political equality does also provide at least one element of intrinsic value, self-respect, but this is only one of the elements of intrinsic value necessary to a fully flourishing human life. Rawls did not see the positive liberties as contributing a broader array of elements of intrinsic value. Thus he wrote, "In a well-governed state, only a small fraction of persons may devote much of their time to politics. There are many other forms of human good" (sec. 36). Yet political equality is a multivalent intrinsic good just as necessary as the negative liberties to full human flourishing.

Most importantly, private and public autonomy cannot be disentangled from one another. Rawls sought, however, to achieve just such a disentanglement, an aspiration that is perhaps imaginable only in contexts of great social homogeneity.

As Rawls saw it, people need political equality in the original position to establish the principles of justice and, by analogy, a basic constitutional structure (sec. 36), which will make it possible for each to pursue his or her own definition of the good life in the context of civil society associations. The result of this constitutional strategy, he hopes, will be a state that does not impose on our efforts to shape a way of life, on our personal autonomy. Nonetheless, Rawls does formulate a concern about how collective decisions can impose on our experience of autonomy, and he also identifies participation as the necessary mode of response to mitigate the experience of imposition. He does not, however, see this problem of the impact of collective decision-making on our personal autonomy as a feature of our membership in the polity. Instead Rawls primarily sees it as a problem inhering in our life within the associations of civil society, where he thinks it is amenable of easy solution. Thus he writes,

> The basic structure is then to secure the free internal life of the various communities of interests in which persons and groups seek to achieve, in forms of social union consistent with equal liberty, the ends and excellences to which they are drawn. People want to exercise control over the laws and rules that govern their association, either by directly taking part themselves in its affairs or indirectly through representatives with whom they are affiliated by ties of culture and social situation. (sec. 82)

Here when Rawls talks about the goods that we derive from our social associations, he comes closest to recognizing the permanent entanglement of personal and public autonomy. Participation is a good that extends beyond self-respect because there is no cure for the experience of imposition on private autonomy other than participation in the crafting of public decisions, not merely in order to protect one's private autonomy but also in order to be a coauthor of its restraints. To be a coauthor in this way, a cocreator of a community's agenda, is an intrinsic, not an instrumental, good. It is the sort of good captured by W. E. B. DuBois when he invoked an aspiration to be a cocreator in the kingdom of culture. Rawls captures this basic dynamic in his description of how participation in our civil associations and their cultural life is a direct expression of our pursuit of autonomy, but he fails to recognize that this description also captures the relationship between citizens and the polity as a whole, not merely their relationship to their own associational groups.

In other words, he envisages a state that can do all the things that states do—make decisions about whether and how to go to war, adjudicate contests when the rights of adversarial parties come into conflict with one another, tax and distribute state revenues in the form of public goods—without tilting the playing field in favor of some conceptions of the good rather than others. But no such state exists—a point being driven home now by controversies over secularism and the veil in France, over marriage equality and the limits on freedom for religious minorities in the United States, and over the confounding correlation between increased protections for gender equality and growing income inequality. Such a "neutral" state, in which participation and the opportunity for influence constitute a discretionary, sacrificeable value, not a necessary good, is imaginable only when the cultural universe of those who hold the levers of power in a state is reasonably close to the cultural universe that characterizes the population governed by the state. In such circumstances, public decisions read as "minimalist" or "neutral" not because they are or aren't minimalist but because they implicitly track the conceptions of the good that predominate within the population.[13] Indeed Rawls more or less admits this in his analysis of the problem of the impositions brought about by social decisions. In the passage above, he argues that we will want to participate in shaping the rules that govern our associations and our communities of interest—that is, participation will be a necessary good—unless that work is done for us by "representatives with whom they are affiliated by ties of culture and social situation" (sec. 82). Cultural homogeneity can make the status of participation as a necessary good of intrinsic value harder to see.

When the distance is greater between the cultural universes and conceptions of the good of those who hold the levers of power in a state and the general population, public decisions will more frequently be experienced as imposing on private autonomy. Public autonomy is a necessary extension of private autonomy, not something separate and separable from it, and in circumstances of cultural heterogeneity this truth is foregrounded. To the degree that private autonomy is intrinsically valuable, so too is public autonomy, even if this fact is more quickly recognized in conditions of felt diversity. If it has sometimes seemed otherwise, that was only because the advocates of private autonomy could rely on a state that tracked their own cultural interests and general conceptions of the good. The ancient and modern liberties are genuinely co-original and co-equal, and a theory of what justice requires must treat the political liberties, or political equality, as indispensable, no less central than freedom of conscience and bodily integrity, to human flourishing.

Rather than building a framework for political judgment, then, in which in real conditions one set of liberties is sacrificeable and another set is not, we should start afresh by investigating what would be required of a theory of justice in which neither set of the liberties was sacrificeable. While agreeing with Rawls that any theory of justice must start by insisting on the provision of equal basic liberties, I redefine that principle in order to eschew any assignment of lower priority to the political liberties and to political equality. Instead I argue that the liberties of the ancients are intrinsically valuable and not simply instrumentally valuable. They structure the activity through which we exercise and experience public autonomy. Given the necessary fact of diversity in all polities, citizens cannot exercise their autonomy only through private action; the exercise of autonomy also requires political participation and participation in civil society. Conditions of heightened diversity make the theoretical point especially visible, but it is a broader human point: the political liberties are intrinsically valuable insofar as autonomy is intrinsically valuable. They are the form autonomy takes.[14]

5. Starting Over with Equality

In public discourse, concerns about inequality or equality are most commonly focused on economic matters or questions of the distribution of material goods — a set of social and economic questions. Rawls's second principle of justice — the difference principle — tackles the question of how to think about just such social and economic questions against a backdrop of political institutions that secure equal basic liberties. But answers about justice in the social and economic domains change once one restores equal priority in a theory of justice to political equality (equal political liberty) alongside the traditional negative liberties: freedom of conscience, freedom of association, and the right to bodily integrity. To see how a view of justice in the social and economic domains must change given a fundamental commitment to political equality, we must elaborate more fully the nature of an analytical starting point in which political equality and public autonomy, on the one hand, and the rights relevant to private autonomy, on the other, are genuinely coequal. Let's return to the basics.

An ideal democracy comprises a population of free and equal citizens, whose equality must first and foremost be understood as a matter of both political equality and equality in the rights constituting private autonomy.[15] Indeed, these two bodies of rights are co-original in further ways that have not yet been specified. The right to association is not, in fact, simply a right of private autonomy, one of the sacred rights of the moderns. If anything, its earliest appearances on the historical register show it fully conjoined to efforts to secure rights of public autonomy. In seventeenth-century England, Dissenters gathered together not merely to celebrate religious rites but also to raise challenges to the legitimate authority of the monarch.[16] They laid claim to a right to association not only to protect freedom of thought but also to protect their political power. In the Bill of Rights of the US Constitution, the right to assemble was closely conjoined to the right to petition political authorities for changes in policies. In our own era, the Chinese government currently imposes great restrictions on the freedom of association not, or not only, to limit freedom of conscience but also to minimize the likelihood that political

solidarities will form capable of challenging its authority.[17] Some rights
that have been identified as elements of negative liberty should, in other
words, properly be reclassified as being components of positive liberty.
This is the first adjustment that comes into view when we launch our investigation of justice from political equality. This adjustment already in-
dicates how elements of the intrinsic value associated with the basic liberties also attach to political equality. The autonomy-satisfying right of
association provides intrinsic value not only in its role as a contributor to
negative liberty but also in its role as an element of positive liberty. When
citizens have political equality, they have both the intrinsic and the instrumental value of democracy.

But, of course, equality is a big concept, and one might immediately
ask if the sense in which these citizens in this ideal democracy are "free
and equal" is limited to the concept of *political* equality. How precisely, on
this argument, do moral equality, social equality, and economic equality
relate to the centrality of political equality? And what is the content of
political equality anyway?

We might begin by saying that human moral equality provides the
foundation for recognizing democracy as both an intrinsic and an instrumental good. Because human beings generally have, as a species property, the capacity for autonomy—not merely choosing their own way of
life but also shaping the necessarily shared aspects of life through participation in politics—democracy is a good thing for them.[18] It supports
the flourishing of human beings as the kind of being they are. Democracy rests on the underlying moral equality that resides in this general
human capacity for autonomy. In *Political Liberalism*, Rawls would describe this capacity for autonomy as consisting of "the two moral powers,
respectively in the capacity for a sense of justice and the capacity for a
conception of the good" (413). Democracy is the only type of polity that
recognizes these capacities; this fact makes it the only type of polity that
can fully support human flourishing. The justice of democracy as a type
of polity therefore derives from its grounding in human moral equality,
but the realization of democracy as a political form also depends on the
achievement of political equality. In other words, equality plays a role
in the conceptualization of democracy at two different points, at least.
Human moral equality justifies democracy; and then political equality
is the necessary instrument of democracy. Importantly, political equality
depends not only on public autonomy—rights of participation, for instance—but also on the traditional components of private autonomy:
rights of association, expression, and freedom of thought. One's public

participation is worth little if it is not grounded in one's own authentic development of a will, and the development of an authentic will requires private autonomy to unfold. Where Rawls sees the pursuit of private autonomy as leading over time to the protection of the political liberties in addition to the "more central liberties," I see the connection flowing the other way around. The pursuit of democracy—which is to say of public autonomy—necessarily brings with it protection of the rights supporting private autonomy.[19] Those negative liberties are necessary to make the positive liberties meaningful.

In sum, human moral equality—which rests in our capacity for autonomy—necessitates political equality (that is, democracy) so that human beings can flourish as the kind of creature that they are. This is how basic human moral equality—which undergirds any rights regime— and political equality fit together.

To go further and consider how political equality relates to matters of social or economic justice, we will next have to examine the content of political equality in greater detail. After we have defined political equality, we can ask the subsequent questions: Given the protection of basic liberties as necessitated by political equality, what will be the dynamics in social and economic realms? And how can these dynamics be directed so as not to undermine the basic liberties and what rests on them, namely, equal political liberty or political equality? This question then proves, upon reflection, to require us to turn our attention again to how we protect basic equal liberties in the first place. For there is more than one way to do this, and some approaches to protecting equal basic liberties are more likely than others to develop dynamics in the social and economic realms that are supportive of political equality. It turns out that the question we have to ask is this: What basic structure protects equal basic liberties in such a way as to generate social and economic dynamics that don't undermine those very liberties? Asking this set of questions will lead us, as we will see, away from Rawls's difference principle and to a new principle: "difference without domination."

6. Defining Political Equality

The time has come to define political equality. Following on the argument of the Declaration of Independence, which makes a coherent philosophical argument about political equality, I take political equality to consist of five phenomena: freedom from domination; egalitarian access to the instrument of government; epistemic egalitarianism; equality of agency based on practices of reciprocity; and cocreation and co-ownership of our political institutions and their broad consequences.[20]

a. Freedom from Domination

To be free from domination, in the argument of Philip Pettit, is to be free from the prospect of arbitrary interference or "reserve control." In his brilliant book *Just Freedom*, Pettit explains freedom from domination with reference to the expression "free rein." If you give a horse free rein, it may be able to go where it wants, but the rider retains "reserve control" and can reassert constraint at any point. Or consider Nora in Henrik Ibsen's play *A Doll's House*. Nora's husband, Torvald, a late nineteenth-century bourgeois gentleman, applies few restrictions to his wife, who is able to spend her time as she pleases. And yet she's unhappy. She is at liberty thanks only to his good graces; she is dominated by his reserve control.

To have freedom from domination requires more than just protection of the basic liberty to choose your religion, political party, associations, and employment. It also requires an equal share of control over the institutions—the laws, policies, procedures—that necessarily interfere with your life but that do so, ideally, only to protect each individual from domination by another, and any group from domination by other groups.

Pettit offers three simple tests for assessing whether freedom from domination exists in a society: the straight-talk test, the tough-luck test, and the eyeball test. Can the people and their representatives speak forthrightly to one another and to other citizens, or do some find themselves bowing and scraping, for instance, to those with deep pockets? If the latter, domination exists. If your side loses a vote in a political dispute, do you have good reason to view it as tough luck rather than as the "sign of a malign will working against you or your kind"? If you do not, again there is domination. And, finally, can citizens look others in the eye "without reason for fear or deference"?

Importantly, a world without domination is not a world without hierarchy nor a world without constraints, but hierarchy and constraints such as law must be legitimate. Whether specific instances of hierarchy and constraint are legitimate depends on procedural questions and on the absence of patterns of domination from the interpersonal engagements that transpire within the framework of the hierarchical institution or legal system. Melvin Rogers's chapter in this volume extends the discussion of the conception of legitimacy that permits us to distinguish between dominating and nondominating forms of hierarchy and law.

b. Egalitarian Access to the Instrument of Government

A democracy consists of the establishment of impersonal forms of corporate decision-making. That is, group decision-making institutions are established whose legitimacy is tied to a conception of "the people" who authorize them and whom they represent. Decision-making power is not tied to any single individual. In antiquity, democracies were the first type of political form to achieve a depersonalization of power, so that, in contrast to a monarchy or oligarchy, it could not be said that political power lay in the hands of this or that particular person or group of people.[21] Democracies can structure these "depersonalizing" institutions in a variety of ways. For instance, the world has seen the direct democracy of the ancient Athenians and the representative democracies of the moderns, in forms both presidential and parliamentarian. The relevant decision-making institutions are typically legislative, executive, and judicial. Executive decision-making includes the regulatory apparatus of executive agencies.

A second important element of political equality is that all citizens have equal access to this decision-making apparatus. We are accustomed to arguing for such equal access in the context of voting rights protections. We are currently engaged in fierce debates about campaign finance law and whether one or another legal regime in this policy domain generates unequal access to the decision-making apparatus. The issue of pro bono provision of defense counsel for the indigent is also relevant here. The question of precisely what institutional arrangements count as ensuring egalitarian access to legislative, executive (including regulatory), and judicial decision-making processes at all levels of the state (federal, state, and local) is open to debate, but the ideal is clear: a pathway to pull the levers of power that is open to *one* should be, in fact as well as in principle, open to *all*, contingent on each individual's acquiring the legitimately established qualifications relevant to the use of that particular lever of power.[22]

c. Epistemic Egalitarianism

A third feature of political equality is what I call epistemic egalitarianism. Like all polities, democracies depend on successful collective learning and knowledge management practices to make good decisions. In contrast to other regime types, they have access to a technique for strengthening collective decision-making, by drawing on the knowledge resources of the whole citizenry.

Human beings are sponges, taking in information about their environment. Some are better sponges than others, but all of us are absorbent. All people are created equal in that we are all born to absorb. Recognizing this fact, we can cultivate collective intelligence that is better than what any individual can achieve. Of course, to say everyone is an equal participant in the project of coming to see the course of human events does not mean that everyone is equally good at it—only that everyone has the capacity to pick up some bit of information, some observation, that is relevant to the whole picture and that no one else will have noticed. Some people will pick up more than others, but everyone picks up something. Experts have a crucial role to play within the larger democratic community, but the value of their contributions should not obscure the fact that contributions are needed from every quarter to achieve a complete view.[23]

Democracies can strengthen our individual and collective capacities to analyze the relation between present and future, and to make related policy judgments, by drawing everyone into the work of understanding the course of human events. By developing egalitarian approaches to knowledge cultivation, they can build a collective intelligence superior to what any individual or even a closed group of experts can achieve. Experts are most valuable when they work hand in hand with a well-educated general population capable of supplying useful social knowledge to deliberations.[24]

This sort of egalitarian epistemic practice can strengthen democratic decision-making, supporting consideration of decisions in the round. Moreover, deploying such practices reinforces political equality. When the knowledge and understanding that flows into a political decision is closely controlled by a limited few, their control of knowledge resources pulls decision-making power to them as well. Broadening the engagement of the citizenry in the discovery, analysis, and deliberation processes that feed into policy-making decentralizes power, supporting political equality. The place of epistemic egalitarianism in political equality thus underscores the need to treat education as a public good, since an effective educational system is necessary to maximize the potential of citizens to participate effectively in the knowledge management processes and deliberations of their democracy. It's not an accident that forty-nine of the fifty US state constitutions include a right to education, and that they commonly ground that right in preparing people for citizenship.[25] A good educational system is an important foundation for realizing political equality, precisely because of the epistemic egalitarianism required of political equality.

d. Reciprocity

The fourth element of political equality concerns egalitarian practices of reciprocity. Justice in human relationships requires the kind of equality expressed by principles of reciprocity. Such principles provide the basis for interaction through which both friends and fellow citizens can achieve equality of agency in relationship with one another.

Whether in friendship or politics, each participant wants a sphere of agency unfettered by others.[26] Each has the capacity to engage, through talk, in a project of responsiveness to make sure that none is encroaching on the sphere of agency of another. The achievement of freedom depends on this egalitarian engagement in a constant recalibration to undo, or re-dress, or fix encroachments. A free people grounds its problem-solving methods on this sort of egalitarian basis in habits of reciprocity. Doing things with words is at the heart of those egalitarian problem-solving methods and of mutual responsiveness. Reciprocity — or mutual respon-siveness — is at the heart of justice.

Two practices define the reciprocity that is at the core of political equality: practices making redress of grievances possible and practices that make it possible to acknowledge and reciprocate benefits that have been supplied to one by one's fellow citizens.[27] No political decision is equally good for all members of the polity, even when all members of the polity have had equal access to the instruments of government and have been equally able to contribute their knowledge to group decision-making practices. Even in these conditions, some members of the polity will incur losses. When settled patterns emerge in who is bearing the losses that result from political decision-making, political equality has come undone. The goal instead is to establish practices that result in po-litical losses circulating through the citizenry over time.[28]

To some extent this is achieved through practices of redress for griev-ances, as in the civil legal system. To another extent this is achieved through legislative and deliberative practices that recognize and recipro-cate sacrifices that some members of the polity bear on behalf of others. This idea of reciprocity identifies the kind of equality that needs to be in play in relations between people in order for freedom to obtain. This is an equality in which when one person does injury to another, the other person can push back and achieve redress so that there can be a balancing of agency in their relations. Securing conditions in which no one domi-nates anyone else requires a form of conversational interaction that rests on and embodies equality in the relationships among the participants. It is not merely that the ideal of equality requires securing conditions free from domination—the first facet of equality that we looked at—but also that equality of agency, achieved through reciprocal responsiveness, itself provides the means for securing freedom. Equality of agency rests on citizens' ability to adopt habits of nondomination in their ordinary interactions with one another; these are habits that in *Talking to Strangers* I have called "political friendship."[29]

e. Co-ownership of Political Institutions

The fifth component of political equality is cultivation in all members of the polity of an understanding that each has an equal ownership share in existing political institutions.[30] This is an ideal of equality as cocreation, where many people participate equally in creating a world together. They do so under conditions of mutual respect and accountability by sharing intelligence, sacrifice, and ownership. The point of political equality is not merely to secure spaces free from domination but also to engage all members of a community equally in the work of creating and constantly re-creating that community. Here the topic of redistricting is relevant, for instance. Current approaches to redistricting that put that work in the hands of political parties rather than in those of the people at large make political institutions the possession of political elites. If instead they are properly understood as the possession of the people themselves, then control over their most basic and routine reorganization should lie with the people directly.

On this expansive definition of political equality, protecting equal basic liberties, including the political liberties, requires securing freedom from domination, equal access to the instruments of government, educational resources that support egalitarian participation by all in the polity's processes of knowledge management and deliberation, a culture of reciprocity and turn-taking, and an asset-based conception of political institutions that assigns the ownership stake in that asset to all citizens and blocks capture of those institutions by a subset of the population. The question, then, of how to design the institutional structure of protections for equal basic liberties so as to generate social and economic dynamics that don't undermine those very liberties turns out to be a question of which versions of basic rights protections support nondomination, equal access to the instruments of government, epistemic egalitarianism, a culture of reciprocity, and a co-ownership conception for political institutions. When we have choices to make among different strategies for protecting equal basic liberties, we should select the options that do a better job with regard to cultivating the five facets of political equality. Then dy-

namics in the social and economic domains will not undermine the equal
basic liberties we sought to secure in the first place.

7. Equal Basic Liberties and the Paradox of Their Potential to Generate Inegalitarian Dynamics

Protecting political liberty requires not merely the provision of the rights
to vote, hold office, and serve on juries but also the freedoms of association and expression that make political participation possible in the first
place. Of course, these latter rights are also valuable as foundations for
the expression of private, and not merely public, autonomy. If we start a
theory of justice from the need to protect equal basic liberties, with the
liberties supporting public autonomy and those supporting private autonomy equally weighted, how should we assess what is required of justice in the social and economic domains?

First and most important, the dynamics of the social and economic
domains cannot be such as to undermine equal basic liberties, including
political liberties. On this point I now break more decisively from Rawls.
While Rawls is willing to say that the basic liberties supporting private autonomy must never be sacrificed for the sake of material well-being, he
does argue that in some circumstances it might be reasonable for people
to forfeit their political liberties, as least temporarily, to achieve material
well-being. In my argument, in contrast, if the ancient and modern liberties are truly given equal weight, then it is also inadmissible for the dynamics in the social and economic realm to unfold in such a way as to
abrogate the political liberties, or political equality, just as it is inadmissible for them to abrogate the rights that support private autonomy. We
need a principle of strict scrutiny. When we protect the negative liberties
of the moderns, are those protections compatible with simultaneous protection of the positive liberties of the ancients? The application of such a
principle of strict scrutiny should permit us to bring the two kinds of liberty into alignment with each other over time.

Here we reach the greatest challenge. How we seek to protect equal
basic rights — and particularly the right to freedom of association — can
generate forms of social and economic difference that often come to be a
source of domination in any given society, ultimately undermining pathways to political equality. We must confront the fact that our choices
about *how* to protect the equal basic liberties already affect the structure
of the social and economic domains.

Segregation is the easy, obvious example of this. The entire structure
of Jim Crow was defended on grounds of the need to protect freedom of

association, an equal basic liberty. Yet from this ostensible protection of a basic liberty flowed a variety of forms of domination. A segregated society, for instance, undermines political equality by establishing patterns of domination and limited access to the levers of power. That said, it does not necessarily undermine private autonomy. This was in effect the meaning of the segregationists' argument that it should be possible to build two separate but equal worlds. Surprisingly, then, and counter to Rawls's own stated view, the segregationist outlook is compatible with the Rawlsian notion that only the rights supporting private autonomy should be considered utterly sacrosanct. But once the political liberties and political equality are also considered sacrosanct, then segregationist social structures are plainly revealed as antithetical to a just society. This example shows the importance of considering the political liberties as equally central to the liberties that protect private autonomy.

Moreover, Jim Crow's effects on the social structure of the United States in the first half of the twentieth century laid down rigid patterns for the distribution of economic benefits. As economic productivity boomed in the mid-twentieth century, its fruits were distributed in patterns determined by the underlying allocations of land and labor controlled through segregation. In other words, the specific protection of an equal basic liberty attempted in the Jim Crow system established a basis for domination of some citizens by others in social, political, and economic domains.

We would now look at the case of segregation and critique it with the argument that in fact the Jim Crow system rested on only a false claim to protect a basic associational liberty. We would point out that in failing to protect the rights of African Americans, Mexican Americans, and Chinese Americans to move freely through society, the Jim Crow system was actually violating their rights of association while putatively protecting those of others. This is indeed the argument Rawls made. Jim Crow may have been protecting the basic liberties of *some*, but it wasn't protecting *equal* basic liberty. One might therefore be tempted to say that in the era of Jim Crow, the only reason the patterns of domination sprang up in the social and economic realms was that equal basic liberties were not in fact protected. But this would be to miss another basic point about the equal basic liberties and their paradoxical potential to generate inegalitarian effects in both the social and the economic realm. Freedom of association does inevitably lead to social difference, and social difference has historically had a high likelihood of generating domination. In the next two sections I will elaborate this point first in relation to the social realm and then in relation to the economic realm.

8. Difference without Domination: Equal Basic
Liberties and the Social Question

A fundamental expression of the right to free association is the right to marry whom one pleases. As people with affinity to one another pair up in marriages, they form the building blocks of units of cultural homogeneity. Regardless of precisely how marriage markets are constituted in different historical and geographic contexts, they have typically generated distinguishable ethnic communities, and there is every reason to think that freedom of association is more likely to reinforce than to undermine that pattern. Scholars of social network theory have identified "homophily," the tendency of those who are like one another to flock together, as a basic building block of human social organization.[31] Even imagining a world in which free association would be protected not only from government intrusion but also from the limitations imposed by social sanction, there is still every reason to think that homophily would drive the formation of distinguishably different social groups.

And where there is social difference there can easily also be domination. Even without antipathy toward out-groups, members of social groups will often focus on gathering opportunities and resources for their own group, on the basis of nothing more than in-group preferences.[32] Social differentiation, in other words, very often connects to opportunity hoarding and other efforts at resource control that can lead to the domination of some groups by others. At its most extreme, protection of free association can generate social differentiation that leads to caste societies—and ironically, these societies are marked by stiff social sanctions that in fact limit free association. The articulation of difference with domination in this fashion undermines a society's prospects for achieving political equality. Consequently, the goal of protecting political equality requires that we ask how we can have the social difference that flows from the protection of negative rights without also generating domination. How can we have difference without domination?

We know what difference with domination is. It is the situation in which patterns of social difference align with some groups having active, or reserve, control over other groups. Difference without domination, therefore, identifies social patterning that does not eventuate in any group's having either direct or reserve control over another group, nor any individual's having direct or reserve control over another merely because of each party's social background. Difference without domination should be the principle guiding our choices about the basic structure,

A Virtuous Circle: Political Equality as the Ground of Justice

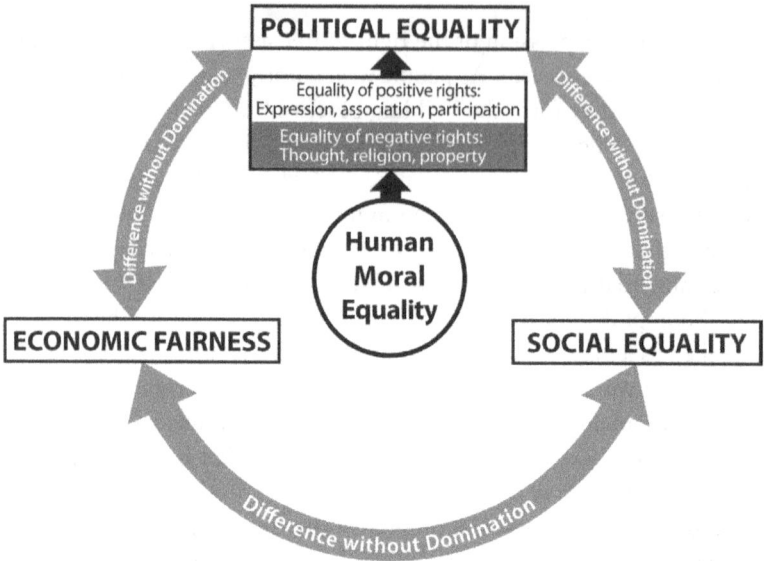

POLITICAL EQUALITY

Equality of positive rights:
Expression, association, participation

Equality of negative rights:
Thought, religion, property

Human
Moral
Equality

ECONOMIC FAIRNESS

SOCIAL EQUALITY

Difference without Domination

Difference without Domination

Difference without Domination

FIGURE 1.1. A virtuous circle: protecting equal basic liberties
with view to difference without domination

the laws and institutions that establish the basic rules of the game for a
society.

Protection of the equal basic liberties must instead be crafted in ways
that ensure protection of those liberties not merely at some imaginary t_1
state of nature, when a society is founded, but also at t_2, t_3, t_4, and so on,
after social difference has developed settled patterns. Only such protections of the equal basic liberties can, in the end, count as protections. This
is the point conveyed by figure 1.1. The idea is that human equality necessitates protections of the equal basic liberties, but these protections must
themselves be crafted so as to meet the standard of difference without
domination if they are to succeed in protecting and not undermining the
equal basic liberties and political equality specifically. Protections of the
equal basic liberties that are crafted in such a way as to meet the standard
of achieving difference without domination in the social and economic
domains should result in social equality and economic egalitarianism.

But what exactly is required of the principle of difference without
domination in the social realm? How can we support social difference
while disconnecting it from domination? The question is what is required
of the basic structure, the fundamental political and social institutions,

such that the social dynamics that emerge out of practices of free association do not articulate with hierarchy and domination and thereby undo
the pathway to political equality.

The solution must lie in identifying features of the institutions of the
basic structure that simultaneously protect free association and work
against the development of phenomena like opportunity hoarding and
group domination. These features of the institutions of the basic structure are those that permit and support difference but without domination. We judge the institutions of the basic structure, then, for their likelihood of spurring difference without domination.

I encapsulate the features of the basic structure that can make the relevant difference under the category of "connected society" institutions.
Scholars of social capital distinguish among three kinds of social ties:
bonding, bridging, and linking. Bonding ties are those (generally strong)
connections that bind kin, close friends, and social similars to one another; bridging ties are those (generally weaker) ties that connect people
across demographic cleavages (age, race, class, occupation, religion, and
the like); finally, linking ties are the vertical connections between people
at different levels of a status hierarchy as in, for instance, the employment context.[33] As I have argued elsewhere, an associational ecosystem
that maximizes bridging ties should minimize the likelihood that social
difference articulates with domination.[34] Constructing an associational
ecosystem that achieves this requires focusing on all of the policies that
impact the use of land and space: transportation, housing, zoning, districting (including both for political representation and for education),
public accommodations, and communications infrastructure (which affects spatiotemporal experiences). The question of how space and land
use is organized affects whether the protection of the right to association
will, over time, support or undermine the equal basic liberties, including the right of association itself. In other words, more already-existing
policies may be directly germane to basic rights protection than we often
realize. The standard of aspiring to achieve difference without domination does not necessarily generate a need for new policies or services.
Instead it requires a review of current policies across domains of social
policy (e.g., transportation policy, housing policy, education policy,
health policy) with a view to assessing how those current policies protect
(or fail to protect) equal basic liberties. Where they fail either to protect
equal basic liberties or to pass a strict scrutiny test for the achievement
of difference without domination, we have found places where we need
to adjust our policies. Whereas many of our current policy domains are
structured by a picture of justice that depends fundamentally on a focus

on the distribution of material goods, I advocate an alternative approach to a policy review based on a picture of justice that depends fundamentally on political equality, or egalitarian empowerment.

A connected society is one in which people can enjoy the bonds of solidarity and community but are equally engaged in the "bridging" work of bringing diverse communities into positive relations while themselves individually desiring and succeeding at forming personally valuable relationships across boundaries of difference. By recognizing that we should choose strategies for protecting the equal basic liberties that also accord with the principle of difference without domination, we bring a heightened salience to policy areas that have long gone overlooked. The goal of acting in this policy space would be the cultivation of an associational ecosystem in which people do have the opportunity to choose their associates in order to realize their personal visions of the good life but also find themselves both routinely interacting with those whom they have not, so to speak, chosen, and routinely obliged to share power in a variety of public contexts with these unchosen others.

9. Difference without Domination: Equal Basic Liberties and the Economic Question

In the economic realm, the focus of policy-making generally falls not on land but on labor and capital. Thus Rawls's difference principle—that any unequal distribution of material goods among members of a polity must in some sense redound to the benefit of the worst off—is usually taken as a justification of redistributive tax policy. The expectation is that institutions that protect equal basic liberties will result in economies in which the rewards of productivity accrue differentially to the owners of capital, the managers, and the laborers. Such a result is acceptable, argues Rawls, only as long as the benefits accruing to the owners and managers are in some fashion beneficial to the worst off, as for instance when the managers' work raises the productivity of the whole economy and the standard of living for the worst off, even as that group falls further behind the owners and managers in income or wealth or both.

By asking the question of how we would build an economy that achieved difference without domination, we once again push the conversation back to the question of how we protect the equal basic liberties in the first place. As in the social realm, we can assume that the protection of equal basic liberties in property, contract, and, again, association will generate difference in the economic realm.[35] But can we protect the equal basic liberties in such a fashion as to avoid the emergence of domination from those forms of difference that do emerge in the economic realm?

As in the social realm, in the economic realm the standard of aspiring to achieve difference without domination does not necessarily generate a need for new domains of policy or services. Instead it requires a review of current policies across domains of economic policy (labor policy, trade policy, the organization of the firm, etc.) with a view to assessing how those current policies protect (or fail to protect) equal basic liberties. Where they fail to protect equal basic liberties or to pass a strict scrutiny test for the achievement of difference without domination, we have found places where we need to adjust our policies. Whereas many of our current approaches to economic policy are structured by a picture of justice that focuses first and foremost on the distribution of material goods, I advocate an alternative approach to a policy review based on a picture of justice that depends fundamentally on political equality, or egalitarian empowerment. Again, use of a strict scrutiny approach with the difference-without-domination principle here is of value.

When we apply this principle to the economic realm, three issues quickly emerge as salient: (1) the organization and operation of the firm and the experience of labor within it; (2) the impact of economic distribution on access to political voice and influence; and (3) whether the distributive shape of the contemporary economy itself relies on forms of decision-making that embed domination within them. With regard to the first, as Elizabeth Anderson has argued, there is the question of how to ensure that the vertical or linking relationships within organizations, like firms or other units of economic activity, are not characterized by domination.[36] Relevant issues can range from compensation, workplace governance, and firm ownership even to matters like assignment of hours and access to time for bathroom breaks. On the second, Rawls put on the table years ago the question of what to do when accumulations of financial capital are converted into forms of political domination and undermine the fair value of political liberty (sec. 36). While efforts to control private giving to campaigns run into conflicts with the liberty of free expression, a reorganization of voting mechanisms around rank-choice voting would redirect the use of campaign funds into more socially productive uses, reducing the power of money in politics without infringing on rights of expression.[37] As for the third, Rawls's difference principle was intended to serve as a constraint in this area. But many scholars have now pointed out how the dramatic increase in income and wealth inequality in developed countries at the end of the twentieth and start of the twenty-first centuries has coincided not so much with a failure by technocratic policymakers to adhere to a principle of that kind as with a decline in the power wielded by labor unions in political decision-making. A focus on political equality gives us more purchase on the challenges facing the pursuit of economic egalitarianism than does Rawls's difference principle.

In short, a focus on achieving difference without domination in the economic realm widens the lens beyond Rawls's redistributive questions and, as in the social realm, requires recognizing a broader swath of the policy landscape than we typically acknowledge as relevant to the question of how to protect equal basic liberties. This is the sense in which the principle of difference without domination is more stringently egalitarian than the difference principle. It establishes a higher standard for our decisions about how we protect our equal basic liberties and pulls a larger swathe of policy under the umbrella of that to which the equal basic liberties pertain.

One other point must also be made about how the difference-without-domination principle affects consideration of questions of economic justice. How we protect our equal basic liberties has an impact on economic outcomes not only directly with regard to how firms operate or with regard to who wields power over economic decisions. Economic outcomes also flow out of our social structures. Recall, again, the example of segregation. That type of social structure itself eventuates in specific inegalitarian patterns in the distribution of material goods. If we seek economic egalitarianism, applying the principle of difference without domination in the social realm is as important as doing so in the economic realm. Particularly in conditions of pluralism, we can achieve an egalitarian economy in which we have managed to achieve difference without domination only if the underlying pluralistic social structure is also egalitarian. The emergence of a connected society in the social realm can be expected, in the inverse of the picture with segregation, to have more egalitarian impacts on patterns in the distribution of economic resources.[38]

Once we see this linkage between the social and economic realms, in relation to the application of the difference-without-domination principle to both and on behalf of political equality, we can finally glimpse the true import of placing equal emphasis on public and private autonomy, on positive and negative liberties, on political equality and personal freedom. When the goal of a theory of justice is above all to protect private autonomy and the capacity of individuals to pursue the good life as they define it, questions of social structure are often seen as separate from the economy and politics. In Rawls's effort to hive off private experience as the thing that justice ought especially to protect, he failed to attend to the

necessary economic and political consequences of how our private social spaces are structured. Critics from Susan Okin to G. A. Cohen have
pointed this out: Okin by emphasizing how Rawls disregarded issues of
justice in the family, Cohen by arguing that Rawls failed to attend to the
issues of justice inherent in our choices of jobs. The connections among
the social, economic, and political realms are invisible only to actors
whose private experiences have not generally been impinged upon by
either the political or the economic realm — namely those who are in the
cultural or political majority or who sit in an economically privileged
position. In contrast, the minoritarian viewpoint is defined by a permanent mutual entanglement of the political, the social, and the economic.
Since politics is defined by pluralism — regardless of the empirical degree
of social heterogeneity in any given polity — a complete theory of justice
must incorporate the view from a minoritarian position. In the veil of
ignorance thought experiment, Rawls's *Theory of Justice* defines a minoritarian perspective abstractly understood out of his account of justice. A
truly universal theory of justice will incorporate this minoritarian viewpoint and therefore start from an acknowledgment of the full and permanent entanglement of private and public autonomy, and from recognition
of the intrinsic value of political equality alongside personal freedom.

10. Conclusion

The time has come to revisit the basic grounds for a theory of justice.
As many have pointed out, Rawls's arguments were too dependent on
an expectation of social homogeneity that drove key features of political life into the background of his consideration. But that expectation
was not merely a problem on the margins. It had a deep consequence.
It led Rawls to place political equality and public autonomy in second
place to the liberties supporting individual autonomy. This is a nonviable
starting point in principle for any discussion of politics, defined as that
activity is by dissensus. As a practical matter, however, the insufficiency
of this starting point shows itself with vivid immediacy in conditions of
great social diversity, where public decisions will routinely impinge on
one's ability to deploy autonomy in fashioning one's life course. In such
contexts, autonomy itself is accessible only through participation in the
collective effort to shape the parameters of a society's life together. As
W. E. B. DuBois put it in the first chapter of *The Souls of Black Folk*, "The
power of the ballot we need in sheer self-defence, — else what shall save
us from a second slavery?" But DuBois's point is not merely instrumental.
It is not merely that the power of the ballot blocks the reemergence of a

socioeconomic institution of enslavement. It is also that the exercise of political power is itself an element of the intrinsically valuable experience of nonslavery, which is to say, of nondomination.

In conditions of demographic diversity, if not in human life generally, human moral equality requires protections for equal basic liberties that always fully encompass the political liberties. Attention to the political liberties will always bring with it attention to the liberties that support private autonomy; the inverse, however, is not true. Once we refocus on protecting the political liberties—for which freedom of association and the other elements of private autonomy are fundamental—we realize that we have to find strategies for protecting the equal basic liberties that preserve them over the long run and that avoid triggering social dynamics that will eventually undermine those liberties themselves. We need strategies for protecting the equal basic liberties that generate egalitarian social and economic spheres; such egalitarian social and economic spheres will anticipate, support, and protect difference but hinder the emergence of any articulation of that difference with domination. The standard we need for identifying policy solutions in the social and economic domain is that we want to be able to choose alternatives that protect the free emergence of social difference but that also disconnect it from domination. Failing that, the dynamics that develop in the social and economic domains will eventually undermine the equal basic liberties even if those dynamics in some sense originally flow from those liberties.

The aspiration to realize a principle of difference without domination should help us select protections for the equal basic liberties that will constitute a genuine and durable foundation for just political, social, and economic institutions.

Notes

1. See Allen, "Toward a Connected Society"; Allen and Pottle, "Democratic Knowledge and the Problem of Faction"; Allen, "Talent Is Everywhere."

2. Amartya Sen explores both of these justifications for democracy and a third "constructive" justification in "Democracy as a Universal Value." By a constructive justification, he has in mind the work that democracies do to generate our preferences and senses of value and direction in the first place; democratic decision-making mechanisms drive social processes that help populations define goals and values in the first place, thereby shaping personal and collective preferences. I agree that democracy can also be justified on this constructivist basis but put that plank of justification aside for the time being.

3. Sen, *Development as Freedom*, chaps. 6 and 7.

4. The focus of my analysis here will be John Rawls, *A Theory of Justice*, in both its original

(1971) and revised editions (1999). Some points of my argument will depend on the differences between the two editions.

5. In "What Is the Point of Equality?" Elizabeth Anderson argued for a reorientation of focus in political philosophy away from the luck egalitarianism spawned by Rawls's view toward a focus on political equality with a view to securing the bases of respect. She writes, "The theory I shall defend can be called 'democratic equality.' In seeking the construction of a community of equals, democratic equality integrates principles of distribution with the expressive demands of equal respect" (289). My essay can be seen as building on Anderson's, insofar as I too change the primary focus from distributive justice to political equality. In contrast to Anderson, however, my interest in doing so has less to do with the need to secure the bases for equal respect and more with the need to secure the functionality (empowerment and nondomination) that political rights secure.

6. Hannah Arendt, for instance, objected to these sorts of abject conceptions of the good of equality, in her case social equality, in her essay "Reflections on Little Rock." This is the one thread of her argument in that essay with which I agree.

7. Rawls, *Political Liberalism*.

8. Rawls, *Political Liberalism*, 5–6, 420.

9. I take the legitimacy of states to depend on, inter alia, their ability to secure certain basic rights and make this argument in my *Talking to Strangers*.

10. Constant, "The Liberty of the Ancients Compared with that of the Moderns."

11. In section 82 Rawls does discuss the emergence of a principle of the nonviolability of political liberties in the well-ordered society. In this and the preceding paragraphs, however, I am suggesting that he has misunderstood the role of principles of nonviolability; they should help us achieve a well-ordered society while we are under nonideal conditions, not be that which we secure with and only with the well-ordered society. Rawls's prioritizations among the basic liberties, and his differential application of a principle of nonviolability to the negative and the positive liberties, establishes a framework for political judgment, which is in itself an ideal framework even if deployed in nonideal circumstances. I am criticizing that framework for political judgment.

12. Earlier in section 32 he has rightly explicated, with reference to Constant, how the long-running arguments over how to define the liberties of the ancients and those of the moderns are really arguments about the relative value of the different basic liberties. Formally he puts the question of relative value to the side, but he nonetheless seems to suggest that he would come down with Constant for the view that freedom of thought and conscience ought not, he argues, to be "sacrificed" to political liberty.

13. Susan Okin made a parallel point concerning Rawls's nonattention to the impact of family structure on justice in *Justice, Gender, and the Family*.

14. A choice not to participate when the avenue of participation is open is also an exercise of autonomy. The intrinsic value of public autonomy can be exercised other than through proactive participation; it can also be exercised through proactive withdrawal. Thus apolitical poets, for instance, can still be said to have access to a good life. Cf. Shelby, "Impure Dissent"; and Arendt, *Men in Dark Times*.

15. For an excellent exposition of the core elements of an ideal of democracy, see Ober, *Demopolis*.

16. Green, *Verdict according to Conscience*.

17. Allen, "Ai Wei Wei and the Art of Protest."

18. This species property argument has predecessors in Aristotle (see Williams, "The

Idea of Equality"; Sen, "Democracy as a Universal Value") and the Declaration of Independence (see Allen, *Our Declaration*).

19. This argument that rights of participation protect rights of private autonomy runs parallel to Sen's argument in *Development as Freedom* that political rights protect economic rights.

20. What follows is a broad-brush paraphrase of my argument in *Our Declaration*. I should note that in the context of this essay I start from the Declaration of Independence not (as is sometimes the case in my writing) because it is an anchor for the US political tradition but because I take it to have made an innovative contribution to political philosophy, and particularly to the philosophy of egalitarianism. Its innovation has been less recognized and less followed up on in the philosophical literature than should have been the case. In particular, I take the Declaration to be articulating a liberal-pragmatist theory of democracy grounded in a conception of human flourishing ("the pursuit of happiness") that it leaves the people themselves to define and judge experimentally and experientially over time, while hedging their experiment with the concept of "rights." This hedge is what makes the view liberal; the experimentalism is what makes it pragmatism. Moreover, this pragmatism does posit a final good ("happiness"), but it does not give that final good a metaphysical ground. Instead the document leaves judgments about happiness to individual people and the people as a whole to be made over time. In this regard the view articulated in the Declaration rests on commitments to both fallibilism and corrigibilism. Finally, it articulates a constructive justification for democracy insofar as it identifies democratic citizenly debate (about principle and about how to organize the powers of government so as to deliver on those principles) as the only means for developing a view about the content of "happiness." The political philosopher who comes closest, I think, to articulating a philosophical view in line with that laid out in the Declaration of Independence is Amartya Sen. John Stuart Mill in *On Liberty* picks up key aspects of the argument about happiness and independent human judgment set out in the Declaration of Independence, but the ultimate reduction of the "happiness" concept to "utility" by the utilitarian tradition reduced the power of the original idea and obscured the original constructivist view about the ongoing creation of definitions of personal and public happiness over time by a deliberating and contestatory democratic people. With this mistake, utilitarianism, and other public philosophies that have flowed from it, fundamentally lost sight of politics, reducing decision-making to the work of aggregating given and static preferences.

21. This brings out the significance of Thucydides's critique of Pericles in the *History of the Peloponnesian War* when the historian says that Athens was a democracy in name only because all the power was really in the hands of one man, Pericles (2.65). Thucydides is seeking to refute the democracy's claim to have achieved a depersonalization of power.

22. This is not quite the same as Rawls's idea that the basic liberties must be protected equally for all even if, due to inequalities in resources, not all have an equal value of political liberty. The rich will have more value from the political liberties available to them. Rawls's solution to the gap between political liberties and actual empowerment is application of the difference principle to the functioning of the basic liberties. He writes, "Taking the two principles together, the basic structure is to be arranged to maximize the worth to the least advantaged of the complete scheme of equal liberty shared by all" (sec. 32).

23. Ober, in *Democracy and Knowledge*, provides the most comprehensive empirical

and theoretical articulation of the importance of epistemic egalitarianism to the success of democracy. See also Farrell and Shalizi, "Pursuing Cognitive Democracy."

24. This has been recognized recently in the United States by the Presidential Commission on Bioethical Issues, which has made collaboration between experts and lay citizens a key feature of its work. See, for instance, the commission's report *New Directions*.

25. Rebell, *Flunking Democracy*, chap. 3.

26. This ideal of equal agency is the cornerstone of Aristotle's concept of rectificatory justice, which he argues for in *Nicomachean Ethics* 5.4, which I explicate in both *World of Prometheus* (chap. 11) and *Talking to Strangers* (pp. 128–30). I have made this idea a core element of my own democratic theory.

27. My account here, articulated fully in my *Talking to Strangers*, is very close to Rawls's argument about the importance of a "sense of justice."

28. Allen, *Talking to Strangers*, chaps. 3, 4, 8, 9.

29. Allen, *Talking to Strangers*, chaps. 3, 4, 8, 9.

30. Nobel Prize–winning economist Herbert Simon made a similar argument that a democracy's political institutions constitute an asset owned by the people as a whole. Moreover, he argued that this commonly owned asset was the source of significant wealth generation in developed democracies, and that that wealth might consequently be allocated to a universal basic income on the grounds that the public owns the asset that generated it. See Simon, "Response to Philippe van Parijs on Universal Basic Income."

31. Granovetter, "The Strength of Weak Ties."

32. Sidanius et al., *The Diversity Challenge*.

33. Granovetter, "The Strength of Weak Ties"; Szreter and Woolcock, "Health by Association?"

34. Allen, "Toward a Connected Society."

35. Robert Nozick provides the classic argument, with Wilt Chamberlain as his example, in "Distributive Justice."

36. Anderson, *Private Government*. Cf. Gould, "Democratic Management and International Labor Rights."

37. Sodonis and Witte, "The Supply Side."

38. See Allen, "A Connected Society."

Works Cited

Allen, Danielle. "Ai Wei Wei and the Art of Protest." *The Nation*, August 29, 2012.

Allen, Danielle. "A Connected Society." *Soundings* 53 (Spring 2013): 103–13.

Allen, Danielle. *Our Declaration: A Reading of the Declaration of Independence in Defense of Equality*. New York: W. W. Norton, 2014.

Allen, Danielle. "Talent Is Everywhere: Using Zip Codes and Merit to Enhance Diversity." In *The Future of Affirmative Action: New Paths to Higher Education Diversity after "Fisher v. University of Texas,"* edited by Richard D. Kahlenberg, 145–59. New York: Century Foundation, 2014.

Allen, Danielle. *Talking to Strangers*. Chicago: University of Chicago Press, 2004.

Allen, Danielle. "Toward a Connected Society." In *Our Compelling Interests: The Value of Diversity for Democracy and a Prosperous Society*, edited by Earl Lewis and Nancy Kantor, 71–195. Princeton, NJ: Princeton University Press, 2016.

Allen, Danielle. *The World of Prometheus: The Politics of Punishing in Democratic Athens.* Princeton, NJ: Princeton University Press, 2002.

Allen, Danielle, and Justin Pottle. "Democratic Knowledge and the Problem of Faction." Knight Foundation White Paper, 2017.

Anderson, Elizabeth S. *Private Government: How Employers Rule Our Lives (and Why We Don't Talk about It).* Princeton, NJ: Princeton University Press, 2017.

Anderson, Elizabeth S. "What Is the Point of Equality?" *Ethics* 109, no. 2 (January 1999): 287–337.

Arendt, Hannah. *Men in Dark Times.* San Diego: Harcourt Brace, 1968.

Arendt, Hannah. "Reflections on Little Rock." *Dissent* 6, no. 1 (1959): 45–56.

Constant, Benjamin. "The Liberty of the Ancients Compared with That of the Moderns." Speech given at the Athéné Royale in Paris, 1819.

Farrell, Henry, and Cosma Shalizi. "Pursuing Cognitive Democracy." In *From Voice to Influence: Understanding Citizenship in a Digital Age*, edited by Danielle Allen and Jennifer S. Light, 211–31. Chicago: University of Chicago Press, 2015.

Gould, Carol. "Democratic Management and International Labor Rights." In *Global Justice and International Labour Rights*, edited by Yossi Dahan, Hanna Lerner, and Faina Milman-Sivan, 266–84. New York: Cambridge University Press, 2016.

Granovetter, Marc S. "The Strength of Weak Ties." *American Journal of Sociology* 78, no. 6 (1973): 1360–80.

Green, T. A. *Verdict according to Conscience: Perspectives on the English Criminal Trial Jury, 1200–1800.* Chicago: University of Chicago Press, 1985.

Nozick, Robert. "Distributive Justice." *Philosophy and Public Affairs* 3, no. 1. (Autumn 1973): 45–126.

Ober, Josiah. *Democracy and Knowledge: Innovation and Learning in Classical Athens.* Princeton, NJ: Princeton University Press, 2008.

Ober, Josiah. *Demopolis: Democracy before Liberalism in Theory and Practice.* Cambridge: Cambridge University Press, 2017.

Okin, Susan. *Justice, Gender, and the Family.* New York: Basic Books, 1991.

Presidential Commission for the Study of Bioethical Issues. *New Directions: The Ethics of Synthetic Biology and Emerging Technologies.* Washington, DC: Presidential Commission for the Study of Bioethical Issues, December 2010. https://papers.ssrn.com/sol3/papers.cfm?abstract_id=2445575, posted June 17, 2014.

Rawls, John. *Political Liberalism.* Exp. ed. Columbia Classics in Philosophy. New York: Columbia University Press, 2011.

Rawls, John. *A Theory of Justice.* Cambridge, MA: Belknap, 1971.

Rawls, John. *A Theory of Justice.* Revised edition. Cambridge, MA: Belknap, 1999.

Rebell, Michael. *Flunking Democracy: Schools, Courts, and Civic Participation.* Chicago: University of Chicago, 2018.

Sen, Amartya. "Democracy as a Universal Value." *Journal of Democracy* 10, no. 3 (1999): 3–17.

Sen, Amartya. *Development as Freedom.* New York: Alfred A. Knopf, 1999.

Shelby, Tommie. "Impure Dissent: Hip Hop and the Political Ethnica of Marginalized Black Urban Youth." In *From Voice to Influence*, edited by Danielle Allen and Jennifer S. Light, 59–79. Chicago: University of Chicago Press, 2015.

Sidanius, James, Shana Levin, Colette van Laar, and David O. Sears. *The Diversity Challenge: Social Identity and Intergroup Relations on the College Campus.* New York: Russell Sage Foundation, 2008.

Simon, Herbert. "Response to Philippe van Parijs on Universal Basic Income." *Boston Review*, October 2000. http://bostonreview.net/forum/basic-income-all/herbert-simon-ubi-and-flat-tax.

Sodonis, Tyler, and Joe Witte. "The Supply Side: Alternative Reform Approaches to Campaign Finance." *Fair Vote*, January 26, 2012. https://www.fairvote.org/citizens-united-rebuttal.

Szreter, S., and M. Woolcock. "Health by Association? Social Capital, Social Theory, and the Political Economy of Public Health." *International Journal of Epidemiology* 33, no. 4 (2004): 650–67.

Williams, Bernard. "The Idea of Equality." In his *In the Beginning Was the Deed: Realism and Moralism in Political Argument*, edited by Geoffrey Hawthorn, 97–114. Princeton, NJ: Princeton University Press, 2009.

2

Race, Domination, and Republicanism

Melvin L. Rogers

1. Introduction

Any effort to understand approaches to justice that rest on principles of nondomination would do well to attend to those who have sought to respond to racial domination. In particular, the resources of nineteenth-century African American political thought have much to offer. In the nineteenth century African American intellectuals, seeking to discover how to undo and ward off racial domination, drew on two different strands of the philosophical tradition of republicanism. In the process they produced a third strand in which republicanism is linked to racial equality. A look at this body of work offers us the chance to recover resources for contemporary projects of justice while also requiring us to revise traditional accounts of when and where republicanism as a political theory has waxed and waned. It will turn out that the work of building a political theory for justice as nondomination also requires undoing forms of domination reflected in the historiographic tradition.

The first strand of republicanism on which key early African American political intellectuals drew emerged from an emphasis placed on the civic character of the citizenry. For African American thinkers, this emphasis directed attention to the character mostly of white citizens and a failure of the republican tradition to foster an appropriate manner of behavior — what I shall call "comportment" — toward their black counterparts. African American thinkers in the early nineteenth century saw exclusion as rooted in white citizens' motivations and attitudes, which in turn shaped the character and the laws of the polity. These thinkers asked the questions of "who are we" and "who ought we to be," understanding such questions to constitute the political community as an ethical enterprise of invention and development rather than thinking that answers might come from the expression of so-called prepolitical values. They did not expect institutions to run on their own but connected the goal of realizing a just society to citizens' comportment. African American writers therefore directed their intellectual energies to the ethos of the American polity, treating laws and institutions as important but also as derivative of the characterological propensities of the nation. Republicanism in this guise has its focus on ideas of civic virtue, political participation, and character as central to a self-determining polity.[1]

The second strand of republicanism deployed by nineteenth-century African American intellectuals is that which defines freedom as nondomination. Use of this strand emerges in expressions of African Americans' desire to escape the internal tyranny of the United States. On republican definitions of freedom, one is free just to the extent that one's bodily movements are not at the arbitrary mercy of another. Republicanism in this guise, as Quentin Skinner and Philip Pettit argue, treats arbitrary power exercised over another as the worst form of enslavement.[2] This iteration of republicanism finds its roots in classical Rome, is rearticulated by Machiavelli during the Renaissance, and is defended by thinkers in the modern period such as James Harrington, Montesquieu, John Adams, and Thomas Jefferson. For this tradition, the security of freedom depends on (a) a republic imposing constitutional constraints that guard against arbitrary power and (b) institutional spaces that allow citizens contestatory power to ensure the proper functioning of a constitutional order. As one commentator explains, for the Romans "full *libertas* [or liberty] is coterminous with *civitas* [or citizenship]."[3] Nineteenth-century African American political thinkers often drew a connection between the two strands, arguing that the characterological orientation emphasized in the first tradition helps to realize and stabilize the institutional meaning of freedom found in the second. That is, civic virtue is the necessary foundation for free institutions that secure nondomination.

African American thinkers added to the meaning of both strands of republicanism. Sometimes the addition consisted of using republicanism's concepts—let's say civic virtue—in a situation or context not otherwise addressed in the tradition. In other instances the contribution involved complicating central concepts in the tradition—for instance, freedom and nondomination—by situating them within a different experiential context. This second approach involved not merely redeploying republicanism but also supplementing its toolbox to expand the range of contexts in which it can be used. The thinkers we will encounter in this chapter developed accounts of civic virtue that sought to embed racial justice in citizens' comportment, and explained how only institutions grounded in that revived conception of civic virtue would finally secure freedom.

Republicanism does not, of course, exhaust the tradition of African American political thought,[4] but it did serve as an important resource for earlier thinkers who contested the reach of white supremacy. There is also a through-line to the present. Contemporary activists in the Black Lives Matter movement often see themselves as trying to transform the ethos of the nation and also often invoke the importance of being free from arbitrary violence and domination. Their project is a continuation of the forms of republicanism that emerged in the nineteenth century. The thrust of this essay will be to explore the connection between the ethos and institutionalization of nondomination as elaborated by nineteenth-century African American political thinkers. We will gain conceptual tools for understanding difference without domination, and also a revised history of political republicanism. It is worth dwelling for a moment on this latter point.

Attending to various figures in African American political thought allows us to avoid the troublesome interpretative claim by contemporary thinkers that by the nineteenth century, republicanism was in retreat or already eclipsed. We need not find ourselves saying, as Pettit does, that "not only did the conception of freedom as non-interference displace the republican idea in the new liberal tradition. It apparently succeeded ... without anyone's noticing."[5] Nor should we be persuaded by Skinner's claim that "with the rise of classical utilitarianism in the eighteenth century," the idea of republicanism "eventually slipped almost wholly out of sight."[6] When we attend to those who fought the ongoing problem of slavery in the United States and the ascendancy of Jim Crow in the wake of the Civil War, we find the language of republicanism very much alive. Recognizing this allows me to advance an important point that remains hidden from view if our primary thinkers are Machiavelli, Harrington, and Jefferson: republicanism as a theory of nondomination, racial equality, and the characterological formation of a democratic people has been with us all along.

Why do conventional histories of republicanism miss this important moment in its history? Despite the neorepublican revival in political theory and history, and the significance of the United States as a primary historical site for understanding the meaning of republicanism, African Americans have been oddly out of view. What slips into the neorepublican revival is an implicit acceptance of criteria of validation of whose thoughts and expressions count as philosophical in the first instance and therefore worthy of historical attention and explication. Unsurprisingly, these criteria of validation are typically connected to those whose social status already accords them standing in philosophical debates. If, however, we treat theoretical reflections regardless of their form of expression or location of social origin as modes of political participation (as this essay does), we need not allow prior criteria of validation to constrain which thoughts count as worthy of explication or whose voices count as worthy of consideration. If we can unshackle ourselves from the chains of preconceived notions of authorial status, we can expand our historical narratives and avoid the blind spot at work in the contemporary neorepublican revival.[7] And we can also, of course, learn something important about race, domination, and republicanism.

As we shall see, two key themes will emerge from the thinkers under consideration in this essay: what is required of civic virtue under conditions of racial domination, and how can a definition of freedom as nondomination be deployed to combat racial domination specifically. Let me provide a review of the conceptual terrain.

What is required of civic virtue under conditions of racial domination? From the 1830s to the 1850s, thinkers such as David Walker, Hosea Easton, Martin Delany, and Frederick Douglass[8]—all black and all abolitionists—redefined civic virtue under conditions of racial exclusion as requiring solidarity among blacks (section 1). They direct their attention to the habits necessary to resist domination. Their writings coupled with the work of churches, newspapers, and literary and benevolent societies built up and out a counterpublic to confront white supremacy and hold at bay "social death," understood as the destruction of bonds of affection and culture and the denial of civic status.[9]

Yet even among them, they disagreed about the political implications of their positions, offering weak and strong versions of racial solidarity.[10] Although Walker is a clear defender of a nascent black nationalism in the form of racial unity, Delany follows the logic of racial solidarity to its end, even endorsing emigration in the 1850s. Here we see a redirection of republicanism's resources that reveals its political potential for redressing the status of African Americans, but the redirection involves these thinkers in developing divergent claims, first, about the possibility of transforming white Americans and second, and consequently, about the fate of African Americans in the United States.

These thinkers also complicate republicanism's commitment to freedom from domination by testing the view in relation to racial exclusion (section 2). The specter of slavery looms large for them, but they saw slavery and its meaning—a master who exercises power at his or her whim—as extending beyond formal practices of enslavement. In their analyses, slavery's reach is dispersed through the cultural sphere[11] of American life, circumscribing African Americans even in instances where there is no obvious master. Douglass succinctly captures the point when he says in 1848, "In Northern States, we are not slaves to individuals, not personal slaves, yet in many respects we are the slaves of the community."[12] African Americans highlight their domination by attending to the imbrication of race and white supremacy. To enjoy liberty requires not merely freedom from the arbitrary whim of particular agents or laws that limit arbitrary power, but a transformation of the system of cultural value in which blacks occupy a lower position of worth. These thinkers desired a form of citizenship found not only in the law but also in the heart.[13] And this could not be achieved by tracking institutional domination alone; it required also attending to the racial domination corrupting the soul of the nation.

When republicanism encounters racialized domination, the following second theme also emerges: *How might we add to the conceptual toolbox such that freedom as nondomination can do its distinctive work for African Americans?* In the republican theories I introduce, freedom is still understood as *nondomination*, but against the backdrop of race these theories require that African Americans acquire freedom through means that go beyond formal positive laws. Here we come up against the limits of republicanism as traditionally understood. Pettit, for instance, identifies the project of republicanism with seeking to satisfy the "range of constitutional constraints associated broadly with the mixed constitution."[14] He links subordination, as the Romans did, to the formal presence of a *dominus* or master. This definition of republicanism and these formal requirements obscure the question addressed in African American political thought. That is, Pettit and the tradition of republicanism more generally fail to deploy a more expansive notion of slavery—one that focuses not on those whose political standing is formally in doubt or denied but on those who were never seen as fit for freedom in the first place. Satisfying one's constitutional standing is a necessary but insufficient indicator of regard. But even in instances where Pettit highlights the importance of norms of proper regard—what he calls civility—he seems to miss that insofar as one's status as a slave is taken to be natural or normal, one will never be a fit object of proper regard, whatever one's formal status might be. Yet being held in regard as a person worthy of freedom is a precondition for the real achievement of republican ideals. A cultural habit of viewing blacks as natural slaves follows from the logic of white supremacy and its historical impact. Under a logic of white supremacy, republican principles can simultaneously be honored and be limited in their application to whites. Focusing on this issue explains why nineteenth-century African American thinkers were concerned to transform the cultural logic of American life. They wished to avoid being the slave of the community, as Douglass says.

Let me make one final point before we begin. A contemporary reader will undoubtedly wonder about the immediate significance of this argument, focused on nineteenth-century African American intellectuals. Yet their cause has come to the fore again. Like many of the thinkers discussed, African American youth involved in the Movement for Black Lives are asking not merely for a change in laws but also, as a condition for sustaining and underwriting a just society, for a deeper change in who we Americans take ourselves to be.

2. Civic Virtue as Racial Solidarity

a. Intimations of Republicanism

It is difficult, if not impossible, to read early African American thinkers and not be struck by the rich literary portraits of American society and the horror of black life therein. The point of such descriptions is to dramatize the differential application of care and concern in American society. In marking the difference between blacks and whites, however, African American thinkers point to the characterological distortion of the citizenry and simultaneously seek to transform it.

This is nowhere more clearly on display than in David Walker's incendiary 1829 *Appeal to the Colored Citizens of the World*—a pamphlet that marks a substantive break with earlier deferential and anti-inflammatory reflections.[15] Walker was born legally free in 1796 to an enslaved father and free mother in Wilmington, North Carolina. During his early years Walker traveled throughout the South, where he witnessed firsthand the horrors of black life. By 1825 he had moved to Boston with the aim of addressing racial domination. He was a respected member of the Boston community in part because of his leadership role in the Massachusetts General Colored Association (MGCA), an organization that sought to unite black Americans and combat domination, because of his membership in the African Masonic Lodge, and because of his work as an agent for the newly established black newspaper *Freedom's Journal*.

The *Appeal* confronts the reader with the tragic details of being black in the United States and, in doing so, calls into question the very humanity of white Americans. "Any man," writes Walker in article 2 of his four-article *Appeal*,

> who is curious to see the full force of ignorance developed among the coloured people of the United States of America, has only to go into the southern and western states of this confederacy, where, if he is not

a tyrant, but has the feelings of a human who can feel for a fellow creature, he may see enough to make his very heart bleed![16]

The invocation of sentiment, captured metaphorically in the bleeding
heart, should not be separated from the theme of character. Walker par-
ticipates in the wider intellectual culture of sentimental appeals central to
early American moral and political thought.[17] In this, he too believes sentimental exchanges reveal "the underlying commonality of human potential across artificial status divides" such as race.[18] He aligns the capacity
for fellow feeling with the image of being a human, and then uses this
as a normative compass to orient readers to the daily treatment of black
people. The aim is to cultivate proper comportment toward harms experienced by black bodies; such proper comportment would in turn produce a just society in which all can share.

Walker directs his reflections to the normative foundation of American life; he agrees in his pamphlet with Hosea Easton's remark in *A Treatise on the Intellectual Character, and Civic and Political Condition of the
Colored People of the United States* (1837) that "a government like this is at
any time liable to be revolutionized by the people, at any and every time
there is a change of public sentiment. This, perhaps, is as it should be."[19]
Like Walker, Easton joined MGCA; he was undoubtedly politicized by
the discrimination and exclusion his family experienced in the 1820s.[20]
But both Walker and Easton knew that institutional organizations were
not the only way to combat exclusion and believed that they should function as a discursive arena in which African Americans sharpened their
ethical and political skills. Easton's invocation of public sentiment expresses an underlying orientation that informs much of African American political thought, from its slave narratives to its political pamphlets
to displays of public protest. All vividly depict conditions of black life in
order to move public sentiment, recognizing the public as the primary authority. The storytelling or narrative mode sought to place white Americans behind the veil so that they might see and feel appropriately. These
efforts capture the aspiration to cultural agency that Allen describes as
one plank of political equality in her chapter. One might also think of the
nineteenth-century connection between narrative and sentimentalism as
a precursor to efforts to reduce implicit bias, such as are described in this
volume by Lai and Banaji. But in the nineteenth-century case, the idea
of the people, foundational to republican discourse, was central to the
effort. For Walker and Easton, this idea had both descriptive and aspirational connotations—that is, a people that is and that may yet be—and

both Walker and Easton depended on this double meaning for the efficacy of their intervention.[21] They sought to engender transformation by
juxtaposing critique of the people as it is to an aspirational picture of the
people that may be.

The emphasis on character and public sentiment was not new, even if
it took on a different articulation in Walker and Easton. Some of its most
important expressions had appeared among classical republican thinkers such as Aristotle and Cicero and were reaffirmed in American thinkers such as Jefferson and Adams. But whereas thinkers such as Jefferson
in particular appealed to character and public sentiment to affirm and
stabilize the white male portion of the polity, which they imagined as
constituting the whole of society, nineteenth-century African American
intellectuals emphasized character and public sentiment to highlight the
fracture at the core of the American *demos*.

The emphasis on character and public sentiment combines with republicanism's commitment to the common good. For Aristotle, Cicero,
Jefferson, and Adams, the stability of the polity depended on proper attentiveness on the part of citizens. They each interpret civic virtue as a
form of attentiveness that leads to the social integration of the community. Citizens must, as Cicero writes in *On Duties*, "fix their gaze so firmly
on what is beneficial to citizens" and "care for the whole body of the republic rather than protect one part and neglect the rest."[22] As Adams explains to political writer Mercy Otis Warren in 1776, civic virtue, or what
he calls public virtue,

> is the only Foundation of Republics. There must be a positive Pas-
> sion for the public good, the public Interest, Honor, Power, and Glory,
> established in the Minds of the People, or there can be no Republican
> Government, nor any real Liberty. And this public Passion must be
> Superior to all private Passions. Men must be ready ... and be happy to
> sacrifice their private Pleasures, Passions, and Interests, nay, their pri-
> vate Friendships and dearest Connections, when they stand in Com-
> petition with the Rights of Society.[23]

Civic virtue infuses and underwrites political participation and grounds
solidarity within the citizenry. There can be no equal institutional compensation, despite James Madison's promises, for deficiencies of civic
virtue.[24] A constitutional order thus depends on the attitudinal orientation of the citizenry, and civic virtue is its crowning achievement.

What, then, is one to do in the face of the differential application of
care and concern? After all, the idea of *common* in the term "common

good" has historically been limited by both racism and patriarchy and thus has often embraced only a portion of the US population. How does one act when one part of the polity is protected but the other is, as Cicero worried, neglected? These questions animate thinkers like Walker and Easton, allowing them to redirect the gaze of republicanism to the condition of internal slavery and the absence of mutual recognition.

Walker and Easton challenge us to confront the commingling of a limited, partial, exclusionary vision of the common good with a vision of freedom that, thanks to the limited picture of the common good, does not guard against domination but entrenches it. The distinction between blacks and whites — the habit of servility by the one and the practice of domination by the other — marks the source of America's moral corruption and with it the clipped wings of republicanism's theoretical possibilities. It is no wonder, then, that Easton, for example, reflects on the "condition and character of the colored people" in the United States and uses the status of black people as the measure of a healthy republic. The long-overlooked writings of nineteenth-century African American intellectuals provide resources to restore republicanism to its full aspirations and potential, a liberation that cannot be achieved on the basis only of work by thinkers more typically associated with that tradition.

Easton worries about the possibility of redeeming the nation. As he says, "But when the subjects of a republican government become morally and politically corrupt, there is but little chance remaining for republicanism." The reason for this, he goes on to say, is that "good laws, and a good form of government, are of but very little use to a wicked people."[25] The term *wicked* will seem archaic, but in this context it is an ethical predicate, denoting an impoverished character. To become the opposite of a wicked people will require the American nation to address the standing of African Americans. And despite his worry, Easton's pamphlet is meant to get the nation to address this issue.

When the analytical frames of republicanism are used to reflect on black subordination and slavery, an injunction to civic virtue does not lead to a requirement of attentiveness to a social whole from which one is excluded. Rather, solidarity *among* the excluded becomes the foundation of civic virtue necessary to respond to the polity as a whole. Civic virtue, now directed to the condition of African Americans, generates a form of solidarity grounded in one's identity. There can be no presumptive retreat to the common good, since its internal meaning at the level of American ethical life is partial, since social integration is determined by that partiality, and since institutional and juridical practices serve to express that domination. This need not imply (although Martin Delany will suggest otherwise) an unbridgeable divide between blacks and whites. But it does mean that actually existing cultures of domination motivate a defense of racial solidarity.

In the nineteenth-century United States, arguments for solidarity among African Americans emerged in two separate spheres—what we might call the *performative* and *explanatory* spheres of early black politics. The first resulted from memory of the Haitian Revolution as a performance of solidarity among slaves and the creation of self-directed organizations—churches, newspapers, literary societies, and benevolent organizations.[26] The Haitian Revolution, in particular, importantly performed the logic of the modern self-understanding otherwise on display in the American and French Revolutions. By "the modern self-understanding" I mean the idea that political deference can no longer be forced or demanded. Rather, political authorization must be tied to reflective assent and answerability in which all may claim to give direction to their own lives.[27] The Haitian capacity for self-governance served as a powerful rejoinder to the historical, philosophical, and scientific "animalization" of black people that otherwise functioned to deny them freedom.[28]

The Haitian Revolution, as we now know, most certainly galvanized black Americans, helping to bring to fruition the organizations identified above. Taken collectively, these organizations functioned as "a parallel discursive arena" in which to "formulate oppositional interpretations" of the identity, interests, and needs of black people.[29] As Samuel Cornish and John Russworm explain to their patrons in the first issue of *Freedom's Journal*, the first African American newspaper, in 1827, "We wish to plead our own cause. Too long have others spoken for us. Too long has the publick been deceived by misrepresentations, in things which concern us dearly."[30] The black counterpublic, however, was not confined to the literate black communities of the Northeast; rather these writers sought to forge a community among the free and enslaved, the literate and illiterate. Hence Walker says, "It is expected that all colored men, women and children, of every nation, language and tongue under heaven, will try to procure a copy of this *Appeal* and read it, or *get someone to read it to them*."[31]

The second, explanatory sphere is captured by the intellectual intervention among the African American intelligentsia—an attempt to *explain* rather than *perform* solidarity. Thinkers such as Walker, Easton, and Delany (among others) most clearly contribute to this second sphere (even as they were often members of the organizations included under the first point). For them, racial solidarity is less of a departure from republicanism and more of an entailment of civic virtue under conditions of racial domination. But racial solidarity comes in weak and strong ver-sions. The difference has less to do with the meaning ascribed by each thinker to "blackness" or the degree to which each offered essentializing definitions of color; instead the weak and strong versions of solidarity flowed from analysis of what each thinker believed was possible for white Americans.[32] This is because chattel slavery (rather than political slavery) would not be easily rectified by the extension of the franchise, since the status of an enslaved person had come to be thought of as consistent with the natural order of things. Chattel slavery thus poses a distinct problem whose resolution depends either on a characterological transformation of those who were once masters or on the acquisition of a separate geo-graphical territory for self-sovereignty.

b. Civic Virtue as Nascent Racial Solidarity: Walker and Easton

How precisely did Walker and Easton understand an account of racial solidarity? To answer this question we need first to get clear about the functioning of racial classification. Briefly, racial classification takes the form of assigning meaning to what Paul Taylor refers to as "human bodies and bloodlines," meaning that permits one to "draw inferences about more distant, often non-physical matters" such as intelligence, imagi-nation, and moral agency.[33] Racial classification in the eighteenth and nineteenth centuries functioned as a global category; these classifications supported broad judgments about particular individuals who fell under specific racial categories. As Jefferson, for example, argued in *Notes on the State of Virginia* of 1787, especially in query 14, regardless of the bio-logical source of a person's blackness, its meaning was of importance for understanding the capacities of African Americans.[34] Although Jefferson advanced it as a "suspicion," no one doubted the force of his claim that "whether originally a distinct race, or made distinct by time and circum-stances, [the blacks] are inferior to the whites in the endowments of body and mind."[35]

Walker and Easton sought to make the globalizing nature of racial classifications their primary target of analysis. The idea is that since race refers to groups rather than individuals, each person's subjective identity was replaced by the larger attributions applied to the race. Thus blacks lit-erally became interchangeable, no matter where they lived in the country. Hence Walker said to his northern readers, "If any of you wish to know how FREE you are, let one of you start and go through the southern and western States of this country, and unless ... you have your free papers, (which if you are not careful they will get from you) ... [they will] sell you into eternal slavery."[36] Notice that Walker does not accept the negative content given to race; rather, he is trying to get his readers to understand how the classification collapses the distinction between the nominally free and the enslaved. With a force that extended well beyond slavery, racial classification was the fundamental problem. (The issues of classification and measurement have been perennially challenging for efforts to move toward worlds where difference does not articulate with domination; the second part of this volume takes up these questions.)

This, of course, clarifies the problems of unfreedom faced by African Americans in the nineteenth century, but the point that I want to emphasize is less about freedom per se and more about the logic of solidarity that emerges from this account. As Walker says, "I advanced it therefore to you, not as a *problematical*, but as an unshaken and forever immovable *fact*, that your full glory and happiness, as well as all other colored people under Heaven, shall never be fully consummated, but with the entire emancipation of your enslaved brethren all over the world."[37] This is a clarion call for solidarity as a fundamental element in securing black liberation. Traditional republicanism would mislead given its emphasis on virtuous activity as an expression of freedom. For African Americans, it would be a mistake to assume that mere individualized self-assertion would suffice to secure freedom or capture freedom's full expression. Because of racial classifications, one's individual subjectivity cannot even come fully into view; a project of transformation through solidarity is necessarily prior to secure the conditions for freedom. (In this volume, Heather Gerken explores what this insight means for political representation.)

What, then, is required to generate and sustain a successful black community? In Walker and Easton's view the answer is coordinated effort with other blacks to resist racial domination and transform the system responsible for it, since African Americans individually are likely to suffer when racial designations are at work. Solidarity in this sense is a functional outgrowth of racial categorization. Measurement and classification are often used for ill but can also, paradoxically, be turned against their ill effects. But we should proceed with care. As Eddie Glaude argues, this view of racial solidarity uses the covering-law universalism of racial classification, but it rejects the essentialism upon which it is based.[38]

For Walker and Easton, just as race is the organizing principle of domination, it becomes the organizing principle that colors civic virtue. If civic virtue is fundamentally about the habits necessary to sustain and realize a political community, it is now particularized in Walker and Easton's hands. Civic virtue in this context does not point toward habits necessary to sustain the American polity as a whole, since that polity is inter-nally divided in any case; rather, civic virtue is racialized, expressing itself as solidarity in order to both fortify African Americans and contest the logic of racism and white supremacy responsible for their unequal status. Ethical and political transformation must first attend to the source of the corruption. Or to put it simply, African Americans must be able to name the problem, and that requires the language of race. If this is right, it is not race understood as a substantive natural kind, but race understood as an experiential outgrowth of domination. If race is the basis for one's exclusion, it must now serve as the foundation for the coordinated efforts of black Americans.

This is nonetheless a weak form of racial solidarity. Walker and Easton's argument endorses racial solidarity as the initial move toward a more racially inclusive society. They hold out the possibility of ethical and political transformation for white Americans. Walker and Easton seek to awaken their white counterparts—to get them to see that in dominating African Americans, they betray the meaning of their republicanism. Thus Easton explains,

> I have taken this course to illustrate the state of a people with a good government and laws, and with a disposition to explain away all their meaning. My conclusions are, that such republicans are capable, like the angel about which I have spoken, to carry out their republican-ism into the most fatal despotism. A republican form of government, therefore, can be a blessing to no people, further than they make hon-est virtue the rule of life.[39]

As contemporary psychologists recognize, and as Lai and Banaji discuss in this volume, inspiring the motivation to change is the mystery element necessary to generate social transformation. Here in the nineteenth cen-tury, intellectuals like Easton wielded rhetorical tools precisely in order to cultivate that motivation to change.

Walker did as well, asking his white counterparts to attend to the language of their Declaration of Independence. "See your Declaration, Americans!!! Do you understand your own language?"[40] Walker, like Easton, intends to generate reflective dissonance that may provoke a re-orientation toward African Americans.[41] In this they are not yet com-mitted to the proposition that white Americans are beyond transforma-tion or that the habit of servility by blacks and the practice of domination by whites fully exhaust the ethos of the nation. Precisely because they do not subscribe to the idea that white supremacy has fully colonized the character of the nation, their advocacy of racial solidarity recommends only a nascent form of group unity that also aspires toward developing a society where all enjoy freedom and equality.

c. Delany, Solidarity, and Emigration

Martin Delany, physician and perhaps the first defender of black nationalism, followed the logic of solidarity further to what appears to be its natural conclusion. But he did so, as we will see, because of how he diagnosed the state of affairs with his white counterparts. Of course Delany's *The Condition, Elevation, Emigration and Destiny of the Colored People of the United States*, published in April 1852, is separated from Walker's *Appeal* by more than two decades and from Easton's *Treatise* by a little less. By the 1850s the racial context was far darker than it had appeared in 1829. This touched Delany personally: he and several other black students were dismissed from Harvard Medical School because of their race. It affected his fellow African Americans directly in the form of the draconian Fugitive Slave Law of 1850. Emerging out of the Compromise of 1850, the law required that slaves who had escaped and found their way to free states were to be captured and returned to their presumptive masters. Delany's text is a direct response to his personal situation, but more significantly to the Compromise and the Fugitive Slave Law, prompting him to argue for emigration.

Delany's interest in the Fugitive Slave Law brings into sharp focus an aspect of his thinking that is not often pursued but that illuminates his sophisticated understanding of the relationship between law and ethical life. Delany views the passage of the law as effectively settling any and all appeals one might make to the polity for inclusion. As he says, "To imagine ourselves to be included in the body politic, except by express legislation, is at war with common sense, and contrary to fact."[42] The reason is that both the passage and the maintenance of the law reveal the ethical norms that guide the polity and underwrite the unequal status of African Americans in the United States.

For Delany, this reveals not a society that has accidentally betrayed itself and that might recover its purpose, as suggested by Walker and Easton, but rather a social and political community built on a fundamental refusal to acknowledge the dignity of African Americans. In short, Walker, Easton, and Delany disagree about the internal normative coherence of American society as it relates to the standing of black persons. Delany thus writes, marking a difference between himself and the earlier thinkers, "We are politically, not of them, but aliens to the laws and political privileges of the country. These are truths—fixed facts, that quaint theory and exhausted moralizing, are impregnable to, and fall harmlessly before."[43] He was, of course, not alone. The publishers of the first black newspaper of Cleveland, Ohio, captured the status of black Americans in the title they selected: *The Aliened American*. The United States, they said in their first issue, had made black Americans into "aliens—through their Law, their Public Opinion and their Community-Regulations."[44] The disagreement between Walker and Easton, on the one hand, and Delany on the other, captures the difficulty involved in diagnosing patterns of domination. When are identifiable forms of domination reversible and when are they not? Any political theory built on pursuit of nondomination must wrestle with this question.

The rejection of political and moral philosophizing and the idea of African American domination as a fixed fact of American life targeted not only thinkers such as Walker and Easton, but also Frederick Douglass, with whom Delany served as a coeditor on Douglass's newspaper *The North Star*. As he says in a letter to Douglass, expressing his disappointment that Douglass did not take notice of his 1852 book in his newspaper, now called *Frederick Douglass' Papers*, "I care but little, what white men think of what I say, write, or do; my sole desire is, to benefit the colored people; this being done, I am satisfied."[45] The implication, of course, was that in taking notice of the work of white Americans, as was the case with Harriet Beecher Stowe's *Uncle Tom's Cabin* published in March 1852, Douglass was committed to the goal of transforming white Americans and thought such a goal possible. Like Walker and Easton, Douglass agreed in 1848 that the main work for black improvement must be "commenced, carried on, and concluded by ourselves," but this did not require one to reject a transformed American polity in which blacks and whites could live.[46] But this, Delany suggests, is to deny the facts on the ground that reveal the alien status of black people in the American context. Whereas Walker, Easton, and Douglass were willing to offer up narratives about African American life, in effect, as therapy for white people, as did Stowe with her sentimentalist blockbuster, Delany rejected that technique because he repudiated any belief that moral improvement was possible for white America.

In contrast, Delany's analysis of the Fugitive Slave Law fueled his argument for emigration. Although this conclusion found support in other writers during the time such as Mary Ann Shadd and James Theodore Holly,[47] we find its most sophisticated articulation in Delany's writing. Delany focused on the Fugitive Slave Law not because he believed law is the exclusive source of equality but because he took the idea of law to be expressive of and to condition the underlying ethos or spirit of the people. The law crystallized the background attitudinal orientation of the citizenry; it was the material expression of the normative identity of the people. As Delany put it, "A people capable of originating and sustaining such a law as this, are not the people to whom we are willing to entrust our liberty at discretion."[48]

Not only were nineteenth-century white Americans capable of bringing into existence a law of domination, but they were also capable of sustaining their commitment to it over time. This marked African Americans as alien to the polity and also marked the polity as alien to them. It was precisely the reach of prejudice, constituting, as it were, the ethical life of American society, that prompted Alexis de Tocqueville to famously remark, "It can happen that a man will rise above prejudices of religion, country, and race, and if that man is a king, he can bring about astonishing transformations in society; but it is not possible for a whole people to rise, as it were, above itself."[49] In his keynote address delivered to the National Emigration Convention of Colored Men in Cleveland, Ohio, in 1854, Delany explains the radical transformation required to change the status of African Americans:

> In the United States, among the whites, their color is made, by law and custom, the mark of distinction and superiority; while the color of the blacks is a badge of degradation, acknowledged by statute, organic law, and the common consent of the people.
>
> With this view of the case—which we hold to be correct—to elevate to equality the degraded subject of law and custom, it can only be done ... by an entire destruction of the identity of the former condition of the applicant.[50]

With "identity" here, Delany has in mind the identity that is ascribed to African Americans by virtue of their race, what he calls the badge of degradation that is instantiated in the political, legal, and cultural life of American society. The identity of white Americans partly comes about, or so Delany suggests, by virtue of this contrast to their darker counterparts. To overcome this condition required that one destroy the badge of degradation, but this also involved, significantly, white Americans' willingness to destroy the legal and customary badge of superiority they were able to flaunt. White Americans needed, in Tocqueville's herculean imagery, to quite literally rise above themselves. Delany doubted this possibility not because he thought it unimaginable but because he believed "ages incalculable" would need to pass in order to claim victory.[51] What untold sacrifices, Delany asks, would need to be made by blacks if they waited for whites to become something other than what they seemed to be? When difference without domination is impossible, the only available avenue is exit or revolution.

This background understanding frames Delany's account of solidarity.[52] The problem required cooperation among blacks to resist domination (here he agreed with Walker, Easton, and Douglass), but it also required a more significant form of racial unity that would eventuate in the founding of an independent state. "To advocate the emigration of the colored people of the United States from their native homes," he writes, "is a new feature in our history, and at first view, may be considered objectionable, as pernicious to our interests. This objection is at once removed, when reflecting on our condition."[53] This is largely because the condition emerged from deep recesses of the American identity that could not easily be changed.

Two things marked Delany's analysis. First, he viewed the nation as effectively beyond transformation because the origination and maintenance of exclusion revealed the underlying character of a people as standing at odds with African American equality. Second, the depth of the problem called into doubt the probable success of any appeals to whites, and instead required a radical affirmation of racial solidarity in the form of emigration. As with Walker and Easton, civic virtue is racialized, but against the backdrop of Delany's analysis, it pointed beyond the shores of the United States. Emigration turns out not to be an affront to republicanism but an outgrowth of its logic.

d. Freedom as Racialized Nondomination

Thus far I have laid out the centrality of civic virtue to republicanism and elucidated how civic virtue was racialized in the hands of nineteenth-century African American intellectuals as a response to background conditions of domination and exclusion. In light of the problem of racism, calls to civic virtue should not function as a mechanism for stabilizing the community as a whole but rather serve as a resource for underwriting and fortifying African Americans. When republicanism is placed within the context of racial exclusion, civic virtue is transformed into racial solidarity. The weak version of this account turns out to be an endorsement of racial unity as the condition for transforming the polity—solidarity as loyalty and in support of the exercise of transforming voice. This strand of republicanism takes seriously the centrality of character but does not yet imagine the character of white Americans as unresponsive to the claim of nonwhites, in this case African Americans. The stronger version of this account also endorses racial unity but as a precondition for constituting a new polity altogether. This stronger version of racialized republicanism also takes seriously the importance of character, but it treats white supremacy as so thoroughly constitutive of American identity that appeals for transformation are nearly impossible. Exit becomes the necessary expression of republican commitments.

Now, in conditions of increased social diversity in countries around the globe and continuing racial inequalities in the United States, once again republicanism need not be displaced, but it is in need of theoretical supplementation in order to properly align freedom as nondomination with the specificity of the conditions confronted by African Americans. Just as in the nineteenth century, republicanism that took seriously the racialized nature of the American polity developed expanded definitions of civic virtue and trenchant analyses of the capacity of the people for characterological transformation, so too must we again expand the tools of republicanism in the twenty-first century. This will involve disconnecting domination from its primary indicator, that of a *dominus* or master, and connecting it more broadly to culture as such than we see in Pettit. Let me briefly sketch Pettit's position before returning to the thinkers we have already considered. With these final moves I hope to distill some insights for thinking about solidarity and difference without domination in contemporary circumstances.

3. Pettit and Republicanism

In his books *Republicanism: A Theory of Freedom and Government* and *On the People's Terms: A Republican Theory and Model of Democracy*, Pettit defends a variant of republicanism that draws from Greek and Roman sources. This version, defined largely by its concern with freedom, argues that "people could enjoy liberty both in relation to one another and to the collectivity, only by being invested with the power and status of the *civis*, or 'citizen.'"[54] To be a citizen comes with a distinct kind of power — a power to hold at bay those who would privately or publicly have you at their arbitrary mercy. In the absence of said power, one is under a condition of domination.

To be dominated, Pettit tells us, involves a relationship in which one person has "(1) the capacity to interfere; (2) on an arbitrary basis; (3) in certain choices that the other is in a position to make."[55] What is significant here is that dominating parties need not use their power; they need only have the capacity to deploy their power over you if they so choose. This is really what it means to be at the arbitrary mercy of another—you never know when the dominating party will act. As stated by Cicero, a figure from whom Pettit draws intellectual energy, "freedom . . . is not a matter of having a just master, but of having none at all." John Locke puts the point more forcefully: "Nobody can desire to have me in his absolute power, unless it be to compel me by force to that which is against the right of my freedom, *i.e.* make me a slave."[56] The primary counterexample to which republicans are drawn, as indicated by Locke's language, is the master-slave relationship. To be a slave is to be at the arbitrary mercy of a master, even if the master is of the benevolent kind.

Notice that this account of domination is not merely about actual interference. On this view, Pettit believes republicanism is far more robust when compared to its liberal alternative. Whereas the tradition of liberalism focuses on actual interference as the test for when freedom is threatened or eclipsed, republicanism, argues Pettit, looks to structural conditions wherein your actions depend on another party's staying his or her hand (be it a private individual or a state official). Although the master-slave relationship is the signature example, domination reverberates across time in other relationships such as the wife who lives at the whim of her abusive husband or a worker whose job is always in danger.

Republicanism counters the danger of domination with three definitive elements of the view. The first is the vision of freedom as nondomination. But how is this realized? It is realized through the second feature: a body of laws that (a) track the interest and concerns of the citizenry and that (b) "satisfy a range of constitutional constraints associated broadly with the mixed constitution." In the event that there is a need to realign state and society with the first two points above, the third feature stipulates that space must be open for citizens to "contest public policies and initiatives."[57] Notice that this account of republicanism is not dissimilar to liberalism, as Pettit implies, since the origin of that tradition can be traced to a desire to remove citizens from a condition of perpetual vulnerability. Entrenchment of liberal rights in a constitutional order subject to periodic electoral realignment and contestation was meant to enable citizens to give direction to their lives rather than having to defer to the whim of elites, monarchs, or religious leaders. That said, if we follow Pettit's analysis we find a more muscular normative understanding of freedom to allow us to do the things outlined above. Thus liberalism and republicanism, as Pettit configures them, both aspire to render citizens free and they both conceive of the rule of law through a constitutional framework as the ideal goal, but they disagree on the robustness of the normative ideal that can ensure that a free and self-governing people remain so constituted.

4. Freedom as Nondomination Reconsidered

This is a very brief sketch of Pettit's argument, and few would deny that domination so understood threatens freedom. Yet it is not clear that this rendering of domination or the response to it addresses the concerns of African Americans. Nor do I think this failure is particular to Pettit's interpretation of the tradition. The reason has to do with the particular kind of slavery to which traditional republicanism is a response—political slavery, not chattel slavery. Recall that in Pettit's account freedom is always explained as an opposition between citizenship and slavery. The historical presumption—and this was at work in Aristotle and Harrington as well as the American framers—was that a status that one was owed was now denied. In Aristotle, explains Mary Nyquist, political slavery derived its meaning "from an opposition between those for whom it would represent a demeaning, traumatic loss and those for whom it was supposed to be natural."[58] This idea continued well into seventeenth-century England, under monarchical rule. While it was true that for the English the monarch was supreme over his subjects, it did not follow that he could do with them as he pleased. Something protected those subjects from the king's domination. That something was cultural views of the worth even of those lowly subjects, an acknowledgment, as Ajume Wingo argues in this volume, of their basic dignity.

During the time of the American Revolution, the idea was not that the colonists were seeking rights they did not have but that they were seeking to reclaim their rightful status as British subjects. For example, in 1774 Jefferson criticized "the wanton exercise of [the King's] power" against the rights of British America.[59] The king's refusal to respond appropriately led the colonists to address him accordingly in the Declaration of Independence: "A prince whose character is thus marked by every act which may define a tyrant is unfit to be the ruler of a Free people." The idea, of course, was (a) that monarchy and the idea of a free people could fit seamlessly together and (b) the king had now acted illegitimately, thus making himself a tyrant or master. From Aristotle to the British monarchy to the American framers, political slavery involved a denial of rightful standing to those to whom it was due. In other words, a dominating figure was defined as one who acted against standing laws and customs or outside the boundaries of constitutional norms. Addressing this situation merely involved proper alignment with standing laws and customs or ensuring the proper functioning of constitutional norms. Hence Jefferson in 1775 longed for "a restoration of our just rights."[60] The Americans, for example, did not create a polity *de novo*; rather, they established a polity that better aligned with norms with which they were familiar. Pettit's republicanism develops out of this strand of thought.[61] This explains why freedom as nondomination is realized through the proper establishment of positive laws and a constitutional order that removes the threat of tyranny, all resting on a basic protection secured by culture.

But if the problem to be addressed by republicanism is not political but chattel slavery, then Pettit's configuration of republicanism is inadequate. Indeed the entirety of the tradition that focuses on political slavery will miss the depth of the problem that African Americans confronted. The problem was not the denial of a status within a political community already acknowledged as one's due, but denial of the very idea that any political status at all might be due to one. For African Americans, the cultural protection of their basic worth or human dignity was absent. For many white republicans, citizenship sat comfortably alongside ideas about natural slavery. Chattel slavery is of a different kind because it is tied to normative claims about racial superiority; it cannot effectively be addressed by the response provided to political slavery. A full account of republicanism, and of freedom as nondomination, must expand to address the conditions of domination that attach to a phenomenon like chattel slavery, namely social death.

To understand what it means to redirect republicanism from a concern merely with political slavery to one that includes chattel slavery, we should focus less on the figure of the master or *dominus* common to both political and chattel slavery and more on the idea that in the first case (political slavery) one's status as a slave is a violation of recognized standing while in the second case (chattel slavery) one's status as a slave is perceived to be natural. One cannot reclaim a status in a community that one never had — a reality that prompted Delany, as noted above, to describe the American polity as being just as alien to blacks as they are to it.[62] This second configuration of republicanism extends well beyond the figure of the master to the domain of culture itself. This is what Douglass has in mind in his 1848 address when he says of nominally free blacks, "In Northern States, we are not slaves to individuals, not personal slaves, yet in many respects we are the slaves of the community."[63]

How ought we to understand this idea of being a slave of the community? This unites the nominally free blacks in northern states with their physically enslaved fellows in the South. To get a handle on this we need

to return to combine Walker's insights with those of Easton. We begin
first with Walker: "If any of you wish to know how FREE you are, let one
of you start and go through the southern and western States of this country, and unless ... you have your free papers, (which if you are not careful they will get from you) ... [they will] sell you into eternal slavery."[64]
With this remark Walker captures how race functions. Its internal content
functions as a universal category to eclipse the subjectivity of individual
blacks and the contextual specificity of their lives.

Easton, understanding precisely how the logic of racial classification
functions, explains that the substantive cultural and ethical meaning of
one's racial designation is an auxiliary to slavery and legal codes of exclusion, following "its victims in every avenue of life."[65] Easton distinguishes in his *Treatise*, as does Walker before him and Douglass after him,
between the institution of slavery and the practices of racial prejudice
to which it is tied, underscoring how the latter lives well beyond even
the penumbra of the former. These thinkers are directing our attention
to the logic of white supremacy as it frames racial categorization. The
logic permeates the cultural zone and therefore extends beyond any specific institutional instantiation, permitting constant reinvention and re-
introduction across evolving institutional forms. This also explains why
blacks traveling in specific states must carry free papers. Travelling with
free papers is meant to render one exempt from the "natural" or "normal"
status of blacks as inferior (per the classification) and therefore to the
stigma of race (i.e., what follows them into every avenue of life), or so one
would think. Walker, Easton, and Douglass thus pointed out the differential application of regard at the heart of the American polity—following
as it does from the supposed differences among races. This differential regard—requiring some but not all to carry papers to prove status against
a presumptive lack of status—conditions laws and institutional practices
and, is in turn, influenced by those very laws and practices. The enormity
of this insidious framework is what caused Delany in the 1850s to aban-
don faith in transformation.

However we understand the differences internal to early African
American political thought, all of these thinkers advanced this argument
about the logic of white supremacy to make a pointed claim to their black
counterparts. It was this: Those who took themselves to be free, let's say,
in the northern states in contrast to the southern states, were deeply
and profoundly confused. The reason was simple. To the extent that one
could not travel freely across all the states, freedom experienced in any
one of the states was an illusion. But notice what is going on here; this

is not merely a claim about the laws on the books. The point is that the position of African Americans as subordinates had been naturalized. Servility had become the normal mode of comportment expected of them, and their freedom was seen as a violation of the natural order. This lives in cultural memory and habituates all those educated therein. Jefferson classically stated the point, even as he contributed to the problem:

> Our children see this [commerce between master and slave], and learn to imitate it; for man is an imitative animal. This quality is the germ of all education in him. From his cradle to his grave he is learning to do what he sees others do. If a parent could find not motive either in his philanthropy or his self-love, for restraining the intemperance of passions toward his slave, it should always be a sufficient one that his child is present. But generally it is not sufficient. The parent storms, the child looks on, catches the lineaments of wrath, puts on the same airs in the circle of smaller slaves, gives loose to the worst of passions, and thus nursed, educated, and daily exercised in tyranny, cannot but be stamped by it with odious peculiarities.[66]

Against this backdrop, freedom thus turns out to be ephemeral, a temporary break from reality that leaves African American liberty without cultural support. Without such support, freedom is not resilient, and for that reason it can hardly be called freedom at all. Psychologists working on implicit bias today should also take this point seriously. There is little hope in changing individual minds if the broader cultural context continuously educates people to hold some in lower regard than others. Moreover, responses to these forms of domination, if confined to the domain of legality, will obscure the deeper problems for standing that are anchored by the cultural context.

Pettit might well respond that traditional republicanism is not as narrow as I describe it as being. After all, he does say that if people do not identify with a republican way of life, it is unlikely that the freedom of persons will remain protected. "The reliable enjoyment of non-domination . . . requires that there are also socially established norms that give an added salience and security and lustre" to the areas of life that are beyond the law. Given this, he continues, "you will not have to depend just on the effectiveness of the law for your freedom as non-domination; you will also be able to put your trust in the power of established norms." Does not this language, Pettit might say, speak directly to the concerns that animate this early tradition of African American political thought? For if such norms exist, "others will be moved to acknowledge your place and your standing, not just by a susceptibility to legal sanction, but also by a spontaneous, culturally reinforced civility."[67]

This is a powerful rejoinder to the criticism I have leveled against the tradition and the necessity for attending carefully to African American intellectuals and their conceptual contributions to it. But we move too quickly if we think Pettit has gone far enough. For citizens must see one another as fit objects of their civility—that is, I must see you as someone to whom proper regard ought to be extended in the first instance, if you are to have the protections of a largely republican culture. The point for these thinkers is not that American society was in need of civility but that African Americans were rarely, if ever, seen as its due recipients. In this context, civility was functioning, but it was delimited in a specific way.

We now need a way to explain the differential application of civility. To get at a proper explanation requires us to see that chattel slavery and the idea of white supremacy served, among other things, as devices of normative distortion. These cultural forms were not anomalies but central to the modern ethical and political imagination. The norm of civility thus ran alongside and was constrained by white supremacy; republicanism reigned but, oddly, was seamlessly connected to whiteness. In fact, given that civility was about a form of courtesy in behavior as informed by republican principles, arguments in defense of abolition and equality for black Americans were often seen as violations of civility. It was this particular characterization of the problem to which African Americans, with their concerns about culture and being the slave of the community, sought to bring into view. For their aim was to bring about an attitudinal transformation to ensure the wide application of republican principles. But the possibility of this attitudinal transformation requires that we treat chattel slavery and the normative framework of white supremacy as foundational to our theorization of freedom. If a restrictive focus on legality is inappropriate for addressing the racialized character of domination because it leaves out the need for cultural transformation, civility also seems inadequate because it fails to address the central logic of white supremacy that can shape civility's functioning without harming republican principles. Each of these republican strategies fails to address how proper regard and standing are frustrated by the naturalized or normalized logic of black servility and white superiority.

The argument of the Black Lives Matter movement is precisely for the overthrow of paradigms that depend on assigning a lower value to the lives of black people than to others. A full-fledged republicanism must begin by recovering a commitment to equal human worth and a presumption that all have political and social standing. Difference without domination begins here, with equal human worth. Only on the basis of such a plank can republicanism's legal strategies and education for civic virtue secure freedom.

Notes

1. For a discussion of republicanism and its reach into American political thought, see Pocock, *The Machiavellian Moment*; and Sellers, *American Republicanism*. Contemporary affinities can be found in Sandel, *Democracy's Discontents*; Dagger, *Civic Virtues*; and Viroli, *Republicanism*.

2. By Skinner: "Machiavelli on the Maintenance of Liberty"; "The Idea of Negative Liberty"; "The Republican Ideal of Political Liberty"; and *Liberty before Liberalism*. By Pettit: *Republicanism*; *On the People's Terms*; and *Just Freedom*.

3. Wirszubski, *Libertas as a Political Ideal at Rome*, 3.

4. For the rich diversity of the tradition of African American political thought see Dawson, *Black Visions*. There are other texts that take up one or more of the traditions attended to by Dawson. A short selection includes West, *Prophesy Deliverance!*; Robinson, *Black Marxism*; Collins, *Black Feminist*; and Glaude, *Exodus!*

5. Pettit, *Republicanism*, 49; cf. Pettit, *On the People's Terms*, chap. 1.

6. Skinner, *Liberty before Liberalism*, 96.

7. Appreciation should be extended to Davide Panagia for helping me understand this point. For a similar argument with which this account is sympathetic see Hesse, "Escaping Liberty."

8. Walker, *Appeal to the Coloured Citizens*, article 2; Easton, *A Treatise on the Intellectual Character*, 63–123; Delany, *The Condition, Elevation, Emigration, and Destiny of the Colored People*.

9. For more on these organizations the reader might consult Horton and Horton, *In Hope of Liberty*, chap. 6; Vogel, *The Black Press*; McHenry, *Forgotten Readers*; Bacon, *Freedom's Journal*; Ball, *To Live an Antislavery Life*; Kantrowitz, *More Than Freedom*. The concept of "social death" in this instance is drawn from Orlando Patterson's analysis of slavery as producing natal and social alienation that excludes the slave not only from the goods of citizenship but also from the goods of social life as such. See Patterson, *Slavery and Society Death*, pt. 1; cf. Brown, "Social Death and Political Life in the Study of Slavery."

10. My language here of "weak" and "strong" version of racial solidarity is inspired by, although not consistent with, Shelby, *We Who Are Dark*, 27.

11. By cultural sphere I do not simply mean E. B. Tylor's "complex whole which includes knowledge, belief, art, morals, law, customs and any other capabilities and habits acquired" by being a member of a society, but also the ways in which culture is a site where power relations originate and are potentially disrupted (Tylor, *Primitive Culture*, 1). This means, of course, that culture will not merely be about political institutions, although those are important, but will permeate all the institutions of social life.

12. Douglass, "An Address to the Colored People of the United States" (1848), 119.

13. The most compelling rendering of this claim is found in Kantrowitz, *More Than Freedom*. Although Neil Roberts would follow neither Kantrowitz nor me in tying the meaning of citizenship to affective states, he does rightly see that for black people under

conditions of chattel slavery the meaning of freedom is not effectively realized through a legalistic framework (see Roberts, *Freedom as Marronage*, esp. chap. 3).

14. Pettit, *On the People's Terms*, 5.

15. On the important rhetorical difference of Walker's text in comparison to earlier appeals by other African Americans see Newman, Rael, and Lapsansky, introduction to their *Pamphlets of Protest*, 1–31, esp. 14.

16. Walker, *Appeal to the Coloured Citizens*, 23.

17. For richer accounts of sentiment in the early American context, see Burstein, *Sentimental Democracy*, and Eustace, *Passion Is the Gale*.

18. Eustace, *Passion Is the Gale*, 15.

19. Easton, *Treatise on the Intellectual Character*, 90.

20. More detail on Easton's upbringing and the details of discrimination experienced is laid out in Price and Stewart, introduction to *To Heal the Scourge of the Prejudice*, 1–47.

21. For more on the account of the people see Canovan, *The People*; Frank, *Constitute Moments*; Rogers, "The People, Rhetoric, and Affect," 190–93.

22. Cicero, *On Duties*, 33. For a more careful analysis of this point that connects Aristotle and Cicero, see Honohan, *Civic Republicanism*, chap. 1.

23. John Adams to Mercy Otis Warren, April 16, 1776, in *The Founders' Constitution*, vol. 1, chap. 18, document 9: http://press-pubs.uchicago.edu/founders/documents/v1c h18s9.html.

24. In fairness to Madison, it is not that civic virtue goes out the window; rather the strong faith that republicans placed in the virtue of humanity must be appropriately chastened. Madison argues that there is sufficient virtue present in humanity to sustain a self-governing society, but not so much virtue that we can do without the structure of constitutional government, whose mechanistic quality can function on its own — see Hamilton, Madison, and Jay, *The Federalist*, nos. 51 and 55. As Gordon Wood explains, the Constitution functioned to "cut through the structure of the states to the people themselves and yet was not dependent on the character of that people"; Wood, *The Creation of the American Republic*, 497.

25. Easton, *Treatise on the Intellectual Character*, 90.

26. On the first point regarding Haiti see the essays found in Jackson and Bacon, *African Americans and the Haitian Revolution*. On the second point, consult note 10.

27. I should not be read as suggesting that this way of legitimizing power was materially realized. It was not. Rather I am noting a changed self-understanding internal to modernity that makes talk of popular assent and individual consent intelligible. This cultural shift is in line with what Jerome B. Schneewind describes as a shift from the "morality of obedience" to the "morality of self-governance"; see Schneewind, *The Invention of Autonomy*, 4.

28. On the process of animalization see Davis, *The Problem of Slavery in the Age of Emancipation*, chap. 1.

29. On the substantive meaning of what is now called a counterpublic, see Fraser, *Justice Interruptus*, 81; cf. Dawson, *Black Visions*, 23–35; Warner, *Publics and Counterpublics*, chap. 2. For a slightly later expression of this in the nineteenth and early twentieth centuries, see the classic text by Brooks-Higginbotham, *Righteous Discontent*.

30. Cornish and Russwurm, "To Our Patrons," *Freedom's Journal*, March 16, 1827, 1.

31. Walker, *Appeal to the Coloured Citizens*, 2 (emphasis added). On the practice of the appeal and the way it affirms the epistemic capacities of black folks, see Rogers, "David Walker and the Political Power of the Appeal."

32. This, of course, marks a departure from Shelby's use of the language of weak and strong. For him "strong" racial solidarity affirms essentialism; Shelby, *We Who Are Dark*, 38–43. For my part, strong racial solidarity is less of a statement about some conception of blackness and more of a claim about the extent to which one's white counterparts are resistant to transformation.

33. Taylor, *Race*, 15–16. See also West, *Prophesy Deliverance*, chap. 2.

34. Jefferson, *Notes on the State of Virginia*, esp. 238.

35. Jefferson, *Notes on the State of Virginia*, 243.

36. Walker, *Appeal to the Coloured Citizens*, 31 (emphasis added).

37. Walker, *Appeal to the Coloured Citizens*, 32.

38. Glaude, *Exodus!*, 54–55, 147–49.

39. Easton, *Treatise on the Intellectual Character*, 92.

40. Walker, *Appeal to the Coloured Citizens*, 78.

41. Walker, of course, was not afraid to threaten violence if white Americans did not transform. But violence functioned as a measure of last resort, and in most instances the invocation was largely meant to exemplify the level of African Americans' commitment to republican liberty. That is, if republican liberty expresses itself as an aversion to practices of domination, a commitment to republican liberty under conditions of unmoved domination justifies a revolution.

42. Delany, *Condition, Elevation, Emigration, and Destiny*, 157.

43. Delany, *Condition, Elevation, Emigration, and Destiny*, 158.

44. Cited in Katrowitz, *More Than Freedom*, 35.

45. Martin Delany to Frederick Douglass, July 10, 1852, in Delany, *A Documentary Reader*, 222. For more on Delany and Douglass's relationship, and Douglass's reception of *Uncle Tom's Cabin*, see Levine, *Martin Delany and Frederick Douglass*; and Levine, "*Uncle Tom's Cabin* in *Frederick Douglass' Paper*."

46. Douglass, "What Are the Colored People Doing for Themselves?" *North Star*, July 14, 1848.

47. Shadd, "A Plea for Emigration" (1852); Holly, "A Vindication of the Capacity of the Negro" (1857).

48. Delany, *Condition, Elevation, Emigration, and Destiny*, 156.

49. Tocqueville, *Democracy in America*, 356.

50. Delany, "Political Destiny of the Colored Race" (1854), in *Documentary Reader*, 248.

51. Delany, "Political Destiny of the Colored Race" (1854), in *Documentary Reader*, 248.

52. It is true that Delany seems committed to underwriting his defense of solidarity with something stronger than this pragmatic argument. After all, he does say that an "original" identity is the solid foundation upon which "the fabric of every substantial political structure in the world" rests and "which cannot exist without it; and so soon as a people or nation lose their original identity, just so soon must that nation or people become extinct"; "Political Destiny of the Colored Race" (1854), in *Documentary Reader*, 250. This is precisely what Tommie Shelby relies on (as well as later, but similar, claims) to illuminate the essentialism in Delany's thinking. The problem, of course, is that the meaning of "original identity" does not amount to much. Delany provides a set of traits that could well be shared, and often are shared, by other "races." If he means, as Shelby suggest, to identify blacks as being accomplished because they were the first to display these traits, that does not mark some essential core of identity as much as it makes a

claim about temporal distinctiveness. On my reading, Delany is less interested in making an essentialist argument about black identity than in cultivating dignity in blacks based on a claim about their capabilities. Their ability to be accomplished is not unlike that of their white counterparts. The intensity of his claim about original identity must be understood against the backdrop of the practice of dehumanization with which black folks must contend.

53. Delany, *Condition, Elevation, Emigration, and Destiny*, 160.

54. Pettit, *On the People's Terms*, 2.

55. Pettit, *Republicanism*, 52.

56. Cicero, *The Republic* 2.43, 2.48–49; Locke, *Two Treatises of Government*, 107.

57. Pettit, *On the People's Terms*, 5, and cf. his chaps. 3–4.

58. Nyquist, *Arbitrary Rule*, 26.

59. Jefferson, "A Summary View of the Rights of British America."

60. Jefferson to John Randolph, August 25, 1775, in Jefferson, *Writings*, 749.

61. Cf. Pettit, *Republicanism*, 32–35.

62. Pettit does say that he takes "citizens in this discussion to comprise, not just citizens in the official sense, but all the more or less settled residents of a state who, being adult and able-minded, can play an informed role at any time in conceptualizing shared concerns and in shaping how the state acts in furthering those concerns"; Pettit, *On the People's Terms*, 75. This move, of course, bypasses the historical problem with which African Americans were concerned—that is, how one achieves formal and informal standing in the eyes of one's fellows.

63. Douglass, "Address to the Colored People of the United States" (1848), 119.

64. Walker, *Appeal to the Coloured Citizens*, 31 (emphasis added).

65. Easton, *Treatise on the Intellectual Character*, 105; cf. Delany, *Condition, Elevation, Emigration, and Destiny*, 154.

66. Jefferson, *Notes on the State of Virginia*, query 18, 257.

67. Pettit, *Republicanism*, 246.

Works Cited

Bacon, Jacqueline. *Freedom's Journal: The First African American Newspaper*. Lanham, MD: Lexington Books, 2007.

Ball, Erica L. *To Live an Antislavery Life: Personal Politics and the Antebellum Black Middle Class*. Athens: University of Georgia Press, 2012.

Brooks-Higginbotham, Evelyn. *Righteous Discontent: The Women's Movement in the Black Baptist Church, 1880–1920*. Cambridge, MA: Harvard University Press, 1994.

Brown, Vincent. "Social Death and Political Life in the Study of Slavery." *American Historical Review* 114, no. 5 (2009): 1232–49.

Burstein, Andrew. *Sentimental Democracy: The Evolution of America's Romantic Self-Image*. New York: Hill and Wang, 1999.

Canovan, Margret. *The People*. Cambridge: Polity, 2005.

Cicero. *On Duties*. Edited by M. T. Griffin and E. M. Atkins. Cambridge Texts in the History of Political Thought. New York: Cambridge University Press, 1991.

Cicero. *The Republic*. Translated by Niall Rudd. New York: Oxford University Press, 1998.

Collins, Patricia Hill. *Black Feminist Thought: Knowledge, Consciousness, and the Politics of Empowerment*. New York: Routledge, 1991.

Cornish, Samuel, and John Brown Russwurm. "To Our Patrons." *Freedom's Journal*, March 16, 1827, 1.

Dagger, Richard. *Civic Virtues: Rights, Citizenship, and Republican Liberalism*. New York: Oxford University Press, 1997.

Davis, David Brion. *The Problem of Slavery in the Age of Emancipation*. New York: Alfred A. Knopf, 2014.

Dawson, Michael. *Black Visions: The Roots of Contemporary African American Political Ideologies*. Chicago: University of Chicago Press, 2001.

Delany, Martin Robison. *The Condition, Elevation, Emigration, and Destiny of the Colored People of the United States*. 1852. Reprint edition, New York: Arno, 1968.

Delany, Martin Robison. *A Documentary Reader*. Edited by Robert S. Levine. Chapel Hill: University of North Carolina Press, 2003.

Douglass, Frederick. "An Address to the Colored People of the United States" (1848). In *Frederick Douglass: Selected Speeches and Writings*, edited by Philip S. Foner, abridged and adapted by Yuval Taylor, 117–21. Chicago: Lawrence Hill Books, 1999.

Douglass, Frederick. "What Are the Colored People Doing for Themselves?" *North Star*, July 14, 1848.

Easton, Hosea. *A Treatise on the Intellectual Character, and the Civil and Political Condition of the Colored People of the United States; and the Prejudice Exercised towards Them*. In *To Heal the Scourge of Prejudice: The Life and Writings of Hosea Easton* (1837), edited by George R. Price and James Brewer Stewart, 63–123. Amherst: University of Massachusetts Press, 1999.

Eustace, Nicole. *Passion Is the Gale: Emotion, Power, and the Coming of the American Revolution*. Chapel Hill: University of North Carolina Press, 2008.

The Founders' Constitution. Edited by Philip B. Kurland and Ralph Lerner. http://press-pubs.uchicago.edu/founders/.

Frank, Jason. *Constitute Moments: Enacting the People in Postrevolutionary America*. Durham, NC: Duke University Press, 2010.

Fraser, Nancy. *Justice Interruptus: Critical Reflections on "Postsocialist Condition."* New York: Routledge, 1997.

Glaude, Eddie. *Exodus! Religion, Race, and Nation in Early Nineteenth-Century Black America*. Chicago: University of Chicago Press, 2000.

Hamilton, Alexander, James Madison, and John Jay. *The Federalist*. Edited by J. R. Pole. Indianapolis: Hackett, 2005.

Hesse, Barnor. "Escaping Liberty: Western Hegemony, Black Fugitivity." *Political Theory* 42, no. 3 (2014): 288–313.

Holly, J. Theodore. "A Vindication of the Capacity of the Negro for Self-Government and Civilized Progress" (1857). In *Pamphlets of Protest: An Anthology of Early African American Protest Literature, 1790–1860*, edited by Richard Newman, Patrick Rael, and Phillip Lapansky, 262–82. New York: Routledge, 2001.

Honohan, Iseult. *Civic Republicanism*. New York: Routledge, 2002.

Horton, James Oliver, and Lois E. Horton. *In Hope of Liberty: Culture, Community, and Protest among Northern Free Blacks, 1700–1860*. New York: Oxford University Press, 1997.

Jackson, Maurice, and Jacqueline Bacon, eds. *African Americans and the Haitian Revolution: Selected Essays and Historical Documents*. New York: Routledge, 2010.

Jefferson, Thomas. *Notes on the State of Virginia* (1787). In *The Life and Selected Writings of Thomas Jefferson*, edited by Adrienne Koch and William Peden, 187–288. New York: Modern Library America, 2004.

Jefferson, Thomas. "A Summary View of the Rights of British America" (1774). In *The Life and Selected Writings of Thomas Jefferson*, edited by Adrienne Koch and William Peden, 293–310. New York: Modern Library America, 2004.

Jefferson, Thomas. *Writings*. Edited by Merrill D. Peterson. New York: Library of America, 1984.

Kantrowitz, Stephen. *More Than Freedom: Fighting for Black Citizenship in a White Republic, 1829–1889*. New York: Penguin, 2012.

Levine, Robert S. *Martin Delany and Frederick Douglass, and the Politics of Representative Identity*. Chapel Hill: University of North Carolina Press, 1997.

Levine, Robert S. "*Uncle Tom's Cabin* in Frederick Douglass' Paper: An Analysis of Reception." *American Literature* 64, no. 1 (1992): 71–93.

Locke, John. *Two Treatises of Government*. 1689. Edited by Ian Shapiro. New Haven, CT: Yale University Press, 2003.

McHenry, Elizabeth. *Forgotten Readers: Recovering the Lost History of African American Literary Societies*. Durham, NC: Duke University Press, 2002.

Newman, Richard, Patrick Rael, and Phillip Lapsansky, eds. *Pamphlets of Protest: An Anthology of Early African American Protest Literature, 1790–1860*. New York: Routledge, 2001.

Nyquist, Mary. *Arbitrary Rule: Slavery, Tyranny, and the Power of Life and Death*. Chicago: University of Chicago Press, 2013.

Patterson, Orlando. *Slavery and Society Death: A Comparative Study*. Cambridge, MA: Harvard University Press, 1982.

Pettit, Philip. *Just Freedom: A Moral Compass for a Complex World*. New York: W. W. Norton, 2014.

Pettit, Philip. *On the People's Terms: A Republican Theory and Model of Democracy*. New York: Cambridge University Press, 2012.

Pettit, Philip. *Republicanism: A Theory of Freedom and Government*. New York: Oxford University Press, 1997.

Pocock, J. G. A. *The Machiavellian Moment: Florentine Political Thought and the Atlantic Republican Tradition*. Princeton, NJ: Princeton University Press, 1975.

Price, George R., and James Brewer Stewart. *To Heal the Scourge of the Prejudice: The Life and Writings of Hosea Easton*. Amherst: University of Massachusetts Press, 1999.

Roberts, Neil. *Freedom as Marronage*. Chicago: University of Chicago Press, 2015.

Robinson, Cedric J. *Black Marxism: The Making of the Black Radical Tradition*. London: Zed Press, 1983.

Rogers, Melvin L. "David Walker and the Political Power of the Appeal." *Political Theory* 43, no. 2 (2015): 208–33.

Rogers, Melvin L. "The People, Rhetoric, and Affect: On the Political Force of Du Bois's *The Souls of Black Folk*." *American Political Science Review* 106, no. 1 (2012): 188–203.

Sandel, Michael. *Democracy's Discontents: Americans in Search of a Public Philosophy*. Cambridge, MA: Harvard University Press, 1996.

Schneewind, Jerome B. *The Invention of Autonomy: A History of Modern Moral Philosophy*. New York: Cambridge University Press, 1998.

Sellers, M. N. S. *American Republicanism: Roman Ideology in the United States Constitution*. New York: New York University Press, 1994.

Shadd, Mary Ann. "A Plea for Emigration, or Notes of Canada West" (1852). In *Pamphlets of Protest: An Anthology of Early African American Protest Literature, 1790–1860*, edited by Richard Newman, Patrick Rael, and Phillip Lapansky, 198–214. New York: Routledge, 2001.

Shelby, Tommie. *We Who Are Dark: The Philosophical Foundations of Black Solidarity*. Cambridge, MA: Harvard University Press, 2005.

Skinner, Quentin. "The Idea of Negative Liberty." In *Philosophy of History: Essays on the Historiography of Philosophy*, edited by Richard Rorty, J. B. Schneewind, and Quentin Skinner, 193–221. New York: Cambridge University Press, 1984.

Skinner, Quentin. *Liberty before Liberalism*. Cambridge: Cambridge University Press, 1998.

Skinner, Quentin. "Machiavelli on the Maintenance of Liberty." *Politics* 18, no. 2 (1983): 3–15.

Skinner, Quentin. "The Republican Ideal of Political Liberty." In *Machiavelli and Republicanism*, edited by Gisela Bock, Quentin Skinner, and Maurizio Viroli, 239–309. Ideas in Context. New York: Cambridge University Press, 1990.

Taylor, Paul. *Race: A Philosophical Introduction*. Malden, MA: Polity, 2004.

Tocqueville, Alexis de. *Democracy in America*. 1835, 1840. Translated by George Lawrence, edited by J. P. Mayer. New York: Perennial Library, 1988.

Tylor, Edward B. *Primitive Culture: Researches into the Development of Mythology, Philosophy, Religion, Art, and Custom*. Vol. 1, 1871. Reprint edition, New York: Cambridge University Press, 2010.

Viroli, Maurizio. *Republicanism*. New York: Hill and Wang, 2002.

Vogel, Todd, ed. *The Black Press: New Literary and Historical Essays*. New Brunswick, NJ: Rutgers University Press, 2001.

Walker, David. *Appeal to the Coloured Citizens of the World*. 1829. Edited by Peter P. Hinks. University Park: Penn State University Press, 2003.

Warner, Michael. *Publics and Counterpublics*. New York: Zone Books, 2002.

West, Cornel. *Prophesy Deliverance! An Afro-American Revolutionary Christianity*. Philadelphia: Westminster Press, 1982.

Wirszubski, Chaim. *Libertas as a Political Ideal at Rome during the Late Republic and Early Principate*. New York: Cambridge University Press, 1968.

Wood, Gordon. *The Creation of the American Republic, 1776–1787*. Chapel Hill: University of North Carolina Press, 1989.

PART 2

Relations before Transactions: New Approaches to Inequality, Justice, & Dignity

3

Crime and Punishment in a Divided Society

Rajiv Sethi

> The degree of civilization of a society can
> be judged by entering its prisons.
> —FYODOR DOSTOYEVSKY (1862)

1. Diagnosing Disparities

If a nation can be judged by the state of its prisons, then a divided nation can surely be judged by the identities of those it chooses to incarcerate. And in the case of the United States, this population is not just staggeringly large but also disproportionately black.

The titles of two influential books provide contrasting perspectives on the role of dominance in generating such disparities in American criminal justice: Michelle Alexander's *The New Jim Crow* and James Forman Jr.'s *Locking Up Our Own*. While Alexander likens current conditions to a time in history where dominance of blacks by whites was codified in laws and openly asserted, Forman tells the story of increasingly aggressive policing and harsher sentencing in Washington, DC, at a time when much of the leadership of the city's political and law enforcement institutions was in African American hands. Taken together, these perspectives reveal a complex underlying reality, the understanding of which requires attention to both the apparatus of punishment and patterns of criminal offending and victimization.

If democratic justice requires the achievement of difference without domination, then a critical task is to distinguish between disparities that emerge from patterns of domination and those that do not. In the former set of cases, a second task emerges of answering the question of how to address and undo that domination. This chapter explores methods for diagnosing these disparities and makes the case that they are connected to forms of domination embedded in the operation of stereotypes, which create incentive structures that generate disparate patterns of offending, victimization, policing, and punishment.

2. The Facts of the Matter

Prior to the late 1970s, the incarceration rate in the United States was roughly stable for several decades at under 200 per 100,000. Then began a steady climb that took the country into uncharted territory. At its peak in 2008, the total number of inmates in jails and prisons stood at 2.3 million, or approximately 760 per 100,000 residents. A further five million individuals were under probation or parole. With the possible exception of Russia, no economically advanced country comes remotely close (National Research Council 2014).

Although the growth of federal prisons was far from negligible over this period, the overwhelming majority of the incarcerated population is held in state and local facilities. That is, individuals enter the criminal justice system most often by running afoul of state and local laws. They are typically arrested by local law enforcement agencies, tried in local courts, judged by local peers, and held in local facilities. Given large differences across jurisdictions in demographic composition, political control, and policy positions—as explored by Heather Gerken in her contribution to this volume—the manner in which domination generates disparities also varies based on local conditions.

What were the main drivers of the rise in incarceration? A number of factors that combined to make the system more punitive were at work: an increased number of admissions for drug crimes, harsher sentences, higher rates of parole revocation, and substantially greater admissions per arrest for violent and property crimes. The last of these factors was due in part to a sharply increased willingness on the part of prosecutors in many jurisdictions to file felony charges for acts that were previously treated less punitively (Raphael and Stoll 2009; Pfaff 2017).

Even as the incarceration rate was rising sharply, the incidence of crimes was falling. For at least twenty-five years, major violent and property crimes have been in decline across all categories. Figure 3.1 shows this trend for homicide, burglary, robbery, and motor vehicle theft, all of which follow roughly the same pattern. There was a sharp rise in crime from 1960 to 1980 and a steady decline from 1990 onward. All four rates are at, or close to, the lowest levels attained over the past five decades, although homicide rates rose quite substantially in percentage terms in 2015 and 2016.

The figure also depicts the imprisonment rate, which appears to have

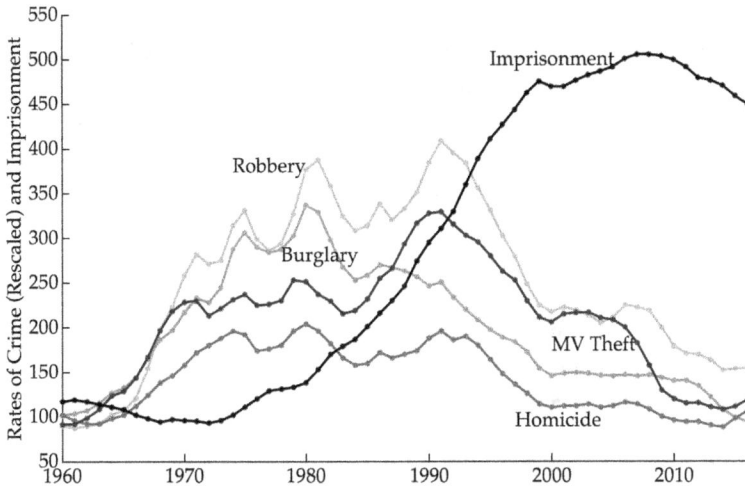

FIGURE 3.1. Trends in crime and punishment, 1960–2016. The imprisonment rate refers to those in state and federal prisons (but not local jails) with sentences of a year or more, per 100,000 persons in the population. Crime rates per 100,000 persons have been rescaled as follows: homicide (×20), robbery (×1.5), motor vehicle theft (×0.5), and burglary (×0.2) as in National Research Council 2014.

become untethered from the rate of offending at around 1990, continuing to rise inexorably for two decades with a momentum of its own.

The population behind bars is demographically quite distinct from the rest of the population along a number of dimensions. Prisoners are overwhelmingly young and male, have fewer years of schooling, and are disproportionately black and Latino. About 93 percent of prisoners were male in 2010, and the imprisonment rate—measured as the number of individuals sentenced to at least a year in state or federal facilities, per 100,000 in the population—was around 70 for women overall, 450 for white men, 1250 for Hispanic men, close to 3,100 for black men, and 7,300 for black men aged thirty to thirty-four (Guerino, Harrison, and Sabol 2011).

At a superficial level, the composition of the prison population simply reflects the degree to which members of different groups engage in activities deemed criminal by the state, as well as biases in the application of the law. Popular diagnoses of the staggering racial disparity in incarceration rates fall broadly into two categories, depending on which of these factors is given prominence.

One approach to diagnosing the disparity emphasizes inequality across groups along dimensions such as income, wealth, employment status, and environmental factors such as childhood lead exposure. These disparities are large but do not come close to matching those in rates of imprisonment. Allowing for biases in the application of the law—such as disproportionate targeting of dense urban populations and the especially severe sanctioning of black offenders—can bridge the gap (Harcourt 2008; Alexander 2010). Dominance plays a central role in explaining disparities in this narrative: both the dominance that accounts for differences in economic and environmental conditions and the dominance embedded in the criminal justice system.

In addition, racially neutral laws such as those targeting drug use, even if enforced without bias, might disproportionately disadvantage black populations because of offending patterns based on the racially segregated social organization of drug markets. Rural and suburban areas are harder to police than more densely populated inner cities, where resources can be concentrated on a few high-value locations. As a result, there can be racially disparate incidence of a seemingly neutral policy of law enforcement. One can have disparate impact even in the absence of disparate treatment: policies can be "fair in form but discriminatory in operation," as Chief Justice Warren Burger observed in a landmark 1971 opinion in *Griggs v. Duke Power Co.*

A very different diagnostic narrative focuses on disparities across groups in rates of offending, attributing these to different propensities for criminality.[1] The emphasis here is on cultural breakdown and moral poverty as root causes, rather than differential incentives, opportunities, and treatment. This essentialist account relies on a belief in differences across groups that are deep, fundamental, and largely impervious to policy in the short run, and has been used to justify *increased* dominance—in the form of more aggressive policing and sentencing—as the only available path to lower crime rates. This appears to be the position of the current administration in the United States.[2]

There are some basic facts about offending and victimization for which these narratives cannot adequately account. Neither the diagnosis based on economic and social inequality nor the essentialist account of disparities in offending can explain why we see large differences across crimes in the racial composition of arrestees. Figure 3.2 shows the black share of arrestees for the eight so-called index crimes, for which the FBI collects and disseminates detailed data.[3] For any given crime, different data points correspond to different years. As is clear from the figure, the racial composition of arrestees varies much more across *crime* than across *time*. For instance, the black share of total arrests for robbery is about twice as great as that for burglary or larceny, even though all of these crimes are primarily motivated by the acquisition of property. Similarly,

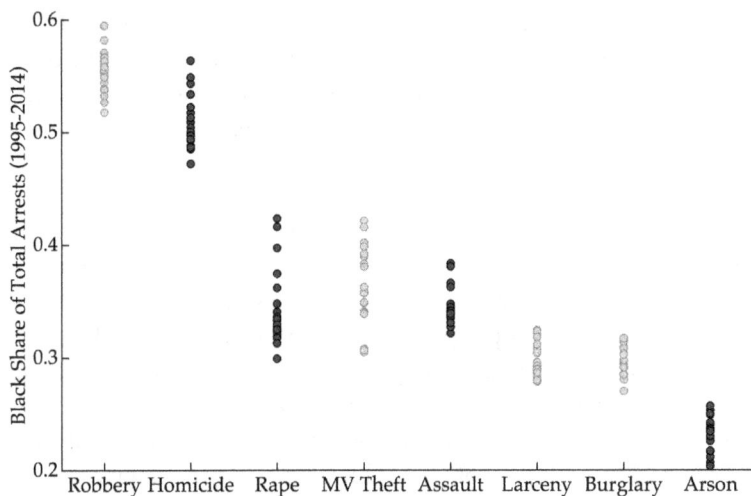

FIGURE 3.2. Black share of total arrests for index crimes, 1995–2014. Crimes motivated primarily by the acquisition of property are shown in lighter gray, even if they involve the threat or use of force (as in the case of robbery).

among violent crimes, the black share of total arrests is much greater for homicide than for aggravated assault.

Any adequate theory of criminal offending must account for not only for the overall incidence of involvement with crime but also the distribution of offending across crime categories. And understanding differences across groups in offending, victimization, and policing requires attention to a particular set of incentives created by the existence of *stereotypes*. Stereotypes are both a consequence of historical dominance and a mechanism for the persistence of disparities in outcomes. In the context of crime and punishment, they permeate interactions at every level.

Consider first how stereotypes affect crime. Robbery is quite different from larceny and burglary because it involves face-to-face interactions in which stereotypes can come into play. And homicide is unique among serious crimes in that it can be motivated by preemptive concerns, driven by the fear of being killed. This fear is contingent on visible characteristics of parties to escalating disputes, and here again stereotypes can loom large, affecting the likelihood of lethal violence.

Similar effects arise in interactions between suspects and law enforcement officers. Fears for one's own safety or that of others is the only legally permissible justification for the use of lethal force by the police under federal law, and these fears can also be sensitive to visible characteristics of the parties involved in a manner conditioned by stereotypes.

Looking at crime through the lens of stereotypes allows us to see rates of offending and victimization as incentive-driven phenomena. This is an "endogenous" account of racial disparity in that characteristics of the agents' interactions with one another themselves generate the disparities. This endogenous account of disparities is therefore distinct from (bio-logical or cultural) essentialism, and also from a crude environmental determinism.

Even so, casual observers often interpret the data generated by the operation of incentives in essentialist terms. This is especially the case when patterns in the data fit prior conceptions of group differences in moral worth. From this perspective, mass incarceration was allowed to build and was tolerated for so long precisely because its impact was felt with disproportionate force within a stigmatized group.

Ironically, stereotypes held by the general public have inhibited a seri-ous exploration of the role of stereotypes in shaping the countless small-scale interactions that give rise to rates of offending, victimization, arrest, and incarceration in the aggregate.

3. Stereotypes at Work: Robbery

When strangers interact, stereotypes inevitably come into play. This is especially the case when the outcome of the interaction can result in sig-nificant profit or damage, as in the case of an attempted robbery or an escalating dispute that could turn violent. Under such conditions, visible traits — including but not limited to racial markers — become salient.

Consider the case of robbery, which begins with a victim selection decision. Among the most important considerations for a potential of-fender is the likelihood of victim resistance. In fact, ethnographic studies of active robbers suggest that beliefs about resistance are given consider-ably greater weight than beliefs about the amount of cash and valuables that a potential victim may be carrying. And such beliefs lead offenders — regardless of whether they are black or white — to exhibit a preference for white victims, who are thought to be more compliant on average.[4]

Indeed, white victims do resist robbers at lower rates and are accord-ingly targeted with greater frequency, even though they tend to carry smaller amounts of cash and valuables than black victims. One reason for lower resistance is that whites are more affluent on average, so the cash on their person is small relative to their overall wealth. But another rea-son — of which offenders are well aware — is that they are especially fear-ful of violence from black offenders. This leads black offenders to prefer white victims, in effect because of a stereotype about a stereotype.[5]

That is, white and black victims on average hold different beliefs about the likelihood that a black offender will try to force compliance in the face of resistance, and offenders are alert to these differences. Such belief differences also show up in the data on implicit association tests, which reveal that about four-fifths of whites and one-third of blacks hold pro-white and anti-black implicit preferences.[6]

The anecdotal and ethnographic evidence on stereotypes is confirmed by data from victimization surveys, which includes both reported and un-reported robberies (O'Flaherty and Sethi 2008). These data indicate that white offenders almost exclusively target white victims, while the victims of black offenders are about equally likely to be white or black. As a result, black-on-white robberies are about twenty times as frequent as white-on-black robberies. This is consistent with the hypothesis that white offenders face unusually high resistance from black victims, while black offenders face high rates of compliance from white victims.

Stereotypes about black male violence also make robbery in general more lucrative relative to burglary or larceny for black offenders. All of these crimes are motivated by the acquisition of property, but since there is no direct contact between victim and offender in the latter cases, stereotypes do not enter the picture. As a result, there are fewer racial differences in incentives to offend when it comes to burglary or larceny. This helps account for the striking difference in arrest rates seen in figure 3.2, which shows that black representation in the pool of arrested robbers is twice as great as that in the pool of arrested burglars and thieves.

This is important because—for a variety of reasons including rapid reporting and eyewitness identification—robbery offenders are significantly more likely to be apprehended and incarcerated relative to those engaged in other crimes of appropriation. In 2009, for instance, there were thirty-one arrests and nine prison admissions for every hundred robberies, while the corresponding figures for burglaries were fourteen and three, and for motor vehicle theft were ten and one (Raphael and Stoll 2013, table 2.2).

Given the greater involvement of black offenders in robbery relative to burglary and motor vehicle theft, whites involved with crimes of appropriation are much less likely to be arrested and imprisoned than are blacks. As a result, the pool of arrestees and prisoners provides a misleading picture of the pool of offenders, reinforcing essentialist notions of criminality in the population at large.

There are, of course, several confounding factors. It is possible that burglaries that are never reported or never solved could have a greater share of black offenders than those resulting in an arrest. One plausible reason for this is that burglaries involving black victims are less frequently reported and less aggressively investigated. Given existing patterns of residential segregation, such burglaries are disproportionately likely to involve black offenders. But segregation cannot explain why robbery so often crosses racial lines when the offender is black but very rarely does so when the offender is white.

Note that the salience of stereotypes is not confined to interactions that cross racial boundaries. In areas with significant class differences among whites, where visible markers such as tattoos can serve as credible signals of class background, robbery rates should be higher than in areas with limited class differences. If those with facial tattoos are feared, they will find robbery lucrative, even in communities that are racially homogeneous.

This incentive-based account of robbery offending and victimization has other implications. The most desperate offenders do not have the luxury of picking and choosing their victims; they will target both blacks and whites, and will often try to force compliance through violence if resisted. Less desperate offenders will selectively target whites, and will often give up and flee if resisted. That is, white victims face a less desperate pool of robbery offenders on average and are therefore less likely to face violence when they do choose to resist. This is precisely what one sees in the data on victim resistance and injury (O'Flaherty and Sethi 2008).

4. Stereotypes at Work: Homicide

Similar considerations can shed light on the sharp difference between homicide and aggravated assault seen in figure 3.2. Homicide is unique among serious crimes in that it can sometimes be motivated purely by preemption: one may kill simply to avoid being killed. Fearful individuals have strong incentives to kill preemptively, and feared individuals are most likely to be killed for this reason. But the level of fear itself depends on prevailing homicide rates, so both high and low rates of killing can be sustained in otherwise similar environments.

This is why homicide rates tend to be so variable across time and space. If a policy intervention or some other change in the environment results in a decline in killing and a concomitant reduction in the level of fear, a positive feedback process starts to operate that can drive rates even lower. Similarly, an uptick in killing that makes people more fearful can result in further increases, as incentives for preemptive killing rise. In the language of economics, there are *multiple equilibria*, so locations that are otherwise similar can end up with very different rates of homicide, each of which is self-reinforcing (O'Flaherty and Sethi 2010b).

Furthermore, the level of fear in an interaction depends not only on the homicide rate in the general area but also on attributes of the individuals involved. In disputes involving strangers or casual acquaintances, visible characteristics such as tattoos, clothing, and racial markers can affect the outcome, just as they can in the case of robbery. Those who are most feared are also more likely to be killed preemptively, and those who are most fearful are also more likely to kill.

In particular, laxity of enforcement against homicide offenders whose victims are black can have significant effects not only on the rate at which blacks are killed but also on the rate at which they kill preemptively. These effects are especially stark when both parties to a dispute are black: if each believes that the other can kill with impunity, then both have preemptive motives to kill (O'Flaherty and Sethi 2010a). Recognizing this only further amplifies the preemptive motive. As noted by Thomas Schelling, "Self-defense is ambiguous when one is only trying to preclude being shot in self-defense" (Schelling 1960).

In her book *Ghettoside*, Jill Leovy describes several individual murder investigations in Los Angeles and makes an explicit connection between low homicide clearance rates and high levels of killing (Leovy 2015). The clearance rate refers to the frequency with which murders are solved and offenders identified. The communities that Leovy describes are simultaneously overpoliced and underprotected: most murders remain unpunished, so conditions are created for both preemptive and retaliatory killing.

Gang symbols and colors can be triggers for violence, sometimes involving tragic misattributions. But gangs as social organizations capable of centralized coercion can also play a role in containing preemptive violence by affording protection to prospective victims and by making more credible the likelihood of retaliation. In fact, many homicide reduction initiatives such as Operation Ceasefire in Boston may be viewed as attempts to secure a coordinated change in beliefs about the likelihood of being killed, thus lowering risk perceptions and preemptive killing (Braga et al. 2001).

These considerations help us understand the recent empirical finding that the expansion of "stand-your-ground" laws causes rates of homicide offending to increase (Cheng and Hoekstra 2013). By raising the likelihood of being killed with impunity, such laws also raise the likelihood of preemptive killing. The argument that stand-your-ground laws should reduce crime in general by making criminals more fearful of lethal victim responses fails to take account of the fact that making people fearful also raises their incentives to kill.

5. Stereotypes at Work: Law Enforcement

On September 4, 2014, upon leaving work, Levar Jones got into his white pickup truck, drove slowly around the corner, and pulled into a gas station. He did not notice that Sean Groubert, a South Carolina trooper, had observed him driving without a seatbelt and had pulled in behind him. After both had exited their vehicles, the officer asked Jones for his license and registration. Jones reached back into his vehicle to grab his wallet, at which point he was shot at several times and suffered a nonfatal bullet wound. The entire incident was captured on the officer's dashcam video.

In a statement announcing the termination of his employment with the South Carolina Department of Public Safety, the director of the agency explained, "Mr. Groubert *reacted to a perceived threat when there was none.*" The officer would later plead guilty to charges of assault and battery.

Whether Jones would have been shot if he were white, or if the officer in question had been black, is impossible to know. But the video of the incident does appear to corroborate the view that the shooting was preemptive and driven by fear. This raises the possibility that the very same stereotypes that make white victims especially fearful of (and hence especially attractive to) black robbery offenders may have been implicated here, in a very different context.

The claim that exaggerated fears of black male violence have led to deaths at the hands of law enforcement officers has been made frequently—from the 1999 killing of Amadou Diallo clutching a wallet mistakenly thought to be a firearm, to that of twelve-year-old Tamir Rice holding a replica pistol in 2014. Sworn statements by officers in such cases, if taken at face value, suggest an extraordinary level of fear. To take one example, Officer Darren Wilson—himself six feet four inches in height and weighing 210 pounds—testified that he "felt like a 5-year-old holding onto Hulk Hogan" when struggling with Michael Brown, whom he subsequently shot dead. The expression on Brown's face was likened to that of a "demon." Incidents such as this currently animate the Black Lives Matter movement.

If exaggerated fears of black male violence are routinely implicated in police killings, then this effect should be discernible in aggregate data. While there is no comprehensive official data on such killings, news organizations such as the *Guardian* and the *Washington Post* have constructed datasets based on public reports. According to the former source, there were a total of 1,145 police killings in 2015 alone, about half of which involved suspects armed with a gun. A further 13 percent of those killed were armed with a knife. Slightly more than half of those killed were white, 27 percent were black, and 17 percent Latino.

Nationwide, the proportion of black victims of police killings is roughly comparable to the proportion of arrestees who are black. Moving from data to diagnosis, Sendhil Mulainathan (2015) interprets this as reflecting an *absence* of significant racial bias in police killings, arguing as follows: "For the entire country, 28.9 percent of arrestees were African-American. This number is not very different from the 31.8 percent of police-shooting victims who were African-Americans. If police discrimination were a big factor in the actual killings (and every place were roughly the same), we would have expected a larger gap between the arrest rate and the police-killing rate. This in turn suggests that removing police racial bias will have little effect on the killing rate."

Mullainathan's argument is roughly this: since any given police-civilian encounter is about as likely to result in a killing when the civilian is black as when the civilian is white, racial bias is unlikely to be playing a major role in the use of lethal force. By this reasoning, black civilians are killed at higher rates relative to their share in the general population because they are encountered and arrested at higher rates, not because any given encounter is more likely to turn lethal. But this assumes that encounters between police and black civilians are as objectively threatening to police, on average, as encounters between police and white civilians. Is the assumption reasonable?

Consider the following three highly publicized police-civilian encounters: the arrest of Henry Louis Gates Jr. on his front porch in 2009, that of Sandra Bland at a traffic stop in 2015, and those of Rashon Nelson and Donte Robinson at a Philadelphia Starbucks in April 2018.[7] Arguably, none of these encounters would have led to arrest—or even have occurred at all—had the civilians not been black. Also, none of these individuals posed a threat to the arresting officers. Arrests of this kind enlarge the pool of black arrestees, but in a manner that lowers the average threat level in the pool. In the absence of police bias, therefore, the ratio of killings to arrests should be lower for black civilians than for white. The parity that Mullainathan highlights could then be indicative of the presence rather than the absence of bias.

This is an entirely hypothetical argument, though it is consistent with anecdotal evidence.[8] To explore the hypothesis statistically, one would need information on the degree of threat involved in each encounter, including those that do not result in lethal force. Such data is hard to come by at the national level, but Roland Fryer (2019) has constructed and examined a dataset for the city of Houston that merges information on officer-involved shootings (including both hits and misses) with records of arrests in categories generally associated with a higher likelihood of justified lethal force. He finds that 58 percent of arrest suspects are black, while 52 percent of suspects shot at by an officer are black. This immediately implies that in the raw data, blacks are *less* likely to be shot in any given encounter. But not all encounters are equally threatening—in the arrest data about half of black suspects "attacked or drew a weapon," while the corresponding proportion for whites was above two-thirds. Once such differences in contextual and behavioral factors are accounted for, Fryer finds no statistically significant effect of suspect race on the likelihood of a weapons discharge, at least for Houston.[9]

What Fryer does find, however, is statistically significant differences across groups in the use of *nonlethal* force. Using data from New York City's "Stop, Question and Frisk" program, he finds that blacks and Latinos are more likely to be held, pushed, cuffed, sprayed, or struck than whites who are stopped. This remains the case even after controlling for a broad range of demographic, behavioral, and environmental characteristics. And using data from a nationally representative sample of civilians, which does not rely on officer accounts, he finds evidence of even larger disparities in treatment.

Such disparities in the use of nonlethal force are important contributing factors to distrust between police and citizens in high-crime neighborhoods. They make it less likely that civilians will step forward to serve as witnesses in the prosecution of homicides and other major felonies. And the belief that others will not come forward as witnesses further reduces the incentive for any one person to testify, since conviction is much less likely without corroboration. This can lead to *collective silence*—no witnesses testify, because they do not expect their testimony to be corroborated (O'Flaherty and Sethi 2010c). Murder clearance rates are accordingly lower, killing occurs with relative impunity, and preemptive motives for killing start to matter. The excessive and discriminatory use of nonlethal force by police thus ends up having indirect lethal effects.

Here's the crux of the matter: an understanding of trends and patterns in American criminal justice is woefully incomplete without attention to the role of stereotypes at every level of the system. Stereotypes affect victim responses to offenders, and for this reason affect offender selection of victims. They affect the extent to which disputes escalate to deadly violence, and the extent to which preemptive motives for killing become salient. They shape interactions between police and citizens, and the use of lethal and nonlethal force. As a result, they affect the willingness of witnesses to come forward, which means that some in our society can be killed with impunity. And stereotypes also matter in feeding public apathy regarding mass incarceration.

6. Stereotypes at Work: Casual Misattributions

The preceding arguments offer an incentive-based account of disparities across groups in offending, victimization, and incarceration, an account that depends crucially on the manner in which individuals are categorized and stereotyped. From this perspective, observed racial differences in offending and victimization need not reflect deep differences in preferences or values between groups. Rather, such disparities may well be the consequence of differences in the strategic situations that members of distinct groups confront.

But unlike behaviors, incentives remain hidden from plain sight, and this can result in what Glenn Loury has called "essentialist causal misattributions" (Loury 2002). That is, behavioral differences across groups can come to be wrongly attributed to deep and largely immutable differences in their nature rather than to flexible and malleable responses to incentives. When one is confronted with the stark racial disparities in arrest and incarceration, the cognitively simplest reaction is simply to ascribe to different groups different propensities for criminality, which is to diagnose incentive-driven phenomena in essentialist terms. That is, group differences that are endogenous to the system are attributed to causes taken to be exogenous and intrinsic to the groups who lag behind. This misattribution underlies the view that the differences we see in incarceration rates do not result from domination and therefore need not inspire us to corrective action.

The point may be illustrated by contrasting racial disparities in imprisonment with gender disparities in education.[10] An underrepresentation of women in science and mathematics is widely viewed as a social calamity, calling for intervention and public action. In contrast, the overrepresentation of men in prison is understood in essentialist terms and does not give rise to calls for urgent corrective measures. The overrepresentation of blacks in prison is widely viewed through the latter essentialist lens rather than through the former structural and incentive-based perspective.

In the context of crime and incarceration, essentialist causal misattributions arise not just because they are cognitively less demanding but also because they are consistent with a superstructure of beliefs that was essential to justifying and legitimizing a system of racial hierarchy, beginning with slavery and continuing through the period of mandated segregation. Formal repeal of these hierarchical systems did not instantly erase the superstructure of beliefs that once gave them legitimacy (Patterson 1982). This concern was paramount in the work of the nineteenth-century African American writers discussed by Melvin Rogers in this volume.

There is a close connection between social epistemology—what people think they know about causation of some social outcome—and social policy: what people are prepared to support in terms of altering the structures that engender the disparity. Essentialist interpretations of criminal offending make it easier for staggering disparities in rates of offending, victimization, and incarceration to be tolerated with acquiescence, instead of giving rise to restless calls for corrective action. Whether we judge difference to be free of domination or attached to domination directs our policymaking and advocacy.

In the absence of essentialist interpretations of the data on criminal offending, the stark racial disparities in incarceration rates and the high levels of confinement in the aggregate would not have enjoyed popular support. That is, the rise in American incarceration would have been considered intolerable were it not for its racial character. Policies serve expressive as well as instrumental ends, and the popularity of vigorous enforcement and harsh sentencing may be due in part to the fact that these initiatives have had a disproportionate impact on blacks (Loury 2008).

The very same stereotypes that shape the behavior of victims and offenders, or parties to a dispute, or police-citizen interactions, can result in apathy on the part of the general public toward the phenomenon of mass incarceration. Mass incarceration may be viewed as a stereotype trap, in which all actors in the system, from low-level offenders and their victims to prosecutors and legislators, act on beliefs that find some confirmation in the data that they observe.

But public apathy toward mass incarceration has started to subside. As can be seen in figure 3.1, incarceration rates have been modestly decreasing for almost a decade. This national trend masks some very significant regional differences.

7. The Push for Decarceration

Over the past decade a number of states have taken steps toward substantially reducing their prison populations. In some cases, such as California, reforms have been forced on the state by lawsuits alleging prison overcrowding and inadequate prisoner healthcare provision (Lofstrom and Raphael 2016). But in others, such as Texas and Georgia, reform has been driven by a rather remarkable change in the conservative orthodoxy on positions related to criminal justice. The transition has involved think tanks and political entrepreneurs with strong conservative credentials that have been able to make a case for a less carceral state (Dagan and Teles 2016). The steep decline in crime across all categories since the early 1990s has facilitated this shift, as has the strain on state budgets in the wake of the financial crisis and the associated collapse in tax revenues. As a consequence, both major political parties have come to support reforms aimed at fewer admissions, earlier release of nonviolent offenders, and more meaningful prisoner reintegration in some states.[11]

Given our claims of essentialist causal misattributions, how are we to interpret the significant steps taken by many states to initiate a process of decarceration? If support for mass incarceration were grounded in its racial character, then how does one account for the loss of support in recent years?

A first step is to note that prosecutor discretion, which was a significant factor in accounting for the rise in incarceration, can also be a force for decarceration. If prosecutors can adopt more punitive postures relative to the past, they can also reverse course and become less punitive. In fact, the decline in incarceration seen nationally since 2008 was foreshadowed by earlier declines in a handful of states. New York and New Jersey led the way with recorded declines of 19 percent and 16 percent respectively in their prison populations over the period of 2000 to 2010 (Guerino, Harrison, and Sabol 2011). Much of this decline came before formal reforms were in place, which John Pfaff interprets as evidence of the importance of prosecutor discretion (Pfaff 2014). More generally, such discretion allows for local exercise of power in ways that can resist and reverse national trends, as Heather Gerken discusses in her contribution to this volume.

But what accounts for the spread to other states of a less punitive regime? One possibility is the changing demographics of prison admissions, which suggest a narrowing of the racial divide, especially in the case of women (Mayer 2013). Figure 3.3 shows percentage changes in the prison population by race and gender over the period 2000 to 2010. The starting values have been normalized to equal 100 for all categories, so the values for subsequent years are relative to this baseline. The change in relative fortunes of white and black women has been dramatic, with the population of white women behind bars rising 40 percent even as that of black women declined by 30 percent.

Similar but more modest trends can be seen among the population of male inmates. And since men constitute the vast majority of the imprisoned population, changes in total incarceration by race closely track

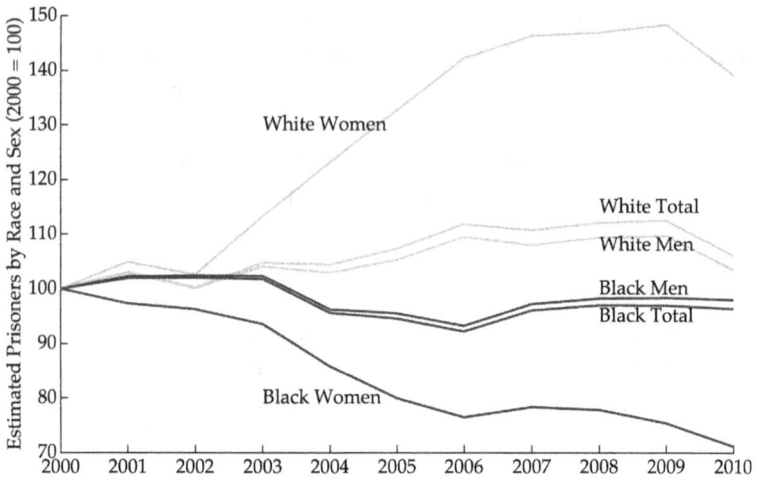

FIGURE 3.3. Trends in imprisonment by race and sex, 2000–2010,
scaled to equal 100 initially in all categories.

changes in male incarceration. Even as arrests for violent, property, and drug crimes fell for blacks during the first decade of this century, property and drug crime arrests increased for whites (Mauer 2013).

These changes mirror declines in other measures of welfare among whites with a high school education or less (Murray 2013; Putnam 2015). For instance, life expectancy for middle-aged whites without a college education has been declining, and again the effect is strongest for women (Case and Deaton 2015; Gelman and Auerbach 2016). The incidence of single parenthood among whites now exceeds the levels that Daniel Patrick Moynihan found so disturbing among blacks fifty years ago.

Once laws and mandatory sentencing requirements are in place, their impact cannot be restricted to particular groups; the demographic reach of these policies will shift over time. For instance, drug laws that initially trap urban users of one drug may subsequently snare rural users of another. And once the demographics of prison admissions are altered, the tolerance for high levels of incarceration may itself diminish as legislators and prosecutors are forced to reassess their understanding of the root causes of criminal offending. Whereas stereotypes supported the acceptance of causal misattribution of innate criminality to African Americans, the same approach to diagnosing the disparity evident in the increased incarceration of white women has not gained traction. Consequently, prosecutors and legislators seek out alternate explanations. It is conceivable that we are witnessing something similar to reform efforts of the

1930s, in which excessive punishment primarily affected white offenders (Muhammad 2011).

While women remain a small part of the total prison population—less than one in ten—they are part of virtually every family in the country. Social segregation by race continues to be extreme, while segregation by gender remains negligible. The rise in white female prison population has undoubtedly touched households and communities that were previously at some distance from the phenomenon of mass incarceration. It has made it tangible and personal. And through chains of social affiliation, these changes in attitude have percolated up to prosecutors, legislators, and governors.

Clearly, the changing composition of the incarcerated class is not the only force driving the movement to soften incarceration policy. Budgetary considerations are clearly significant, as is the small-government philosophy that has allowed decarceration to become acceptable within conservative circles. This is especially true in states with limited electoral competition, where there is little need to characterize opponents as being weak on crime (Dagan and Teles 2016). Nevertheless, to some degree decarceration initiatives could well be a response to facts that challenge stereotype-based essentialist views of criminal offending. As Lai and Banaji argue in this volume, exposure to counterstereotypical information can reduce the power of stereotypes.

How might we exit mass incarceration's stereotype trap? An unexpected change in the underlying facts can give rise to a perceptual disequilibrium, a counterstereotypical experience. This can force people to adjust the causal structure they place on the world. These changes then reveal themselves not only in shifting laws and explicit policies but also in routine decisions by prosecutors on countless individual cases. This is the largely untold part of the mass incarceration (and incipient decarceration) story. Wherever domination rests on stereotypes, difference without domination should gain traction to the degree that we encounter counterstereotypical facts.

8. What Can Be Done?

If democratic justice requires finding a pathway to the achievement of difference without domination, the work can proceed only with tools of positive social science that can analyze disparities, or patterns of difference, to determine which ones in fact flow from practices of domination. To do this work, we have added to the diagnostic tools by arguing for pay-ing attention to how stereotypes shape incentives. Where our tools turn up patterns of domination, we must then turn to the question of what corrective measures are available. With regard to mass incarceration, we need to ask how we can break out of the stereotype trap.

One approach to breaking out of the trap is to focus on changing beliefs when these are at variance with the underlying facts. In this volume, Lai and Banaji argue that black-white differences in implicit associations arise in part from the fact that black respondents have more positive exposure to black friends and family, and "the ultimate source of experience: themselves." This suggests that segregation in social contact is a key driver of differences across groups in beliefs. In fact, significant belief differences across groups exist on a number of issues, including the religion and birthplace of Barack Obama, the existence of racial discrimination in everyday life, the origins of the AIDS virus, and the selective targeting of black public officials for prosecution.[12] These differences are held in place by social segregation in everyday life, a point underscored by Lai and Banaji.

Policy interventions that target social segregation in a free society are not easily conceived. Nonetheless, there is considerable heterogeneity *within* groups in levels of exposure to other groups, and screening for such attributes, or building them through training programs, could make stereotypes less salient in law enforcement practices. Lowering discrimination in the use of nonlethal force while simultaneously increasing the clearance rate for homicides and other serious felonies would also have clear benefits. These two initiatives are intertwined: reduced harassment of innocents should make witnesses more likely to step forward, which in turn should help reduce homicide rates.

However there are limits to what policy interventions alone can accomplish. As Melvin Rogers describes in his contribution to this volume, an important strand of nineteenth-century African American thought treated "laws and institutions as important but also as derivative of the characterological properties of the nation. . . . To enjoy liberty requires not merely freedom from the arbitrary whim of particular agents or laws that limit arbitrary power, but a transformation of the system of cultural value in which blacks occupy a lower position of worth. These thinkers desired a form of citizenship found not only in the law but also in the heart."

Rogers quotes Frederick Douglass, who argued in 1848 that even those African Americans who were "not slaves to individuals" were yet "in many respects . . . slaves of the community." By analogy, one might argue today that even those who are not behind bars are in many respects prisoners of the community. Changing this would require a break with essential-ist interpretations of incentive-based phenomena. Perhaps a first step is to simply clarify the role that incentives play in shaping the patterns of crime and punishment that currently confront us.

Acknowledgments

I thank Danielle Allen, Marcellus Andrews, Eric Bottorff, Glenn Loury, Brendan O'Flaherty, Rohini Somanathan, and the other contributors to this volume for extremely helpful comments on an earlier version. Natalie Kozlova and Sophie Rothman provided valuable research assistance.

Notes

1. See Bennett, DiIulio, and Walters 1996, for example.

2. See, for instance, Horwitz and Zapotosky 2017.

3. The distinction used by the FBI in its statistical reporting is between violent crimes (homicide, rape, aggravated assault, and robbery) and property crimes (burglary, larceny, arson, and motor vehicle theft). For some purposes it is more useful to classify by motive, as is done in the figure: robbery, larceny, burglary, and motor vehicle theft are crimes of appropriation, while the rest are crimes of destruction. See O'Flaherty and Sethi 2019 for further justification and additional evidence.

4. See Wright and Decker 1997 for a detailed ethnographic study of active robbery offenders.

5. As one offender puts it in Wright and Decker's ethnographic study, "[Whites] got this stereotype, this myth, that a black person with a gun or knife is like Idi Amin or Hussein. And [a] person [who believes] that will do anything [you say]."

6. See Banaji and Greenwald 2013 and the contribution of Lai and Banaji to this volume.

7. Bland took her own life in a jail cell following her arrest, while the others had all charges dropped. See Ogletree 2010; Nathan 2016; and Dias, Eligon, and Oppel 2018, respectively, for discussions of these three cases.

8. See Dias et al. 2018 for a number of similar examples.

9. Houston is an unusual city when it comes to police use of lethal force, so care must be taken in drawing broader implications from this. For instance, in the *Guardian* data, whites in Houston were more likely to be killed by police than blacks in New York City over the 2015 to 2016 period (O'Flaherty and Sethi 2019).

10. This example is discussed at length in Loury 2004.

11. At the federal level, the trend appears to be in the opposite direction (Horwitz and Zapotosky 2017). However, as noted above, most prisoners are convicted under state laws and held in state facilities.

12. See Sethi and Yildiz 2012 for a survey of the evidence and a theoretical model of belief revision in the face of unobserved biases.

Works Cited

Alexander, Michelle. 2010. *The New Jim Crow: Mass Incarceration in the Age of Color-blindness*. New York: New Press.

Banaji, Mahzarin R., and Anthony G. Greenwald. 2013. *Blindspot: Hidden Biases of Good People*. New York: Delacorte.

Bennett, William, John DiIulio, and John Walters. 1996. *Body Count: Moral Poverty—and How to Win America's War against Crime and Drugs*. New York: Simon & Schuster.

Braga, Anthony A., David M. Kennedy, Elin J. Waring, and Anne Morrison Piehl. 2001. "Problem-Oriented Policing, Deterrence, and Youth Violence: An Evaluation of Boston's Operation Ceasefire." *Journal of Research in Crime and Delinquency* 38 (3): 195–225.

Case, Anne, and Angus Deaton. 2015. "Rising Morbidity and Mortality in Midlife among White Non-Hispanic Americans in the 21st Century." *Proceedings of the National Academy of Sciences* 112 (49): 15078–83.

Cheng, Cheng, and Mark Hoekstra. 2013. "Does Strengthening Self-Defense Law Deter Crime or Escalate Violence? Evidence from Expansions to Castle Doctrine." *Journal of Human Resources* 48 (3): 821–54.

Dagan, David, and Steven M. Teles. 2016. *Prison Break: Why Conservatives Turned against Mass Incarceration*. New York: Oxford University Press.

Dias, Elizabeth, John Eligon, and Richard A. Oppel Jr. 2018. "Philadelphia Starbucks Arrests, Outrageous to Some, Are Everyday Life for Others." *New York Times*, April 17, 2018.

Forman, James, Jr. 2017. *Locking Up Our Own: Crime and Punishment in Black America*. New York: Farrar, Straus and Giroux, 2017.

Fryer, Roland. 2019. "An Empirical Analysis of Racial Differences in Police Use of Force." *Journal of Political Economy* 127 (3): 1210–61.

Gelman, Andrew, and Jonathan Auerbach. 2016. "Age-Aggregation Bias in Mortality Trends." *Proceedings of the National Academy of Sciences* 113 (7): E816–E817.

Guerino, Paul, Paige M. Harrison, and William J. Sabol. 2011. "Prisoners in 2010." December, NCH 236096. Washington, DC: Bureau of Justice Statistics.

Harcourt, Bernard E. 2008. *Against Prediction: Profiling, Policing, and Punishing in an Actuarial Age*. Chicago: University of Chicago Press.

Horwitz, Sari, and Matt Zapotosky. 2017. "Sessions Issues Sweeping New Charging Policy." *Washington Post*, May 12.

Leovy, Jill. 2015. *Ghettoside: A True Story of Murder in America*. New York: Spiegel & Grau.

Lofstrom, Magnus, and Steven Raphael. 2016. "Prison Downsizing and Public Safety." *Criminology and Public Policy* 15 (2): 349–65.

Loury, Glenn C. 2002. *The Anatomy of Racial Inequality*. Cambridge, MA: Harvard University Press.

Loury, Glenn C. 2004. "The Anatomy of Racial Inequality: The Author's Account." *Review of Black Political Economy* 32 (2): 75–88.

Loury, Glenn C. 2008. *Race, Incarceration, and American Values*. Cambridge, MA: MIT Press.

Mauer, Marc. 2013. *The Changing Racial Dynamics of Women's Incarceration*. Washington, DC: Sentencing Project.

Muhammad, Khalil Gibran. 2011. "Where Did All the White Criminals Go? Reconfigur-
ing Race and Crime on the Road to Mass Incarceration." *Souls* 13 (1): 72–90.
Mullainathan, Sendhil. 2015. "Police Killings of Blacks: Here Is What the Data Say."
New York Times, October 16.
Murray, Charles. 2013. *Coming Apart: The State of White America, 1960–2010*. New York:
Three Rivers.
Nathan, Debbie. 2016. "What Happened to Sandra Bland?" *The Nation*, April 21.
National Research Council. 2014. *The Growth of Incarceration in the United States:
Exploring Causes and Consequences*. Edited by Jeremy Travis, Bruce Western, and
Steve Redburn. Washington, DC: National Academies.
O'Flaherty, Brendan, and Rajiv Sethi. 2008. "Racial Stereotypes and Robbery." *Journal
of Economic Behavior and Organization* 68 (3–4): 511–24.
O'Flaherty, Brendan, and Rajiv Sethi. 2010a. "Homicide in Black and White." *Journal of
Urban Economics* 68 (3): 215–30.
O'Flaherty, Brendan, and Rajiv Sethi. 2010b. "Peaceable Kingdoms and War Zones:
Preemption, Ballistics and Murder in Newark." In *The Economics of Crime: Les-
sons for and from Latin America*, edited by Rafael Di Tella, Sebastian Edwards, and
Ernesto Schargrodsky, 305–53. Chicago: University of Chicago Press.
O'Flaherty, Brendan, and Rajiv Sethi. 2010c. "Witness Intimidation." *Journal of Legal
Studies* 39 (2): 399–432.
O'Flaherty, Brendan, and Rajiv Sethi. 2019. *Shadows of Doubt: Stereotypes, Crime and the
Pursuit of Justice*. Cambridge, MA: Harvard University Press.
Ogletree, Charles. 2010. *The Presumption of Guilt: The Arrest of Henry Louis Gates Jr. and
Race, Class and Crime in America*. New York: St. Martin's.
Patterson, Orlando. 1982. *Slavery and Social Death*. Cambridge, MA: Harvard Univer-
sity Press.
Pfaff, John F. 2014. "Escaping from the Standard Story." *Federal Sentencing Reporter* 26
(4): 265–70.
Pfaff, John. 2017. *Locked In: The True Causes of Mass Incarceration and How to Achieve
Real Reform*. New York: Basic Books.
Putnam, Robert D. 2015. *Our Kids: The American Dream in Crisis*. New York: Simon &
Schuster.
Raphael, Steven, and Michael A. Stoll. 2009. "Why Are So Many Americans in Prison?"
In *Do Prisons Make Us Safer? The Benefits and Costs of the Prison Boom*, 27–72. New
York: Russell Sage Foundation.
Schelling, Thomas C. 1960. *The Strategy of Conflict*. Cambridge, MA: Harvard Univer-
sity Press.
Sethi, Rajiv, and Muhamet Yildiz. 2012. "Public Disagreement." *American Economic
Journal: Microeconomics* 4 (3): 57–95.
Wright, Richard, and Scott H. Decker. 1997. *Armed Robbers in Action: Stickups and Street
Culture*. Chicago: Northeastern University Press.

4

The Psychology of Implicit Intergroup Bias and the Prospect of Change

Calvin Lai and Mahzarin Banaji

1. Introduction

Over the course of evolution, human minds acquired the breathtaking quality of consciousness that gave our species the capacity to regulate behavior. Among the consequences of this capacity was the possibility of internal dialogue with oneself about the consistency between one's intentions and actions. This facility to engage in daily rituals of deliberative thought and action is so natural to our species that we hardly reflect on it or take stock of how effectively we are achieving the goal of intention-action consistency. We do not routinely ask at the end of each day how many of our actions were consistent with the values so many individuals hold: a belief in freedom and equality for all, in opportunity and access for all, in fairness in treatment and justice for all.

Even if we wished to compute the extent to which we succeed at this task, how would we go about doing it? As William James (1904) pointed out over a century ago, the difficulty of studying the human mind is that the knower is also the known, and this poses difficulties in accessing, in modestly objective fashion, the data from our own moral ledger. Ask and you will learn that people believe themselves to be good moral actors who may not be perfect but are largely behaving as they wish they would (Aquino and Reed 2002). This result is especially likely when we probe people's attitudes and beliefs about social groups (Banaji and Greenwald 2013). And yet since the implicit revolution (Greenwald and Banaji 2017), data from the social and behavioral sciences have repeatedly shown significant discrepancies between the lack of expression of conscious prejudice and stereotypes and data on group disparities in hiring and promotion, medical treatment, access to financial resources, education, and basic living conditions (e.g., by gender, age, race, ethnicity, sexuality). In this chapter we report on what is known from psychological science about the mental limits to fair treatment, with a special focus on what we know about the possibilities for change in mind and behavior.

A humble three-pound organ, the brain, gives rise to the grandest thinking apparatus, called the mind. *Beliefs* and *attitudes* originate here, and these thoughts and feelings shape societies and the course of civilization itself. Among the most significant roles that beliefs and attitudes play is to help humans formulate concepts of good and bad, right and wrong. Modern humans in democratic societies set a premium on particular values: freedom, equal opportunity, and fairness. These values are broadly deemed to be the foundations of a just society. And yet as scientists like ourselves have studied the extent to which *implicit* or unconscious attitudes and beliefs subvert these ideals, we have discovered just how early in life, how quickly, and how subtly they do so. For this reason, any discussion about social difference without domination must begin with understanding the act of an individual mind making ordinary and everyday decisions about others—decisions about core features such as a person's worth, competence, and goodness.

A quick glance at the past century of race relations in the United States reveals dramatic changes in how Americans think about race. Racially egalitarian principles infuse American laws and institutions. The workplace, transportation, and public spaces in many parts of the country are visibly more diverse in race and ethnicity. In quite a reversal of the America of only a few decades ago, major corporations, governmental agencies, and NGOs publicly promote their commitment to egalitarian merit-based treatment. They showcase their commitment through the affinity groups they sponsor, the awards they receive for being leaders on diversity, and the representations of groups among their ranks who were previously absent from their industry. Healthcare systems devote time and attention to reducing disparities in health outcomes. Educational institutions set aside sizable funding to ensure that the most meritorious can attend. Government agencies, whether they involve law and law enforcement, labor, health, education, housing, or the military, speak enthusiastically about their efforts to increase access and opportunities. Indeed the military, in its amicus brief for the Supreme Court cases on affirmative action, *Gratz v. Bollinger* and *Grutter v. Bollinger* (Becton et al. 2003), made the case that diversity in the military is necessary for the military to do its job—to keep the country safe. These principles are also present in public discourse with demands for civil speech that does not rely on group-based prejudices and stereotypes and chastising of social media expressions of views that curtail freedom, opportunity, and fairness in treatment of all.

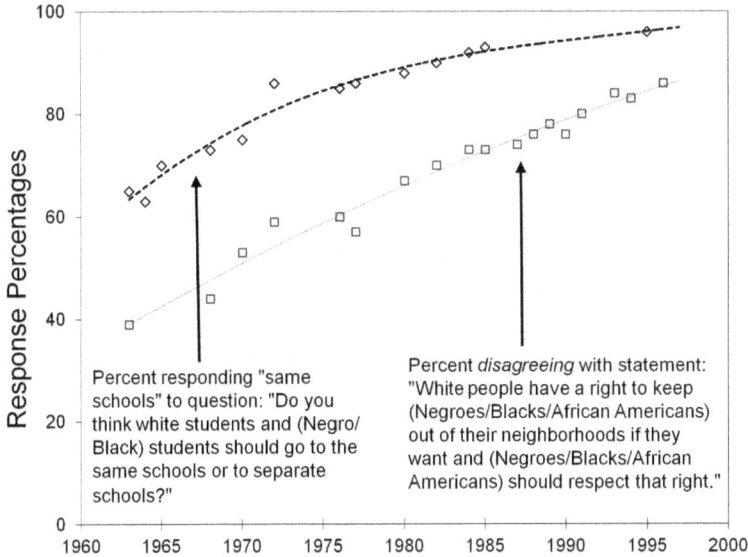

FIGURE 4.1. White Americans' increasing support for racial integration (1963–1996). Data source: H. Schuman et al., *Racial Attitudes in America* (Cambridge, MA: Harvard University Press, 1997), table 3.5A.

These public shifts in opinions and actions that characterize race relations today are simultaneously reflected in private shifts in attitudes and beliefs. A series of studies focused on racial/ethnic stereotypes known as the Princeton Trilogy shows this change most dramatically. At various moments beginning in the 1930s, social psychologists asked white American undergraduates to report privately on what they believed to be true of various racial/ethnic groups. In 1933, 75 percent of students endorsed the stereotype that black Americans were lazy (Katz and Braly 1933). In 1951 that percentage was reduced by more than half, to 31 percent (Gilbert 1951). By 2001 the percentage was cut by two-thirds more: only 12 percent of white students reported that African Americans were lazy (Madon et al. 2001).

Similar research on white Americans' opinions about various policies have been conducted over the decades, and those opinions have changed dramatically as well. Figure 4.1 shows four decades of results for white Americans' answers to two questions, one about school segregation and another about residential segregation. In the early 1960s only about 60 percent of white Americans supported racial integration in schools. By 1995 support for school integration had grown to almost 100 percent. Shortly after, the question was removed from surveys because the answers ceased to be informative. Similar increases in support were found for racial integration of neighborhoods. Whereas only 40 percent of white Americans supported housing integration in the early 1960s, more than 80 percent did so by the 1990s.

A conclusion from studies like these is that racial animus has largely disappeared. There is good reason to believe that such responses are not "just for show" but that Americans have changed their privately held conscious attitudes and beliefs as well. But this account belies the continued presence of discrimination in American life. There is a mismatch between the attitudes and beliefs that are expressed and the facts of black lives. Focusing on race alone, we have many examples of racial segregation (Iceland, Weinberg, and Steinmetz 2002), job discrimination (Bertrand and Mullainathan 2004), and inequalities in access to basic constitutional rights and their entailments—from education (US Dept. of Education 2016) to housing (US Census 2015), employment (US Bureau of Labor Statistics 2016), and health (LaVeist 2003).

A large tradition of research addresses this disconnect between what people say and what they do. Our particular strand of this research has looked at the earliest possible feelings and thoughts that can be measured behaviorally[1] with the intent of measuring less conscious forms of racial attitudes and beliefs. This research tells a different story about how present-day Americans think and feel about social groups (Banaji and Greenwald 2013; Devine 1989; Macrae and Bodenhausen 2000; Gawronski and Payne 2010). Much of the research on implicit cognition taps into introspectively unidentified thoughts using measures that examine the strength of association between a *concept* (e.g., black or white) and an *attribute* (e.g., good-bad, smart-dumb, rich-poor) by relying on the relative speed to make pairings between the concept and attribute. Using a variety of methods to get at these associations has led to a striking set of discoveries. Among the most central of these discoveries is that within the same individual mind there exist multiple actors: a deliberative decision-maker who aspires to egalitarian ideals and a less conscious partisan who is attentive to the similarity, familiarity, and social standing of those who are judged. Such lack of consistency within the same mind is psychologically interesting and morally consequential. It is easier to understand that a society may consist of people who vote for equal opportunity and fairness in treatment and those who do not. But to discover that one and the same mind can hold these differing values is perplexing. It raises questions such as why such mental states exist, where they come from, how pervasive they are, and their range of influence.

To set a manageable scope for our discussion, and because research on implicit social cognition has been covered elsewhere (Gawronski and

Payne 2010), we focus on a particular thread of this research: implicit associations and their openness to change. To understand the possibilities and limits of change is profoundly important for understanding human minds in social context and for serving as a foundation for the discussion in this volume about how difference is to be attended to within democratic societies. Social policies may seek to address the many divisions and segments of any society, but the work is incomplete unless we consider the mental barriers to equal treatment. Our intent is to lay bare what we know today in order to provoke a discussion about the standards we set for ourselves when we say that we value providing equal access and fair treatment.

2. The Implicit Association Test

The most commonly used method to measure implicit group-based cognition is the Implicit Association Test (IAT; Greenwald, McGhee, and Schwartz 1988). In the Race IAT, participants begin by seeing images appear on the screen. Some images represent the faces of people of African origin, whereas others represent the faces of people of European origin. The participant's task is to sort faces into one of two categories using a key on a standard computer keyboard: "Black people" or "White people." Then the participant learns to classify words into two categories, "good" and "bad" words, also using the same two keys on the keyboard. The two tasks after that require combining race categories and valence attributes (see figure 5.2). Participants complete combined blocks of trials where they are presented with all four types of images and words (black faces, white faces, bad words, and good words). In one set of blocks, participants must mentally associate white + good and black + bad by using a common key to respond to the pair. In a different set of blocks, participants must make the opposite association of white + bad and black + good. A measure of ease or effort is obtained by measuring the relative speed with which the two types of pairings are made. In mathematical terms, a score for the Race IAT is computed with the following equation (RT = reaction time):

$$\frac{\text{mean (RT pairing white \& bad/black \& good)} - \text{mean (RT pairing white \& good/black \& bad)}}{\text{standard deviation (Overall RT)}}$$

The idea that the speed of a response tells us about the strength of mental association is noncontroversial, beginning with the insight that reaction time could be used as a measure of mental processes from the Dutch scientist Franciscus Donders (1868). Two concepts that are closely associated in the mind are responded to more quickly than two concepts that are less associated. To the extent that there is a stronger association between white + good / black + bad than between white + bad / black + good, the test reveals faster response to the former pairings than the latter. A majority of white Americans are faster in pairing white + good / black + bad, suggesting that white Americans tend to hold relatively more pro-white/anti-black implicit preferences (Nosek, Banaji and Greenwald 2002; Nosek et al. 2007a).

The IAT's methodological limitations have been well documented. A commonly observed challenge is the possibility that the order in which blocks are administered may matter. That is, people who are first assigned to associate white + good and black + bad may perform differently on the IAT than people are first assigned to associate white + bad and black + good. To address this possibility, IAT standard practice is to randomly assign people to receive one order or the other so that it can be statistically controlled for (Nosek, Greenwald, and Banaji 2005). Another common concern is whether the images and words used to represent the categories may bias the results. To address this, researchers often take care to use images and words that are clear and representative of the categories they seek to represent (Nosek, Greenwald, and Banaji 2005). Over ten potential constraints to the IAT's validity have been identified, and many of these have been addressed through methodological refinements or are routinely taken into account in the interpretation of results (see Nosek, Greenwald, and Banaji 2007b for a full review).

The IAT has been used in hundreds of psychological laboratories as well as having been available online since 1998 (see Nosek, Banaji, and Greenwald 2002; implicit.harvard.edu). From these data we know that implicit biases are pervasive and often larger in magnitude than those observed on self-report measures (Nosek et al. 2007a). In the aggregate, visitors to Project Implicit show implicit preferences in favor of culturally dominant groups. In addition to showing a pro-white/anti-black implicit preference, participants show implicit preferences for the concept straight rather than gay, thin rather than overweight, and young over elderly. Data also show implicit stereotypes associating career with men and home with women and European American with the concept American more than Native American with American. Data also show associations of Black American with danger and White American with safety (Correll et al. 2007a; Donders, Correll, and Wittenbrink 2008).

We know that although there is a dissociation between consciously

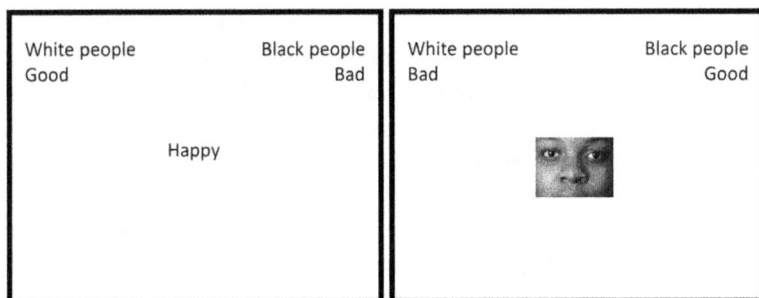

FIGURE 4.2. The Race Implicit Association Test.

expressed attitudes and the data on the IAT, the two measures are nevertheless correlated. Implicit and explicit racial attitudes are moderately
correlated at $r = .31$ (Cohen 1992; Nosek et al. 2007a). At the same time,
they are psychologically distinct from each other, with each type of attitude accounting for unique statistical variance (Cunningham, Nezlek,
and Banaji 2004).

Sethi (this volume) suggests that such implicit stereotypes might play
a role in how criminal offenders select victims and in issues of how the
law is enforced. He extends the argument about stereotypes to explain
how they create incentive structures and how these incentive structures
create larger social patterns. Sethi's argument, and Loury's argument in
The Anatomy of Racial Inequality (2002), shows how mental barriers to
equal treatment can come to be linked to the divisions in society that
social policy often seeks to address.

What are the factors that seem to predict preference for one group or
another? For many decades, psychological research has shown the power
of group membership in group attitudes and beliefs. We like our own
kind, we believe our own group to be superior to others, and we are more
willing to justify advantages to our own group over other groups. It is received wisdom that in-group favoritism is ubiquitous and accounts for a
large share of one's group preferences. But recognition that not all groups
show equally robust in-group preference is not new (see Jost and Banaji
1994; Jost, Banaji, and Nosek 2004). Groups that sit higher in the social
hierarchy tend to show greater in-group–favoring attitudes and beliefs
than those who sit lower in the social hierarchy.

Research on implicit social cognition has tested the contributions of
group membership and recognition of social hierarchy. Based on a simple
in-group favoritism account, members of two different groups, say black
and white people, should show equal and opposite preferences for their
own group over the other. For instance, white participants are expected

to show pro-white preference and black participants are expected to show equal and opposite pro-black preference because such preferences reflect in-group favoring attitudes. In contrast, third-party participants such as Asians should show neutrality on a black-white Race IAT because they do not belong to either group. From a *social standing* account, the test should reflect the degree to which a group has greater standing in society. This account would suggest that all groups would show a stronger pro-white implicit bias, reflecting the existence of higher status of white Americans in American society.

Examining the data can unpack the relative weight of both accounts. Among white participants at Project Implicit (total $N = 1,716,521$), 73 percent show a pro-white implicit preference, 16 percent show no overall preference, and 11 percent show a pro-black preference, which is consistent with both *in-group preference* and *social standing* accounts (Nosek et al. 2007a; Xu, Nosek, and Greenwald 2014).

To get better traction on the relative contribution of these accounts, we can look at the data of black participants (total $N = 279,612$). If implicit preference reflects in-group membership, then the data from black participants should be the mirror image of that of white participants with 73 percent of black participants showing pro-black implicit preference and 11 percent showing pro-white implicit preference. In contrast, if implicit preference reflects social standing, then the data should be near-identical to white participants with 75 percent showing pro-white implicit preference and 10 percent showing pro-black preference. The actual results show the presence of both factors on implicit attitudes. Forty percent of black participants show pro-black implicit preference, 35 percent of black participants show pro-white implicit preference, and 25 percent show no overall preference. Although black participants show slightly more pro-black preference than do white participants, the striking result here is the lack of the sort of in-group preference that is observed in the data from white participants. Knowledge of blacks' lower standing in society is visible in the implicit preferences of black participants themselves (despite black participants' self-reporting robust preferences for their own group).

Asian participants (total $N = 135,338$) also show pro-white preference almost at the level of white participants: 69 percent show a pro-white implicit preference, 13 percent show a pro-black implicit preference, and 18 percent show no overall preference. These results again show the importance of social standing in implicit attitudes. Theoretically, Asians could have shown neutrality on the white-black test of implicit attitude, but they did not. Together, results from these three groups suggest that two factors account for implicit preferences: *in-group favoritism* is visible in the data of white and black participants; *social standing* is visible in the far lower in-group preference of black Americans and the lack of neutrality among Asians. This simultaneous contribution of in-group favoritism and social standing is evident on other tests of implicit bias as well. For example, Christian Americans show stronger implicit preference for their own religion compared with Jewish Americans and Muslim Americans, and straight individuals show stronger preferences for straight people than gay individuals do for gay people (Axt, Ebersole, and Nosek 2014; Nosek et al. 2007a; Westgate, Riskind, and Nosek 2015).

The signature result from this research is the gap between what we explicitly report when asked about our feelings toward various social groups and what is observed on such tests of implicit attitudes. White participants report less explicit in-group preference than they show on measures on implicit preference, whereas black participants report more in-group preference on survey measures than they reveal on measures of implicit preference. From such data, investigators have concluded that self-reported attitudes are products of reflection to a greater extent, whereas implicit attitudes are products of impulse to a greater extent. When the two are not in sync, implicit and explicit attitudes reveal a psychological dissociation—a schism between two parts of the same mind.

3. Implicit Bias and Behavior

Measures of implicit cognition have been used to predict behavior in many domains, from racial discrimination to mental health to consumer preferences (Cameron, Brown-Iannuzzi, and Payne 2012; Carlsson and Agerstrom 2016; Greenwald et al. 2009; Oswald et al. 2013). Although most studies measuring the link between implicit cognition and behavior are laboratory based, interest has also focused on whether measures of implicit cognition can predict behavior in naturalistic settings. As an example of such a study, researchers evaluated how cashiers interacted with managers in a chain of French grocery stores (Glover, Pallais, and Pariente 2016). Managers in this study took an IAT assessing the degree to which they associated Europeans and North Africans with being good or poor employees. The researchers also measured the work performance of majority white and minority North African employees. On average, minority and majority cashiers performed about equally well. However, this differed based on who the presiding manager was during a particular work shift. When the presiding manager's anti-minority bias was low, the African cashiers performed better than white cashiers. When the presiding manager's anti-minority bias was high, African cashiers performed worse than white cashiers. African cashiers (but not white cashiers) who were scheduled to work when the manager on duty had high anti-minority bias were more likely to be absent from work, left work earlier, scanned items at the counter more slowly, and took more time between customers.

These racial biases in employee management extend to hiring. In a field experiment, researchers sent over 1,500 resumes to positions listed in job ads in Sweden (Rooth 2007). These resumes were matched to be almost identical except for two words: the name of the applicant, which signaled whether the applicant was Swedish or Arab. The study found that simply having an Arabic-sounding name reduced the probability of an interview callback by 9 percent. Moreover, implicit racial/ethnic stereotypes were predictive of biases in the callback rate even though explicit racial/ethnic attitudes and stereotypes were not.

Implicit biases are also implicated in critical life-and-death decisions to shoot (or not shoot) criminal suspects. In one series of studies, participants played a simulated game by observing images of white and black men situated in everyday places like parks or city sidewalks. In the simulation, some of the men are armed with guns, while others are unarmed and carrying mundane objects like wallets or cell phones. Participants are instructed to press a button to "shoot" (if the man is holding a gun) or press another button, "don't shoot" (if the man is not holding a gun). Research on civilian participants finds that they tend to mistakenly shoot unarmed black targets more than unarmed white targets (Correll et al. 2002). Similar research on police officers finds that the racial shooting bias depends on the types of experiences that police officers have, such as whether they primarily interact with members of the community or with gang members (Correll et al. 2007b; Sim, Correll, and Sadler 2013), whether they are fatigued (Ma et al. 2013), and what the interaction is like (James, Vila, and Daratha 2013).

Implicit cognition also predicts how we make sense of political information. One study examined political partisans and independents within the United States (Hawkins and Nosek 2012). Participants read about two competing special education policies, one proposed by the Democrats, the other by Republicans. Political independents were found to be mixed in their support of these policies, with some preferring the Democrat version and others the Republican one. However, this mixed support did not indicate an objective appraisal of policy facts. Independents who implicitly identified with Democrats (Republicans) were more likely to support policies proposed by the Democratic (Republican) Party, regardless of policy details. The significance of this result of course rests on

Redesigning the	Changing	Self-Regulating
↓	↓	↓
Situation →	Implicit Associations →	Behavior

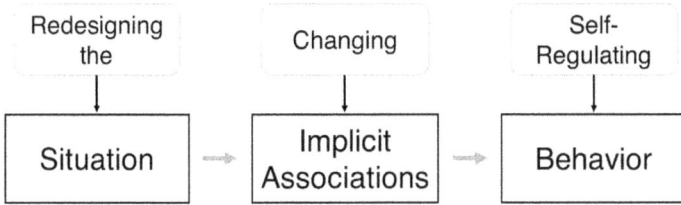

FIGURE 4.3. Three "locations" for addressing the impact of implicit bias.

the fact that the participants believe themselves to be independent. Implicit cognition may provide a window into patterns of behavior that are missed by explicit endorsements and can reflect hidden partisan affiliations (Dennis 1988; Keith et al. 1992).

Implicit biases predict how voters seek and consume political media. Undecided voters in northern Italy took an IAT assessing implicit attitudes toward integrating Turkey into the European Union (EU; Galdi et al. 2012). These implicit attitudes predicted how voters selectively exposed themselves to biased information. Undecided voters who had more pro-integrationist implicit attitudes were more likely to choose to read pro-integrationist news articles, leading to more pro-integrationist conscious attitudes. Meanwhile, undecided voters who had more anti-integrationist implicit attitudes were more likely to choose to read anti-integrationist news articles, leading to more anti-integrationist conscious attitudes.

The impact of implicit biases on discrimination has generated considerable interest in understanding how to combat them (e.g., Sethi, this volume). But how does one do so? In this chapter we analyze the process of change by focusing on aspects of the situation that can elicit or retard the expression of implicit bias, on the actual implicit associations themselves, and on conscious strategies for self-regulation. These three "locations" — situations, mental associations, and regulation — may serve as a useful way to organize what is currently known about the process of changing biases as they affect the allocation of opportunities and interpersonal dealings (see figure 4.3).

4. Three Approaches to Addressing Implicit Bias

a. Redesigning Situations

The concept of an *affordance* is an old chestnut in psychological theorizing, originally proposed by J. J. Gibson (1979), who promoted the idea that specific physical objects, situations, and the environment create specific possibilities for action. Open spaces "afford" walking, a thread "affords" sewing, handles "afford" turning. In other words, particular objects directly drive particular actions. In a loose way, we suggest that social situations "afford" or prompt particular behaviors. Situations can create or demand behavior that relies on use of group-based information to a greater or lesser extent. Here we give two examples of features of situations that can be designed to promote or hinder use of social group information.

Blinding. Many group memberships are signaled to us by visual and auditory cues. In most cases a person's gender, ethnicity, and age are easily available from visual and auditory perception. Even a person's name can cue us about one's group memberships. As dozens of audit studies in the field show, merely knowing a person's name can lead to group-based discrimination. Studies exist in the domains of hiring (Bertrand and Mullainathan 2004), financial access and remuneration (Ayres, Vars and Zakariya 2005; Ladd 1998), and healthcare (Kugelmass 2016) that reveal the role of an individual's group membership in decisions made about them.

To the extent that attributes of a person such as their name, physical body, dress, and speech produce discrimination, it is worth considering when such cues are undesirable and should be removed from perception. As one example, a highly cited case study of symphony orchestras suggests that blind auditions (i.e., using a curtain to visually block musicians from view of selecting judges) led to increased hiring of female musicians (Goldin and Rouse, 2000). There is no question that blinding decisionmakers to individual demographic characteristics can remove the pernicious and privileging effects of irrelevant information. In modern democracies, many will agree that if a prospective employee's group membership enters into decision-making about the individual's competence and thwarts two ideals—the ideal of selecting the best possible employee and the ideal of fair treatment—it is in a society's interest to consider corrective measures.

If we wish to evaluate competently, removing irrelevant information is clearly a good practice. But current practices seem largely unaffected by the evidence. A recent study found that law firms were much more likely to invite male applicants from high-income backgrounds for an interview than equally qualified female applicants, or male applicants from low-income backgrounds (Rivera and Tilcsik 2016). Another recent study shows that African Americans are 16 percent less likely to be accepted as renters than white Americans on Airbnb, a short-term housing rental service (Edelman, Luca, and Svirsky 2017). Such studies suggest that if access to cues for inferring characteristics like a person's gender, race, or social class are hidden from view, evaluators will home in on the criteria that matter most for job performance. Consider the field experiment described above, where CVs with Arabic-sounding names were 9 percent less likely to get an interview callback than CVs with Swedish-sounding names (Rooth 2007). To combat subtle biases like these, institutional policies may mandate the removal of names from job applications in some rounds of hiring. In 2010 Germany's Federal Anti-Discrimination Agency conducted a field experiment testing the effects of procedural blinding (Krause, Rinne, and Zimmermann 2012). Some companies used anonymized job applications and other companies did not. The researchers found that procedural blinding worked: companies that used anonymized job applications reduced bias against women and migrant applicants in many cases.

As the reader may have already guessed, blinding is possible only in limited circumstances such as grading in the classroom and reading applications for jobs. And even in these circumstances, it is not airtight. Information about one's group membership can indirectly leak through. We take this up shortly in describing many interactions in which human decisionmakers cannot avoid a person's group information. Moreover, differences in training may be helpful to consider. Say two candidates are only slightly different in skill but the one with slightly less skill has had far less schooling; in such a case it may be smart to select the slightly less skilled candidate, who likely has great potential to soar with training or experience. Such decisions cannot be implemented in blind reviews where differences of all kinds are explicitly obscured.

Reducing subjectivity. When the criteria for making a decision are ambiguous or uncertain, and when the decision requires reliance on one's judgment (e.g., a gut feeling, or a sense of what is expected to work best), biased judgments are to be expected (Darley and Gross 1983). To understand the extent to which minds will bend to create the outcome that is wished for rather than the outcome that rewards merit, consider a series of studies by E. L. Uhlmann and G. L. Cohen (2005). Participants were tasked with selecting one of two candidates, Michael and Michelle, for promotion to the position of police chief. All the materials for Michael and Michelle were identical, with one difference. One set of participants learned that Michael is known for his practical knowledge (street smart), while Michelle is known for being formally educated (book smart). After reviewing the candidates, these participants were more likely to select Michael for promotion, citing his street smarts as essential to success as a police chief.

Another set of participants in the same experiment also evaluated

Michael and Michelle but were alerted to the opposite attributes: Michael was formally educated (book smart) and Michelle was the practical one (street smart). If participants were evaluating solely on credentials, then one would expect that these participants would now pick Michelle, given that the quality of being street smart was prized. However, that was not the outcome. Participants in this group were also more likely to pick Michael, citing formal education as essential to success as a police chief.

These results demonstrate the slipperiness of decision-making criteria that allow us to hire the candidate we want while believing that we are selecting based on objective criteria. Participants' notions of what qualities mattered for the position were confabulated in order to confirm their gendered preference in a highly gendered profession.

To combat this tendency, the researchers ran the study again but made a small change to the procedure. Participants reported what qualities were important to being a police chief before selecting a candidate instead of after. When participants pre-committed to a set of criteria, they were more consistent with the qualities they reported as important. Regardless of gender, people who prioritized being streetwise picked the streetwise candidate, and people who prioritized being educated picked the educated candidate. This finding shows that constraining decision-makers to objective criteria can powerfully reduce bias.

Benefits and risks. The social situation can expand or contract the degree to which biases in individual minds can be expressed. When possible during important decisions, information about irrelevant group memberships should not be present, as it can lead individual minds away from fairness and merit-based selection. Blinding does not require active effort from the decisionmaker. It simply removes distracting information to produce decisions that are more in line with one's conscious values. Once instituted, blinding procedures can become routine and require little effort to maintain.

Redesigning situations can also be effective, because they have wide-reaching influence on unwanted biases. First, blinding or objective criteria can counter the effects of social knowledge well beyond the biases of which one is aware. For instance, blinding names in job applications may block evaluators from acting on race and gender biases but also more subtle biases like those of age, social class, and implicit egotism (e.g., liking a name that shares the same first initial as yours; Pelham, Carvallo, and Jones 2005; Polman, Pollmann, and Poehlman 2013).

More broadly, these strategies can prevent general cognitive biases. For example, use of objective criteria can eliminate the possibility of biases that arise from subjective judgment such as confirmation bias (the tendency to interpret evidence as confirming of one's existing beliefs; Nickerson 1998), framing effects (the tendency to react to information differently based on how it is presented; Tversky and Kahneman 1981), or primacy and recency effects in memory (the tendency to remember the first and last things in a series better than the things in the middle; Murdock 1962). These strategies add new tools to the toolbox for assuring fair treatment. Policymakers can identify situations where bias might interfere, and introduce procedural changes to prevent bias (Thaler and Sunstein 2009).

Despite their advantages, blinding and removing subjectivity from selection suffer from several limitations. As noted, blinding is simply not possible in the many situations that demand face-to-face interactions. Even if an individual actor wishes to de-bias herself by eliminating group membership information, such knowledge can intrude through the many channels that constitute the stream of information: voice, photos, and hearsay.

Implicit biases emerge from cues that are subtle and of which the perceiver is unaware. Having the foresight to anticipate potentially biasing behavior and implementing a fix can be a demanding requirement. Among these issues is the possibility that blinding increases failure to take potential into account at the time of decision-making as opposed to preexisting accomplishment. In the field experiment described above (Krause, Rinne, and Zimmerman 2012), some cases of blinding led to *increased* bias against women and/or migrants (see also Behaghel, Crépon and Babanchon 2015). In those cases, increased bias may result from removing information about demographics, when that prevents the possibility of enacting compensatory measures like affirmative action or undertaking forms of holistic review that take prior opportunities into account in order to assess potential. Thankfully, this is a tractable issue. If institutions seek to employ blinding but also desire to increase diversity, then blinding could be supplemented with counterweights that promote diversity-related outcomes. For example, a technology start-up that is composed of 80 percent men could choose to include applicant gender as a criterion in hiring when constructing objective hiring criteria. That would increase the probability of women being hired, all else being equal.

b. Changing Implicit Associations

The human mind has acquired distinctive ways of processing information over the course of evolutionary time. The mind has developed specific ways of attending to the world and perceiving and forming inferences about the world based on the partial information provided by experience. Our effort is directed toward what we might do, given these features of the mind, in the context of the values that characterize democracies today. Based on the evidence we reviewed early in this chapter on the presence of implicit group-based associations that exist without conscious animus, an obvious location to conceive of change is in the status of those associations themselves.

The logic goes something like this: We form good habits all the time. We didn't wear seatbelts but now we do. We didn't pay attention to the threat from smoking, but now we do. We learned to brush our teeth each morning and night even if we are incredibly tired. The list of human achievements in the small things that keep us healthy are similar to the many changes we have made to our social lives, in which we obey ordinary rules of conduct, such as who has the right of way on the road, and courtesies we practice all the time of standing in lines, giving people time to make an argument, and so on. The brains of humans today who routinely perform these actions are no different from those of their ancestors who did not, but our *minds* are unrecognizably different.

Psychology as a discipline placed the concept of "learning" at the center of the field early in its history, and we have an enormous amount of knowledge about how we learn and change. If implicit associations are in part a reflection of the world in which we live and if these associations are also likely to be causes of how we act, it is worth attempting to understand how and when changing implicit associations is possible. If the very activation of particular implicit associations is reduced, the influence of bias might be reduced as well (Lai, Hoffman, and Nosek 2013). Unlike explicit attitudes (e.g., stating that one doesn't like members of group X), implicit attitudes and beliefs have a unique pattern of learning that needs specific attention (Gawronski and Bodenhausen 2006 and 2011).

One such theory of learning suggests that implicit biases reflect the sheer accumulation of associations between stimuli in the environment (Rydell and McConnell 2006). A direct method to change implicit biases, then, is exposure to stimuli that counter existing associations. Just as with learning that emerges from classical conditioning (Bouton 2007; Pavlov 1927; Staats and Staats 1958), interventions present participants with dozens or hundreds of new pairings between a concept (like race or gender) and attributes (like good/bad, strong/weak; e.g., Bar-Anan, De Houwer, and Nosek 2010; De Houwer, Thomas, and Baeyens 2001; Karpinski and Hilton 2001; Olson and Fazio 2001). Interestingly, these con-

Procedure category		k	g [95% CI]
Stereotype-defying info		58 (28)	-0.25 [-0.33, -0.16]
Stereotype-confirming info		34 (27)	0.17 [0.06, 0.28]
Reduce via indirect methods		81 (28)	-0.23 [-0.31, -0.15]
Increase via indirect methods		22 (27)	0.08 [-0.05, 0.20]
Egalitarian goals		65 (12)	-0.27 [-0.36, -0.18]
Anti-egalitarian goals		11 (12)	0.20 [0.03, 0.38]
Threatening values/identity		32 (7)	0.21 [0.08, 0.34]
Affirming values/identity		9 (2)	-0.09 [-0.33, 0.14]
Positive mood/emotion		11 (8)	-0.07 [-0.25, 0.11]
Negative mood/emotion		6 (12)	-0.14 [-0.36, 0.08]
Deplete mental resources		20 (1)	0.20 [0.01, 0.38]

-0.6   -0.3   0   0.3   0.6
Change in implicit bias vs a control condition

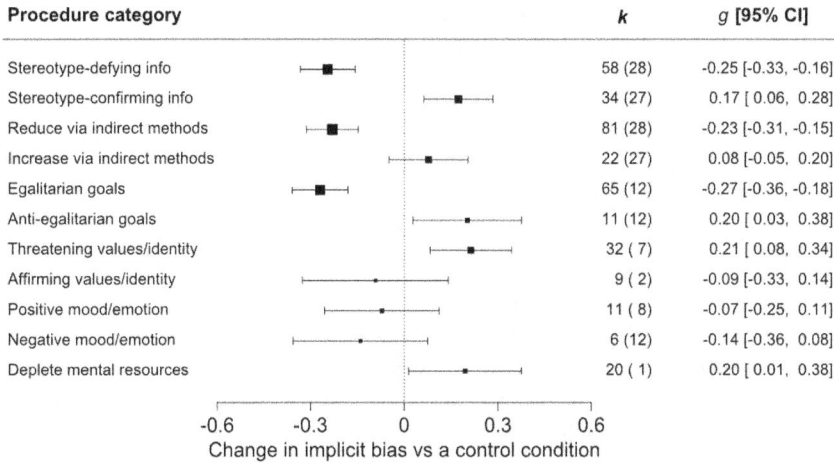

FIGURE 4.4. Forest plot of comparisons between each approach and a control condition on implicit intergroup bias, in which k gives the number of study samples that directly (or indirectly, listed in parentheses) compare the approach and a control condition, and g gives the standardized mean difference between an approach and a control condition and its 95 percent confidence interval. Larger effect sizes reflect greater increases in implicit bias relative to a control condition. See Forscher 2018 for a complete description of the methods and analyses.

ditioning trials often change implicit attitudes without affecting explicit attitudes and give credence to the view that implicit associations arise from distinct mental processes that operate by a unique set of rules. For example, M. A. Olson and R. H. Fazio (2006) presented participants with positive images and words paired with black faces and negative images and words paired with white faces. Exposure to these pairings reduced implicit racial attitudes immediately, and this effect persisted two days later. In contrast, explicit racial attitudes remained unchanged.

A more elaborate version of presenting new associations to change existing attitudes is to create encounters with people or media images that defy stereotypes. Mere exposure to well-liked black people (e.g., Nelson Mandela, Michael Jordan) and disliked white people (e.g., Charles Manson, John Gotti) can reduce the typical pro-white/anti-black bias (Dasgupta and Greenwald 2001; Joy-Gaba and Nosek 2010). Even imagining a counterstereotypical person can reduce implicit stereotyping, as was the case when college students were asked to imagine working for a woman as their boss even for a few minutes (Blair, Ma, and Lenton 2001). Changing implicit associations through exposure to counterstereotypical information is one method of many. A recent meta-analysis (Forscher, Lai, et al. 2019) compared 492 experiments that study implicit bias change, of which 313 tested experimental manipulations on topics relevant to inter-group relations. Figure 4.4 shows a forest plot synthesizing the results of these 313 intergroup studies across eleven approaches.

Overall, changes in implicit associations were small but robust. How-ever, the magnitude of change depended heavily on the type of approach used to change implicit intergroup biases. An initial set of approaches in-volved experiences with stereotype-defying information (like the above) or stereotype-confirming information. These two approaches were effec-tive at reducing and increasing implicit associations, respectively. A sec-ond class of approaches sought to change implicit associations indirectly by targeting higher-level mental states and beliefs that are not directly related to the implicit association—for example, taking the perspective of a member of another group or being led to feel powerful or high-status (Guinote, Willis, and Martellotta 2010; Richeson and Ambady 2003). In-direct approaches that sought to reduce implicit associations were effec-tive at doing so, although indirect approaches that sought to increase im-plicit biases were not consistent at doing so. These results suggest that implicit biases are not merely products of brute force associations; they can also be changed by higher-level mental states and beliefs.

A third class of approaches activated egalitarian or antiegalitarian motivations or goals. Egalitarian motivations or goals were effective at reducing implicit biases, and antiegalitarian motivations or goals were effective at increasing them, suggesting that implicit biases are sensitive to the motivations or goals that individuals carry with them into social situations (e.g., Lun et al. 2007; Stewart and Payne 2008). A fourth class of approaches involved threatening or affirming ones' values or identi-ties. Echoing decades of work on intergroup threat (Stephan and Stephan 2000), threatening one's values or identity was effective at increasing im-plicit bias against members of other groups (e.g., Frantz et al. 2004). In sharp contrast, affirming one's values or identities did not have an overall effect on implicit intergroup biases (e.g., Rudman, Dohn, and Fairchild 2007; Walton et al. 2015).

A final set of approaches looked at general mental states. Emotions and moods such as happiness and sadness did not have an overall effect in changing implicit intergroup biases (e.g., Kuppens et al. 2012). However, depleting mental resources did. In these studies, participants were led to feel mental fatigue or mental load, and this mental state increased the expression of implicit biases. These studies suggest that tiredness, stress, and other mental states that constrain one's ability or motivation to think things through can enhance the effects of implicit bias.

These results are important. They teach us that implicit attitudes and beliefs are malleable. Even well-known and well-practiced habits of mind are able to stretch in opposite directions with brief and minimal interventions. It is illustrative that a few minutes of a variety of minor interventions can produce a reappraisal after a lifetime of learning that one group is superior to another.

Long-term change in implicit bias. Studies like these have raised the question whether implicit attitudes are amenable to long-term change. Unfortunately, most studies use short-term interventions that examine change over the course of a single experimental session lasting an hour or so. Only 18 out of the 313 experiments summarized above examined effects over a longer period, such as several days or weeks.

In a recent series of studies, we sought to address this lack with experiments that compared the impact of eighteen brief interventions to reduce implicit racial attitudes (Lai et al. 2014 and 2016). Of these eighteen, nine were effective at reducing implicit attitudes immediately. The most effective intervention leveraged exposure to counterstereotypical exemplars to cut implicit preferences by half.

However, none of these nine interventions had persistent effects on implicit preferences after several days. Post intervention, participants returned to baseline levels of implicit preferences. These results are not necessarily surprising. Human minds have evolved to change in response to experiences that are potent, adaptive, or repeatedly practiced. The interventions used in the studies lacked many of these properties. They were mild, brief, and unlikely to be sustained in environments that routinely confirm existing biases. Being sensitive to context but able to snap back to default ways of thinking is exactly what an intelligent system should do. And this of course suggests just how difficult the project of changing attitudes and beliefs is. To understand how permanent changes in implicit biases can happen, one must investigate research that undertakes changes in implicit bias after subjecting it to robust intervention.

Long-term experiences with people outside of one's own group is one of the most studied and effective approaches to reducing prejudice, both implicit and explicit (Allport 1954; Pettigrew and Tropp 2006). In one study, researchers took advantage of a natural experiment where white college freshmen were randomly assigned to a black or white roommate and found that those that lived with a black roommate showed reduced implicit racial bias at the end of the first semester of living together (Shook and Fazio 2008). Another study looked at gender stereotypes by studying how going to a women's single-sex college related to gender stereotypes (Dasgupta and Asgari 2004). They assessed female students during the beginning of their first and second years of college, half of whom attended a women's liberal arts college, and half of whom attended a coeducational liberal arts college. At the start of college, students in both colleges showed the same level of gender stereotypes associating men more with leadership than women. Over the course of their first year, the implicit gender-leader stereotypes of women at the women's college had dissipated, whereas the implicit stereotypes of women at the coeducational college had increased. Interestingly, this difference in stereotyping was explained not by the single-sex versus coeducational structure of the institution but rather by the extent to which students had been exposed to female faculty members—the greater the number of courses taken with female faculty, the lower the gender-leader bias. Having greater exposure to female professors, an event more likely at the women's college, had shifted implicit gender-leader stereotypes away from the cultural norm.

Another way to assess the impact of long-term experiences is to track changes at the cultural level. A deep analysis of attitude IATs at the Project Implicit website was recently undertaken (Charlesworth and Banaji 2019) using 4.4 million tests of implicit and explicit attitudes that were measured continuously from 2007 to 2016. Comparative analysis using time series models examined whether the United States has changed in attitudes toward six social groups: age, disability, race, skin tone, sexual orientation, and body weight. Within that decade, all explicit attitudes show change toward neutrality. Implicit attitudes have also changed toward neutrality in three domains: implicit preferences for straight vs. gay people (33 percent), implicit preferences for white vs. black people (17 percent), and implicit preferences for light-skinned vs. dark-skinned people (15 percent). In contrast, other implicit attitudes remain unchanged (age, disability) or even moved away from neutrality (body weight). These data show that implicit attitude change is possible. We cannot isolate the causes of why sexuality, race, and skin tone attitudes have changed toward neutrality, but we speculate that their change may be related to the intense social dialogue that has surrounded questions of sexuality and race relative to other social categories in the United States in the early decades of the twenty-first century. Some initial evidence suggests that at least for race, reductions in implicit racial preferences were associated with the rise of the Black Lives Matter movement (Sawyer and Gampa 2018). This suggests that active political discussion, disagreeable as the discussion may be, has had the effect of reducing implicit bias.

In this volume, Sethi also presents a case of a durable intervention resulting from a natural experiment—the increasing rates of the incarceration of women—and argues that it has made a durable difference for explicit attitudes about punishment.

These long-term studies of implicit attitudes provide insight into the kinds of interventions that are likely to change and not change implicit attitudes. Although such comparisons do not provide clear explanations for some implicit attitudes changing and others remaining stable, they do allow us to hypothesize about the conditions that are necessary for change to occur.

Benefits and risks. If change in anti-gay bias is an example of the change that is possible even with robust negative attitudes, media exposure, personal contact, and legal progress cannot be underestimated as vehicles of change. As psychologists, we are interested in change at the level of the individual mind. We are aware that one can choose to create the conditions of social life that will produce shifts in attitudes and beliefs. The path we walk every day can be chosen rather than passively accepted. If the will exists, one can shape experiences in such a way that positive associations with otherwise negative social categories can be created through media exposure and personal experience. The power of counterstereotypes is not to be underestimated, and if counterstereotypical encounters become typical, shift in attitudes and beliefs will follow. What has been learned can be unlearned, or learned in a new mold. But this is neither easy to implement nor achievable through a few experiences. The stuff of life—where we live, whom we encounter and in what capacity, who are the objects of our intimacy, and what representations of them we choose to present to our senses—all these phenomena contribute to the formation and re-formation of attitudes and beliefs, and to some extent they are within our own control.

Although it is possible, to expect that individuals will change their habits and their experiences at the level of minuscule threads of daily experience, and to do so on a large scale, is unreasonably optimistic. There are few incentives to do so, there are few "manuals" that show the way, and there are many daily experiences that oppose change. Existing group memberships, such as religious, political, and ethnic identities, are viewed around the world as sacred, and explicit negative attitudes toward those from another group are common in many of them. This being the case, it is important to consider the role of mechanisms other than individuals' volunteering to change individual minds. In many social sciences that are not as focused on the individual as psychology is, the idea of measuring progress and creating change has always been considered at the more macro level of groups, institutions, laws, and governance. As we consider the evidence on implicit cognition, it is clear that if individuals are largely unaware of their own mental states and of the fact that their behavior is not in line with their own intentions and values, levers of change other than individual minds must be activated.

Institutions in democracies have the power to shape environments to elicit the attitudes and beliefs their citizens aspire to but fall short on. Institutions that control housing, education, business, healthcare, and the law can take up the challenge of creating implicit bias-reducing experiences that a society willingly acknowledges to be in the public interest. This focus on institutions becomes a necessity when such an aspiration is combined with knowledge of the deep bounds of the rationality of individual decision-making. If a society believes that all its citizens deserve equal opportunity, then institutions may fill in the gaps created by the limits of individual decision-making. Achieving difference without domination may require us to activate the representational power latent in our institutions themselves.

c. Self-Regulating Behavior

In the animal kingdom, certain species dominate. The gargantuan blue whale eats up to 2.2 tons of food each day. The nimble cheetah can run at seventy miles per hour. The sage tortoise can outlast the lives of humans many times over. And yet humans are the species we are because we have the gift of conscious thought. Among the functions of conscious thought is the ability to exert control over behavior, even if the mind has an opposing preference. Humans are champions of holding their tongue, suppressing maladaptive emotions, and delaying gratification to seek a greater later reward. Our ability to self-regulate flexibly exceeds that of any other species. In the domain of bias reduction, the Self-Regulation of Prejudice (SRP) Model has been proposed (Monteith 1993; Monteith et al. 2002; Monteith and Mark 2005; Monteith and Mark 2009; Monteith, Parker, and Burns 2016) to explore this phenomenon. The model elucidates several consequences of becoming aware that one did something biased. These consequences are affective (the experience of negative emotions such as guilt or shame), behavioral (inhibition of the biased behavior), and cognitive (reflection on the situation and the mental states associated with biased thought or behavior). A combination of these is expected to lead to the development of mental control. Practice with such routines creates learning that leads to inhibition of biased behavior, prospective reflection on how to behave differently, and the achievement of nonbiased behavior.

Of course self-regulation is never foolproof. Failures to control one's own biases can arise at any point. Social actors may fail to realize that they are acting in a biased way to begin with. Or social actors may fail to prevent themselves from acting on their biases, fail to experience negative emotions about being biased, or fail to reflect on why they may be biased. Social actors may also fail to establish mental control or fail to remember to enact mental control in a future event where they are potentially biased. To counteract these many self-regulation failures, we propose two evidence-based strategies: looking into the bias blind spot and implementation intentions.

Looking into the bias blind spot. A near-necessary condition for bias self-regulation is awareness that one's own behavior is biased. This sounds simpler than it is. The singular psychological obstacle to awareness is the inability to introspect accurately about the origins of one's own thoughts and feelings (Nisbett and Wilson 1977). This tendency to fail to see bias in one's own judgments despite being able to perceive bias in others' judgments is known as the *bias blind spot* (Pronin, Lin, and Ross 2002). People can consciously search their thoughts for biased processing but very rarely find any indication of it (Pronin and Kugler 2007).

Just as humans cannot introspect accurately about their level of blood pressure or a developing cancer (and rational individuals must rely on external methods to learn about the workings of their bodies), so too with hidden mental content. One can imagine that efforts to educate about the existence of implicit bias and how it influences behavior might translate into successful regulation. Of course such efforts to educate rely on the assumption that many individuals in modern democracies will aspire to behavior change if they are made aware that their current behavior is unaligned with their values and aspirations.

Implicit bias is most likely to influence behavior when individuals lack the motivation or ability to deliberate (Fazio and Olson 2014). The motivation to deliberate can arise from motivations to be accurate (e.g., Schuette and Fazio 1995), being accountable for a behavior (e.g., Sanbonmatsu and Fazio 1990), concerns about being viewed favorably (e.g., Fazio et al. 1995), or motivations to act without prejudice (e.g., Dunton and Fazio 1997). The ability to deliberate can be impeded by factors such as mental fatigue (Govorun and Payne 2006), time pressure (Ranganath, Smith, and Nosek 2008), alcohol use (Bartholow, Dickter, and Sestir 2006), or age-based cognitive decline (Gonsalkorale, Sherman, and Klauer 2009). Greater self-insight into when one is most likely to act on implicit bias can combat these influences. A major caveat to this recommendation is the dearth of evidence examining the effectiveness of raising awareness about unconscious bias. We are aware of only one experiment that has done so. It found that a 2.5-hour workshop for university faculty raising awareness about gender bias led to increased self-efficacy in combating gender bias (Carnes et al. 2015).

Implementation intentions. Awareness of biased behavior does not eliminate the biased behavior in question. One must also act to replace it with nonbiased behavior. This can be difficult in practice. A surprisingly effective strategy to bridge this gap between values and action is implementation intentions (Fujita 2011; Gollwitzer 1999; Gollwitzer and Sheeran 2006). Implementation intentions are "if-then" plans that link a situational cue with a behavioral response (e.g., "if event X happens, then I will do Y"). Setting an if-then plan creates a mental association between the cue and response, making effortful behavior more automatic and unconscious (Bayer et al. 2009; Gollwitzer and Brandstätter 1997). Despite their simplicity, implementation intentions have improved outcomes across many types of self-regulation problems, including exercise and dieting (e.g., Luszczynska, Sobczyk, and Abraham 2007), recycling (Holland, Aarts, and Langendam 2006), and smoking cessation (Armitage 2007). Importantly, they have also successfully reduced the expression of implicit biases (Lai et al. 2014, 2016; Mendoza, Gollwitzer, and Amodio 2010; Stewart and Payne 2008). Although it is difficult to imagine that the strategy would succeed, research has shown setting an if-then implementation intention to think a counterstereotypical thought when they see a black person reduced the expression of implicit bias for at least two months after the implementation intention was taught (Monteith, Parker, and Burns 2016).

Benefits and risks. Self-regulation strategies are flexible and can be tailored to many areas of bias. Compared to efforts to reduce implicit bias, efforts to self-regulate are more likely to result in effective behavior change because the behavior and self-control are more closely linked. Efforts to promote bias regulation give agency to individuals who seek to treat people of different groups fairly, although they may be avoided by individuals who do not share such commitments (Kulik et al. 2007). In the policy realm, education initiatives could be used to inform individuals about approaches for successful self-regulation. Public campaigns, school curricula, and other social media can orient people to simple tips like implementation intentions for controlling unwanted behavior.

5. Conclusion

The human mind is limited in its ability to apply the ideals of freedom, opportunity, and fairness equally to all, or to treat all with dignity, as Wingo also elaborates in this volume. This limitation must be recognized if we are to enter into any discussion of creating a better society. Evidence of implicit bias has raised the bar on the challenges faced by modern democracies consisting of a plurality of social groups with differing histories, power, and potential futures. Understanding that we can discriminate against others even when we have no intention to harm is difficult to grasp and even harder to solve, given legal systems founded on the idea of intent as pivotal in determining justice. However, recent discoveries show that pernicious effects of implicit bias need not be inevitable. The research we have reviewed shows individual minds to be sensitive to change, given the right inputs. We hope that this approach to securing positive social change can aid in the project of safeguarding diverse societies.

Note

1. By "behaviorally" we mean any action outside of neural and physiological responses. By that definition, survey responses and responses on reaction time tasks are behaviors.

Works Cited

Allport, G. W. 1954. *The Nature of Prejudice.* Cambridge, MA: Addison-Wesley.

Armitage, C. J. 2007. "Efficacy of a Brief Worksite Intervention to Reduce Smoking: The Roles of Behavioral and Implementation Intentions." *Journal of Occupational Health Psychology* 12 (4): 376–90.

Aquino, K., and A. Reed II. 2002. "The Self-Importance of Moral Identity." *Journal of Personality and Social Psychology* 83 (6): 1423–40.

Axt, J. R., C. R. Ebersole, and B. A. Nosek. 2014. "The Rules of Implicit Evaluation by Race, Religion, and Age." *Psychological Science* 25 (9): 1804–15.

Ayres, I., F. E. Vars, and N. Zakariya. 2005. "To Insure Prejudice: Racial Disparities in Taxicab Tipping." *Yale Law Journal* 114 (7): 1613–74.

Banaji, M. R., and A. G. Greenwald. 2013. *Blindspot: Hidden Biases of Good People.* New York: Random House.

Bar-Anan, Y., J. De Houwer, and B. A. Nosek. 2010. "Evaluative Conditioning and Conscious Knowledge of Contingencies: A Correlational Investigation with Large Samples." *Quarterly Journal of Experimental Psychology* 63 (12): 2313–35.

Bartholow, B. D., C. L. Dickter, and M. A. Sestir. 2006. "Stereotype Activation and Control of Race Bias: Cognitive Control of Inhibition and Its Impairment by Alcohol." *Journal of Personality and Social Psychology* 90 (2): 272–87.

Bayer, U. C., A. Achtziger, P. M. Gollwitzer, and G. Moskowitz. 2009. "Responding to Subliminal Cues: Do If-Then Plans Facilitate Action Preparation and Initiation without Conscious Intent?" *Social Cognition* 27 (2): 183–201.

Becton, J. W., et al. Consolidated Brief of Lt. Gen. Julius W. Becton Jr. et al. as Amici Curiae in Support of Respondents, in *Grutter v. Bollinger*, et al., *Gratz and Hamacher v. Bollinger*, et al., nos. 02-241, 02-516 February 19, 2003.

Behaghel, L., B. Crépon, and T. L. Barbanchon. 2015. "Unintended Effects of Anonymous Resumes." *American Economic Journal: Applied Economics* 7 (3): 1–27.

Bertrand, M., and S. Mullainathan. 2004. "Are Emily and Greg More Employable Than Lakisha and Jamal? A Field Experiment on Labor Market Discrimination." *American Economic Review* 94 (4): 991–1013.

Blair, I. V., J. E. Ma, and A. P. Lenton. 2001. "Imagining Stereotypes Away: The Moderation of Implicit Stereotypes through Mental Imagery." *Journal of Personality and Social Psychology* 81 (5): 828–41.

Bouton, M. E. 2007. *Learning and Behavior: A Contemporary Synthesis*. Sunderland, MA: Sinauer Associates.

Cameron, D. C., J. L. Brown-Iannuzzi, and B. K. Payne. 2012. "Sequential Priming Measures of Implicit Social Cognition: A Meta-analysis of Association with Behavior and Explicit Attitudes." *Personality and Social Psychology* 16 (4): 335–50.

Carlsson, R., and J. Angerström. 2016. "A Closer Look at the Discrimination Outcomes in the IAT Literature." *Scandinavian Journal of Psychology* 57 (4): 278–87.

Carnes, M., P. G. Devine, L. B. Manwell, A. Bryars-Winston, E. Fine, C. E. Ford, . . . and M. Palta. 2015. "Effect of an Intervention to Break the Gender Bias Habit for Faculty at One Institution: A Cluster Randomized, Controlled Trial." *Academic Medicine* 90 (2): 221–30.

Charlesworth, T., and M. R. Banaji. 2019. "Patterns of Change in Implicit and Explicit Attitudes I: Long-Term Change and Stability from 2007–2016." *Psychological Science* 30 (2): 174–92.

Cohen, J. 1992. "A Power Primer." *Psychological Bulletin* 112 (1): 155–59.

Correll, J., B. Park, C. M. Judd, and B. Wittenbrink. 2002. "The Police Officer's Dilemma: Using Ethnicity to Disambiguate Potentially Threatening Individuals." *Journal of Personality and Social Psychology* 83 (6): 1314–29.

Correll, J., B. Park, C. M. Judd, and B. Wittenbrink. 2007a. "The Influence of Stereotypes on Decisions to Shoot." *European Journal of Social Psychology* 37 (6): 1102–17.

Correll, J., B. Park, C. M. Judd, B. Wittenbrink, M. S. Sadler, and T. Keesee. 2007b. "Across the Thin Blue Line: Police Officers and Racial Bias in the Decision to Shoot." *Journal of Personality and Social Psychology* 92 (6): 1006–23.

Cunningham, W. A., J. B. Nezlek, and M. R. Banaji. 2004. "Implicit and Explicit Ethnocentrism: Revisiting the Ideologies of Prejudice." *Personality and Social Psychology Bulletin* 30 (10): 1332–46.

Darley, J. M., and P. H. Gross. 1983. "A Hypothesis-Confirming Bias in Labeling Effects." *Journal of Personality and Social Psychology* 44 (1): 20–33.

Dasgupta, N., and S. Asgari. 2004. "Seeing Is Believing: Exposure to Counterstereotypic Women Leaders and Its Effect on the Malleability of Automatic Gender Stereotyping." *Journal of Experimental Social Psychology* 40 (5): 642–58.

Dasgupta, N., and A. G. Greenwald. 2001. "On the Malleability of Automatic Attitudes: Combating Automatic Prejudice with Images of Admired and Disliked Individuals." *Journal of Personality and Social Psychology* 81 (5): 800–814.

De Houwer, J., S. Thomas, and F. Baeyens. 2001. "Association Learning of Likes and Dislikes: A Review of 25 Years of Research on Human Evaluative Conditioning." *Psychological Bulletin* 127 (6): 853–69.

Dennis, J. 1988. "Political Independence in America, Part I: On Being an Independent Partisan Supporter." *British Journal of Political Science* 18 (1): 77–109.

Devine, P. G. 1989. "Stereotypes and Prejudice: Their Automatic and Controlled Components." *Journal of Personality and Social Psychology* 56 (1): 5–18.

Donders, F. C. 1868. "On the Speed of Mental Processes." Translated by W. G. Koster, 1969. *Acta Psychologica* 30: 412–31.

Donders, N. C., J. Correll, and B. Wittenbrink. 2008. "Danger Stereotypes Predict Racially Biased Attentional Allocation." *Journal of Experimental Social Psychology* 44 (5): 1328–33.

Dunton, B. C., and R. H. Fazio. 1997. "An Individual Difference Measure of Motivation to Control Prejudiced Reactions." *Personality and Social Psychology Bulletin* 23 (3): 316–26.

Edelman, B. G., M. Luca, and D. Svirsky. 2017. "Racial Discrimination in the Sharing Economy: Evidence from a Field Experiment." *American Economic Journal: Applied Economics* 9 (2): 1–22.

Fazio, R. H., J. R. Jackson, B. C. Dunton, and C. J. Williams. 1995. "Variability in Automatic Activation as an Unobtrusive Measure of Racial Attitudes: A Bona Fide Pipeline?" *Journal of Personality and Social Psychology* 69 (6): 1013–27.

Fazio, R. H., and M. A. Olson. 2014. "The MODE Model: Attitude-Behavior Processes as a Function of Motivation and Opportunity." In *Dual Process Theories of the Social Mind*, edited by J. W. Sherman, B. Gawronski, and Y. Trope, 155–71. New York: Guilford.

Forscher, P. S., C. K. Lai, J. R. Axt, C. R. Ebersole, M. Herman, P. G. Devine, and B. A. Nosek. 2019. "A Meta-analysis of Procedures to Change Implicit Measures." *Journal of Personality and Social Psychology* 117 (3): 522–59.

Frantz, C. M., A. J. C. Cuddy, M. Burnett, H. Ray, and A. Hart. 2004. "A Threat in the Computer: The Race Implicit Association Test as a Stereotype Threat Experience." *Personality and Social Psychology Bulletin* 30 (12): 1611–24.

Fujita, K. 2011. "On Conceptualizing Self-Control as More than the Effortful Inhibition of Impulses." *Personality and Social Psychology Review* 15 (4): 352–66.

Galdi, S., B. Gawronski, L. Arcuri, and M. Friese. 2012. "Selective Exposure in Decided and Undecided Individuals: Differential Relations to Automatic Associations and Conscious Beliefs." *Personality and Social Psychology Bulletin* 38 (5): 559–69.

Gawronski, B., and G. V. Bodenhausen. 2006. "Associative and Propositional Processes in Evaluation: An Integrative Review of Implicit and Explicit Attitude Change." *Psychological Bulletin* 132 (5): 692–731.

Gawronski, B., and G. V. Bodenhausen. 2011. "The Associative-Propositional Evaluation Model: Theory, Evidence, and Open Questions." *Advances in Experimental Social Psychology* 44: 59–127.

Gawronski, B., and B. K. Payne, eds. 2010. *Handbook of Implicit Social Cognition: Measurement, Theory, and Applications.* New York: Guilford.

Gibson, J. J. 1979. *The Ecological Approach to Visual Perception.* Boston: Houghton Mifflin.

Gilbert, G. M. 1951. "Stereotype Persistence and Change among College Students." *Journal of Abnormal and Social Psychology* 46 (2): 245–54.

Glover, D., A. Pallais, and W. Pariente. 2016. "Discrimination as a Self-Fulfilling Prophecy: Evidence from French Grocery Stores." Unpublished manuscript.

Goldin, C., and C. Rouse. 2000. "Orchestrating Impartiality: The Impact of 'Blind' Auditions on Female Musicians." *American Economic Review* 90 (4): 715–41.

Gollwitzer, P. M. 1999. "Implementation Intentions: Strong Effects of Simple Plans." *American Psychologist* 54 (7): 493–503.

Gollwitzer, P. M., and V. Brandstätter. 1997. "Implementation Intentions and Effective Goal Pursuit." *Journal of Personality and Social Psychology* 73 (1): 186–99.

Gollwitzer, P. M., and P. Sheeran. 2006. "Implementation Intentions and Goal Achievement: A Meta-analysis of Effects and Processes." *Advances in Experimental Social Psychology* 38 (6): 69–119.

Gonsalkorale, K., J. W. Sherman, and K. C. Klauer. 2009. "Aging and Prejudice: Diminished Regulation of Automatic Race Bias among Older Adults." *Journal of Experimental Social Psychology* 45 (2): 410–14.

Govorun, O., and B. K. Payne. 2006. "Ego-Depletion and Prejudice: Separating Automatic and Controlled Components." *Social Cognition* 24 (2): 111–36.

Greenwald, A. G., and M. R. Banaji. 2017. "The Implicit Revolution: Reconceiving the Relation between Conscious and Unconscious." *American Psychologist* 72 (9): 861–71.

Greenwald, A. G., D. E. McGhee, and J. K. L. Schwartz. 1998. "Measuring Individual Differences in Implicit Cognition: The Implicit Association Test." *Journal of Personality and Social Psychology* 74 (6): 1464–80.

Greenwald, A. G., T. A. Poehlman, E. L. Uhlmann, and M. R. Banaji. 2009. "Understanding and Using the Implicit Association Test: III. Meta-analysis of Predictive Validity." *Journal of Personality and Social Psychology* 97 (1): 17–41.

Guinote, A., G. B. Willis, and C. Martellotta. 2010. "Social Power Increases Implicit Prejudice." *Journal of Experimental Social Psychology* 46 (2): 299–307.

Hawkins, C. B., and B. A. Nosek. 2012. "Motivated Independence? Implicit Party Identity Predicts Political Judgments among Self-Proclaimed Independents." *Personality and Social Psychology Bulletin* 38 (11): 1441–55.

Holland, R. W., H. Aarts, and D. Langendam. 2006. "Breaking and Creating Habits on the Working Floor: A Field-Experiment on the Power of Implementation Intentions." *Journal of Experimental Social Psychology* 42 (6): 776–83.

Iceland, J., D. H. Weinberg, and E. Steinmetz. 2002. *Racial and Ethnic Segregation in the United States, 1980–2000*. Washington, DC: US Government Printing Office, US Census Bureau.

James, W. 1904. "Does 'Consciousness' Exist?" *Journal of Philosophy, Psychology and Scientific Methods* 1 (18): 477–91.

James, L., B. Vila, and K. Daratha. 2013. "Results from Experimental Trials Testing Participant Responses to White, Hispanic and Black Suspects in High-Fidelity Deadly Force Judgment and Decision-Making Simulations." *Journal of Experimental Criminology* 9 (2): 189–212.

Jost, J. T., and M. R. Banaji. 1994. "The Role of Stereotyping in System-Justification and the Production of False Consciousness." *British Journal of Social Psychology* 33 (1): 1–27.

Jost, J. T., M. R. Banaji, and B. A. Nosek. 2004. "A Decade of System Justification Theory: Accumulated Evidence of Conscious and Unconscious Bolstering of the Status Quo." *Political Psychology* 25 (6): 881–919.

Joy-Gaba, J. A., and B. A. Nosek. 2010. "The Surprisingly Limited Malleability of Implicit Racial Evaluations." *Social Psychology* 41 (3): 137–46.

Karpinski, A., and J. LK. Hilton. 2001. "Attitudes and the Implicit Association Test." *Journal of Personality and Social Psychology* 81 (5): 774–88.

Katz, D., and K. Braly. 1933. "Racial Stereotypes of One Hundred College Students." *Journal of Abnormal and Social Psychology* 28 (3): 280–90.

Keith, B. E., D. B. Magleby, C. J. Nelson, E. A. Orr, M. C. Westlye, and R. E. Wolfinger. 1992. *The Myth of the Independent Voter*. Berkeley: University of California Press.

Krause, A., U. Rinne, and K. F. Zimmermann. 2012. "Anonymous Job Applications of Fresh Ph.D. Economists." *Economics Letters* 117 (2): 441–44.

Kugelmass, H. 2016. "'Sorry, I'm Not Accepting New Patients': An Audit Study of Access to Mental Health Care." *Journal of Health and Social Behavior* 57 (2): 168–83.

Kulik, C. T., M. B. Pepper, L. Roberson, and S. K. Parker. 2007. "The Rich Get Richer: Predicting Participation in Voluntary Diversity Training." *Journal of Organizational Behavior* 28 (6): 753–69.

Kuppens, T., T. V. Pollet, C. P. Teixeira, S. Demoulin, S. Craig Roberts, and A. C. Little. 2012. "Emotions in Context: Anger Causes Ethnic Bias but Not Gender Bias in Men but Not Women." *European Journal of Social Psychology* 42 (4): 432–41.

Ladd, H. F. 1998. "Evidence on Discrimination in Mortgage Lending." *Journal of Economic Perspectives* 12 (2): 41–62.

Lai, C. K., K. M. Hoffman, and B. A. Nosek. 2013. "Reducing Implicit Prejudice." *Social and Personality Psychology Compass* 7 (5): 315–30.

Lai, C. K., M. Marini, S. A. Lehr, C. Cerruti, J. L. Shin, J. A. Joy-Gaba, . . . B. A. Nosek. 2014. "Reducing Implicit Racial Preferences: I. A Comparative Investigation of 17 Interventions." *Journal of Experimental Psychology: General* 143 (4): 1765–85.

Lai, C. K., A. L. Skinner, E. Cooley, S. Murrar, M. Brauer, T. Devos, . . . B. A. Nosek. 2016. "Reducing Implicit Racial Preferences: II. Intervention Effectiveness across Time." *Journal of Experimental Psychology: General* 145 (8): 1001–16.

LaVeist, T. A. 2003. "Racial Segregation and Longevity among African Americans: An Individual-Level Analysis." *Health Services Research* 38 (6.2): 1719–34.

Loury, G. C. 2002. *The Anatomy of Racial Inequality*. Cambridge, MA: Harvard University Press.

Lun, J., S. Sinclair, E. R. Whitchurch, and C. Glenn. 2007. "(Why) Do I Think What You Think? Epistemic Social Tuning and Implicit Prejudice." *Journal of Personality and Social Psychology* 93 (6): 957–72.

Luszczynska, A., A. Sobczyk, and C. Abraham. 2007. "Planning to Lose Weight: Randomized Controlled Trial of an Implementation Intention Prompt to Enhance Weight Reduction among Overweight and Obese Women." *Health Psychology* 26 (4): 507–12.

Ma, D. S., J. Correll, B. Wittenbrink, Y. Bar-Anan, N. Sriram, and B. A. Nosek. 2013. "When Fatigue Turns Deadly: The Association between Fatigue and Racial Bias in the Decision to Shoot." *Basic and Applied Social Psychology* 35 (6): 515–24.

Macrae, C. N., and G. V. Bodenhausen. 2000. "Social Cognition: Thinking Categorically about Others." *Annual Review of Psychology* 51: 93–120.

Madon, S., M. Guyll, K. Aboufadel, E. Montiel, A. Smith, P. Palumbo, and L. Jussim. 2001. "Ethnic and National Stereotypes: The Princeton Trilogy Revisited and Revised." *Personality and Social Psychology Bulletin* 27 (8): 996–1010.

Mendoza, S. A., P. M. Gollwitzer, and D. M. Amodio. 2010. "Reducing the Expression of Implicit Stereotypes: Reflexive Control through Implementation Intentions." *Personality and Social Psychology Bulletin* 36 (4): 512–23.

Monteith, M. J. 1993. "Self-Regulation of Prejudiced Responses: Implications for Progress in Prejudice Reduction Efforts." *Journal of Personality and Social Psychology* 65 (3): 469–85.

Monteith, M. J., L. Ashburn-Nardo, C. I. Voils, and A. M. Czopp. 2002. "Putting the Brakes on Prejudice: On the Development and Operation of Cues for Control." *Journal of Personality and Social Psychology* 83 (5): 1029–50

Monteith, M. J., and A. Y. Mark. 2005. "Changing One's Prejudiced Ways: Awareness, Affect, and Self-Regulation." *European Review of Social Psychology* 16 (1): 113–54.

Monteith, M. J., and A. Y. Mark. 2009. "Self-Regulation and Prejudice Reduction." In *Handbook of Prejudice, Stereotyping, and Discrimination*, edited by T. Nelson, 507–20. New York Psychology Press.

Monteith, M. J., L. R. Parker, and M. D. Burns. 2016. "The Self-Regulation of Prejudice." In *Handbook of Stereotyping, Prejudice, and Discrimination*, edited by T. D. Nelson, 409–32. New York: Psychology Press.

Murdoch, B. B. 1962. "The Serial Position Effect of Free Recall." *Journal of Experimental Psychology* 64 (5): 482–88.

Nickerson, R. S. 1998. "Confirmation Bias: A Ubiquitous Phenomenon in Many Guises." *Review of General Psychology* 2 (2): 175–220.

Nisbett, R. E., and T. D. Wilson. 1977. "Telling More Than We Can Know: Verbal Reports on Mental Processes." *Psychological Review* 84 (3): 231–59.

Nosek, B. A., M. R. Banaji, and A. G. Greenwald. 2002. "Harvesting Implicit Group Attitudes and Beliefs from a Demonstration Website." *Group Dynamics* 6 (1): 101–15.

Nosek, B. A., A. G. Greenwald, and M. R. Banaji. 2005. "Understanding and Using the Implicit Association Test: II. Method Variables and Construct Validity." *Personality and Social Psychology Bulletin* 31 (2): 166–80.

Nosek, B. A., A. G. Greenwald, and M. R. Banaji. 2007. "The Implicit Association Test at Age 7: A Methodological and Conceptual Review." In *Social Psychology and the Unconscious: The Automaticity of Higher Mental Processes*, edited by J. A. Bargh, 265–92. New York: Psychology Press.

Nosek, B. A., F. L. Smyth, J. J. Hansen, T. Devos, N. M. Lindner, K. A. Ranganath, . . . M. R. Banaji. 2007. "Pervasiveness and Correlates of Implicit Attitudes and Stereotypes." *European Review of Social Psychology* 18 (1): 36–88.

Olson, M. A., and R. H. Fazio. 2001. "Implicit Attitude Formation through Classical Conditioning." *Psychological Science* 12 (5): 413–17.

Olson, M. A., and R. H. Fazio. 2006. "Reducing Automatically Activated Racial Prejudice through Implicit Evaluative Conditioning." *Personality and Social Psychology Bulletin* 32 (4): 421–33.

Oswald, F. L., G. Mitchell, H. Blanton, J. Jaccard, and P. E. Tetlock. 2013. "Predicting Ethnic and Racial Discrimination: A Meta-analysis of IAT Criterion Studies." *Journal of Personality and Social Psychology* 105 (2): 171–92.

Pavlov, I. P., ed. 1927. *Conditional Reflexes: An Investigation of the Physiological Activity of the Cerebral Cortex*. London: Oxford University Press.

Pelham, B. W., M. Carvallo, and J. T. Jones. 2005. "Implicit Egotism." *Current Directions in Psychological Science* 14 (2): 106–10.

Pettigrew, T. F., and L. R. Tropp. 2006. "A Meta-analytic Test of Intergroup Contact Theory." *Journal of Personality and Social Psychology* 90 (5): 751–83.

Polman, E., M. M. Pollmann, and T. A. Poehlman. 2013. "The Name-Letter-Effect in Groups: Sharing Initials with Group Members Increases the Quality of Group Work." *PLOS ONE* (11): e79039.

Pronin, E., and M. B. Kugler. 2007. "Valuing Thoughts, Ignoring Behavior: The Intro-spection Illusion as a Source of the Bias Blind Spot." *Journal of Experimental Social Psychology* 43 (4): 565–78.

Pronin, E., D. Y. Lin, and L. Ross. 2002. "The Bias Blind Spot: Perceptions of Bias in Self versus Others." *Personality and Social Psychology Bulletin* 28 (3): 369–81.

Ranganath, K. A., C. T. Smith, and B. A. Nosek. 2008. "Distinguishing Automatic and Controlled Components of Attitudes from Direct and Indirect Measurement Meth-ods." *Journal of Experimental Social Psychology* 44 (2) 386–96.

Richeson, J. A., and N. Ambady. 2003. "Effects of Situational Power on Automatic Racial Prejudice." *Journal of Experimental Social Psychology* 39 (2): 177–83.

Rivera, L. A., and A. Tilcsik. 2016. "Class Advantage, Commitment Penalty: The Gen-dered Effect of Social Class Signals in an Elite Labor Market." *American Sociological Review* 81 (6): 1097–1131.

Rooth, D. O. 2007. *Implicit Discrimination in Hiring: Real World Evidence.* IZA Discus-sion Paper 2764.

Rudman, L. A., M. C. Dohn., and K. Fairchild. 2007. "Implicit Self-Esteem Compensa-tion: Automatic Threat Defense." *Journal of Personality and Social Psychology* 93 (5): 798–813.

Rydell, R. J., and A. R. McConnell. 2006. "Understanding Implicit and Explicit Atti-tude Change: A Systems of Reasoning Analysis." *Journal of Personality and Social Psychology* 91 (6): 995–1008.

Sanbonmatsu, D. M., and R. H. Fazio. 1990. "The Role of Attitudes in Memory-Based Decision Making." *Journal of Personality and Social Psychology* 59 (4): 614–22.

Sawyer, J., and A. Gampa. 2018. "Implicit and Explicit Racial Attitudes Changed during Black Lives Matter." *Personality and Social Psychology Bulletin* 44 (7): 1039–59.

Schuette, R. A., and R. H. Fazio. 1995. "Attitude Accessibility and Motivation as Deter-minants of Biased Processing: A Test of the MODE Model." *Personality and Social Psychology Bulletin* 21 (7): 704–10.

Schuman, H., C. Steeh, L. Bobo, and M. Krysan. 1997. *Racial Attitudes in America.* Rev. ed. Cambridge, MA: Harvard University Press.

Shook, N. J., and R. H. Fazio. 2008. "Interracial Roommate Relationships an Experi-mental Field Test of the Contact Hypothesis." *Psychological Science* 19 (7): 717–23.

Sim, J. J., J. Correll, and M. S. Sadler. 2013. "Understanding Police and Expert Perfor-mance: When Training Attenuates (vs. Exacerbates) Stereotypic Bias in the Deci-sion to Shoot." *Personality and Social Psychology Bulletin* 39 (3): 291–304.

Staats, A. W., and C. K. Staats. 1958. "Attitudes Established by Classical Conditioning." *Journal of Abnormal and Social Psychology* 57 (1): 37–40.

Stephan, W. G., and C. W. Stephan. 2000. "An Integrated Threat Theory of Prejudice." In *Reduce Prejudice and Discrimination,* edited by S. Oskamp, 23–46. Mahwah, NJ: Lawrence Erlbaum Associates.

Stewart, B. D., and B. K. Payne. 2008. "Bringing Automatic Stereotyping under Con-trol: Implementation Intentions as Efficient Means of Thought Control." *Person-ality and Social Psychology Bulletin* 34 (1): 1332–45.

Thaler, R. H., and C. R. Sunstein. 2009. *Nudge: Improving Decisions about Health, Wealth, and Happiness.* New Haven, CT: Yale University Press.

Tversky, A., and D. Kahneman. 1981. "The Framing of Decisions and the Psychology of Choice." *Science* 211 (4481): 453–58.

Uhlmann, E. L., and G. L. Cohen. 2005. "Constructed Criteria Redefining Merit to Justify Discrimination." *Psychological Science* 16 (6): 474–80.

US Bureau of Labor Statistics. 2016. *Labor Force Statistics from the Current Population Survey.* http://www.bls.gov/cps/cpsaat11.htm.

US Census. 2015. *Homeownership Rates by Race and Ethnicity of Householder.* http://www.census.gov/housing/hvs/data/ann15ind.html.

US Department of Education, National Center for Education Statistics. 2016. *The Condition of Education 2016.* http://nces.ed.gov/pubsearch/pubsinfo.asp?pubid=2016144.

Walton, G. M., C. Logel, J. M. Peach, S. J. Spencer, and M. P. Zanna. 2015. "Two Brief Interventions to Mitigate a 'Chilly Climate' Transform Women's Experience, Relationships, and Achievement in Engineering." *Journal of Educational Psychology* 107 (2): 468–85.

Westgate, E., R. G. Riskind, and B. A. Nosek. 2015. "Implicit Preferences for Straight People over Lesbian Women and Gay Men Weakened from 2006 to 2013." *Collabra* 1 (1): 1–10.

Xu, K., B. Nosek, and A. G. Greenwald. 2014. "Psychology Data from the Race Implicit Association Test on the Project Implicit Demo Website." *Journal of Open Psychology Data* 2 (1): e3.

5

Human Dignity and Modern Democracies

Ajume Wingo

In the early nineteenth century, Benjamin Constant introduced his distinction between the "liberty of the ancients" and the "liberty of the moderns." Constant drew interesting and important distinctions between the demanding and exclusive sense of ancient liberty and the more expansive modern conception.

In this paper I consider a similar distinction we might draw between the democracy of the ancients and that of the moderns. Like Constant's distinction with respect to liberty, the distinction I wish to draw regarding democracy is largely a matter of its scope. For the ancients, democracy was a local system adapted to the characteristics of a particular society and that society's own structure and traditions, whereas the modern variety purports to be universal in character.[1] I argue that the logic of modern democracy so conceived has a significant effect on citizens by both drawing "outsiders"—the disenfranchised and the oppressed—into the polity as active participants, and pressuring "insiders"—those with the most influence within the system—to allow those outsiders in. As a consequence, while the membership in a democratic polity was for the ancients an unproblematically exclusive status, we moderns are, simply by being moderns, theoretically committed by democratic principles to a continuing search for ways to broaden the category of full members of our democratic polity.

The recent Black Lives Matter (BLM) movement is a vivid illustration of the logic of modern democracy at work. It also illustrates how considerations of *equal dignity* drive this universalizing tendency of modern democracy. For purposes of this paper, I consider "dignity" to be a measure of an individual's actual ability to represent himself or herself in the polity.[2] A polity that is committed to the goal of equal dignity thus seeks to confer equal standing with regard to voice and influence. This paper is about what is distinctive about the democracies of the moderns (in contradistinction with the ancients) and the perils democratic governments face if they ignore the calls of the disenfranchised. At the same time, I suggest that pursuing the goal of achieving equal dignity for all entails significant costs that cannot be ignored if we hope to realize the promise of dignity-based democracy.

1. Democracy, Ancient and Modern

The idea of democracy is an ancient one, dating at least to fifth-century BCE Athens. The focus of the ancient democracy was on a certain kind of citizen—in the case of Athens, the freeborn Athenian male. The state invested in material, legal, and intellectual resources to ensure that citizens enjoyed full civic dignity but was indifferent to the civic lives and dignity of the noncitizens among them. On the Athenian view, the rights and privileges of democracy were owed to citizens of democratic communities but not to people in general.

There is no inconsistency in the exclusive nature of such ancient democracies, for in its most general sense, democracy is just a system of government in which decisions about who gets what and when and how are made by *recognized members* of the state. On the ancient conception, status as a recognized member of the state was restricted to "sons of the soil"—Athenian men and their male descendants. Of course those recognized members of the polity shared the same physical space with enslaved people, women, laborers, the indigent, and immigrants who were excluded from any role in governing.

Significantly, the equality among the Athenian "insiders"—free males—was a device adopted for political purposes, not a recognition of some deep fact about those individuals. As Jeremy Waldron says in *Dignity, Rank, and Rights*:

> The Athenians adopted a legal principle of treating one another as equals, not because of any moral conviction about real equality between them, but because such a principle made possible a form of political community they could not otherwise have. For their engagement in the joint enterprise of politics, the community created for each of them an artificial *persona*—the citizen—that could take place on the public stage, presenting them as equals for political purposes. The community did this using artificial techniques like the equal right to speak in the assembly, the equality of votes, the equal liability to be drafted into a jury, and so on.[3]

Beginning in the seventeenth and eighteenth centuries, however, the notion of democracy was transformed. The natural rights framework underlying the Declaration of Independence and America's War for Independence, for instance, made democratic appeals generally available, not just to citizens of existing democracies invoking their already-recognized rights but also to those who had ambitions of self-government. A similar presumption of democracy as a universal system of rights similarly animated the French Revolution, the Declaration of the Rights of Man, and the Haitian Revolution, and shaped the growth of popular democracy in the United States through the nineteenth century and elsewhere, culminating in the United Nations' Declaration of Human Rights following the Second World War.

Given how long we've lived with this modern conception of democracy, it is easy to forget how revolutionary it was and what underlies that revolutionary character. For many, the link between democracy and procedural features like universal suffrage and equal opportunity to run for office is simply analytic: it is part of the meaning of the word *democracy*.

But as the example of ancient democracy shows, there is no such necessary link between democracy and the range of individuals who enjoy the status of recognized members of that democracy. To the extent that the conception of democracy and an inclusive conception of citizenship have been united, that has been the result of *dignity* emerging as the paramount political good in modern democracies. This focus on dignity, I believe, is what gives modern democracy its distinctive character and grounds many of the West's traditions relating to efforts to confer civic dignity upon the disenfranchised, upon the indigent, and (at least in principle) upon *all* human beings.

Unlike the ancient conception, the modern conception of democracy puts pressure on those states that purport to be democracies to support (or at least to *appear* to support) efforts to dignify their least powerful members. No government that calls itself a democracy in modern times can afford to be indifferent to the dignity of its subjects, at least for the sake of appearances. In many cases the inexorable logic of respect for dignity has led states, however slowly and however reluctantly, to invest heavily in dignity-sustaining goods such as material goods, civic education, equalization of opportunities, and equal protection of rights and freedom.

Equally distinctive to modern democracy is that outsiders—the formerly disenfranchised or those who do not feel they yet enjoy the full benefits of democracy—are demanding that their states carry through on the promises of democracy: as Martin Luther King Jr. put it, they are demanding that the promissory note of democracy be honored. The logic (if not always the practice) of modern democracy, then, is to put the focus of modern democracies on those human beings whose dignity has been injured by injustices that have muted their voices and rendered them largely invisible within the political realm. In the United States, this group of human beings would include the descendants of former slaves, Native Americans, women, indigents, and new immigrants.

What is revolutionary about the democracy of the moderns (in contradistinction to the democracy of the ancients) is its universality—its presumption that *all* human beings, not just "insiders," are entitled to dignity. As a consequence of this universality, its central traditions and institutions are, intentionally or not, ones that reach out to those "outsiders" and induce them to demand entry as their right.

Documents like the Declaration of Independence, the Constitution of the United States, the United Nations Declaration of Human Rights, the Declaration of Women's Rights, and the French Declaration of the Rights of Man are not just statements of principle for those communities that produced them. They also speak to those who do *not* enjoy the rights and privileges they articulate, telling them that they are entitled to demand those rights and privileges and that they deserve a state that respects their dignity.

From the perspective of ancient democracy, this is a radical proposition. For the ancients, democracy was parochial, a system to empower citizens—the "insiders"—but not one that by its own nature sought to expand the scope of citizenship. Democracy for the ancients was a walled city intended to protect the privileges of the natives against the barbarians without. Outsiders may be tempted to breach the walls, but they can have no expectation of a right to enter, nor will the natives be disturbed by any nagging doubts about their right to exclude those outside.

2. Defining Dignity-Based Modern Democracy

I have claimed above that we should understand modern democracy as the result of an underlying commitment to universal dignity. Here I want to suggest why that should be.

As suggested above, democracy (whether ancient or modern) can be thought of generally as a system in which recognized members of the polity govern that polity. That is, democracy is a system of procedures for making governing decisions, such as voting procedures, requirements for running for office, and perhaps the separation of powers and authority of different governmental institutions.

But as the fact of ancient democracy itself proves, there is nothing in this procedural conception of democracy itself that dictates who the "recognized members" of the polity are. Those same procedures can be adopted within a polity that restricts "recognized members" to free white males (as in the antebellum United States) just as well as within a polity with a much broader franchise.[4]

The universalizing nature of modern democracy is that those procedural features are tied to a (presumptively) universal fact about humans. That is, we are all believed to have a right, by virtue of being human, to participate democratically in our polities.[5] One may see the various efforts to ground democratic principles on shared universal human qualities (such as the common desires for certain basic goods) as evidence of how the logic of modern democracy is intrinsically imperial, pushing its frontiers ever farther to bring outsiders within the application of its governing procedures.

The formal, procedural features of democracy, then, constitute a kind of frame around a picture. The picture is dignity, a good owed to all persons whether they live in a democratic polity or not. The proper aesthetic function of a frame is to lead the viewer to the picture by focusing the viewer's attention. A frame that focuses attention to itself is, aesthetically speaking, a bad frame. An aesthetically well-made frame appears invisible or disappears for the picture. What is distinctive about this aesthetic metaphor of the relationship of democracy to dignity is that it gives equal weight to both. Given this, democratic procedures are a means of achieving dignity. The fact that all are entitled to dignity is what drives efforts to install democratic procedures and to expand the ambit of this inclusiveness.

In the eighteenth century the turbulent storm of modern democratic revolution was already sweeping through the Western world, starting with the American Declaration of Independence (1776), the French Revolution (1789), and the Haitian Revolution (1791–1804); it continued with the American Civil War and then the civil rights movement of the 1960s. The storm was propelled by the castaways of various Western societies seeking a system of government that would recognize and confer dignity upon them. The Declaration of Independence and US Constitution (as reconceived by Abraham Lincoln) convey that idealized commitment to framing a system of government that could yield dignity for all and that generated a constant pressure to expand the scope of application for those principles.[6]

But if the ties between dignity and democracy help to explain the character of modern democracy, the nature of dignity itself is less than clear. In particular, the notion of dignity does not seem amenable to objective measurement in the same way that other political goods (such as welfare, as measured by income, wealth, or other indices of health or happiness) appear to be. As I argue below, one of the potential problems posed by modern democracy is that the good it seeks to promote—dignity—is not just very expensive but also possibly not measurable by any objective standard. As a result, there may be no clear way to resist unreasonable demands by certain individuals that they be accorded equal dignity.[7]

To clarify the challenge raised by the concept of dignity, I will offer a comparative consideration of the ideal as it operates in African and Christian belief systems. There is some arbitrariness to my comparative choice, but I choose to conduct this investigation in relation to the intellectual traditions that I know best, and to provide a comparative interlude for the volume as a whole.

3. Dignity in African and Christian Society

Let's start the search for the meaning of the term *dignity* and an understanding of the implications using dignity as a fundamental political good with how the concept of dignity is used by the people of Nso in Cameroon. *Dignity* in Lamso (the language spoken by the people of Nso) is a highly social and political term. The word for dignity is *viwir*, which literally means "the people." Indeed, there is a saying in Nso that "a person is a person because of a person" to highlight the intrinsically social nature of *viwir*. The stem of the word is *wir*, which translates variously as "human being" or "person." As that suggests, *wir* is an ambiguous term: *wir* as a human being signifies a human entity, but *wir* as a person signifies a human entity as a participating member of society. In the former sense, *wir* refers to a biological category; in the latter sense, it is (to use Locke's term) a forensic term referring to an entity subject to moral judgment of value and desert.

The word *viwir* signifies a person as a doer, or a person with what Waldron calls "uprightness of bearing"—a dignified and forthright physical carriage and appearance.[8] The word is applied to an especially distinguished subset of Cameroonians—dignitaries. These dignitaries are models of Nso citizenship who adorn themselves in costly regalia, a walking staff, and specially designed hats bearing feathers from the rarest species of birds (the feathers are the monopoly of the state). They walk and sit upright and look others straight in the eye—something taught to the young, who are praised for exuding *viwir* when they walk upright and look at the foreheads of other people when in communication with them.

Dignity in Nso is a shared quality—again, all children are encouraged to exhibit it—and there is a shared core to the concept. This is the entitlement of each individual to security, or to the assurance of the inviolability of one's life. An implication of this right to the inviolability of life is the right to proper care for the human body, which includes a right to a respectful burial and handling of the human corpse. All humans thus enjoy an equal right to be treated in a dignified manner by virtue of their status as *wir* in the biological sense.

But dignity among the Nso also has a more nuanced—and exclusive—dimension that arises from *wir* as referring to persons who, despite sharing a common biological structure, are distinguished for their moral qualities or character. Along this dimension, dignity is distributed unequally through different social ranks. The *virwir*, or dignitaries, described above occupy a higher rank than others by virtue of their responsibilities and behavior in society. That difference in rank is the result of their extraordinary efforts as contributing members who shoulder the ironically "joyful" burden of creating and sustaining their society. The joy is ironic because it flows out of the sleepless nights and active days of taking care of societal affairs. The dignitary's recompense comes not in material form but in social recognition or honor. This allocation of dignity is fundamentally an aesthetic matter involving the distribution of a resource for noninstrumental enjoyment. Among the Nso, then, there is a meaningful difference between dignitaries and the rest of the polity, in that the former have a more active, purposeful role in the operation of their polity than the latter—the former *make* their world, while the latter merely live in it. Not all Nso, but only the dignitaries, earn the ironic joyfulness of being, in Allen's vocabulary in this volume, cocreators in the kingdom of culture.

Dignity in the ancient Western world, like dignity in Nso, rested on a concept of honor and its unequal distribution. Ancient Greek and Nso are thus similar in that they both have at least two levels of society. First, there were people with dignity, honored heroes who helped make the world. Second, there were people who merely lived in a world created by others. The concept of dignity applied to both groups but with differentiated application.

The rise of Judaism, Christianity, and Islam introduced a new understanding of dignity that was not just universal but was equally distributed among all of God's children. The founders of these religions— "immortals" as I have referred to them elsewhere[9]—created a perspective on the world that focused on universally shared bases of dignity and attempted to remake the world to realize that potential for all. Thus at the center of their teachings is the doctrine that all human beings—and most specifically the outcasts—are created equal and in the image of God. Their lives matter. While Judaism dealt with the lives of particular outcasts, Jesus's message was even more broadly inclusive. (Of course Jesus knew that when the outsider was rescued, everyone would thereby be protected. His was perhaps an early application of the "maximin principle," as was the Akan[10] principle that "all human beings are the children of God and none the child of earth.")

The Western humanistic tradition—and, I would argue, much of our modern idea of democracy—owes a debt to Christianity for this focus on the dignity of all persons. The humanistic narrative of Christianity starts with the revelation of the divine being in the human flesh of Jesus. God in the person of Jesus Christ dwelled among us in circumstances of poverty, humiliation, and humility.[11] In the Sermon on the Mount, Jesus overturned the preexisting pagan hierarchy of dignity, saying, "Blessed are the poor in spirit, ... the pure in heart, ... the meek, [and] the merciful."[12] His embrace of lepers and his association with outcasts and sinners were fundamentally at odds with the Greek and Roman worldviews, where social status was everything, where if you had no social status you were invisible to the polity—a nobody.[13] According to theologian David Bentley Hart, one of the innovations of Christianity was its focus on care for the least well off: "Christianity placed charity at the center of its spiritual life as no pagan cult ever had and raised the care of widows, orphans, the sick, the imprisoned, the poor to the level of the highest of religious obligation."[14] And it did so with a simple imperative—"Thou shalt love thy neighbor as thyself"—that both embodied the principle of reciprocity and dispensed with the need for complex rules or codes. As Peter Wehner notes,

> Accounts of how Jesus interacted in this messy, complicated, broken world, through actions that stunned the people of his time, allow us to learn compassion in ways that being handed a moral rule book never could.
>
> For one thing, rule books can't shed tears or express love; human beings do. Seeing how Jesus dealt with the religious authorities of his day (often harshly) and the sinners and outcasts of his day (often tenderly and respectfully) adds texture and subtlety to human relationships that we could never gain otherwise.[15]

Not surprisingly, then, Christians and Christian principles of charity, humility, and compassion for especially those most disadvantaged in society have played important roles in ending slavery and segregation and con-

tinue to fuel efforts to end human trafficking and abortion, and to alleviate suffering and want the world over.

4. Dignity and Democracy of the Moderns

While the Christian conception of dignity dramatically expanded the
notion of dignity as compared to how the Nso and the ancients conceived
of it, even the Christian conception excluded many. True, the vision of
humanity united as beings made in the image of God represented a radical view as compared to much of what the ancient world offered. But the
implementation of that vision was left to the whims of church elites and
other parties with their own agendas.

The modern conception of dignity may be seen as an effort to ground
the universal nature of dignity on a foundation less divisive than religion
(e.g., on species membership or on shared rational capacities). With the
building up of political institutions that (at least in principle) give every
individual a voice in governance, the hope is that those institutions will
more faithfully serve the purpose of supporting the dignity of all. Allen's
difference-without-domination principle, for instance, starts out with a
claim about what human beings share—a need for flourishing through
autonomy—and then argues that participation is necessary to secure the
conditions of dignity. In other words, modern democracy has two aims
concerning the use of dignity (and Allen's chapter is an example of this
effort): (1) to secure belief in universal human dignity and (2) to operationalize that belief in inclusive political institutions.

5. Modern Democracies and Dignity in Practice

How well do modern democracies succeed with respect to these two
aims? As adumbrated above, the political history of the democracy of
the moderns started in eighteenth-century Europe. The forerunners included the likes of John Locke,[16] Jean-Jacques Rousseau,[17] and Immanuel
Kant. Kant defined dignity in his *Groundwork of the Metaphysics of Morals*
in terms of the unique, nonfungible nature of a person or thing:

> In the Kingdom of ends everything has either a price or a dignity. What
> has a price can be replaced by something else as its equivalent; what,
> on the other hand, is raised above price and therefore admits of no
> equivalent has a dignity. Now, morality is the condition under which
> alone a rational being can be an end in itself.... Hence morality, and

humanity insofar as it is capable of morality, is that which alone has dignity.[18]

While the Christian basis for equal dignity lies in the claim that all persons are the creation of God, the Kantian basis is in persons' capacity to be moral. Despite the different bases for dignity on those conceptions, the Christian and Kantian conceptions share a very broad and inclusive view of who has dignity and what facts about an individual confer dignity.[19]

Just as Christianity underscored the universal value and dignity of human life by reversing the usual hierarchies ("So those who are last now will be first then, and those who are first will be last"), the moderns achieved a similar result. Jeremy Waldron describes this "transvaluation of values" in late eighteenth-century romantic poetry:

> One begins with an idea of dignity associated with the high rank of some humans (compared to others), and then one *reverses* that ordering ironically or provocatively to claim that the high rank of some is superficial or bogus and that it is the lowly man or the virtues of very ordinary humanity that enjoy true dignity. The *Oxford Dictionary* cites a passage from William Wordsworth to illustrate this: "True dignity abides with him alone, [w]ho, in the silent hour of inward thought, [c]an still suspect, and still revere himself, [i]n lowliness of heart."[20]

Waldron cites Robert Burns as the real master of this move with the reversal of rank and dignity in the fourth stanza of "For A' That and for A' That."

> A prince can [make] a belted knight,
> A marquis, duke, an' a' that;
> But an honest man's abon his might,
> Gude faith, he maunna fa' that!
> For a' that, an' a' that,
> Their dignities an' a' that;
> The pith o' sense, an' pride o' worth,
> Are higher rank than a' that.[21]

The rank of individuals (in the traditional sense used by Burns here) is meaningful only as part of a conventional structure that is independent of an individual's "true" worth or dignity. Within that conventional structure, a prince can confer rank—can make a man a knight, a marquis, or a duke. But the prince cannot make "an honest man" with "pith o' sense, an' pride o' worth," for such qualities are not just a matter of rank and convention but exist (if at all) in the individual.

According to Waldron, Burns's use of "dignities" in the above poem represents a sea-change in the way *dignity* is used, enabling it to become a leading concept of *universal* rights (as opposed to special privileges), and bringing into the realm of rights what James Whitman has called "an extension of formerly high-status treatment to all sectors of the population."[22]

Of course, Waldron does not claim that this sea-change eliminated the notion of rank. Rather, he argues that the notion of rank was put to work in the service of dignity. Waldron's hypothesis is that "the modern notion of human dignity involves *upwards* equalization of rank, so that we now try to accord to every human being something of the dignity, rank, and expectation of respect that was formerly accorded to nobility." In the modern notion of dignity, "we are not like a society that has eschewed all talk of caste; we are like a caste society with just one caste (and a very high one at that). Every man a Brahmin. Every man a duke, every woman a queen."[23] The modern conception of equal dignity compels us to try to treat persons' rank—the position they occupy in society—in a way commensurate with their (equal) level of dignity. In short, we are compelled to *level-up* citizens by respecting their dignity equally.

6. Leveling-Up Dignity

As Waldron sees it, then, modern democracies have achieved the first aim of modern democracies with respect to the use of dignity by formulating a secular version of the universal Christian conception of dignity. But have modern democracies succeeded in their further aim of developing political institutions to operationalize that universal secular conception?

Waldron has rather less to say about how exactly actual states should go about leveling-up the dignity of their citizens. And perhaps for good reason, for this is a particularly thorny problem. As Waldron acknowledges, there is an irony in the very thought of having to take affirmative steps to develop and support a property—dignity—that is presumed to be universal. For example, human rights charters tell us that dignity is inherent in the human person, but they also command us to make heroic efforts to establish everyone's dignity through the protection of far-reaching lists of civil, political, social, and economic rights. It is likely that those efforts will impose material and political costs—but how heroic must those efforts be? And if the dignity of citizens of one polity depends (as it well might) on the dignity accorded by that polity to those beyond its borders, are there any principled limits on whose dignity a democratic state is responsible for supporting?

If the logic of dignity-based democracy creates the imperative to level-up individuals in terms of their dignity, it remains to be determined how—or even *if*—that imperative can be performed. One difficulty for knowing how to level-up human beings with respect to dignity is epistemological. There are myriad inequalities in real life, and the combined effect of those inequalities on dignity may be difficult to discern. Banaji and Lai's essay in this volume provides significant evidence that inequality in social circumstances does routinely lead us to pay differential regard to one another. Yet because this effect operates at the level of implicit bias, we are not always able to discern the sources of harms to dignity. Further, even the most ardent advocate of equal dignity probably has to acknowledge that individuals' dignity—their receipt of positive regard from others—depends at least in part on their own efforts. To the extent that background inequalities do or do not undermine those individual efforts, it may be difficult to determine when particular individuals are responsible for their situations (and so may have to live with the consequences).

One way modern democracies attempt to support dignity is through *public recognition*, for example, by devoting attention and public resources to meeting the needs of particular groups in a way that publicly affirms the state's interest in those groups. Some measures can be relatively inexpensive. For example, the recent proposal to replace Andrew Jackson on the front of the twenty-dollar bill with Harriet Tubman would be a relatively inexpensive but quite prominent way for the United States to make a statement as to the significance of African Americans and women in its history. (That said, in the end it proved too *politically* expensive to accomplish.)

But other ways of supporting dignity will be much more expensive—and not just in a financial sense. By committing itself to supporting dignity, the state takes on a debt to be discharged, the kind of debt to which Martin Luther King Jr. referred in his "I Have a Dream" speech. In short, a state committed to the equal dignity of its citizens creates, if not a legally enforceable obligation, an expectation that often motivates citizens to make demands on their representatives and to hold those representatives responsible when they fail to satisfy those demands.

Among the expectations that citizens in a dignity-based modern democracy develop is that their state (a) has a commitment to protecting and sustaining the life, and the *good* life, of each citizen, and (b) has an almost single-minded commitment to leveling-up marginalized or disenfranchised members of the state.

The first expectation arises from the very reason states came to be in the first place. Aristotle characterized it well: "The polity comes into existence for the sake of mere life, but it continues to exist for the sake of the good life" (*Politics* 1.2.1252b.27–30). The first part of the expectation adumbrated by Aristotle is common to any enterprise that calls itself a state or a polity. Protections from physical harm and assurances of the bodily integrity of each member of the polity are the principal reasons for states to exist. Not surprisingly, then, one of the hallmarks of a state is institutions like armed forces and police forces for the protection and assurance of mere life, or the kind of life that humanity shares with all other organisms as a species of living thing. At this level of protection and assurances, there is no room for any kind of utilitarian trading of the bodily integrity of an individual citizen. The bodily integrity of a citizen is, simply put, inviolable and sacrosanct. A state that is incapable of satisfying this expectation is no state at all but merely a Hobbesian jungle.[24]

The expectation of protection of the *good* life, of course, goes beyond mere security. The people of Nso, who have particularly nuanced conceptions of life, death, and the continuum between those extremes, speak of "life in life," a life spent not just in obtaining the necessities of biological life but one engaged in social, political, and other communal projects. So significant to the people of Nso is "life in life" that they say that "not death but death in life is what is to be regretted." For the Nso, it is not mere life but this "life in life" that is to be cherished. "Life in life" is an aesthetic life,[25] a life in which persons are, like the Nso dignitaries discussed above, active in making their world and so should be distinguished from the "socially dead," who merely live in the world as is. Since the basic requirement of aesthetic life is the ability of human beings to make their world their own way, the basic freedoms and rights are integral to the concept of human dignity. "Life in life" is about achieving a status of being a cocreator in the kingdom of culture.

Importantly, in Nso culture this has both a public and a private dimension. The public dimension is comprised of certain venues—the agora, courthouses, public parks, sport arenas, public entertainment sites, businesses, town hall venues (like the ones that Jane Mansbridge writes so well about), and schools—where "dignizens"[26] can appear to see and be seen, hear and be heard, and in general, sense and be sensed by others. This accords with the Nso conception of dignity as *viwir* with its roots in the term meaning "the people" or "peers."[27]

The private dimension consists of areas shielded from the public gaze in which much of our less dignified human activity takes place. In Nso, these are places for basic biological functions such as sleeping, defecation, and bathing, as well as for "higher" functions such as sex, mourning, and care of the ill—all functions and actions that present persons as particularly vulnerable or undignified. Nso dignitaries also use their private space to don their regalia and distinctive feathered hats for public appearances (much as a judge puts on her robe in her chambers before entering her public courtroom). Privacy thus functions as an important defense against harm to dignity and as protection from degradation, insult, and contempt, and so is in service of the realm of "life in life" or aesthetic life. In other words, this rich concept of dignity serves as the basis not only for public, participatory rights, but also for private rights that are foundational to public standing—or dignity and nondomination.

For the Nso, degradation, insults, and contempt are threats not to the biological life but to the aesthetic life ("life in life") or dignity of the victim. Such *aesthetic harm* or *expressive harm* (as Michael Rosen refers to it)[28] presents the victim as a mere animal and so treats him or her as devoid of dignity. Those who witnessed on YouTube the hanging of Saddam Hussein, the photos of prisoners in Abu Ghraib, the brutal murder of Muammar Gadhafi, or murders of hostages by ISIS can see what aesthetic harm means.[29] The project of difference without domination—or of dignity—is very demanding in that it may extend so far as to require protection from insult.

The second expectation of a modern democratic society is that it will have a single-minded commitment to elevating those with no rank or lower ranks to the highest rank comparable with similar ranks for everyone. As I have argued above, modern democratic states are committed to dignity as the paramount political good, and so to the project of leveling-up all citizens to the highest level of dignity compatible with equal dignity for all. Thus, a general condition of any policy in a modern democratic society—be it one addressing poverty, the environment, prison overcrowding, or fiscal policy—is that it should tend to level-up the indigent and the marginalized (which in the case of the United States, would include blacks, Native Americans, LGBTQ individuals, and women).

7. What the Modern Democratic State Expects of Its Citizens

In order to understand how the state should respond to its own dignitarian harms against citizens, we must pause for a moment to review what the democratic state itself expects from citizens. As I will argue in my discussion of the Black Lives Matter movement, the state most clearly is responsible for addressing dignitarian harms when citizens have them-selves met the expectations of the state, for there is an element of reci-procity in the dignitarian project. That is, the state makes the opportu-nity for dignity available by offering citizens the means of participation; citizens must avail themselves of those means for creating dignity if their claims to dignitarian harms are to have force.[30]

What a modern democratic state expects from its members does not differ that much from what the ancient democracies expected. Citizens are expected to exhibit (1) a commitment to nonviolence and respect for politics as an end in itself; (2) self-representation; (3) self-enforcement of the laws applying to oneself; and (4) self-ownership of governing (i.e., individuals must accept that they have ownership interests in the state and its governance, and so are responsible for its actions, as is everyone else).

a. Commitment to Nonviolence and to Politics as an Aesthetic Good

Politics — and in particular modern dignitarian democratic politics — is an alternative to violence. It is a state in which human beings attempt through often heated but *nonviolent* means to persuade others to make particular policy choices. That the commitment to politics is a commit-ment to nonviolent means (at least in one's dealing with political peers) was evident for the ancient Greeks, who relegated violence to the sphere of international relations and noncitizens. A similar view of politics as a disavowal of violence was expressed by John Stuart Mill, who insisted that "liberty, as a principle, has no application to any state of things an-terior to the time when mankind have become capable of being improved by free and equal discussion. Until then, there is nothing for them but implicit obedience to an Akbar or a Charlemagne if they are so fortunate as to find one."[31] Mill viewed rational discussion — not violence — as the heart of politics.[32]

b. Self-Representation

Speaking and acting for oneself is critical both to dignity and to citizen-ship in a democratic state. Self-representation was particularly important to citizenship in ancient democracies, which were geographically small and homogeneous. In such states, members regularly associated with one another on a face-to-face basis so that representation was necessarily *self-representation.*

In larger, more diverse democracies such as the United States, there are perhaps fewer opportunities for self-representation when it comes to major issues of policy. Still, the legitimacy of democratic institutions relies on citizens' seeing themselves as having a voice in the direction the state takes, however small that voice might be. As Judge Learned Hand wrote, having even a small voice in public affairs creates a special relationship between the citizen and democratic state: "I should miss the stimulus of living in a society where I have, at least theoretically, some part in the direction of public affairs. Of course I know how illusory will be the belief that my vote determined anything but nevertheless when I go to the polls I have a satisfaction in the sense that we are all engaged in a common venture."[33] What Judge Hand recognized was the role of self-representation in realizing one's dignity. It is the dignity of being autonomous and a rights-bearer or being properly sui juris.

The role of self-representation as a basis for dignity is no small matter. As I have indicated in my discussion of the Nso, dignity is a matter of being active in creating and affecting one's society—it is not given but taken.[34] To the extent that self-representation constitutes even a theoretical influence on the direction of the state and the course of the citizen's life, such activity helps to sustain both the legitimacy of the democratic state and the dignity of the citizen.[35]

c. Self-Enforcement of the Law

Dignity as self-representation goes along with the self-application of law. As Waldron argues, law is the placeholder of dignity. Dignitary action is action that accords with living with others in an orderly, lawful manner. This does not mean that one cannot act spontaneously while respecting the dignity of others; indeed, as I have argued elsewhere, to be a free citizen of a democracy is to be a "maker of surprises."[36] Rather, what the modern democratic state expects of its citizens is that they will exercise some degree of self-control, deliberation, and consideration for the rights, autonomy, and dignity of others. Lon Fuller expressed this well in *The Morality of Law*:

> To embark on the enterprise of subjecting human conduct to rules involves ... a commitment to the view that man is ... a reasonable agent, capable of understanding and following rules.... Every departure from the principles of law's inner morality is an affront to man's dignity as a responsible agent. To judge his actions by unpublished or retrospective laws, or to order him to do an act that is impossible is to convey ... your indifference to his power of self-determination.[37]

The law counts on bearers of dignity to follow the law themselves, not to be compelled to adhere to rules by an ever-present threat of force. As Waldron tells us, ruling by law in a democracy is "quite different from (say) herding cows with a cattle prod or directing a flock of sheep with a dog. It is quite different too from eliciting a reflex recoil with a scream of command."[38]

Such self-enforcement of the law requires citizens to understand not just the letter of the law but the rationale behind laws. Thus the dignitarian Nso society insists that individuals represent themselves before the court of law; even the deaf and the blind are required to speak and act on her own behalf. Only in very rare cases of *alieni juris*, the mentally challenged, and people with clinical congenital shyness in public are represented. Otherwise it is a matter of dignity that one's story be heard in one's own voice.

d. Self-Ownership

The idea of self-ownership is fundamental to modern dignitarian liberal societies. At its core, it is the idea (one closely related to that of self-representation) that individuals think of themselves as responsible for what happens to them. This is not the view that one's successes and failures are totally self-determined, but an assumption that one must look to one's own resources and abilities before appealing to those of another.

Such self-reliance helps support each citizen's self-concept as autonomous, capable, and active—in short, as having dignity. And from the perspective of the democratic state, having confidence that citizens have such an attitude can make it easier to solve the epistemic problem described in section 6 above by knowing that citizens who are struggling have exhausted their own abilities and are genuinely in need of support.

8. The Matter of Black Lives in Perspective

As I noted at the outset, the democracy of the ancients is remarkably different from that of the moderns in its *modes of inclusion* of the formerly marginalized or the outcasts. While the inclusion of ancient Athenians was restricted to the Athenian freeborn male, the democracy of the moderns since at least the eighteenth century did something revolutionary by including (even if at first only in theory) all human beings in the higher rank of dignity.

One thing the recent Black Lives Matter movement has highlighted is that supporting dignity often requires seeing things from the point of view of the group whose dignity has been injured. For instance, critics of BLM have often argued that the movement is misdirected (intentionally or not) against the police because police violence against blacks is dwarfed by criminal violence by blacks against blacks. Statistically speaking, fatal police shootings make up a much larger proportion of white and Hispanic homicide deaths than of black homicide deaths.[39] Given that, why should a few publicized shootings cause outrage among the African American population and lead to the creation of a movement — BLM — directed at the state? Glenn Loury has recently made this point, saying that these crime statistics indicate that BLM may be "barking up the wrong tree."[40]

Even if we assume these statistics are correct, one cannot help but think that they do not really address the grievances of BLM. That is, even if blacks in America face larger and deadlier problems than police violence, there is something particularly degrading in violence by state actors and the aftermath of that violence.

Recall that BLM was born after the shooting of an unarmed eighteen-year-old black man, Michael Brown, at the hands of a Ferguson police officer, Darren Wilson. The shooting itself does not stand out from other police shootings of young unarmed black men. But perhaps the reason for the movement that grew up after it was the assault on Brown's dignity as his dead body lay unattended for hours, at first out in the open and only later partially draped with a white cloth. His body was denied that elementary privacy that he was entitled to as a member of a modern dignitarian democratic society. As a twenty-one-year-old black resident of Ferguson, Alexis Torregrossa, said, "They shot a black man, and they left his body in the street to let you all know this could be you. To set an example, that's how I see it."[41]

In a sense, then, it wasn't the shooting so much as the state's indifference to the shooting that set BLM into motion. Recognizing that, however, demands looking beyond the statistics and seeing the actions of the state through the eyes of those whose dignity has been insulted and asking what standard they are calling the state to.

9. The Cost of Undoing the Expressive or Aesthetic Dignity Harm

As I have tried to suggest above, it is reasonable for participants in BLM (and other Americans) to expect a modern democratic state like the

United States to make efforts to avoid dignitarian insults like that which led to the formation of BLM. Further, there is a strong case to be made that for the most part, BLM is making its demands of the state in ways that respect modern democratic processes. Members of BLM are using their voices to persuade leaders and authorities to act and using time-honored methods of protest and public demonstrations to advance their cause. They are representing themselves, speaking and acting for themselves. BLM, then, may reasonably be seen as engaged in the honorable tradition of abolitionists, suffragettes, and civil rights workers that have helped broaden the scope of democracy in the United States over its entire history and to level-up the dignity of those in the bottom ranks.

One should understand, however, that this process of leveling-up is not without risks to the democratic structure. Just as we should challenge those who (perhaps in good faith, perhaps not) question the validity of BLM and similar movements, I think it fair to pose a challenge to those who support the leveling-up program to recognize the cost of such a commitment to according equal dignity to everyone.

And there surely *is* a cost to this program. History suggests that the reason ancient states that cared about the dignity of their citizens remained small was probably not because they couldn't expand but because dignity as a political good is very expensive. Similarly, part of the reason that colonialism and imperialism collapsed may have been that as the colonized—prompted by the inexorable logic of modern democracy—started to demand dignity, the imperialists and colonizers realized the colonies were no longer cost effective and so withdrew.

What would it take, realistically speaking, to level-up everyone in America? At the very least, it would likely call for a variety of symbolic gestures, such as new monuments to prominent woman and racial minorities on the scale of the monument to Martin Luther King Jr. on the Mall in Washington, DC, and the redesign of currency and other such emblems. And it will certainly also call for more significant economic costs for services and policies that Loury listed in his lecture referred to above, such as

> universal early childhood education, scattered site public housing, massively increased spending on mental health care for the indigent, revamped criminal justice policies, a guaranteed minimum income for all American families, public jobs as employer-of-last-resort, higher per capita expenditure on the education of those from the least advantaged home environment.[42]

Calling for leveling-up every human being—or even just every resident member of a single society—to a high dignity rank surely is no small matter.

Abraham Lincoln and others in his administration and the Union Army recognized during the Civil War that you cannot actually dignify by freedom a people born into slavery without significant investments (hence the slogan "forty acres and a mule").[43] Undoing the expressive or aesthetic dignitarian harm to achieve the dignitarian society that Lincoln dreamed of would require a massive and expensive expressive civic education directed not only at blacks but also at whites and all other citizens. Banaji and Lai point to the sort of intervention that would be necessary when they write, "Institutions in democracies have the power to shape environments to elicit the attitudes and beliefs their own citizens aspire to but fall short on. Institutions that control housing, education, business, healthcare, and the law can take up the challenge of creating implicit bias–reducing experiences that a society willingly acknowledges to be in the public interest."

But are the efforts needed for this leveling-up project even possible? Even in a rich state like the United States, resources are not unlimited. What will the consequences be when a state that has succeeded in instilling the expectation of equal dignity by raising up those who are worst off simply cannot satisfy that expectation? And is it realistic to expect that equalizing dignity is solely a matter of leveling *up*, rather than leveling some *down*? Might it be that modern dignitarian democracy with its promise of leveling all human beings to a higher plane of equal dignity is not doing more harm than good by raising false expectations?

What I've argued here is that while the various measures, great and small, that a democratic state may take to support the dignity of its citizens are implied by the logic of dignity-based democracy, there is no assurance that those measures will satisfy the expectations of citizens. Apart from the epistemological problem described in section 6 concerning the reasonable limits on what the state must do to support dignity, there is bound to be opposition to any comprehensive leveling-up program.

Such a program would likely require dramatic redistribution of income and wealth—something that is bound to generate enormous resistance. And redistribution of income and wealth may not even be the most serious obstacle to achieving equal dignity where dignity is supported by comparing one's own status to that of those who are perceived to be *less* dignified. This is the case for the Nso dignitaries I have described above, whose special status appears to rest heavily on the contrast between their appearance and demeanor—their posture, regalia, and attitude—and that of the rest of the community. It is likely that the sense of dignity among many in modern democratic states is similarly dependent on there being some against whom they can be favorably compared. In that case, the leveling-up program will require not just redistribution of goods but reeducation of many individuals to instill a sense of dignity that does not rest on comparisons with others.

I highlight these challenges not as a criticism of dignity-based democracy but to make clear the types of problems that friends of inclusive modern democracy must confront. Having a realistic understanding of the cost of democratic principles is a key element in managing the expectations of citizens who rightfully have come to rely on the promise of equal dignity. Only by balancing those expectations and capacities will modern democracies have a chance to achieve a state in which, in the words of Waldron, "everyone's maltreatment—maltreatment of the lowliest criminal, abuse of the most despised of terror suspects—can be regarded as a sacrilege," a violation of human dignity that (to borrow Edmund Burke's memorable phrase) ten thousand swords must leap from their scabbards to avenge.

Notes

1. By "democracy of the moderns," I am referring to its theoretical underpinnings and principles, e.g., that all humans should have dignity, rather than what modern politicians are doing in specific situations.

2. So conceived, one's dignity may be thought of as depending on one's standing within a particular polity. I do not, of course, claim that there is no more objective or intrinsic sense of dignity.

3. Waldron, *Dignity, Rank, and Rights*, 20.

4. Josiah Ober, in his *Demopolis: Democracy before Liberalism in Theory and Practice* (2017), usefully distinguishes the core concepts that define democracy from those that define liberalism and discusses various historical examples of nonliberal democracies (e.g., ancient Greece) and nondemocratic liberal states (e.g., the Austro-Hungarian Empire).

5. Allen makes just such an argument in her chapter in this volume.

6. For a detailed discussion of how Lincoln managed to redefine our national purposes and the relationship between the Declaration and the Constitution, see Wills, *Lincoln at Gettysburg*. See also my discussion of that analysis in Wingo, *Veil Politics in Liberal Democratic States*.

7. Allen argues in this volume that difference without domination is a necessary feature of justice in modern democracies. If we approach equality of dignity as domination wanes, the difficulties in finding an objective measure of equal dignity may also apply to any attempt to measure reductions in domination.

8. See Waldron, "Dignity, Rights, and Responsibilities," 1127.

9. Wingo, "Immortals in Our Midst."

10. The Akan are an ethnic group in Ghana and Ivory Coast.

11. Wehner, "Christmas Revolution."

12. Wehner, "Christmas Revolution."

13. Wehner, "Christmas Revolution."

14. Hart, quoted in Wehner, "Christmas Revolution."

15. Wehner, "Christmas Revolution."

16. In his *Two Treatises of Government*, Locke wrote that there is

nothing more evident, than that creatures of the same species and rank, promiscu-
ously born to all the same advantages of nature, and the use of the same faculties,
should also be equal one amongst another without subordination or subjection.
. . . [Since we are] furnished with like faculties, . . . there cannot be supposed any
such subordination among us that may authorise us to destroy one another, as
if we were made for one another's uses, as the inferior ranks of creatures are for
ours. (2.4, 2.6; pp. 269–71; also quoted in Waldron, *Dignity, Rank, and Rights*, 44)

17. In the *Social Contract*, Rousseau is very clear about equality of all:

Every man having been born free and master of himself, no one else may under
any pretext whatever subject him without his consent. To assert that the son of a
slave is born a slave is to assert that he is not born a man. . . . In respect of riches,
no citizen shall ever be wealthy enough to buy another, and none poor enough to
be forced to sell himself. (33)

18. Kant, *Groundwork to the Metaphysics of Morals*, 84–85 (4:435 of the Prussian
Academy edition of Kant's works).

19. I will not belabor the history of the meaning of dignity, which has been reviewed in
detail by Jeremy Waldron in his Tanner Lectures. See Waldron, *Dignity, Rank, and Rights*.

20. Waldron, *Dignity, Rank, and Rights*, 32.

21. Burns, quoted in Waldron, *Dignity, Rank, and Rights*, 32.

22. Waldron, *Dignity, Rank, and Rights*, 33.

23. Waldron, *Dignity, Rank, and Rights*, 33, 34.

24. This respect for the body in modern democratic society is evident from the work
of the framers of the United Nations Declaration of Human Rights. In the 1950s, for example, the American lawyer Luis Kutner advocated an international writ of habeas corpus to protect individual human beings against unlawful detention around the world. See
Kutner, "A Proposal for a United Nations Writ of Habeas Corpus"; Kutner, *World Habeas
Corpus*, 266 (draft of a "Treaty-Statute of International Court of Habeas Corpus"). See
also Williams, "Idea of Equality," in his *Problems of the Self*, 230–49.

25. For discussions of the concepts of "life in life" and the aesthetic life, see Wingo,
"Aesthetics of Freedom" and "Immortals in Our Midst."

26. I use this word to designate a dignified citizen. Not all citizens in modern democracies possess acknowledged dignity, and not all who have dignity are citizens in the ancient parlance.

27. This goes hand in hand with the concept of Ubuntu as John Mbiti puts it: "I am
because we are and since we are therefore I am." In the Nso, it is said that the Fon (king)
is the people and the people is the Fon; or they will say, the Fon is the Fon because of the
people and the people are the people because of the Fon.

28. For a detailed account of expressive or symbolic harm, see Waldron, *Dignity, Rank, and Rights*, 95–97, and Rosen, *Dignity*.

29. See Waldron (*Dignity, Rank, and Rights*) at 97: "One of the features that have characterized many of the violent and destructive acts of the twentieth century has been the humiliation and symbolic degradation of the victims. We can find examples in the Nazi concentration camp, the Soviet gulag, Cambodia, or the Balkans. It seems to be the fact about human nature that human beings are able more easily to engage in the most violent behavior towards one another if at the same time they can expressively deny the humanity of their victims."

30. To the extent that citizens have a responsibility to attempt to satisfy the expectations of the state, that will similarly depend on the extent to which the state is meeting citizens' expectations. A state that fails to provide for the good of its citizens will at some point forfeit the loyalty and support of its citizens, just as citizens who do not do what they can to support their dignity could at some point forfeit their entitlement to further support from the state for their dignity.

31. Mill, *Utilitarianism*, 79.

32. Arendt, *Crisis of the Republic*, 155: "Power and violence are opposites; where one rules absolutely, the other is absent. Violence appears where power is in jeopardy, but left to its own course it ends in power's disappearance."

33. Quoted by Waldron, *Dignity, Rank, and Rights*, as quoted in Dworkin, *Freedom's Law*, 343.

34. This is particularly clear in Nso where it is taught that freedom, rights, and dignity are "power and power," or, as the people of Nso say, are literally "in the blood." Nso dignitarians partake in blood rituals designed to prepare them to be willing to sacrifice their own (biological) life rather than suffer a loss of dignity. See Wingo, "Immortals in Our Midst."

35. In a recent decision, the United States Supreme Court in *Husted v. A. Philip Randolph Institute* upheld a state law purging voting rolls of citizens who fail to respond to a notice seeking confirmation that they still live in the district in which they are registered to vote and do not vote in either of the next two elections following that notice. This decision may be seen as indicating the type of minimal expectations a democratic state might reasonably have of its citizens, i.e., that they would take the affirmative action of either actually participating in an election over the course of four years or of responding to an inquiry concerning their eligibility to vote.

36. See Wingo, "A Free Person as a Maker of Surprises."

37. Quoted in Waldron, *Dignity, Rank, and Rights*, 52.

38. Waldron, *Dignity, Rank, and Rights*.

39. In 2015 police officers killed 662 whites and Hispanics and 258 blacks. In 2014 there were 6,095 black homicide deaths compared with 5,397 homicide deaths for whites and Hispanics, and almost all of the black homicide victims were perpetrated by black killers. Further, according to the Bureau of Justice Statistics, blacks were charged with 62 percent of all robberies, 57 percent of murders, and 45 percent of assaults in the 75 largest US counties in 2009, though they made up roughly 15 percent of the population there. See MacDonald, "Myth of Black Lives Matter."

40. Loury, in a lecture at the Southern Sociological Society Annual Meeting, April 15, 2016, which he titled "Remarks on Racial Inequality and Black Lives Matter."

41. Hunn and Bell, "Why Was Michael Brown's Body Left There for Hours?"

42. Loury, "Remarks on Racial Inequality and Black Lives Matter," 13.

43. Of course that gesture was never realized. Rogers's chapter analyzes how African American intellectuals in the nineteenth century wrestled with this disappointment.

Works Cited

Arendt, Hannah. *Crisis of the Republic*. New York: Harcourt Brace Jovanovich, 1969.

Dworkin, Richard. *Freedom's Law: The Moral Reading of the American Constitution*. Cambridge, MA: Harvard University Press, 1996.

Hunn, David, and Kim Bell. "Why Was Michael Brown's Body Left There for Hours?" *St. Louis Post-Dispatch*, September 14, 2014.

Kant, Immanuel. *Groundwork to the Metaphysics of Morals* (1785). In his *Werke*, edited by Paul Menzer, 4:387–463. Berlin: Academy of Sciences, 1903.

Kutner, Luis. "A Proposal for a United Nations Writ of Habeas Corpus and International Court of Human Rights." *Tulane Law Review* 28 (June 1954): 417–41.

Kutner, Luis. *World Habeas Corpus*. Dobbs Ferry, NY: Oceana, 1962.

Locke, John. *Two Treatises of Government*. London, 1689.

Loury, Glenn. "Remarks on Racial Inequality and Black Lives Matter (or, What's a Self-Respecting Intellectual to Do?" Lecture given at Southern Sociological Society annual meeting, April 15, 2016.

MacDonald, Heather. "The Myth of Black Lives Matter." *Wall Street Journal*, February 12, 2016.

Mill, John Stuart. *Utilitarianism, On Liberty, Considerations on Representative Government, Remarks on Bentham's Philosophy*. Edited by Geraint Williams. London: J. M. Dent, 1993.

Ober, Josiah. *Demopolis: Democracy before Liberalism in Theory and Practice*. Seely Lectures. Cambridge: Cambridge University Press, 2017.

Rosen, Michael. *Dignity: Its History and Meaning*. Cambridge, MA: Harvard University Press, 2018.

Rousseau, Jean-Jacques. *The Social Contract* (1762). Baltimore: Penguin Books, 1968.

Waldron, Jeremy. *Dignity, Rank, and Rights*. Edited by Meir Dan-Cohen. Oxford: Oxford University Press, 2009.

Waldron, Jeremy. "Dignity, Rights, and Responsibilities." *Arizona State Law Journal* 43, no. 4 (Winter 2011): 1107–36.

Wehner, Peter. "The Christmas Revolution." *New York Times*, December 25, 2015, A27.

Williams, Bernard. *Problems of the Self: Philosophical Papers 1956–1972*. Cambridge: Cambridge University Press, 1973.

Wills, Garry. *Lincoln at Gettysburg: The Words That Remade America*. New York: Simon & Schuster, 1992.

Wingo, Ajume. "The Aesthetics of Freedom." In *New Waves in Political Philosophy*, edited by Boudewijn de Bruin and Christopher Zurn, 198–220. New York: Palgrave Macmillan, 2009.

Wingo, Ajume. "A Free Person as a Maker of Surprises." Unpublished manuscript.

Wingo, Ajume. "The Immortals in Our Midst: Why Democracies in Africa Need Them." *Journal of Ethics* 19, no. 3 (December 2015): 237–55.

Wingo, Ajume H. *Veil Politics in Liberal Democratic States*. Cambridge: Cambridge University Press, 2003.

6

Relations before Transactions

A PERSONAL PLEA

Glenn Loury

Prologue. Consider the following imagined dialogue between two black American social scientists—one a technically oriented economist like myself and the other an ethnographically oriented sociologist with radical political leanings:

EC: (*chanting, but otherwise sitting still*) Relations before transactions. Relations before transactions. Relations before transactions. Relations before transactions.

SOC: (*enters with a start—alarmed*) What's wrong, my friend? Why are you saying that? You must be the culprit who pilfered my copy of Bourdieu last week!

EC: No, I am not. Who's Bourdieu, anyway? One of those airy French sociologists you always fawn over? It's my mantra; I'm meditating. Very calming. You should try it sometime.

SOC: (*ignoring the dig*) I meditate all the time, man. I'm the one who belongs to a profession fraught with anxiety, remember? But what's your excuse?

EC: Well, I've been having a recurrent nightmare of late, and I want it to stop. My shrink thinks that meditation could help.

SOC: Who's your shrink?

EC: Oh, this brother was my roommate at Swarthmore. Brilliant dude; works a lot with gunshot victims, inner-city types involved in gangs, the drug trade and so on. He thinks they're making passive suicide attempts; writes books on hopelessness, self-loathing, falling into an existential abyss; cites Freud, Nietzsche, and de Sade. Strange guy, but brilliant. He gave me the mantra; promised it would help; said I should repeat it slowly while sitting very still and taking deep breaths.

SOC: Perhaps. But, remember what I told you about those pizzas—not a good idea after midnight. And did you say de Sade? Anyway, tell me, what's the dream?

EC: Oh, it's awful. I'm back in grad school. I'm sitting in my usual place right at the front of the class. The professor poses what he says is an important question. He's invited one of us to the board to work out an answer. I get there first and proceed to fill the board with equations. Finally I arrive at what must be the solution. My derivation is far too elegant not to be true. I turn to explain myself to the rest of the class. Just then, I realize that I've forgotten the original question! I rack my (very large) brain, but for the life of me, I can't recall it. The class begins to snicker. They're a ruthless bunch when they smell blood. The guffaws and catcalls grow louder. It's humiliating, just humiliating. (*begins to tremble uncontrollably*)

SOC: (*comforting his friend*) Yeah, I can see that. It's got to be tough being the smartest person in the room but without a clue as to what's the point. You ought to stick with this shrink, though. Dreams can be very revealing, you know. But I'm not sure I get the mantra. And what was the professor's question, anyway?

EC: He had asked us to explain how durable racial inequality in the United States can be squared with the premises of modern economic theory, without making any assumption of innate racial inferiority and without postulating any unexplained preferences for own-group associations.

SOC: That's a damned good question! It's a tough one, too. You're telling me you ran to the board to take that one on? Brave man. (*fools jump in where angels fear to tread, he thinks ...*)

EC: Well, to be honest, in the dream I always start to the board before he finishes posing the question. Happens the same way every time. I can't stop myself ... (*the trembling returns*)

SOC: (*in a bright tone, hoping to shift to a happier subject*) So what was your elegant solution?

EC: Oh, I'd love to tell you. But it's hopeless, because you'd never understand the mathematics!

(*At this, the sociologist takes offense and storms off angrily. The economist yells after him.*)

EC: Besides, I'm not sure I believe it anymore myself. Anyway, my shrink gave me this mantra and it seems to be helping. (*Returns to his chanting*) Relations before transactions. Relations before transactions. Relations before transactions. Relations before transactions ...

Thus ends the dialogue.

1. Relations before Transactions: A Conceptual Framework
   for Thinking about "Race" and Racial Inequality

Over these last forty years I have expended considerable effort trying to explain—to myself and to the world—why the subordinate status of African Americans persists in the United States. Some of this thinking was summed up in my 2002 monograph *The Anatomy of Racial Inequality*. That book sketched a theory of "race" applicable to the social and historical circumstances of the United States. It speculated about why racial inequalities persist. And it advanced a conceptual framework for thinking about social justice in matters of race. It was one part social science, one part social criticism, and one part social philosophy—themes that were pursued in successive chapters titled "Racial Stereotypes," "Racial Stigma," and "Racial Justice"—deriving from a synonymous series of lectures I had given at Harvard's DuBois Institute. As it turns out, my work on this question of the persistence of racial inequality has led me to upend a key premise of my discipline. Economics generally puts transactions at the center of its analysis. But my arguments in *Anatomy* have, over time, led me to see something that I was not yet able to articulate in that book: relations precede transactions. My goal in this paper will be to explain that core idea—an idea that has become foundational for this volume as a whole—and its implications. To explain this mantra—relations before transactions—I will reprise some core arguments from *Anatomy*. To expand on the implications of this mantra, I will go beyond it. Finally, I will argue that in our historical moment, well beyond that evolutionary moment where geographical separation was the most important explanatory factor for human difference, the human difference that we call "race" is necessarily the result of domination, in the form of racial stigma. Difference without domination, the normative ideal espoused in this volume, raises the possibility that in a world that had achieved such an outcome, and only in such a world, race would cease to exist. That is a big claim. It will take me some time to explain what I am getting at. I begin with a reprise of *Anatomy*.

2. The Concept of Race

I wish to fix ideas for the argument to come by briefly reviewing some ideas from *Anatomy of Racial Inequality*. I agree with the UCLA sociologist Rogers Brubaker, whose 2006 book *Ethnicity without Groups* has much impressed me: one ought never to invoke racial aggregates as subjects of social analysis unreflectively. So please bear with me. I assure

you, the relevance of this introductory conceptual excursion will be clear
soon enough.

A theoretical discussion of this kind properly starts with an account of
the phenomenon of "race" itself. (To speak of racial inequality is necessarily to speak of "race.") Why do people take note of and assign significance to the skin color, hair texture, and bone structure of other human
beings? How have the superficial markings on human bodies taken on
social significance to the extent that people routinely partition the field
of human subjects they encounter into groups, with this sorting convention based on these subjects' possessing some observable bodily mark?
This is a universal feature of human societies. But why should this be
so? I proposed (acknowledging in advance that there was no great origi-
nality in this) to conceive of "race" as being socially constructed—as a
conventional, not a natural, category. For me, the term race refers to in-
delible and heritable marks on human bodies of no intrinsic significance
in themselves which nevertheless have through time come to be invested
with social expectations that serve a certain kind of so-called rational
choice-making, and social meanings that are more or less durable.

Notice that when talking about "race" in America, or anywhere else
for that matter, we are actually dealing with two distinct processes: one
is categorization, the other is signification. Categorization entails sorting
people into cognitively manageable subsets on the basis of bodily marks
and differentiating one's dealings with such persons accordingly. It is a
cognitive act, an effort to comprehend the social world around us. By contrast, signification is an interpretative act—one that associates certain
connotations or social meanings with those categories. So both informa-
tional and symbolic issues are at play. Or, as I like to put it, when we speak
about "race," we are really talking about "embodied social signification."[1]

This social-cognitive conception of "race" can be instructively con-
trasted with acts of biological taxonomy—the sorting of human beings
based on presumed variations of genetic endowments across what had
been geographically isolated subpopulations. Such isolation was the
human condition until recently on an evolutionary time scale, and it led
to genetically distinct populations whose histories can still be traced in
the genome of contemporary populations in our age of mobility, even
as the (always proportionally minimal) genetic differentiation among
human populations recedes. Whether the term race can be used to identify human subpopulations from that moment of geographic isolation in
evolutionary history is a contested question. What I am emphasizing here
is that using "race" as a category of social cognition is conceptually distinct from the more dubious use of the concept for purposes of biologi-

cal taxonomy: to establish the scientific invalidity of "race" demonstrates neither the irrationality nor the immorality of invoking racial classification as acts of social cognition. So it is in this social constructivist spirit that I shall employ the concept here, with an emphasis on the negative interpretative/symbolic connotations that are attached to "blackness" in the United States.[2] Given this theoretical understanding of "race," what, then, might one say about the causes of persistent racial inequality? The all-important conclusion in *Anatomy* turned on a distinction I proposed between "reward bias" and "development bias."

3. Rethinking Racial Discrimination: Reward Bias versus Development Bias

Fundamental to my approach in *Anatomy* was the distinction between *racial discrimination* and *racial stigma*. Discrimination is about how blacks are treated, while stigma is about how blacks are perceived. Furthermore, I argued that what I called *reward bias* is now a less significant barrier to the full participation of African-Americans in US society than is what I called *development bias*. *Reward bias* is focused on disadvantageous treatment of black people in formal transactions that limits their rewards for skills and talents presented to the market. *Development bias* references impediments that block access for black people to those resources that are necessary to develop their skills and to refine their talents but are conveyed through informal social relations.

Thus while *reward bias* is grounded in racially discriminatory transactions, *development bias* is ultimately rooted in racially stigmatized social relations, since many of the resources that foster human development can become available to persons only as the byproduct of race-influenced informal social interactions. Another way of putting this is that reward bias is a reflection of *discrimination in contract* whereas, by contrast, development bias is a reflection of *discrimination in contact*.

Obviously, these two kinds of bias are not mutually exclusive: acquisition of skills can be blocked by overt acts of discrimination. Moreover, maintaining a regime of market discrimination that comes under pressure from the forces of economic competition may require employing informal instruments of social control.[3] Still, while both kinds of bias promote racial inequality, this is a useful distinction, for whereas the moral problem presented by *reward bias* is straightforward and calls for an uncontroversial remedy via laws against discrimination, *development bias* presents a subtler, more insidious ethical challenge — one that may be difficult to remedy via public policies in any manner that is likely to gar-

ner majoritarian support. This difficulty has both a cognitive and an ethical dimension. From a cognitive point of view, observers may find it difficult to distinguish between blocked developmental opportunities and
limited capacities, or distorted values, when confronted with a racially
stigmatized group's poor social performance. In terms of ethics, citizens
who find "transactional discrimination" associated with reward bias to be
noxious, may be less offended by the covert and subconscious "relational
discrimination" underlying development bias.[4]

For the project of this volume, the problems that flow from developmental bias could not be more important. If the goal is difference without domination, and developmental bias makes it difficult for social observers to distinguish between blocked developmental opportunities and
limited capacities or distorted values, what confidence can we have that a
society can develop the capacity to diagnose domination accurately? Do
we not live currently in a society characterized by an incapacity to see the
effects of domination, insofar as they manifest in development bias? Re-
latedly, while we have honed our ability to spot, challenge, and mitigate
reward bias, do we bring the same capacities to the judgment of relational
discrimination—those forms of social relationship that generate difference out of the stuff of domination?

It turns out that the economist's shrink, in that opening dialogue, with
the mantra "relations before transactions" was directing our attention
to the unspoken upshot of *Anatomy*. He was pointing toward the idea
that the persisting subordinate position of blacks in the economy—as
manifest to some extent in reward bias—is best thought of as deriving
from our stigmatized status in the society, that is, from developmental
bias, and not the other way around. This means that if we were somehow
able to put an end to all reward bias, we would not solve racial inequality;
we would not bring an end to difference with domination. As long as
there is relational discrimination, we will see developmental bias, and
with it racial inequality—difference with domination. In short, a focus on
racially discriminatory economic transactions doesn't cut deeply enough;
one must also consider the consequences of racially stigmatized social
relations. Stigma inhibits blacks' access to those networks of social affiliation where developmental resources are most readily appropriated.
On this view, the problem of persisting inequality is not mainly a racially
antagonistic marketplace or administrative state that refuses to reward
black talent or to accord blacks an equal citizenship—as had been the
case in decades past. Rather, the mantra's claim is that today's problem
derives mainly from a race-tinged psychology of perception and valua-
tion (as discussed by Lai and Banaji in this volume)—a way of seeing

black people that at some level withholds from them a presumption of an equal human worth. And so a racial group's stigmatized status in the social imagination — *and, crucially, in its own self-understanding* — may come to be rationalized and socially reproduced as a result of its subordinate position in the economic order — creating a vicious circle. Here we have a world where the notions of racial dignity, an end to racial subordination, racial honor or pride (and an end to shame) resonate powerfully. *These are the solutions* — not the project of nondiscrimination.

4. Social Capital and the Inequality-Producing Effects of Racial Stigma

To spell out the full implications of the recognition that relations are prior to transactions, and fully condition the parameters of possible transactions, I must reprise also some of the arguments that preceded *Anatomy* and even laid the foundation for it. A quarter-century earlier, in my 1976 doctoral dissertation written at MIT, I had the good fortune to coin the term "social capital."[5] To my everlasting benefit, the great sociologist James S. Coleman — in his 1990 treatise *Foundations of Social Theory* — credited me (along with writer Jane Jacobs)[6] as the concept's originator. What is more, distinguished political scientist Robert Putnam cited me to this same effect in his classic text *Making Democracy Work*. As it happens, I first used this concept in an analysis of persistent racial inequality in the United States. By discussing how I came to coin the term "social capital," I can further illuminate this contrast I am drawing between informal social relations and formal economic transactions — between reward and development bias — as mechanisms perpetuating the subordinate position of black people in the United States. This should drive home the point I am trying to make about how economics as a discipline might reorient itself.

In that dissertation, thinking as an economist, I wanted to contrast my concept of "social capital" with the more familiar idea of "human capital." Human capital theory attempts to account for variation in the earnings capacities of persons in society, explaining such unequal labor market outcomes by analogy with the well-developed theories of investment in economics — assuming competitive markets and rational choice by forward-looking individuals, analyzing "investment" decisions in light of agents' time preferences, their anticipated rates of return, and available alternatives for the use of their time. In a word, human capital theory imports into the study of human inequality an intellectual framework that had been well developed in economics to explain investment decisions by firms—a framework that focuses on the analysis of formal economic transactions.

Put simply, my point in that 1976 dissertation was that associating business with human investments is merely an analogy, not an identity—particularly if one seeks to explain persistent racial disparities. I argued that important things were overlooked in the human capital approach, things having to do with informal social relations. I emphasized two central aspects of this incompleteness, and these have come to form the basis of my argument for placing relations before transactions.

First, I stressed that *all human development is socially situated and mediated*. That is, I argued that development of human beings occurs inside social institutions. It takes place as between people, in the context of human interactions. The family, the community, the school, the peer group—such institutions of human association are where human development occurs. As a consequence, many of the resources essential to human development—the attention that a parent gives to her child, for example—are not *alienable*. For the most part, developmental resources are not "commodities." Most development is not for sale. Instead, structured connections between individuals create the context within which developmental resources come to be allocated to individual persons. Opportunity travels along the synapses of these social networks. The resulting allocation of resources need not be responsive to prices, and neither need it necessarily be economically efficient. Development of human beings is not the same as corporate investment. As a result, it may not always be a good metaphor, or a good analogy, to reason as though this were so.

The family is one such institution. This point is fundamental since processes of human development begin before birth. The decisions a mother makes—about how closely to attend to her health and nutrition during pregnancy, for instance—will alter the neurological development of her fetus. This and myriad other things I could name all come together to shape the experience of this newly born infant, who will mature one day to become a human being and about whom it will be said that he or she has this or that much productivity, as reflected in wages or the scores manifested on some cognitive examination. They are not machines, and their "productivities"—that is, their behavioral and cognitive capacities—are not merely results of some mechanical infusion of material resources. Rather, these capacities are byproducts of social processes that were mediated by networks of human affiliation and connectivity, and this is fundamentally important for understanding persistent racial disparities. That was my first point about the incompleteness of human capital theory. In relation to this volume, it has the consequence of meaning that if difference without domination is to be achieved, it will be achieved outside of markets. Why? Because relations precede transactions. Any effort to pursue justice exclusively through attention to the transactional distribution of material goods will fail for having failed to understand the fundamentally relational character of human development.

My second observation was that, as mentioned previously, *in our historical era, what we are calling "race" is mainly a social, and only indirectly a biological, phenomenon; consequently, "race" itself is endogenous to social relations, a dependent, not independent, variable.* In an open society where individuals live in proximity to one another, the persistence across generations of racial differentiation between large groups of people provides irrefutable evidence of a profound separation between the racially defined networks of social affiliation within that society. There would be no "races" in the steady state of any dynamic social system unless, on a daily basis and in regard to their most intimate affairs, people paid assiduous attention to the boundaries separating themselves from racially distinct others. Over time "race" would cease to exist unless people chose to act in a manner so as biologically to reproduce the variety of phenotypic expression that constitutes the substance of racial distinction.

"Race" is a socially produced equilibrium outcome; it is something we are making. Thus if the goal is to understand durable racial inequality, we will need to attend in some detail to the processes that cause "race" to persist as a fact of life in the society under study. For such processes almost certainly will not be unrelated to the allocation of human developmental resources in that society. In the contemporary world of mobility and proximity, race just is, I suggest, difference *with* domination.

Here, then, is my second point, in a nutshell: The creation and reproduction of "race" as a feature of society rests upon a set of beliefs and conceptions about identity held by people in that society—beliefs about who they are and about the legitimacy of conducting intimate relations (and here I do not only mean sexual relations, though I do mean that too) with racially distinct others. My impulse to contrast *human* and *social* capital in 1976 was based on the conviction that beliefs of this kind will affect the access various persons enjoy to the informal resources that individuals need to develop their human potential. What I was calling "social capital" was therefore a critical component in the creation of what economists routinely referred to as "human capital." Any theory of persistent racial inequality would be incomplete if it failed to consider interactions between social processes ensuring the reproduction of racial difference in that society, on the one hand, and those processes facilitating human development, on the other hand. We needed to talk about "social capital" as well as "human capital" if we were to understand persistent socioeconomic disparities between racial groups in the United States.

For example, let's assume my child is musically talented. Having seen her at the keyboard, I know that she could be a great pianist one day. But she needs a teacher, and I have no money for a teacher. Suppose I go to the banker with the following proposal: "My daughter here is destined to be a great pianist one day. Invest in fifteen years of lessons, and I'll repay you with 10 percent of her royalties for the first twenty-five years of her performance career." Such a contract is unlikely to be written, because it is not enforceable. As a result, that talented kid never gets the lessons. The human capital loans market is incomplete. Even if we were to accept the idea that physical and human investment are a good analogy, a corporate entity might be able to borrow against future earnings, while an individual would have a much more difficult time doing so.

Now, let us change this hypothetical so that my child has the talent and gets the lessons but won't practice.[7] A number of reasons might explain this. Anthropologist John Ogbu has argued that historically oppressed groups often evolve notions of identity that cut against the grain of their societies—*oppositional identities*.[8] Embrace of an oppositional identity can inhibit a young person from doing the things that are essential to fully develop his or her human potential. Sociologist Angel Harris has challenged Ogbu's arguments about the existence of oppositional identities, marshaling significant bodies of evidence for the existence of strong aspiration in historically oppressed communities. He has argued that school and pedagogic practices reduce the achievement of students from marginalized backgrounds.[9]

Given such a situation, I wish to ask, Do kids in a dysfunctional peer group simply have the wrong utility functions? How can that possibly be the end of our analysis? *It is a mistake to attribute the dysfunctional behavior of any historically oppressed group of people to their simply having the wrong preferences when their "preferences" have emerged from a set of historical experiences reflecting the larger society's social structures and activities.* When ethnic communities and their local cultures are not integrated across boundaries of race in a society, racial inequalities are likely to persist even in the face of effective enforcement of laws against racial discrimination in the formal areas of employment, housing, and credit markets. In the end, persistent racial disparities derive from complex, morally ambiguous, and difficult-to-regulate phenomena embodying and reflecting what people see as the *meanings* that give significance to their lives and from the nature of the social networks to which those meanings give rise.[10]

This is why I have always been dissatisfied with economic approaches to understanding racial discrimination in the United States within which the social significance of racial categories plays no operational role in the theory. Generating such theories is massively ahistorical. Of course, as a theoretical exercise one can elaborate a price theory for markets where traders are averse to doing business with some group marked with an X and where it won't matter what the X signifies — of the sort that the great Gary Becker did in his classic book from the 1950s. Even in 1969 I had the vague sense that Becker's theory was incomplete, that this incompleteness was stark and graphic when one considers the question of race in America, and that the context for human development and human investment was racially tinged and unequal because structures of social connectedness were — and still are — racially disparate. I could see that "race" ("blackness") was (and is) not some arbitrary marker, some X, merely a differentiator. Rather this symbol is laden with historically generated meanings particular to American society — meanings that, as history would have it, carry a stigmatizing, negative, degrading, and subordinating connotation. Race *is* difference with domination. What I am talking about here is, in short, "racial stigma." It creates and maintains developmental bias. It ensures the ongoing existence of difference *because* of domination.

5. Implications of "Racial Stigma" for the "Culture versus Structure" Debate

This point about racial stigma is fundamental for me. Without this insight, one may make a mistake. One may say, as many more or less conservative commentators have in effect said, "Look at recent immigrants from Asia and even from Latin America. They too have been victims in various ways. And yet they have advanced in our society even as the blacks of inner-city Detroit, Chicago, Philadelphia, Baltimore, New Orleans, Los Angeles, Oakland ... continue to lag. Whatever is wrong with those people?" Without appreciating that some bodily marks signify things — negative things, "otherness" things — that influence the chance for people bearing those marks to develop their human capacities; without seeing this, one may attribute the backwardness of these people who have been stigmatized to their "essence." One will say, in effect, "It must be something about 'those people,' not about us, that causes them to be so backward." One will eschew social and political and moral responsibility for their plight. Either one will conclude that their failure to develop their human potential reflects the absence of such potential in the first place (and we have books on the shelf making that argument), or one will decide upon this narrative: "Their failure is due to their backward culture which, sadly but inevitably—what more can we do?—causes them to lag behind." Yet black people are not the authors of the stigma that engenders the developmental bias against them. When we understand that the way people come to value things or make decisions is created via interactions in society, then their flourishing, or lack thereof, reflects on society as a whole. It reflects on an *us* that encapsulates the whole of society, not on an othered *them*.

My concern here is to warn against a mistake one can make—a cognitive mistake, a mistake in the analysis of society—about the extent to which racial inequality is a reflection of cultural differences between insular groups of people, instead of being the product of a system of social interactions knitting us together in a seamless web. Putting it directly and succinctly: *imputing a causal role to what one takes to be intrinsic cultural traits of a subordinate racial group, while failing to see the systemwide context out of which dysfunctional cultural patterns have emerged, is a significant error of social cognition.* That members of a particular group seem to routinely perform less well on a set of transactions of interest is a matter not of a cultural essence but of the weave of social relations that has (or has not) prepared the members of that group for those transactions. More importantly, the relevant failure is not a failure of market mechanisms.

The symbols signifying racial difference are freighted with important connotations that have adverse effects on a person's opportunities to develop his or her skills. Specifically in the US context, "blackness" has meanings associated with it that are stigmatizing. This stigma inclines people to a presumption against the merits of persons bearing the mark. It causes people to start out doubting the assumption that the stigmatized one is "like us." It leads an observer to be reticent to enter into intimacy with such a person. The result is a social allocation of developmental resources that results in developmental bias. This social allocation is not like a market-mediated allocation.

I hold that people don't make social judgments by means of straightforward benefit-cost calculations. They often act on identity considerations. They ask such questions as, Who am I? How then ought I to live? With whom should I associate? And when ought I to extend to this "other" a benefit of the doubt? Inequality is the outcome of a system of nonmarket social interactions such as these that entangle us all together in a seamless web.

Consider, finally, one example to illustrate this basic point: *race, marriage, and the family.* I mentioned out-of-wedlock birthrates among blacks. This issue actually illuminates how we can take "culture" as if it were simply there when it is, in fact, something that we're producing, all of us. So let us talk about marriage, the family, and childbearing. A person looking at gender relations between black people in the United States — at divorce, out-of-wedlock childbearing, and so forth—might be inclined to comment, "Ah, just look at how they are living." But I would urge us to consider intermarriage rates between the races in the United States. They remain quite low, though they have risen in recent decades.[11] Now I cast no aspersions. It might be that black women are getting proposals from white men and are turning them down. I don't know. But I do know that in the equilibrium there's a low rate of cross-boundary mating between these two groups, and I strongly suspect that this fact has implications for human development, for resources available to children, and for the generation and transmission of wealth. Moreover, it has implications for the dating and mating market among African Americans, because blacks are a small minority of the population—roughly one in eight Americans. So if white men and black women were marrying at a higher rate, black men and black women would be interacting in a different way. How? I don't know exactly. That's not my point. That would be a study. Mine is a higher-level insight, to wit: observing a social equilibrium in which black and white subpopulations exhibit different out-of-wedlock birthrates and, on the basis of that observation, imputing the difference to something called "black culture," reflects a failure to see how the intraracial marriage market is nested within a larger context, where a higher rate of cross-boundary mating could substantially alter intraboundary behavior. So what one could take to be "culture" just might turn out to be "structure" after all. What was seen to be a characteristic of "those people"—why don't they marry? why do they bear their children in such a disorderly manner?—just might turn out to be a question about marriage markets in the society as a whole. We could also put it this away and say, from the perspective of the white population, that the question turns out to be about *us*: why do *we* avoid intimacy with *them*? I use these words—*us, we, them*—to make a point about how stigma operates. It operates in the very definition of who the social "we" is.

How a society answers the question, who are *we*? is a very significant issue, as Melvin Rogers eloquently explicates in this volume. It is certainly an important question in the United States today. Who are *we*? Whose country is it? When we talk about crime, violence, school failure, urban decay, prisons, etc., are these matters that, in the back of our minds, can be understood as *us* against *them*? Because if it is US against *them*, anything is possible. It becomes possible to say about those people languishing in the ghettos of our great cities, "That's not my country. That's some third world thing." (This was actually said during the flood of New Orleans after Hurricane Katrina. But it's a lie. Black people in New Orleans have been there for 250 years. They're not aliens. They're as American as you can get, as American as anybody can be. That was *us* down there crawling up on the rooftops. That was *us* huddled in the Superdome. That was *us*.) I maintain that these problems are a quintessentially American affair, not simply a measure of the inadequacy of "black culture." They reflect *our* social inadequacy, I wish to argue. And I buttress that argument by observing the incompleteness of human capital theory, by insisting that human developmental processes are socially contextualized, and by stressing that "race" plays a foundational part in all of this. That is what I mean when I, as an economist, nevertheless insist on placing relations before transactions!

6. Conclusion: Who Are "We" in America?

Relations before transactions. Thinking in this way helps to account for the durable racial inequality with which America is still encumbered. Consider the poor central-city dwellers who make up perhaps a quarter of the African American population. In the face of the despair, violence, and self-destructive folly of so many of these people, it is morally superficial in the extreme to argue, as many commentators have done, that "if those people would just get their acts together like many of the poor immigrants, we would not have such a horrific problem in our cities." To the contrary, any morally astute response to the "social pathology" of American history's losers would conclude that while we cannot change our ignoble past, we need not and must not be indifferent to the contemporary suffering issuing directly from that past, for which we all bear some collective responsibility in the form of the texture of our social relations.

While we should not ignore the behavioral problems of this so-called underclass—of some of the results of difference emergent from domination—we should discuss and react to them as if we were talking about our own children, neighbors, and friends. This is an American tragedy. *It is a national, not merely a communal, disgrace.* Changing the definition of the American *we* is the first step toward rectifying the relational discrimination that afflicts our society. The achievement of difference without domination is possible only in societies in which all members of that society are embraced among *us*.

Notes

1. A self-conscious awareness that the marks on one's body may convey profound significations to the others one encounters in society may be an impediment to one's psychological health—particularly in a place like the United States where, because of the need to justify chattel slavery in a nation self-consciously defining itself as "the land of liberty," the mark of "blackness" has, over the course of the last two centuries, come to be infused with long-enduring derogatory significations.

2. Of particular interest to me is the possibility that powerful and derogatory social meanings may come to be associated with the bodily marks that define "race" in American society, and that such meanings may even be internalized by persons identifying with a stigmatized racial group—even people like me, who might hope to study such matters more or less scientifically. How, I ask, does one achieve the objective observer's stance while enmeshed in the tangled web of identities, fealties, and conflicting narratives which is the nature of racial discourse in America?

3. For example, norms against trading with stigmatized "others" may be established and enforced via threats of social ostracism for those violating the norm.

4. For example, they may object if a white police officer treats black youths unfairly, but say nothing at all when white families flee an integrating residential community because of their exaggerated fear of the threat they perceive from "black crime."

5. Loury, "Two Essays in the Theory of the Distribution of Income."

6. See Jane Jacobs's book *The Economy of Cities.*

7. Some evidence (see, e.g., Austen-Smith and Fryer, "An Economic Analysis of 'Acting White'") supports the view that in the United States today, some part of the difference in intellectual preparedness of youngsters across racial lines turns on the fact that black peer groups discourage their members from the doing of what is necessary to fully develop their intellectual talents—seeing this as betraying their racial identity—thereby fostering a so-called oppositional identity.

8. See Ogbu's 2008 edited volume *Minority Status, Oppositional Culture and Schooling.*

9. See Harris, *Kids Don't Want to Fail.*

10. See also Morton, "Reasoning under Scarcity."

11. See, e.g., Romano, *Race Mixing.*

Works Cited

Austen-Smith, David, and Roland Fryer. "An Economic Analysis of 'Acting White.'" *Quarterly Journal of Economics* 120, no. 2 (May 2005): 551–83.

Brubaker, Rogers. *Ethnicity without Groups.* Cambridge, MA: Harvard University Press, 2006.

Coleman, James S. *Foundations of Social Theory.* Cambridge, MA: Harvard University Press, 1990.

Harris, Angel L. *Kids Don't Want to Fail: Oppositional Culture and the Black-White Achievement Gap.* Cambridge, MA: Harvard University Press, 2011.

Jacobs, Jane. *The Economy of Cities.* New York: Vintage Books / Random House, 1970.

Loury, Glenn C. *The Anatomy of Racial Inequality.* Cambridge, MA: Harvard University Press, 2002.

Loury, Glenn C. "Two Essays in the Theory of the Distribution of Income." PhD diss., Department of Economics, Massachusetts Institute of Technology, 1976.

Morton, Jennifer M. "Reasoning under Scarcity." *Australasian Journal of Philosophy* 95, no. 3 (2017): 543–59.

Ogbu, John, ed. *Minority Status, Oppositional Culture and Schooling*. Sociocultural, Political, and Historical Studies in Education. New York: Routledge, 2008.

Putnam, Robert. *Making Democracy Work*. Princeton, NJ: Princeton University Press, 1993.

Romano, Renee. *Race Mixing: Black-White Marriage in Postwar America*. Cambridge, MA: Harvard University Press, 2003.

PART 3

The Limits of Mirroring: New Approaches to Representation, Measurement, & Membership

7

Overrepresentation

ASIAN AMERICANS AND THE CONUNDRUMS
OF STATISTICAL MIRRORING

Ellen D. Wu

"Is Harvard Unfair to Asian-Americans?" The *New York Times* headline made me do a double take. The date was November 25, 2014.[1] The op-ed responded to a lawsuit filed the previous week by a group called Project on Fair Representation. The organization alleged that the university's objective of racial "balancing" in its student body unfairly discriminated against high-achieving applicants of Asian ancestry.[2]

This was the morning after a St. Louis County grand jury decided not to indict white police officer Darren Wilson for the shooting death of eighteen-year-old Michael Brown, a young African American man. The verdict impelled distraught protests by area residents in the streets of Ferguson, Missouri—Brown's home and the scene of his murder. Local law enforcement retaliated with disturbingly militarized responses.

Something about the juxtaposition of Ivy League admissions and police brutality felt jarring. A question of access to elite privilege seemed almost frivolous next to a literal and terrifying matter of life and death. It was as if the two issues did not reside in the same political and moral universe. Writer Nicole Chung (@nicole_soojung) captured my uneasiness when she tweeted, "idk maybe today wasn't the best day to run this in the print edition, @nytimes."[3]

Yet it may be precisely this strange divergence that points to a novel avenue for charting the US racial order in recent times. How do we make sense of this disconnect, the radically different fates of two groups that

For generous help with sources, concepts, and research support, I thank Nicole Chung, Heather Gerken, Indiana University's US History Workshop, National Endowment for the Humanities, David Null, John Skrentny, University College London Institute of the Americas, Thuy Tran Wu, Indiana University's US History Workshop, and especially Danielle Allen, Rohini Somanathan, and the participants in the Harvard University Edmond J. Safra Center for Ethics' Workshop on Diversity, Justice, and Democracy.

ostensibly started out on the same side of the color line as nonwhite "minorities" a half century ago? What might this history reveal about the reconfiguration of social and political alignments in the wake of the civil rights movement?

1. Asian Americans, Affirmative Action, and the Puzzle of Proportional Representation

The black freedom struggle drove the nation to reconcile the yawning chasm between its egalitarian ideals and its exhaustive white supremacy. A suite of policy correctives appeared to tackle the crisis: civil rights legislation, busing, and affirmative action.[4] At the grassroots level, sweeping challenges to the status quo imagined alternative ways of being that would unshackle oppressed peoples from the intertwined destructions of racism, capitalism, and imperialism.[5]

The upheavals of this period begat the "Asian American," a self-identity inspired by Black Power and the Vietnamese masses' quest for self-determination. Those who marched under the banner of "Asian American" did so as an unapologetic quarrel with the United States.

They rejected its history of dispossessing, exploiting, and dehumanizing "Third World" persons at home and abroad. They touted a kinship with other peoples of color, calling for worldwide liberation from myriad forms of injustice. At the same time, "Asian American" signaled a guarded embrace, a claim to belong to the very community that they trenchantly critiqued.[6]

With these proclamations, Asian Americans demanded that others acknowledge them as such—semantically, culturally, and institutionally. But they discovered that their yearning for meaningful recognition on their own terms would not be simply a matter of swapping out the old ("Oriental" and the like) for the new. To be hailed as "Asian Americans" from the 1960s onward required legibility within the racial management apparatus of the day.[7] Asian Americans would need to be visible within the framework of affirmative action.

Pressured by the black freedom movement's vitality, federal authorities haltingly adopted untested approaches to secure equal opportunities for people of color beginning in the early 1960s. "Affirmative action" unfolded in a piecemeal manner, fuzzy in its conceptions of unfairness, its protocols, and its intended outcomes. This imprecision extended to its target populations as well. African Americans were indisputably the main focus. However, initial moves by bureaucrats in the 1950s to track employer discrimination also collected data on "other minority" workers: "Spanish Americans, Orientals, Indians, Jews, Puerto Ricans, etc." By 1962 a revision of the federal contract compliance survey forms clarified "Negro, Spanish-American, Oriental, and American Indian" as quasi-official "minority" groups, setting the template for future affirmative action initiatives.[8]

The exact meaning of "minority," though, would remain unsettled. In the 1960s and 1970s, the notion of "minority" was stretchy, denoting at once head counts, victims of discrimination, and social difference, especially distance from whiteness.[9] Its amorphousness presented a serious conundrum for Asian Americans as they sought to clarify their standing in the post-1960s racial order. Subscribers to the Asian American Movement saw themselves as sharing in the historical traumas of white supremacy with Native Americans, Latinos, and African Americans. Thus they saw themselves as entitled to access opportunities and resources made available via affirmative action. So to them it made sense to situate themselves on the "minority" side of the burgeoning majority-minority divide.

More influential decision-makers did not agree. As affirmative action spread, policymakers readily presumed that African Americans (and to a lesser extent Hispanics and Native peoples) were indeed "minorities" and thus appropriate beneficiaries. But Asian Americans perplexed them. Quantitative indicators of socioeconomic wellbeing suggested that Asian Americans stood apart from other "minority" groups despite their minuscule numbers, the historical patterns of anti-Asian racism, and their racial distinctiveness. Did Asian Americans count as "minorities" for the purposes of compensatory justice? Or had they, as Assistant Secretary of Labor Daniel Patrick Moynihan put it in 1965, "ceased to be colored"?[10]

Confronted with this mismatch, affirmative action's early architects lurched clumsily toward wobbly compromises. Herbert Hammerman, the first chief of the Equal Employment Opportunity Commission (EEOC)'s reports unit, suggested in 1967 that the agency bypass the tracking of Asians in its monitoring of apprenticeships and referral unions for affirmative action purposes. The population was too minuscule to bother about and also demonstrably immune from discrimination, in his view. All of his colleagues agreed, Hammerman later recounted, but the chair stated his unwillingness to "take the political heat" that the removal would surely inflame.[11]

Similar proposals soon surfaced in various contexts. In some instances, planners linked the definition of "minority" more tightly to "disadvantage" and "underrepresentation." In these scenarios, Asian Americans were dropped completely from "minority" categorization (as Hammerman had urged)—and, thereby, systemic efforts to redress racism. Another approach decoupled "minority" status from assumed "disadvantage." Doing so meant that Asian Americans might continue to be recognized as a racial minority group—a concession to the Asian American Movement and to the multiplying exhortations for "diversity"[12]—but one not necessarily in need of remedial succor. Either way, the solutions began to sap Asian Americans' claims to affirmative action eligibility by removing them from the realm of the "disadvantaged," "underutilized," and "underrepresented" in terms of both policy and rhetoric.

While irregular and inconclusive, these maneuvers laid the groundwork for the cultural branding of Asian Americans as "overrepresented" in the coming decades: minority self-starters wholly capable of unassisted upward mobility. Their numbers on elite college campuses and in select professions provided the empirical evidence.

Troubled by these developments, Asian American activists confronted the peculiar dilemma of trying to prove their credentials as bona fide minorities. Disputing insinuations of their "overrepresentation," they fought assiduously to convince university administrators and government officials of their rightfulness as an "underrepresented" population.

Arguing for their underrepresentation, however, left intact assumptions of proportional representation as *the* fundamental tenet of fairness in the age of affirmative action.[13] Americans have understood "representation" as an integral part of democracy—an unalienable right—since the Revolutionary era.[14] While there has been vigorous debate on its proper meanings and forms, one of the prevailing paradigms has been the notion that the makeup of legislative assemblies ought to reflect accurately the composition of the citizenry at large.[15] Initially, fans of proportional representation championed it as a means to political equality, a guarantee that the voices of ideological minorities would be heard in the course of political deliberations.[16]

In the mid-twentieth century, policymakers applied proportionality thinking to civil rights reforms.[17] To them it made pragmatic sense; the period's mass culture increasingly valued quantitative social-scientific evidence as the most reliable insight into society's problems.[18] Such an emphasis encouraged government officials to mobilize statistics to prove the existence of discrimination in various arenas—not only ones that were most overtly about politics and citizenship (voting rights, jury representation) but also in distributive and social realms (housing, employment, education).[19] As affirmative action spread, statistical mirroring became entrenched as the default measure of racial inequality and racial progress.[20] The closer the racial makeup of a given organization (a workplace, a school, etc.) paralleled the percentages in the community as a whole, however defined, the better.

In certain respects, the proportionality doctrine has convincingly demonstrated the embedded and enduring racial inequalities in the United States beyond the end of formal segregation. Critics of the US criminal justice system have productively reoriented the national debate on crime, policing, and mass incarceration by exposing glaring disparities between nonwhites and whites.[21] Black and Latino/a individuals make up 59 percent of all US prisoners despite constituting only one-quarter of the general population.[22] African Americans across the socioeconomic spectrum have a higher likelihood of imprisonment than individuals of all other races in the United States.[23] The overwhelmingly disproportionate numbers of incarcerated African Americans, as Michelle Alexander has famously argued, constitutes what is effectively "the New Jim Crow," a racial caste system updated for the late twentieth century and early twenty-first.[24]

Still, proportionality is an imperfect vehicle for both measuring and achieving equity for people of all races. Statistics themselves are not transparent, objective reflections of material reality. They are instead socially generated information systems, products of ideological forces, political intentions, and epistemological assumptions.[25] The very act of determining deviations from proportions-as-they-should-be (the number of white employees should not exceed X; the number of African American students has not yet reached Y) necessitates agreed-upon racial categories to be monitored and racial inequities to be addressed. But how are these racial categories and racial inequities to be defined? Which are to be accepted as legitimate and worthy of redress within the purview of a particular project such as criminal justice, hiring, or admissions? These decisions are subject to competing metrics, situational pressures, and political disagreements — inconsistencies that invite the possibility of stoking disparities and injustices rather than solving them.

The case of Asian Americans underscores these confounding puzzles and pitfalls. The boundaries of "Asian American" itself have fluctuated over the years with the arrival of new immigrant and refugee streams. People with roots in the Pacific islands, South Asia, and the Middle East have sometimes but not always been included under this umbrella. Collapsing a broad mix of individuals into this demographic monolith has glossed over all kinds of differences — socioeconomic, cultural, religious, ideological, experiential. These blind spots have kept the state and other institutions from recognizing disparities both within "Asian America" as well as those between Asian Americans and other racial groups. The reliance on numbers to authenticate problems means that the absence of data or lack of "statistical significance" makes it tough to demonstrate the existence of specific injustices.

The slaying of six Sikh Americans at their Oak Creek, Wisconsin, gurdwara in August 2012 sharply illustrates these gaps. Islamophobia in the United States has spiked since the events of September 11, 2001, with Muslim, Sikh, South Asian, and Arab immigrant communities all experiencing heightened surveillance, discrimination, animosity, and violence. Notably, the Federal Bureau of Investigation did not explicitly tag hate crimes against Sikhs, Hindus, or Arabs until 2015, categorizing them instead as "anti-Islamic," "anti-Asian," or "other." Paramjit Kaur Saini was one of the six killed at Oak Creek. Her son Harpeet Singh Saini subsequently appeared before the US Senate Committee on the Judiciary to plead: "Senators, I came here today to ask the government to give my mother the dignity of being a statistic. The FBI does not track hate crimes against Sikhs. My mother and those shot that day will not even count on a federal form. We cannot solve a problem we refuse to recognize." His testimony helped push the agency toward more refined data collection.[26]

Yet data alone cannot right all racial wrongs; sometimes data exacerbates or even spawns them.[27] For Asian Americans, statistical data and proportionality thinking—core components of the affirmative action regime—have resulted, inadvertently, in a new constellation of difficulties. Selective interpretations of quantitative indices have fixed the stereotype of Asian Americans as exceptional, accomplished strivers immune to racial barriers. In policy deliberations, media accounts, and grassroots mobilizations, various interested parties have deployed the conceit of Asian American "overrepresentation" for a range of political ends—left, center, and right—including moves to defend, expand, and now abolish affirmative action. Curiously, just as the "underrepresentation" of minority bodies has been framed as a problem, so too has the "overrepresentation" of Asian Americans. Analytically, politically, and ethically, Asian American "overrepresentation" calls into question—if not upending altogether—reigning approaches to representation, fairness, and racial justice at the dawn of the twenty-first century.

2. Campus Crusades

The crux of Asian American "overrepresentation" evolved in fits and starts at the intersections of state policy, higher education, and community activism. Stereotyping of Asian Americans as the "model minority"—a racial group distinct from whites but lauded as well-assimilated, up-

wardly mobile, politically nonthreatening, and definitively not-black[28] —
first emerged between World War II and the mid-1960s. With the advent
of affirmative action, university and college administrators grafted this
racial common sense onto the proportional representation principle. The
result was an institutional invisibility that infuriated Asian American college students across the country.

Asian Americans at the University of Wisconsin–Madison (UW) em-
blematized this outrage. Graduate student Donna S. Tamanaha took the
unusual step of calling on US congresswoman Patsy T. Mink to resolve a
campus dispute in February 1974. Tamanaha explained that she and fellow members of the fledgling UW Asian Union had joined other students
of color to push UW to "make education more responsive to so-called minorities." But Asian Americans faced a unique hurdle: the "reluctan[ce]"
of the administration to consider them formally as an "ethnic minority."
Without this recognition, Asian Americans felt "excluded" from recruitment and admissions, financial aid, counseling, and the curriculum, "systematically ignored" because they lacked political clout. They hoped that
an intervention from Mink, the first Asian American female elected to
Congress and a vocal champion of racial justice, might tip the balance
in their favor.[29]

Several months earlier Tamanaha had confronted UW chancellor H. Edwin Young, pointedly asking if the institution included Asian
Americans in its affirmative action outreach.[30] She may have known the
answer but had perhaps sought explicit documentation to fuel the Asian
Union's mission. The reply from the chancellor's office confirmed the
divergence: UW counted "Asian-Americans" separately from whites but
did not include them in campus affirmative action programs.[31]

To justify this omission, the chancellor's office leaned on proportionality logic. The 173 Asian American students at UW composed 0.5 percent of the student body (34,866). Asian Americans (30) made up 0.47
percent of the total classified staff (6328) and 4.20 percent of all academic employees (229 of 5360). Moreover, the proportion of "Oriental
or Other Non-White" workers in Dane County, home to UW, amounted
to roughly 0.5 percent. Based on these tabulations, Asian Americans were
neither "underutilized" nor "underrepresented." Academic staff were "ap-
preciably more numerous than their numbers in the local population
would predict." Federal guidelines stipulated the development of affirmative action enterprises for "underutilized" ethnic minority groups; demographically speaking, Asian Americans did not fit the bill. The administration hastened to note, however, that Asian Americans could apply on
a need basis for the same grant monies open to *all* minority students, and

that UW was "fully committed to insure equal opportunity for all groups including Asian-Americans."[32]

The university's stance roiled the Asian Union. They asked the Japanese American Citizens League (JACL), the nation's foremost Asian American civil rights organization, to intercede. Tom Hibino, director of the league's Midwest regional office, contacted Chancellor Young to "strongly protest" the university's treatment of "minority groups" such as in the unilateral shuttering of UW's Native American, Latino, and Afro-American student centers. Emphasizing the "necessity of self-determination," Hibino connected the "insensitivity" of the closings to the university's "failure" to address the "needs" of its Asian Americans. Had administrators been lulled by the fallacy that "Asian Americans have 'made it'"?[33]

When JACL's rebuke yielded nothing, the Asian Union turned to Congresswoman Mink. She quickly urged Chancellor Young, UW's president and dean of students, and Governor Patrick Lucey to regard Asian American students as "an ethnic minority." Their inclusion in minority-targeted recruitment, admissions, financial aid, and counseling and the teaching of "Asian studies" were "vital elements" in "ensuring an important and meaningful education."[34] Mink also persuaded her Wisconsin colleagues Senator Henry S. Reuss and Representative Robert W. Kastenmeier to jump into the fray.[35]

The UW responses elaborated on the previous exchange with Tamanaha. Chancellor Young assured Mink that the University "recognized" Asian Americans as an "ethnic minority." He verified their eligibility for financial aid, tailored counseling, and extending the undergraduate time-to-degree to five years as part of various programs for "minority/disadvantaged students." The caveat, though, was that Asian Americans often did not "require" such "remedial assistance." Furthermore, the proportion of Asian American students at UW (0.5 percent) and faculty (3.2 percent) exceeded that of the ratio in the Wisconsin labor force (0.2 percent). For these reasons UW did not make "special recruitment efforts."[36]

UW president John Weaver fleshed out the justification in his reply to Representative Kastenmeier. Reiterating the chancellor's argument, he emphasized the presence of Asian American students, staff, and faculty "in far greater proportions" in relation to the populations of Madison and Wisconsin. The administration contended that Wisconsin's Asian Americans "have not suffered the same deprivations as many Blacks, Chicanos, and Native Americans." Weaver saw "little evidence" that the state's Asian Americans had been "victims of discrimination either economically or educationally." Weaver also nodded to the extra complication of "defining this group" given that many were "naturalized United States citizens" rather than native-born. He acknowledged the Asian Union's demands, but given the evidence at hand plus "limited" available funding, the administration did not find it "necessary or appropriate" to heed them for now.[37]

The Asian Union fired back, resoundingly rejecting the university's defense. "Supposedly we've reached our quota. We're almost overutilized, according to the Affirmative Action Office," Tamanaha retorted sarcastically.[38] Her peers articulated a host of frustrations, including pervasive feelings of "alienation," the need for "solidarity," and the "confusion" by outsiders of Asian Americans with "Asians."[39] Most disturbingly, the Asian Union perceived the administration's decision-making as a flawed process based on racist assumptions ("villainous Fu Manchus" and "studious, docile, ever-smiling Charlie Chans") rather than "real needs."[40] Tamanaha stressed that the faulty "success myth—and it is a myth—has been perpetuated so that many people just ignore us." More than that, it upheld the fiction of an attainable "American Dream" for racial minorities.[41]

But puncturing the "success myth" presented its own conundrum. Claims of Asian American mobility were "untrue to begin with," Tamanaha argued. "None of the statistics prove that." Yet even as she invoked quantitative measures to disprove racial typecasting, fellow traveler Jack Tchen called them into question altogether. "The University's analysis of racism is purely statistical, it doesn't get at the real problem," he insisted.[42]

Tchen's exasperation foretold the existential troubles that Asian Americans would repeatedly collide with as they struck against invisibility. At institutions of higher learning across the United States—the University of Michigan, the University of Colorado School of Law, Stanford University, and the Ford Foundation Fellowship program, among others—Asian Americans strove to be identified as "minorities." Some took years, even decades, to attain this status. (The University of Chicago, for one, waited until 2004.)[43] Crucially, however, many attempts flopped. Asian Americans' hunger for recognition within the affirmative action paradigm could not escape the dominant logic of proportionality and its concomitant statistical indexing.

3. Bakke: Unanswered Questions

The spottiness of Asian Americans' affirmative action eligibility spurred community spokespersons to intervene in *Regents of the University of*

California v. Allan Bakke (1978), the Supreme Court case that tested the legality of racial considerations in university admissions. They feared two dire outcomes: first that the Supreme Court might declare University of California, Davis School of Medicine's special admissions program—and therefore affirmative action writ broadly—unconstitutional; and second that even if the justices green-lighted affirmative action, Asian Americans would be unequivocally shut out.

In anticipation, the fledgling Asian American Bar Association of the Greater Bay Area (AABA) submitted an amicus brief to address the two concerns.[44] Like dozens of other organizations, AABA saw race-based admissions programs as critical to realizing "meaningful and effective" integration.[45] But what distinguished AABA's statement from the other briefs supporting UC Davis was its impassioned entreaty that "Asian Americans have suffered and continued to suffer from invidious racial discrimination."[46] Speaking directly to *Bakke*, AABA carefully emphasized the community's protracted struggles in education and employment. In San Francisco and Los Angeles, 15 percent of Asian American minors still attended racially segregated schools, with those lacking English fluency particularly suffering "deprivation of equal protection."[47] Those who managed to graduate found themselves underemployed, underpaid, or nearly absent from professional circles.[48] Law was a standout example of "patent underrepresentation," with Asian Americans composing 1 percent of the US population but only 0.3 percent of the nation's attorneys.[49] Taken together, the evidence "demonstrate[d] beyond any reasonable doubt the lingering effects of past racial discrimination against Asian Americans."[50]

AABA presciently forecast doubts about Asian Americans' suitability for "minority-sensitive"[51] programs scattered throughout the *Bakke* deliberations. Executive branch officials raised the question as they edited the Department of Justice (DOJ)'s amicus brief siding with the University of California. Stu Eizenstat (President Jimmy Carter's chief domestic policy adviser) and Bob Lipshutz (White House counsel) worried that a draft "inartfully" implied that Asians did not belong in special admissions, even as they conceded that discrimination against Asians in medicine might have already been "redressed." At the same time, they cautioned that "limit[ing] affirmative action to African Americans was both "legally and politically unsound"—though they had in mind blowback from the "Hispanic community," not Asian Americans.[52]

DOJ's finalized brief displayed this ambivalence. It built a case for affirmative action by furnishing data to illustrate that people of color lived with the "pervasive effects of past discrimination" such as rates of unemployment and indigence higher than those of whites.[53] But Asian Americans were a striking aberration. There were markedly lower percentages of Asians (Japanese, Chinese, Filipino) either jobless or living below the poverty line as compared to African Americans and Hispanics. Asians also had much higher levels of education and a greater proportion of white-collar workers—surpassing even whites on these measures.[54] In medicine, DOJ found "no apparent under representation." Asian Americans comprised 0.75 percent of the nation's total population in 1970 but 2 percent of US medical students and 3.6 percent of all physicians in the United States in 1973.[55] DOJ did acknowledge, though, that anti-Asian racism might linger in "subtle forms" such as relatively lower medical school acceptance rates in contrast to whites.[56]

Despite this caveat, DOJ wondered why Asian Americans fell under the purview of UC Davis Medical School's targeted selection when "substantial numbers" had been admitted without affirmative action. In 1973, Asian Americans had claimed 13 of the 84 "regular" spots. That percentage (15.48 percent) far exceeded the proportion of Asian American bachelor's degree holders in California (6 percent).[57] "Although it may well be that disadvantaged Asian-American persons continue to be in need of the special program to overcome past discrimination, the record is silent on that question," DOJ ruminated.[58]

Why was DOJ even concerned with Asian Americans? It may well be that Justice attorneys were not trying to single them out per se. They probably predicted (rightly so, in retrospect) that Asian American anomalies would attract the unwanted attention of affirmative action opponents. So even as the DOJ argued for the constitutionality of taking race into account in admissions decisions, it suggested sending the case back to the trial court to reconsider the specific conditions at UC Davis Medical School. More details were needed to determine whether or not it had operated in a constitutionally permissible manner. In this context, the inclusion of Asian American applicants was one of several "unresolved serious questions" to be reinvestigated by the lower court.[59]

Nonetheless, Asian Americans did feel singled out. Alarmed, the DC-area Asian Pacific American Federal Employee Council (APAFEC) immediately dispatched a rebuttal to Attorney General Griffin B. Bell. APAFEC underlined the monumental stakes of DOJ's handiwork: with it, the federal government had become "the first participant in a case of the *Bakke* type to single out Asian/Pacific Americans from other minority groups for a constitutional challenge to their participation in a minority program."[60] The brief had "cast doubt" on the government's intentions for Asian Pacific Americans. A ruling that disqualified them from minority admissions initiatives would "gravely jeopardize" their eligibility for affirmative action across the board.[61] The council demanded to know how the Carter administration might "limit the damage" to existing efforts.[62]

APAFEC appended a detailed "Fact Sheet" to correct the misinformation that had undermined Asian/Pacific Americans' claims to inclusion in affirmative action. The Fact Sheet scolded DOJ for its "misleading or irrelevant suggestions" that Asian/Pacific Americans were "too well off to suffer the effects of past discrimination." Many newcomers were under- or unemployed. Language barriers and unauthorized immigration made it tough to collect reliable information on Asian/Pacific Americans.[63] Communities shouldered burdens of violent crime, educational gaps, and deficiencies in public service outreach. Asian/Pacific Americans were "under-represented," not to mention "underpaid and underranked" in a range of professions.[64]

APAFEC also took issue with the brief's statistical distortions. DOJ had cited the 9,920 Asian doctors in the US, 3.6 percent of all practicing MDs, to show that there was "no apparent under representation of Asian-American persons" in medicine. But this claim was "grossly inflated." Because 9,796 of the 9,920 were foreign-born, Asia-trained physicians, it was "absurd" to deduce that opportunities for medical education abounded for Asian/Pacific Americans.[65] Additionally, Justice had slighted Koreans, Asian Indians, Samoans, Vietnamese, Hawaiians, Pakistanis, and Cambodians by relying on skewed data limited in scope to Chinese, Japanese, and Filipinos.[66]

And if Asian Pacific Americans were totally axed from affirmative action? The fate of their standing had harmful implications reaching beyond the community. A ruling that separated Asian/Pacific Americans from other racial minority, women's, and civil rights groups might "'divide and conquer'" coalitions that "promote[d] the common goal of equality for all."[67]

APAFEC's missive rallied Asian Americans around the country to denounce the brief as "callous and unfounded" and to proclaim their "right" to be codified as a "minority in need of assistance."[68] Community envoys rushed from California to Washington, DC, to lobby key players in the days before the *Bakke* oral arguments, scheduled for October 12, 1977. The nine delegates represented a cross-section of constituencies: Chinese for Affirmative Action, Japanese American Citizens League, and the Filipino American Democratic Club, Asian Inc., Asian American Bar Association of the Greater Bay Area, and the University of California, Berkeley's Asian American Studies Program. Speeding through the

White House, DOJ, and Capitol Hill, the intrepid band insisted on an "immediate retraction" of the "erroneous and devastating statements." It blasted the government for its "false assumptions and indifferent attitudes toward the needs of Asian Americans."[69]

The frantic mobilization yielded mixed results. Doug Huron, White House associate legal counsel to President Carter and liaison to the Justice Department for *Bakke*, conceded that the commentary was "inconclusive" and possibly damaging to Asian American interests. Yet he agreed only to pass along their apprehensions to DOJ. Terry Adamson, special assistant to the attorney general, was less sympathetic. He disputed the charges that the brief wounded Asian Americans, instead saying that their atypicality indicated good reason to remand the case back to the lower court. Adamson did, however, pledge to confer with Solicitor General Wade McCree, who would represent the United States before the Supreme Court. Frustrated at their lack of muscle, one of the emissaries reflected that "sympathetic and just arguments are no substitutes for real or perceived political power necessary to bring change."[70]

Then, unexpectedly, the delegates received a bit of good news: Solicitor General McCree had backpedaled. McCree told the justices that the DOJ did not intend to boot Asian Americans from special admissions; the brief meant only to gesture to the "sparseness of the record" on anti-Asian discrimination. Meanwhile, California senator Alan Cranston had urged the DOJ to spell out its policy on Asian Americans and affirmative action.[71]

In the end, however, the definitive clarification sought by Asian American community leaders never materialized. The Carter administration did not officially define Asian Americans as a "disadvantaged" racial group entitled to corrective outreach. Such an endorsement might have served as legal armor fending off future misgivings about their standing in the affirmative action schema.

The Supreme Court only muddled the situation even more. The justices latched on to DOJ's insinuation that Asian Americans might not be "underrepresented." Chief Justice Warren Burger and Associate Justice Lewis Powell both inquired about the "29.1% " of all Asian Americans who held white-collar positions, a figure "substantially higher than their proportion of the total population." McCree explained that the figure was a "generic" one that did not break down into specific ethnic groups, and that the numbers for any one might be much lower. Justice Powell pushed back: "Well, on its face, the 29 percent hardly would support any ready conclusion that there's pervasive discrimination against people of

Asian ancestry, isn't that so?" Again, McCree restated how "sparse" relevant data was with regard to Asian Americans. Seemingly unconvinced,
Chief Justice Burger then wondered whether or not "Orientals, as one
identifiable group, have been disadvantaged." Associate Justice William
Rehnquist chimed in, wanting more specificity: "Is there anything in this
record to show that there are not a substantial number of Orientals in
medicine, in teaching, and in law?" Rehnquist answered himself: "Probably higher than in any of the other categories."[72]

The final *Bakke* verdict, delivered June 1978, reflected this skepticism.
The Supreme Court hedged in a 5–4 split. It decreed that the use of explicit racial quotas in admissions vetting was unconstitutional but also
that race could be one of a number of acceptable considerations in the
interest of "the attainment of a diverse student body."[73] Delivering the
touchstone opinion, Associate Justice Powell ruminated on the tricki-
ness of drawing bright lines between "majority" and "minority" for the
purposes of affirmative action, as both concepts "necessarily reflected
temporary arrangements and political judgments."[74] It was imperative
that institutions justify their divisions. He pointed to UC Davis Medical
School as a problematic example, noting that the university was "unable"
to say why only African Americans, Latinos, American Indians, and Asian
Americans were special admissions eligible. The "inclusion" of Asians
was "especially curious" given that "substantial numbers" had been accepted via standard admissions.[75] The messaging by APAFEC and the
delegation had not trickled up far enough.

In grappling with the "fraught" mechanics of designating "preferences," Powell recalled the remarks of Associate Justice William Douglas
weighing in on *DeFunis v. Odegaard* (1974), an earlier affirmative action
case involving the University of Washington law school. Warning of
the problem of "determin[ing] whether an individual is a member of a
favored group," Douglas had predicted the possibility of endless "competing claims." Japanese Americans, excluded from Washington's affirmative action outreach at the time, were a prime example. How was their
eligibility to be determined? Should the ugly history of anti-Japanese animosity matter if Japanese Americans currently made up 2 percent of the
state's population *and* 2 percent of the bar—a perfect statistical mirror?
Such a scenario prophesied future battles hinging on the characterization of Asian Americans as an "overrepresented" minority group. It au-
gured how Asian Americans would increasingly challenge proportionality as a foundational premise of affirmative action—and racial justice
more broadly—after *Bakke*.[76]

4. The 1980s: Overrepresentation Gains Traction

In *Bakke*'s wake, Anthony Kahng, a founding member of the nonprofit Asian American Legal Defense, conducted a postmortem for the community magazine *Bridge* with any eye toward the fallout for Asian Americans.[77] Kahng fervently dismissed the Supreme Court's doubts about including Asian Americans in special admissions. He shot down DOJ's initial claim of "no apparent underrepresentation" of Asian Americans in medicine by spotlighting the distinction between the homegrown and the foreign-born and educated.[78] "How can we explain the irony of the situation in which some disadvantaged Asian Americans students are excluded from the special admissions program because our 'imported' Asian doctors *overrepresent* in the medical profession?" he fumed.[79]

The objection was indeed ironic. Pointing to the "overrepresentation" of immigrant professionals to deflate DOJ's judgment reinforced the idea that certain groups' access to desirable and scarce resources and opportunities could be a problem in need of restraint. (To be fair, Kahng attacked the "profit-motivated medical industry" for recruiting from Asia as a source of cheaper labor rather than opening up medical careers to greater numbers of Americans. Moreover, he noted, foreign personnel commonly faced discrimination in the US workplace.)[80] Kahng's analysis was also prophetic. As trans-Pacific migration flows continued unabated, driven by the exigencies of US capital, Asians would become more tightly associated with the irritant of overrepresentation.

The casting of Asian Americans as "overrepresented" stuck in the 1980s as demographic shifts collided with diversity imperatives and Asian American vigilance around the issue of undergraduate admissions. Prominent universities coast to coast fell under scrutiny when Asian American whistleblowers dug for empirical evidence of bias against Asian applicants. In 1983 Brown University's Asian American Association investigated its own institution and ascertained that the acceptance rate of Asian Americans lagged well behind overall percentages—a clear indication of "prima facie racial discrimination."[81] Brown administrators justified this discrepancy by claiming that Asian Americans were already "overrepresented" in the student body.[82] Brown's Asian American Association also partnered with the East Coast Asian Student Union (ECASU), an interschool network, to compare circumstances across twenty-five different campuses. ECASU detected parallel trends up and down the Atlantic seaboard. Even as applications from Asian Americans had jumped over the past five years, their matriculation numbers had hardly budged.[83]

The 1984 decision by the University of California, Berkeley (UCB) to drop Asian Americans from affirmative action in admissions further cemented the notion of Asian American "overrepresentation" in mainstream culture. A decade earlier the state legislature had charged the university with composing its undergraduate student body to "reflect" the ethnic, gender, and socioeconomic balance of California's high school graduates. As the state's population continued to boom, demand for seats at the most elite campuses (UCB and UCLA) outpaced availability. Administrators realized that they would need to revamp the admissions formula, up until then based primarily on academic criteria, to fulfill the state mandate for African Americans and Latinos in particular. They opted to weigh more heavily "underrepresentation," now treated interchangeably with "disadvantage."[84] At the same moment, UCB saw a steep decline in Asian American enrollment—a 21 percent drop from the previous year, despite the university's own projections to the contrary.[85]

Suspecting that discrimination was at play, Asian American watchers pressed the administration for accountability and "fair representation." Ever on guard, Berkeley professor Ling-chi Wang (one of the nine-member 1977 *Bakke* delegation) mustered the Asian American Task Force on University Admissions to probe the reasons for the plummet. For Wang and his allies, affirmative action was *not* the cause; rather, it was absolutely necessary "to correct past injustices."[86] The task force accused the university of purposely redesigning its vetting protocol to discourage Asian American admittees. It claimed that criteria such as a minimum SAT verbal score, the foreign-language requirement and the use of "supplemental criteria" (extracurricular involvement) hurt otherwise "highly qualified" immigrant, refugee, and non–native English-speaking Asian aspirants.[87]

As at Brown, UC officials held that Asian Americans had exceeded their demographic benchmark.[88] "Asians are overrepresented by three times their high school population. How will the university justify overrepresenting Asians at the expense of others?" asked Frank S. Baratta, Berkeley's research coordinator for admissions and services. His explanation suggested a sense of misplaced entitlement: "But because they've been overrepresented over the years, they've come to expect more of the same."[89] University of California president David Gardner made clear that "the Caucasian student" was now threatened as a new underrepresented group. "Changes are needed because Asians comprise more than 20 percent of the undergraduate enrollment at UC campuses but make up only six percent of the state's population," he warned.[90]

By the mid-1980s, audits of Asian American overrepresentation had spilled far beyond rarefied ivory-tower settings. Media outlets took interest in the "astonishing... extent to which Asian-Americans have become prominent out of all proportion to their share of the population."[91] Some even reframed overrepresentation as something to be praised, factual proof of the immigrant dream much like Jews in the earlier twentieth century.[92] "No matter what their route, young Asian Americans ... are setting the educational pace for the rest of America and cutting a dazzling figure at the country's finest schools," marveled *Time's* 1987 cover story "The New Whiz Kids." "By almost every educational gauge, young Asian Americans are soaring"—from math SAT scores to GPAs, amount of hours spent on homework, numbers of advanced high school courses, graduation rates, and enrollments such as Berkeley's "astonishing 25%."[93] Journalistic accounts were often sympathetic to Asian Americans' claims of stereotyping, discrimination, and quotas ("they're all pre-med, and there are too many").[94]

Conservative commentators in particular pounced on the opportunity to deploy Asian American "overrepresentation" to swipe at affirmative action. "Racial preference is now being used against the wrong people," lamented Daniel Seligman in *Fortune* (1989). "In the pregnant word at the core of affirmative action logic, they are 'overrepresented' on campus." Seligman found ceilings on Asian American enrollments distasteful. He used this as a jumping-off point to assert that limits on the "'best and ablest'" white students—that is, affirmative action—were absurd too.[95] This tethering of the overrepresentation and affirmative action critiques was a shrewd rhetorical move, one that would return with renewed vigor in the new millennium.

5. The "New Asian American Civil War"

After a relative calm in the 1990s and early 2000s,[96] the Asian American admissions controversy bubbled up once again. On the surface, the latest iteration echoes older ones. Once again Asian Americans are accusing universities of unlawful discrimination, rooted in false stereotypes. As before, they seek federal intervention to right perceived wrongs and to ensure fairness and equal opportunity. And like its forerunner, the resuscitation revolves largely around the question of Asian American "overrepresentation."[97]

But this is not simply history repeating itself. There are two arresting distinctions. First, *non-Asians* in addition to Asian Americans have been at the forefront of making discrimination claims and seeking government intervention. Second, the Asian Americans now most animated by the admissions question have called for the abolition—rather than expansion—of affirmative action. So not only has the cast of characters switched up, but the normative worldviews of those crying foul today also clash with those of their 1970s and 1980s predecessors.

Asian Americans' status as an "overrepresented"—and wronged—minority now serves as a linchpin of affirmative action *takedowns* by opponents who have not otherwise taken a deep interest in the Asian American community. Mentioning anti-Asian discrimination conveniently allows for a critique of racial considerations as harmful to *minorities* as well as whites. In 2008 Abigail Fisher, a white woman, charged the University of Texas with refusing her entry because of her race. *Fisher v. University of Texas* eventually found its way to the Supreme Court in 2012. In her suit she invoked Asian Americans—whom she depicted as similarly victimized—no fewer than twenty-two times. Fisher argued that they, like whites, encountered racial roadblocks in an affirmative action–minded selection system designed to prioritize African Americans and Hispanics.[98] The Supreme Court first remanded Fisher back to the lower court for review in 2013, and in 2016 finally ruled in 4–3 favor of the university. In a heated dissent, Justice Samuel Alito reproached the majority—which had not found Texas's protocol guilty of discriminating against Asian Americans—for reasoning that "defies the laws of mathematics." Perhaps, he suggested, they brushed it off as "benign" since Asian Americans were "overrepresented" at UT.[99]

Conservative diehard Edward Blum had masterminded *Fisher* as part of a bigger plan to demolish affirmative action and voting protections for racial minority groups.[100] In 2005 Blum, who is white, founded the Project on Fair Representation, a self-described nonprofit venture "designed to support litigation that challenges racial and ethnic classifications and preferences in state and federal courts."[101] As *Fisher* stalled, Blum—not only the father but also director and sole member of the Project on Fair Representation—devised an offshoot named Students for Fair Admissions to advance his agenda from another vantage point: that of Asian Americans.

Students for Fair Admissions has ingeniously repurposed the notion of overrepresentation, placing Asian Americans at the center of its ambition to "restore the original principles of our nation's civil rights movement." Its goal is to eliminate race and ethnicity as factors in college admissions.[102] Blum launched three websites to recruit Asian Americans: Harvard University Not Fair; The University of North Carolina at Chapel Hill Not Fair; and The University of Wisconsin–Madison Not Fair. The homepage of each one conspicuously features a closeup photo of what look to be Asian American college students—library bookshelf in the background, laptop open, notebook in hand—looking pensive or determined. Next to it, a suggestive, bolded proposition: "Were you denied admission to Harvard [or UNC or UW]? It may be because you're the wrong race."[103]

In November 2014, with some 125 members on board, Students for Fair Admissions (SFFA) sued Harvard for violating the Fourteenth Amendment (guaranteeing equal protection) and Title VI of the 1964 Civil Rights Act (barring discrimination on the basis of race, color, and national origin in programs and activities receiving federal financial assistance) by intentionally discriminating against Asian Americans. Recalling the institution's infamous anti-Semitism in the 1920s and 1930s, the lawsuit accused Harvard of "engaging in a campaign of invidious discrimination by strictly limiting the number of Asian Americans it will admit each year and by engaging in racial balancing year after year."[104] SFFA alleged that the school's "holistic" admissions approach "disguise[s] the fact it holds Asian Americans to a far higher standard than other students and essentially forces them to compete against each other for admission"— a practice tantamount to "'illegitimate racial prejudice or stereotype.'"[105]

SFFA portrayed Harvard's treatment of Asian Americans as deeply worrisome and unjust. (It quoted Henry Rosovsky, a former dean of the Faculty of Arts and Sciences, who once apparently described them as "no-doubt the most over-represented group in the university.") After some forty years of "intentional discrimination" against Asian Americans, Harvard continued to "artificially limit the number of Asian Americans to whom it will offer admission" despite "stronger qualifications" compared to "all other" racial groups, including whites.[106] "Ironically, then," SFFA concluded, "the most *underrepresented* group of admitted students relative to the applicant pool is the most *overrepresented* racial or ethnic group among top academic performers."[107]

How did this happen? SFFA blamed "racial balancing," or the engineering of cohorts "to ensure proportional representation of the various racial and ethnic groups present in Harvard's student body."[108] The goal was not to achieve "diversity"—itself a noble pursuit—but rather to "keep white enrollment more than twice as high as Asian-American enrollment." Indeed if the admissions process were not rigged against Asian Americans, Harvard would actually be *more* diverse because the student body would have more Asians and fewer whites.[109] (Reminiscent of the 1970s and 1980s Asian American activists, SFFA also made the point that Asian Americans themselves were an eclectic lot. Harvard's regard of them as not only interchangeable but "overrepresented" unjustly flattened this variation.)[110]

The solution to this injustice, then, was to eliminate "racial preferences" in admissions altogether. Implementing "race-neutral alternatives," such as the recruitment of poor and disadvantaged students or taking into account parental education, wealth, or even zip code, would still guarantee "diversity" on campus.[111]

Skeptics castigated Blum's brainchild as a cover for hobbling affirmative action rather than a sincere interest in Asian American civil rights.[112] 18MR (short for "18 Million Rising"), a progressive Asian American network, immediately circulated an online petition in protest: "Q: Why does this man think he can speak for Asian American students? A: He thinks we won't realize we're pawns in his racist agenda. . . . *Support affirmative action today.*"[113]

Yet Blum had clearly tapped into a discontent already seeping through many Asian American circles. Yale University freshman Jian Li filed a complaint with the Department of Education's Office of Civil Rights in 2006, claiming that Princeton University had discriminated against him in the admissions process by treating his Chinese ethnicity as a liability. The school had denied him a spot despite his impeccable credentials in part because of preferences for African Americans and Latinos (as well as legacy applicants and athletes). "Theoretically, affirmative action is supposed to take spots away from white applicants and redistribute them to underrepresented minorities," Li said. "What's happening is one segment of the minority population is losing places to another segment of minorities, namely Asians to underrepresented minorities."[114]

In 2011 an unnamed Indian American youth—also the son of immigrants—raised a similar grievance against Princeton as well as Harvard.[115] The Office of Civil Rights combined the second case with Li's in a wider probe of Princeton's admissions practices. (It closed the Harvard investigation after the young man withdrew his accusation.) After years of scrutiny, OCR finally determined in September 2015 that there was "no evidence of the different treatment of Asian applicants."[116]

By then, however, the issue had transcended isolated individuals and energized sizable numbers of Asian Americans. For the first *Fisher v. University of Texas* Supreme Court hearing in 2012, five Asian American organizations submitted objections to race considerations in college admissions. Among them was the National Federation of Indian American Associations, an umbrella covering some two hundred entities nationwide.[117] In May 2014, Chinese American organizations, including lobbying group 80–20 Educational Foundation and the Silicon Valley Chinese Association, rallied more than a hundred thousand individuals to block the passage of California's SCA-5. The legislation would have allowed for the reinstatement of race-conscious admissions in the state's public universities and colleges — outlawed in 1996 by California's Proposition 209.[118]

On the heels of the SFFA lawsuit, sixty-four groups merged as the Coalition of Asian-American Associations to voice their own quarrel with the Department of Justice and the Department of Education's Office of Civil Rights in May 2015.[119] Parroting SFFA, the coalition charged Harvard with "systematic discrimination" against Asian applicants.[120] Like SFFA, it wanted racial stereotypes, biases, quotas, and balancing to be purged from the university's admissions assessments.[121] (The document replicated chunks of SFFA's suit, suggesting that Blum served as a spiritual if not an in-real-life political adviser.)

Notably, the coalition reframed Asian American overrepresentation into a salute to Asian American over*achievement*. The paper highlighted Asian Americans' "rapid growth" since the 1970s and 1980s, a trend driven by the normalization of relations between the People's Republic of China and the technology industry boom. Both factors propelled the spike in "well-educated" Asian (especially Chinese) immigrants focused on their children's education and, therefore, "high-performing Asian American students." The coalition piled on example upon example of prestigious academic awards earned by these youth nationwide. Asians made up only 11 percent of California's high school students but 60 percent of the state's National Merit Scholarship semifinalists; the "over-representation" in New York was similarly "enormous," with Asian American students — many from impoverished backgrounds — making up one-third of the state's top scorers. This "massively disproportionate" ratio held true across a range of competitions, from the US Math Olympiad Team to the Intel Science Talent Search and the US Presidential Scholars.[122]

Their dazzling accomplishments, however, had not yielded more coveted spots on Ivy League campuses. In fact, the coalition asserted, the very opposite had occurred. Asian Americans suffered two "distinct disadvantage[s]." They were not counted as "under-represented minorit[ies]" eligible for affirmative action. More than that, if applicants too closely resembled the Asian stereotype (high math and science scores, mediocre English scores, skimpy extracurriculars, future doctors/engineers/scientists), admissions officers were likely to "treat you as part of the 'Asian invasion.'" Students not rejected outright were forced to "compete against other Asian applicants . . . rather than against the applicant pool as a whole."[123] The upshot? At Harvard, Asian Americans (17 percent) were *"massively underrepresented* ... in relation to their share of the applicant pool" and "in relation to the share of the highly qualified portion [46 percent] of Harvard's applicant pool."[124]

All told, these misalignments evinced the "shocking ... violat[ion]" of Asian American "civil rights" by Harvard and its elite counterparts. This "patently unconstitutional" activity recalled the historical malevolence of the 1882 Chinese Exclusion Act and the internment of Japanese Americans during World War II. The coalition beseeched federal authorities to arbitrate. It averred that race has no place in admissions (though it grudgingly admitted that class might be considered). "Illegal" discrimination not only threated Asian Americans but imperiled "meritocracy, one of the fundamental values that make America the greatest nation in the world."[125]

While the coalition claims to speak for all Asians in the United States, the reality is far messier. Independent journalist Emil Guillermo has dubbed affirmative action the "new Asian American civil war," a wedge issue "practically nuclear, an atom splitter for the community."[126] After the coalition leveled its objections against Harvard, 130 *other* Asian American groups spoke out in defense of affirmative action.[127] But that did not detract from the event's significance as the first time so many Asian Americans rallied to contest affirmative action on the national stage. In May 2016, emboldened with double the number of cosigners, the coalition similarly faulted Yale, Brown, Columbia, and Cornell Universities and Dartmouth College of acting in the same unscrupulous manner as Harvard.[128]

The SFFA/coalition's muscular pushback has gained dramatic momentum, placing Asian Americans squarely in the eye of the firestorm. In August 2017 the US Department of Justice announced that it would begin probing, if not litigating, "intentional race-based discrimination" in college and university admissions in response to the coalition's complaint of anti-Asian conduct.[129] Within months, Harvard grudgingly relinquished six years' worth of confidential records pertaining to 160,000 applicants to DOJ for scrutiny.[130]

Blum and his collaborators (allowed access due to the ongoing lawsuit) mined the documents for ammunition. They found that Asian American hopefuls ranked the highest among all racial and ethnic groups in terms of academics, standardized test scores, extracurricular activities, and alumni interview ratings. But the same contenders were hobbled by "holistic" admissions criteria such as "positive personality" traits. Not least, SFFA pointed to a 2013 internal study by Harvard that had projected Asian

Americans would have constituted 43 percent of the incoming class if such nonacademic criteria had been factored out—incontrovertible evidence of anti-Asian evaluation patterns, SFFA charged. Harvard rebuffed the allegations as "dangerously inaccurate," disavowed any racial discrimination in its screening process, and flagged a 29 percent hike in the admissions rate of Asian Americans over the previous decade.[131]

Those who were already convinced that Asians were unfairly saddled with a racial "tax" or "penalty" in the college admissions chase swatted away this counterargument. The 80-20 Educational Foundation, a coalition affiliate, celebrated the confirmation of its longtime suspicions of anti-Asian bias: "Harvard didn't have to publish its admissions data [back] then. So it could hide behind lies and myths and make suckers out of those establishment-centric AsAms. However, thanks to the lawsuit filed by SFFA, which forced Harvard to show its admission data, Harvard's discrimination against AsAms has been thoroughly exposed."[132]

In this tug-of-war between the SFFA/coalition bloc and "establishment-centric AsAms"—presumably the more traditionally civil rights–oriented stakeholders—the former now wields significant power in fashioning the narrative around Asian Americans and race. Their influence—boosted by political winds shifting in their favor[133]—has forced the opposition to take the defensive. Leading social scientists, for instance, launched the AAPI Data project in 2013 to provide "rigorous and accurate" policy research and analysis of Asian American and Pacific Islander demographic information to journalists, public officials, and the general public.[134] Their messaging— and that of other center-left Asian American institutions[135]—consistently accentuates the fact that the majority of Asian Americans support affirmative action.[136] The question is: if quantitative data helped to generate this predicament, can it also help to eradicate it?

The conundrum of Asian American "overrepresentation" remains as contentious and inconclusive as it has been from its beginnings. The disagreements rooted in this characterization accentuate the deadlock when fairness is primarily measured in terms of body counts. The notion that racial groups can be "underrepresented" or "overrepresented" has been decidedly useful in drawing attention to the sprawling barriers that have long thwarted opportunity and dignity for African Americans. But statistical mirroring also founders because its rationale holds to the same standard myriad situations and peoples with different histories, desires, and approaches to enfranchisement and justice. It straitjackets a problem that is inherently fluid. The challenge for Americans in the twenty-first century will be to figure out a more flexible yardstick for determining and achieving equity, one that can retain proportionality thinking where it supports accurate diagnoses of domination but also move beyond it where it does not.

6. Coda

The national outcry seeking "#Justice4Liang" that erupted as a counterpoint to the Black Lives Matter movement exposed a jarring incongruity between Asian Americans and African Americans. Peter Liang, a twenty-seven-year old Chinese American New York Police Department officer, fatally shot Akai Gurley in a stairwell of the Louis H. Pink Houses housing project in Brooklyn on November 20, 2014. Gurley, a twenty-eight-year old African American man, was unarmed at the time. Liang was charged with manslaughter three months later.

Chinese Americans across the United States—largely recent immigrants who are educated professionals[137]—decried Liang's indictment, conviction, and sentencing. As of April 2016, some 123,000 signatures had been collected on the White House petition "Demand Brooklyn District Attorney Kenneth P. Thompson to withdraw indictment against Asian minority Office Peter Liang!"[138] Demonstrations in more than thirty cities took place in February 2016. His backers argued that Liang was not given a fair shake by the criminal justice system. They maintained that prosecutors used him as a "scapegoat" because of his Asian ancestry. In their view, Liang suffered harsher scrutiny than white officers did in similar situations.[139] He became the first NYPD officer in more than ten years to be found guilty for an on-duty killing—a tragic twist on over-representation.

Observers quickly noted the weight of the protests. The scale seemed remarkable for a population not generally associated with political activity.[140] Such a huge mobilization had not been seen among Asian Americans of any ethnicity since the 1992 Los Angeles riots, when many Korean businesses were destroyed. Marchers bore placards bearing famous civil rights slogans ("Injustice anywhere is a threat to justice everywhere").[141] "Enough is enough. It's time we should get the same treatment, the same respect, as everyone else," one of the organizers asserted.[142] Yet plainly this was not a tidy, miniaturized parallel to the black freedom movement. As Jay Caspian Kang mused in the *New York Times Magazine*, "No amount of nuance or qualification or appeal to Martin Luther King will change the fact that the first massive, nationwide Asian-American protest in years was held in defense of a police officer who shot and killed an innocent black man."[143]

For those Asian Americans who believe that their community *must* rally behind Black Lives Matter—see #Asians4BlackLives[144]—these developments have been intensely frustrating and alarming. They have also not been surprising. The history of Asian Americans and affirmative action both previewed and fed this rupture. Tellingly, some Peter Liang supporters had cut their political teeth on the successful 2014 drive to block the reinstatement of affirmative action in California's public post-secondary institutions (SCA-5). Others have tried to torpedo the dis-aggregation of "Asian American" demographic data along ethnic lines (a move they view as hurting their children's chances in college admissions)[145] and consideration of race in the selection criteria for New York City's elite public schools.[146]

But fracturing can be constructive as well as destructive. It may well be that this moment steers us in untrodden directions, testing innovative approaches for reckoning with centuries of white supremacy, centuries that ironically also hold the history of abolitionism. In the days after Ferguson, progressive activist Soya Jung urgently beckoned those of us who exist in the gaps between blackness and whiteness: "Our options are invisibility, complicity, or resistance, and black rage is a clarion call for standing on the correct side of the color line, for reaping the collective rewards of justice."[147]

Notes

1. The online edition of this op-ed by Yascha Mounk is dated November 24, 2014.

2. *Students for Fair Admissions, Inc., v. President and Fellows of Harvard College*, December 17, 2014.

3. Twitter, November 25, 2014, 6:04 a.m., https://twitter.com/nicole_soojung/status/537245524458737664.

4. For contrasting takes ("top-down" versus "bottom-up" narratives on the spread of affirmative action), see Graham, *Civil Rights Era*; McLean, *Freedom Is Not Enough*.

5. See for instance Payne, *I've Got the Light of Freedom*; Ransby, *Ella Baker and the Black Freedom Movement*; Joseph, *Waiting 'til the Midnight Hour*.

6. Omatsu, "The 'Four Prisons' and the Movements of Liberation"; Maeda, *Chains of Babylon*; Ishizuka, *Serve the People*; and Chang, foreword to Ishizuka, *Serve the People*.

7. On the long history of racial management by the governments of the world's developed economies, see Hanchard, *Spectre of Race*.

8. Orlans, "Politics of Minority Statistics"; Skrentny, *Minority Rights Revolution*.

9. Gleason, "Minorities (Almost) All."

10. Wu, *Color of Success*, 244. Moynihan referred specifically to Chinese and Japanese Americans.

11. Hammerman, "Affirmative-Action Stalemate," 131. Hammerman used this example to argue against Nathan Glazer's proposal to eliminate Hispanics and Asians from affirmative action categories, a move that "would not be acceptable now or in the foreseeable future."

12. Loss, *Between Citizens and the State*, 165–234.

13. John D. Skrentny notes that proportional representation is a "hallmark" of affirmative action. See Skrentny, *Minority Rights Revolution*, 87; and Anderson, *Pursuit of Fairness*, 124–25.

14. Pitkin, *Concept of Representation*, 3.

15. Pitkin, *Concept of Representation*, 8, 10, 60–91.

16. Urbinati, *Representative Democracy*, 40–42. On "voice" and minority populations, see Williams, *Voice, Trust, and Memory*.

17. Skrentny, *Ironies of Affirmative Action*, 162–63.

18. Igo, *Averaged American*, 5.

19. Skrentny, *Ironies of Affirmative Action*, 127–33, 142–44.

20. Skrentny, *Minority Rights Revolution*, 87; Anderson, *Pursuit of Fairness*, 124–25.

21. See for example Alexander, *New Jim Crow*; Coates, "Black Family in the Age of Mass Incarceration."

22. Hinton, *From the War on Poverty to the War on Crime*, 5.

23. Hinton, *From the War on Poverty to the War on Crime*, 5.

24. Alexander, *New Jim Crow*, 1–19.

25. On statistics as discourse, see Starr, "Sociology of Official Statistics"; Porter, *Trust in Numbers*. Muhammad, *Condemnation of Blackness*; and Igo, *Averaged American*, are incisive examples of the cultural and social impact of statistics in the twentieth-century United States.

26. Iyer, *We Too Sing America*, 21–22.

27. See for instance Muhammad, *Condemnation of Blackness*, 1–14.

28. Wu, *Color of Success*, 2.

29. Donna S. Tamanaha, letter to Patsy Mink, February 10, 1974, Folder 10, Box 673, Mink Papers. The UW Asian Union coalesced in the spring and summer months of 1973, and in fall 1973 it registered officially as a campus organization. The UW newsletter *Rice Paper* noted that a prior Asian American group had existed at UW but had "dissolved over the anti-war issue." "Madison Asian Union," *Rice Paper* 1, no. 1 (Summer 1974): 5–6, MSU, Radicalism Collection.

30. D. Tamanaha Miller, Asian American Students, letter to Chancellor H. Edwin Young, August 24, 1973, Edwin Young papers, Series 4/21/1, Chancellor Edwin Young, General Subject Files, Box 143, Folder Minority Students, General, UWM. Special thanks to David Null for locating the primary sources from the University of Wisconsin–Madison University Archives.

31. Cyrena N. Pondrom, letter to D. Tamanaha Miller, August 30, 1973, Edwin Young papers, Series 4/21/1, Chancellor Edwin Young, General Subject Files, Box 143, Folder Minority Students, General, UWM.

32. Pondrom to Tamanaha Miller, August 30, 1973.

33. Tom Hibino, letter to Edwin Young, November 29, 1973, Edwin Young Papers, Series 4/21/1, Chancellor Edwin Young, General Subject Files, Box 143, Folder Minority Students, General, UWM. On minority programs at UW ca. 1971, see Merritt J. Norvell Jr., "Madison Campus: Operative Committees Concerned with Equal Education Opportunities," 1971, unpublished report, UWM. On the closing of the minority student centers, see UW Office of the Dean of Students, memorandum to "Members of the University Community," August 24, 1973, Edwin Young Papers, Series 4/21/1, Chancellor Edwin Young, General Subject Files, Box 143, Folder Minority Students, General, UWM.

34. Patsy T. Mink, letter to Edwin Young, February 25, 1974, Folder 10, Box 673, Mink papers.

35. Henry S. Reuss, letter to Edwin Young, March 1, 1974, Edwin Young Papers, Series 4/21/1, Chancellor Edwin Young, General Subject Files, Box 143, Folder Minority Students, General, UWM; Robert W. Kastenmeier, letter to Edwin Young, March 4, 1974, Edwin Young Papers, Series 4/21/1, Chancellor Edwin Young, General Subject Files, Box 143, Folder Minority Students, General, UWM.

36. Edwin Young to Patsy Mink, February 28, 1974, Folder 10, Box 673, Mink papers. See also Patrick J. Lucey to Patsy Mink, March 19, 1972, Folder 10, Box 673, Mink Papers.

37. John C. Weaver, letter to Robert W. Kastenmeier, March 18, 1974, Edwin Young Papers, Series 4/21/1, Chancellor Edwin Young, General Subject Files, Box 143, Folder Minority Students, General, UWM.

38. Haskett, "Asian Union Works for Minority Status."

39. Haskett, "Asian Union Works for Minority Status."

40. Haskett, "Outreach for Asian Students."

41. Haskett, "Asian Union Works for Minority Status."

42. Haskett, "Outreach for Asian Students."

43. Moesel, "Asian Student[s] Gain Minority Status."

44. AABA amicus brief at 2. Lee, "De-minoritization of Asian Americans," is a pioneering study on the historical trajectory of Asian Americans' "minority" status between the 1960s and 1980s. I use several of the same sources as she does, particularly in regard to *Bakke*. I am also interested in similar questions, such as the evolution in Asian Americans' "minority" status. Lee argues that Asians effectively became "de-minoritized" in the UC system's admissions policies. In contrast, I argue the "overrepresentation" is a more useful analytical category (despite its problems as a policy category) because it underscores the continuing nonwhiteness of Asians and the anxieties that have accompanied the prospect of "too many" Asians.

45. AABA amicus brief at 3.

46. AABA amicus brief at 5.

47. AABA amicus brief at 12–13, 15.

48. AABA amicus brief at 13–14.

49. AABA amicus brief at 15–16 (also quoted in Lee, "De-minoritization of Asian Americans," 137).

50. AABA amicus brief at 16.

51. AABA amicus brief at 1.

52. Stu Eizenstat and Bob Lipshutz, memorandum to Jimmy Carter, subject: The Bakke Brief, September 6, 1977, Folder: Bakke Case, 9/77, Container 33, Series: Hamilton Jordan's Confidential Files, Office of the Chief of Staff Files, Carter Presidential Library, http://www.jimmycarterlibrary.gov/digital_library/cos/142099/33/cos_142099_33_07-Bakke_Case_9-77.pdf (hereafter Carter Library).

53. US DOJ amicus brief at 3.

54. US DOJ amicus brief at 46–47n51(also cited in Lee, "De-minoritization of Asian Americans," 138–39).

55. US DOJ amicus brief at 46–47n51 (also cited in Lee, "De-minoritization of Asian Americans," 138–39).

56. US DOJ amicus brief at 47 n51.

57. US DOJ amicus brief at 70–71 (also cited in Lee, "De-minoritization of Asian

Americans," 139). US DOJ amicus brief at 71n82 noted, "The record contains no information with respect to the reason for including Asian-Americans in the special admissions
program, and the University's brief does not discuss Asian-American applicants." DOJ
also noted that the 1974 application form asked applicants whether or not they wished
be considered "minority" applicants but did not explicitly define "minority." A separate section on the application, however, asked applicants, "How do you describe your-
self?" with the available choices being white, Black/Afro American, American Indian,
Mexican-American or Chicano, Oriental/Asian-American, Puerto Rican (Mainland),
Puerto Rican (Commonwealth), Cuban, Other; US DOJ amicus brief, 10n10.

58. US DOJ amicus brief at 70–71 (also cited in Lee, "De-minoritization of Asian
Americans," 139).

59. US DOJ amicus brief at 67–74. Ackerman, "Legality of Voluntary Affirmative
Action," noted this point at 60. Thanks to Heather Gerken for this insight.

60. APAFEC Fact Sheet, 1, Carter Library. Lee, "De-minoritization of Asian Americans," 139–40, also cites the APAFEC fact sheet.

61. APAFEC Fact Sheet, 1.

62. Stephen Thom to Griffin Bell, September 30, 1977, Folder: Asian-Americans [in-
cludes Bakke Case Material] 2/77–10/77 [O/A 4467], Box 60, Office of Public Liaison
(Costanza), Carter Library. Lee, "De-minoritization of Asian Americans," 139–40, also
cites Thom to Bell.

63. APAFEC Fact Sheet, 2–3.

64. APAFEC Fact Sheet, 4–5.

65. APAFEC Fact Sheet, 3.

66. APAFEC Fact Sheet, 3.

67. APAFEC Fact Sheet, 5.

68. "Asian Community Criticizes Government Bakke Brief," 1; "Protest Bakke Brief
Statements," 2.

69. Wang, "White House Hears Asian American Views on Bakke," 1.

70. Wang, "White House Hears Asian American Views on Bakke."

71. Wang, "Government Modifies Stand in Bakke Case Argument," 1–3.

72. Supreme Court exchange recounted in Kahng, "University of California v. Bakke
... Who Won?," 4–14. Lee, "De-minoritization of Asian Americans," 142, also cites Kahng.

73. *Regents of the University of California v. Bakke*, 438 US 265 at 311 (1978) (hereafter
University of California v. Bakke).

74. *University of California v. Bakke* at 295.

75. *University of California v. Bakke* at 309n45 (also cited in Lee, "De-minoritization
of Asian Americans," 141).

76. *University of California v. Bakke* at 297n37.

77. Kahng, "University of California v. Bakke ... Who Won?," 8.

78. Kahng, "University of California v. Bakke ... Who Won?," 8.

79. Kahng, "University of California v. Bakke ... Who Won?," 9 [emphasis added].

80. Kahng, "University of California v. Bakke ... Who Won?," 8–9.

81. Takagi, "From Discrimination to Affirmative Action," 580. Takagi elaborated on
this article in *The Retreat from Race*, which remains the definite study of Asian Americans
and the 1980s admissions debate.

82. Takagi, "From Discrimination to Affirmative Action," 582.

83. Ho and Chin, "Admissions Impossible," cited in Takagi, "From Discrimination to
Affirmative Action," 579–80.

84. Douglass, "Anatomy of Conflict," 127–28.

85. Takagi, "From Discrimination to Affirmative Action," 580.

86. Wang, "Anti-Asian Exclusivism at Univ. of California, Berkeley," *East West*, October 30, 1985, 7–8.

87. Takagi, "From Discrimination to Affirmative Action," 580–82.

88. Douglass, "Anatomy of Conflict," 128; Takagi, "From Discrimination to Affirmative Action," 582–83.

89. Takagi, "From Discrimination to Affirmative Action," 582–83.

90. Takagi, "From Discrimination to Affirmative Action," 582–83.

91. Bell, "Triumph of Asian-Americans."

92. Bell, "Triumph of Asian-Americans"; David Brand, "New Whiz Kids"; "New 'Open Door' at Berkeley"; Winnick, "America's 'Model Minority'"; Shaw, "Counting Asians."

93. Brand, "New Whiz Kids."

94. Brand, "New Whiz Kids"; Levine and Pazner, "On Campus Stereotypes Persist"; Galloway et al., "New 'Open Door' at Berkeley"; Buderi, "Berkeley's Changing Student Population"; Holden, "Concern in Washington."

95. Seligman, "Quotas on Campus."

96. On the role of Asian Americans in affirmative action debates at the University of California and University of Michigan, see Omi and Takagi, "Situating Asian Americans in the Political Discourse on Affirmative Action"; Lee, "De-minoritization of Asian Americans," 145–46.

97. Wang, "Anti-Asian Exclusivism at Univ. of California, Berkeley."

98. Baynes, "Asian American Rift over Supreme Court Affirmative Action Case," Reuters, August 14, 2012.

99. *Fisher v. University of Texas at Austin et al.*, 579 U.S. ___ (2016) at 25, 136 S.Ct. 2198, 195 L.Ed.2d 511 (2016). For an analysis of Asian Americans' amicus briefs for Fisher, see Poon and Segoshi, "Racial Mascot Speaks."

100. Biskupic, "Special Report: Behind US Race Cases, a Little-Known Recruiter"; Biskupic, "Litigious Activist's Latest Cause."

101. Project on Fair Representation website, https://www.projectonfairrepresentation.org/about/ (accessed April 22, 2016).

102. Students for Fair Admissions website, https://studentsforfairadmissions.org/about/ (accessed April 22, 2016).

103. harvardnotfair.org, uncnotfair.org, and uwnotfair.org websites (accessed April 22, 2016).

104. "Project on Fair Representation Announces Lawsuits Challenging Admissions Policies at Harvard Univ. and Univ. of North Carolina–Chapel Hill," Project on Fair Representation. SFFA sued the University of North Carolina the same day, although the UNC lawsuit was not framed specifically as a grievance about discrimination against Asian Americans. But it otherwise raised the same objections as the Harvard lawsuit.

105. Complaint, Students for Fair Admissions, Inc. v. President & Fellows of Harvard Coll., 308 FRD 39 (D. Mass. 2015) (No. 14-cv-14176), at 4 [hereafter SFFA Complaint].

106. SFFA Complaint at 43, 47, 69.

107. SFFA Complaint at 47 (emphasis added).

108. SFFA Complaint at 67.

109. SFFA Complaint at 70.

110. SFFA Complaint at 87–88.

111. SFFA Complaint at 72–75.

112. Mencimer, "Meet the Brains behind the Effort to Get the Supreme Court to Rethink Civil Rights."

113. 18Million Rising, "Edward Blum, We Won't Be Used for Your Racist Agenda!"

114. Golden, "Is Admissions Bar Higher for Asians at Elite Schools?"; Carroll, "Rejected Applicants Alleges Bias against Asians."

115. Golden, "Harvard Targeted in US Asian-American Discrimination Probe."

116. Schmidt, "Federal Investigation Finds No Anti-Asian Bias in Princeton Admissions."

117. Schmidt, "Indian-American Groups Urge Supreme Court to End Race-Conscious Admissions"; Baynes, "Asian American Rift over Supreme Court Affirmative Action Case."

118. Concerned Californians, "Vote No to SCA 5!"; Huang, "SCA 5: A Political Coming of Age for Chinese-Americans"; "Not Black and White"; Yang, "Asian Americans Would Lose Out under Affirmative Action."

119. The Coalition of Asian-American Associations later changed its name to Asian American Coalition for Education.

120. "More Than 60 Asian American Organizations File Complaint against Harvard University"; Coalition of Asian-American Associations, "Complaint against Harvard University and the President and Fellows of Harvard College for Discriminating against Asian-American Applicants in the College Admissions Process," 3 (hereafter Coalition Complaint).

121. Woolf, "Why Are So Many Asian Americans Missing Out on Ivy League Schools?"

122. Coalition Complaint, 4–7.

123. Coalition Complaint, 28–29.

124. Coalition Complaint, 41 (emphasis added).

125. Coalition Complaint, 45–46.

126. Guillermo, "New Asian American Civil War over Affirmative Action?"

127. Noriega, "Asian-American Groups Split over Affirmative-Action Complaint."

128. Asian American Coalition for Education, "130+ Asian American Organizations Filed Civil-Rights-Violation Complaint against Yale University, Brown University and Dartmouth College."

129. Savage, "Justice Dept to Take On Affirmative Action in College Admissions"; Hartocollis and Saul, "Affirmative Action Battle Has New Focus"; Horowitz and Brown, "Justice Department Plans New Project to Sue Universities over Affirmative Action Policies"; Savage, "Asian-Americans' Complaint Prompted Justice Inquiry of College Admissions."

130. Hartocollis, "Harvard Agrees to Turn Over Records amid Discrimination Inquiry."

131. Hartocollis, "Asian-Americans Suing Harvard Say Admissions Files Show Discrimination"; Korn and Hong, "In Harvard Affirmative Action Suit, Filings to Provide Rare Look at Admissions Process"; Hartocollis, "Harvard Rated Asian Americans Lower on Personality Traits, Suit Says."

132. Woo, "Beyond a Doubt—Harvard Discriminates!" (emphasis in original).

133. Anderson and Balingit, "Trump Administration Moves to Rescind Obama-Era Guidance on Race in Admissions."

134. As of July 2018, AAPI Data is directed by founder Karthick Ramakrishnan. The two senior researchers are Janelle Wong and Jennifer Lee.

135. National Council of Asian Pacific Americans, "NCAPA Reaffirms Support for Diversity in Higher Education Admissions."

136. Ramakrishnan and Wong, "Survey Roundup: Asian American Attitudes on Affirmative Action."

137. Wong, "Scapegoated?"

138. "Demand Brooklyn District Attorney Kenneth P. Thompson to withdraw indictment against Asian minority Officer Peter Liang!" An identical petition dated February 12, 2016, garnered more than 101,000 signatures; there is no way to tell if the same individuals signed both petitions. Petitions are archived at https://petitions.obamawhitehouse.archives.gov/?page=3.

139. Justice for Peter Liang website (accessed April 29, 2016).

140. Kang, "How Should Asian Americans Feel about the Peter Liang Protests?" *New York Times Magazine*, February 23, 2016; Wang, "'Awoken' by N.Y. Cop Shooting, Asian American Activists Chart Way Forward," *NPR Code Switch*, April 23, 2016.

141. Bain and Connelly, "Asian and Black Communities Square Off over Cop Prosecution," *New York Post*, February 20, 2016.

142. Rojas, "In New York, Thousands Protest Officer Liang's Conviction."

143. Kang, "How Should Asian Americans Feel about the Peter Liang Protests?"

144. Wang, "'Awoken' by N.Y. Cop Shooting, Asian American Activists Chart Way Forward."

145. Wong, "Scapegoated?"; Mak, "You're Asian Right? Why Are You Even Here?"; Wang, "Racist Bill?"

146. Asian American Coalition for Education, "AACE Condemns de Blasio's Proposed Changes on NYC Specialized High School Admissions Process"; Harris and Hu, "Asian Groups See Bias in Plan to Diversify New York's Elite Schools."

147. Jung, "Why Ferguson Matters to Asian Americans."

Works Cited

ARCHIVAL WORKS

Carter Library = Jimmy Carter Presidential Library and Museum. Atlanta, GA
    Asian and Pacific American Federal Employee Council (APAFEC). "The Bakke Case and Asian Pacific Americans," fact sheet, 1977, 1. Folder: Asian-Americans [includes Bakke Case Material] 2/77–10/77 [O/A 4467], Box 60, Office of Public Liaison (Costanza).
    Stephen Thom to Griffin Bell, September 30, 1977, Folder: Asian-Americans [includes Bakke Case Material] 2/77–10/77 [O/A 4467], Box 60, Office of Public Liaison (Costanza).
    Stu Eizenstat and Bob Lipshutz, memorandum to Jimmy Carter, subject: The Bakke Brief, September 6, 1977, Folder: Bakke Case, 9/77, Container 33, Series: Hamilton Jordan's Confidential Files, Office of the Chief of Staff Files.
Library of Congress, Manuscripts Division
    Patsy T. Mink Papers, 1883–2005. MSS84957.
Michigan State University Libraries, Special Collections, Radicalism Collection
    "Madison Asian Union," *Rice Paper* 1, no. 1 (Summer 1974): 5–6. E184.06 R53.
University of Wisconsin-Madison (UMW) University Archives

Young, Edwin, Papers. Series 4/21/1, Chancellor Edwin Young, General Subject Files, Box 143, Folder Minority Students, General.

Legal Cases and Briefs

Asian American Bar Association (AABA), Greater Bay Area. Brief as Amicus Curiae Supporting Petitioners, *Regents of the University of California v. Bakke*, 438 US 265 at 2 (1978).

Coalition of Asian-American Associations. "Complaint against Harvard University and the President and Fellows of Harvard College for Discriminating against Asian-American Applicants in the College Admissions Process." Submitted to Office of Civil Rights, US Department of Education, and Civil Rights Division, US Department of Justice, May 15, 2015. http://asianamericanforeducation.org/wp-content /uploads/2015/09/Complaint-Against-Harvard-University.pdf.

Fisher v. University of Texas at Austin et al, 579 US ___ (2016) at 25, 136 S.Ct. 2198, 195 L.Ed.2d 511 (2016). Online at https://www.supremecourt.gov/opinions/15pdf /14–981_4g15.pdf.

Regents of the University of California v. Bakke, 438 US 265 at 311(1978).

SFFA Complaint: Complaint, *Students for Fair Admissions, Inc. v. President & Fellows of Harvard Coll.*, 308 FRD 39 (D. Mass. 2015) (no. 14-cv-14176). Available at https:// studentsforfairadmissions.org/project-on-fair-representation-announces-lawsuits -challenging-admissions-policies-at-harvard-univ-and-univ-of-north-carolina -chapel-hill/.

Students for Fair Admissions, Inc., v. President and Fellows of Harvard College (Harvard Corporation); and The Honorable and Reverend the Board of Overseers, December 17, 2014. US District Court for the District of Massachusetts, Boston Division. Available online at https://www.projectonfairrepresentation.org/case/students-for-fair -admissions-v-harvard-university/ (accessed November 21, 2016).

US Department of Justice (DOJ). Brief, as Amicus Curiae, *Regents of the University of California v. Bakke*, 438 US 265 (1978).

Books, Articles, and Web Posts

18Million Rising. "Edward Blum: We Won't Be Used for Your Racist Agenda!" Online petition. http://action.18mr.org/blockblum/ (accessed September 2, 2016).

Ackerman, David M. "The Legality of Voluntary Affirmative Action: Analysis of *Bakke v. The Regents of the University of California*." Congressional Research Service, November 18, 1977.

Alexander, Michelle. *The New Jim Crow: Mass Incarceration in the Age of Colorblindness*. New York: New Press, 2010.

Anderson, Nick, and Moriah Balingit. "Trump Administration Moves to Rescind Obama-Era Guidance on Race in Admissions." *Washington Post*, July 3, 2018.

Anderson, Terry. *The Pursuit of Fairness: A History of Affirmative Action*. New York: Oxford, 2004.

Asian American Coalition for Education. "130+ Asian American Organizations Filed Civil-Rights-Violation Complaint against Yale University, Brown University &

Dartmouth College." May 23, 2016. http://asianamericanforeducation.org/en/pr
_20160523/.
Asian American Coalition for Education. "AACE Condemns de Blasio's Proposed
Changes on NYC Specialized High School Admissions Process." June 6, 2018.
http://asianamericanforeducation.org/pr_20180606/.
"Asian Community Criticizes Government Bakke Brief." EastWest, October 5, 1977, 1.
Bain, Jennifer, and Eileen A. J. Connelly. "Asian and Black Communities Square Off
over Cop Prosecution." New York Post, February 20, 2016. http://nypost.com/2016
/02/20/10000-protesters-rallying-in-support-of-ex-cop-peter-liang/.
Baynes, Terry. "Asian American Rift over Supreme Court Affirmative Action Case."
Reuters, August 14, 2012.
Bell, David A. "The Triumph of Asian-Americans." New Republic 193 (July 15–22): 1985,
24–31.
Biskupic, Joan. "A Litigious Activist's Latest Cause: Ending Affirmative Action at Har-
vard." Reuters, June 8, 2015. http://www.reuters.com/investigates/special-report
/usa-harvard-discrimination/.
Biskupic, Joan. "Special Report: Behind U.S. Race Cases, a Little-Known Recruiter."
Reuters, December 4, 2012.
Brand, David. "The New Whiz Kids." Time, August 31, 1987, 42–46, 49, 51.
Buderi, Robert. "Berkeley's Changing Student Population." Science, August 18, 1989,
694–96.
Carroll, Kate. "Rejected Applicants Alleges Bias against Asians." Daily Princeto-
nian, November 13, 2006. http://dailyprincetonian.com/news/2006/11/rejected
-applicant-alleges-bias-against-asians/.
Chang, Jeff. Foreword to Ishizuka, Serve the People, v–vii.
Chung, Nicole. Twitter post. November 25, 2014, 6:04 a.m. https://twitter.com/nicole
_soojung/status/537245524458737664.
Coalition of Asian-American Associates. "More Than 60 Asian American Organizations File Complaint against Harvard University." Press release, May 15, 2015. http://
asianamericanforeducation.org/en/pr_20150515/.
Coates, Ta-Nehisi. "The Black Family in the Age of Mass Incarceration." Atlantic, October 2015. https://www.theatlantic.com/magazine/archive/2015/10/the-black
-family-in-the-age-of-mass-incarceration/403246/.
Concerned Californians. "Vote No to SCA 5!'" Online petition to California State
Assembly, Change.org. https://www.change.org/p/california-state-assembly-vote
-no-to-sca-5-3 (accessed April 26, 2016).
"Demand Brooklyn District Attorney Kenneth P. Thompson to Withdraw Indictment
against Asian Minority Officer Peter Liang!" petition to Obama White House, created February 17, 2015. https://petitions.obamawhitehouse.archives.gov/petition
/demand-brooklyn-district-attorney-kenneth-p-thompson-withdraw-indictment
-against-asian-minority-officer-peter-liang (accessed January 22, 2019).
Douglass, John Aubrey. "Anatomy of Conflict: The Making and Unmaking of Affirmative Action at the University of California." In Color Lines: Affirmative Action, Immigration, and Civil Rights Options for America, edited by John Skrentny, 127–28. Chicago: University of Chicago Press, 2001.
Galloway, Joseph L., et al. "The New 'Open Door' at Berkeley." US News and World
Report, June 5, 1989, 13.

Gleason, Philip. "Minorities (Almost) All: The Minority Concept in American Social Thought." *American Quarterly* 43, no. 3 (September 1991): 392–424.

Golden, Daniel. "Harvard Targeted in US Asian-American Discrimination Probe." *Bloomberg News*, February 2, 2012. http://www.bloomberg.com/news/articles /2012-02-02/harvard-targeted-in-u-s-asian-american-discrimination-probe.

Golden, Daniel. "Is Admissions Bar Higher for Asians at Elite Schools?" *Wall Street Journal*, November 11, 2006.

Graham, Hugh Davis. *The Civil Rights Era: Origins and Development of National Policy, 1960–1972*. New York: Oxford University Press, 1990.

Guillermo, Emil. "The New Asian American Civil War over Affirmative Action?" Asian American Legal Defense and Education Fund blog, May 14, 2015. http://aaldef.org /blog/emil-guillermo-the-new-asian-american-civil-war-over-affirmative-action .html.

Hammerman, Herbert. "Affirmative-Action Stalemate: A Second Perspective." *Public Interest*, Fall 1988, 130–34.

Hanchard, Michael G. *The Spectre of Race: How Discrimination Haunts Western Democracy*. Princeton, NJ: Princeton University Press, 2018.

Harris, Elizabeth A., and Winnie Hu. "Asian Groups See Bias in Plan to Diversify New York's Elite Schools." *New York Times*, June 5, 2018.

Hartocollis, Anemona. "Asian-Americans Suing Harvard Say Admissions Files Show Discrimination." *New York Times*, April 4, 2018. https://www.nytimes.com/2018/04 /04/us/harvard-asian-admission.html.

Hartocollis, Anemona. "Harvard Agrees to Turn Over Records amid Discrimination Inquiry." *New York Times*, December 1, 2017. https://www.nytimes.com/2017/12 /01/us/harvard-justice-department-discrimination.html.

Hartocollis, Anemona. "Harvard Rated Asian Americans Lower on Personality Traits, Suit Says." *New York Times*, June 15, 2018. https://www.nytimes.com/2018/06/15 /us/harvard-asian-enrollment-applicants.html.

Hartocollis, Anemona, and Stephanie Saul. "Affirmative Action Battle Has New Focus: Asian Americans." *New York Times*, August 2, 2017. https://www.nytimes.com/2017 /08/02/us/affirmative-action-battle-has-a-new-focus-asian-americans.html.

Haskett, Mary Ellen. "Asian Union Works for Minority Status." *Daily Cardinal*, April 5, 1974, 4.

Haskett, Mary Ellen. "Outreach for Asian Students." *Daily Cardinal*, September 27, 1954, 1–2.

Hinton, Elizabeth. *From the War on Poverty to the War on Crime: The Making of Mass Incarceration in America*. Cambridge, MA: Harvard University Press, 2016.

Ho, David, and Margaret Chin. "Admissions Impossible." *Bridge*, Summer 1983, 7–8, 51,

Holden, Constance. "Concern in Washington." *Science* 245, no. 4919 (August 18, 1989): 694–95.

Horowitz, Sari, and Emma Brown. "Justice Department Plans New Project to Sue Universities over Affirmative Action Policies." *Washington Post*, August 1, 2017.

Huang, Josie. "SCA 5: A Political Coming of Age for Chinese-Americans." scpr.org blog, posted March 21, 2014. http://www.scpr.org/blogs/multiamerican/2014/03 /21/16152/sca-5-chinese-americans-immigrants-asian-americans/.

Igo, Sarah E. *The Averaged American: Surveys, Citizens, and the Making of a Mass Public*. Cambridge, MA: Harvard University Press, 2007.

Ishizuka, Karen. *Serve the People: Making Asian America in the Long Sixties*. London: Verso, 2016.

Iyer, Deepa. *We Too Sing America: South Asian, Arab, Muslim, and Sikh Immigrants Shape Our Multiracial Future*. New York: New Press, 2015.

Joseph, Peniel. *Waiting 'til the Midnight Hour: A Narrative History of Black Power in America*. New York: Henry Holt, 2006.

Jung, Soya. "Why Ferguson Matters to Asian Americans." *Race Files* blog, posted August 20, 2014. http://www.racefiles.com/2014/08/20/why-ferguson-matters-to-asian-americans/.

Kahng, Anthony. "University of California v. Bakke ... Who Won?" *Bridge*, Fall 1978, 4–14.

Kang, Jay Caspian. "How Should Asian Americans Feel about the Peter Liang Protests?" *New York Times Magazine*, February 23, 2016. http://www.nytimes.com/2016/02/23/magazine/how-should-asian-americans-feel-about-the-peter-liang-protests.html?_r=0.

Korn, Melissa, and Nicole Hong. "In Harvard Affirmative Action Suit, Filings to Provide Rare Look at Admissions Process." *Wall Street Journal*, June 13, 2018.

Lee, Sharon S. "The De-minoritization of Asian Americans: A Historical Examination of the Representations of Asian Americans in Affirmative Action Admissions Policies at the University of California." *Asian American Law Journal* 15 (January 2008): 129–52.

Levine, Art, with Irit Pazner. "On Campus Stereotypes Persist." *US News and World Report*, March 28, 1988, 53.

Loss, Christopher. *Between Citizens and the State: The Politics of American Higher Education in the 20th Century*. Princeton, NJ: Princeton University Press, 2011.

Maeda, Daryl J. *Chains of Babylon: The Rise of Asian America*. Minneapolis: University of Minnesota Press, 2009.

Mak, Aaron. " 'You're Asian Right? Why Are You Even Here?' " *Politico*, August 23, 2016.

McLean, Nancy. *Freedom Is Not Enough: The Opening of the American Workplace* Cambridge, MA: Harvard University Press and the Russell Sage Foundation, 2006.

Mencimer, Stephanie. "Meet the Brains behind the Effort to Get the Supreme Court to Rethink Civil Rights." *Mother Jones*, March/April 2016. http://www.motherjones.com/politics/2016/04/edward-blum-supreme-court-affirmative-action-civil-rights.

Moesel, Andrew. "Asian Student[s] Gain Minority Status." *Chicago Maroon*, January 23, 2004. http://chicagomaroon.com/2004/01/23/asian-student-gain-minority-status/.

Mounk, Yascha. "Is Harvard Unfair to Asian-Americans?" *New York Times*, November 25, 2014, A27. The online edition of this article is dated November 24, 2014.

Muhammad, Khalil Gibran. *The Condemnation of Blackness: Race, Crime, and the Making of Modern Urban America*. Cambridge, MA: Harvard University Press, 2010.

National Council of Asian Pacific Americans (NCAPA). "NCAPA Reaffirms Support for Diversity in Higher Education Admissions." June 27, 2018. http://www.ncapaonline.org/ncapa_reaffirms_support_for_diversity_in_higher_education_admissions.

"The New 'Open Door' at Berkeley." *US News and World Report*, June 5, 1989, 13.

Noriega, David. "Asian-American Groups Split over Affirmative-Action Complaint." *Buzzfeed*, May 19, 2015.

Norvell, Merritt J., Jr. "Madison Campus: Operative Committees Concerned with Equal Education Opportunities." Unpublished report, 1971, University of Wisconsin–Madison.

"Not Black and White: Asians Object to Affirmative Action." *Economist*, March 22, 2014.

Omatsu, Glenn. "The 'Four Prisons' and the Movements of Liberation: Asian American Activism from the 1960s to 1990s." In *The State of Asian America: Activism and Resistance in the 1990s*, edited by Karin Aguilar San Juan, 19–69. Boston: South End, 1994.

Omi, Michael, and Dana Takagi. "Situating Asian Americans in the Political Discourse on Affirmative Action." Special issue, *Representations* 55 (Summer 1996): 155–62.

Orlans, Harold. "The Politics of Minority Statistics." *Society* 26, no. 4 (May-June 1989): 24–25.

Payne, Charles. *I've Got the Light of Freedom: The Organizing Tradition and the Mississippi Freedom Struggle*. Berkeley: University of California Press, 1995.

Pitkin, Hanna Fenichel. *The Concept of Representation*. Berkeley: University of California Press, 1967.

Poon, O. A., and M. Segoshi. "The Racial Mascot Speaks: A Critical Race Discourse Study of Asian Americans and *Fisher vs. University of Texas*." *Review of Higher Education* 42 (Fall 2018): 235–267.

Porter, Theodore M. *Trust in Numbers: The Pursuit of Objectivity in Science and Public Life*. Princeton, NJ: Princeton University Press, 1995.

Project on Fair Representation. "Project on Fair Representation Announces Lawsuits Challenging Admissions Policies at Harvard Univ. and Univ. of North Carolina-Chapel Hill." https://studentsforfairadmissions.org/project-on-fair-representation -announces-lawsuits-challenging-admissions-policies-at-harvard-univ-and-univ-of -north-carolina-chapel-hill/ (accessed April 22, 2016).

Project on Fair Representation website. https://www.projectonfairrepresentation.org /about/ (accessed April 22, 2016).

"Protest Bakke Brief Statements." Editorial. *EastWest*, October 12, 1977, 2.

Ramakrishnan, Karthick, and Janelle Wong. "Survey Roundup: Asian American Attitudes on Affirmative Action." *Data Bits*, blog for AAPI Data, June 18, 2018. http:// aapidata.com/blog/asianam-affirmative-action-surveys/.

Ransby, Barbara. *Ella Baker and the Black Freedom Movement: A Radical Democratic Vision*. Chapel Hill: University of North Carolina Press, 2003.

Rojas, Rick. "In New York, Thousands Protest Officer Liang's Conviction." *New York Times*, February 20, 2016. http://www.nytimes.com/2016/02/21/nyregion/in-new -york-thousands-protest-officer-liangs-conviction.html?_r=0.

Savage, Charlie. "Asian-Americans' Complaint Prompted Justice Inquiry of College Admissions." *New York Times*, August 2, 2017. https://www.nytimes.com/2017/08 /02/us/politics/asian-americans-complaint-prompted-justice-inquiry-of-college -admissions.html.

Savage, Charlie. "Justice Dept to Take On Affirmative Action in College Admissions." *New York Times*, August 1, 2017. https://www.nytimes.com/2017/08/01/us/politics /trump-affirmative-action-universities.html.

Schmidt, Peter. "Federal Investigation Finds No Anti-Asian Bias in Princeton Admissions." *Chronicle of Higher Education*, September 23, 2015.

Schmidt, Peter. "Indian-American Groups Urge Supreme Court to End Race-Conscious Admissions." *Chronicle of Higher Education,* May 30, 2012.

Seligman, Daniel. "Quotas on Campus." *Fortune,* January 30, 1989, 205–6.

Shaw, Peter. "Counting Asians." *National Review,* September 25, 1995, 50.

Skrentny, John David. *The Ironies of Affirmative Action: Politics, Culture, and Justice in America.* Chicago: University of Chicago Press, 1996.

Skrentny, John D[avid]. *The Minority Rights Revolution.* Cambridge, MA: Belknap / Harvard University Press, 2002.

Starr, Paul. "Sociology of Official Statistics." In *The Politics of Numbers,* edited by William Alonso and Paul Starr, 7–57. New York: Russell Sage Foundation, 1987.

Students for Fair Admissions website. https://studentsforfairadmissions.org/about/ (accessed April 22, 2016).

Takagi, Dana Y. "From Discrimination to Affirmative Action: Facts in the Asian American Admissions Controversy." *Social Problems* 37, no. 4 (November 1990): 578–92.

Takagi, Dana Y. *The Retreat from Race: Asian-American Admissions and Racial Politics.* New Brunswick NJ: Rutgers University Press, 1992.

Urbinati, Nadia. *Representative Democracy: Principles and Genealogy.* Chicago: University of Chicago Press, 2006.

Wang, Hansi Lo. "'Awoken' by N.Y. Cop Shooting, Asian American Activists Chart Way Forward." NPR *Code Switch,* April 23, 2016.

Wang, Hansi Lo. "'Racist Bill'? Chinese Immigrants Protest Effort to Collect More Asian American Data." NPR, August 5, 2017.

Wang, L. Ling-chi. "Anti-Asian Exclusivism at Univ. of California, Berkeley." *EastWest,* October 30, 1985, 7–8.

Wang, Ling-chi. "Government Modifies Stand in Bakke Case Argument." *EastWest,* October 26, 1977, 1–3.

Wang, Ling-chi. "White House Hears Asian American Views on Bakke." *EastWest,* October 12, 1977, 1.

Williams, Melissa S. *Voice, Trust, and Memory: Marginalized Groups and the Failings of Liberal Representation.* Princeton, NJ: Princeton University Press, 1998.

Winnick, Louis. "America's 'Model Minority.'" *Commentary,* August 1, 1990, 22–29.

Wong, Julia Carrie. "'Scapegoated'? The Police Killing That Left Asian Americans Angry—and Divided." *Guardian,* April 18, 2016. http://www.theguardian.com/world/2016/apr/18/peter-liang-akai-gurley-killing-asian-american-response.

Woo, S. B. "Beyond a Doubt—Harvard Discriminates!" 80-20 National Asian American Educational Foundation e-newsletter, July 2, 2018 (in author's possession).

Woolf, Nicky. "Why Are So Many Asian Americans Missing Out on Ivy League Schools?" *Guardian,* May 24, 2015. http://www.theguardian.com/us-news/2015/may/24/why-are-so-many-missing-out-on-ivy-league-schools.

Wu, Ellen D. *The Color of Success: Asian Americans and the Origins of the Model Minority.* Princeton, NJ: Princeton University Press, 2014.

Yang, Yunlei. "Asian Americans Would Lose Out under Affirmative Action." *Los Angeles Times,* October 1, 2014. http://www.latimes.com/opinion/opinion-la/la-ol-affirmative-action-sca5-asian-americans-20141001-story.html.

8

Second-Order Diversity

AN EXPLORATION OF DECENTRALIZATION'S
EGALITARIAN POSSIBILITIES

Heather K. Gerken

One of the great puzzles for democratic theory is what a democracy owes its minorities. Minorities, after all, are supposed to lose in a majoritarian system, but we worry about the fate of democracy's consistent losers. Most work on this subject focuses on providing an adequate baseline of minority rights and ensuring that minorities have "voice" within the system. Occasionally some will imagine more robust opportunities for minority governance such as consociationalism,[1] group rights,[2] or even "taking turns" in governing.[3] For the most part, however, democratic theory has stuck with the assumption that the best—perhaps the only—model for distributing power fairly is to give electoral minorities influence, but not control, over democratic decisions.

Our thinking on democratic equality has been stymied by two mistaken assumptions. The first is that a democratic system is unitary. Theorists have traditionally written about the power that minorities should wield in *the* legislature or *the* electorate. They view power as unitary, and it's no wonder that they can only imagine minorities speaking truth *to* power rather than *with* it. That's why scholars have emphasized the need to give minorities voice and votes, and diversity has become the touchstone of success. When scholars use the term *diversity*, they usually mean that a decision-making body should roughly mirror the composition of the relevant population from which it draws its members; it should "look like America," to borrow one of President Clinton's more evocative phrases.[4]

The truth—like our system of governance—is more complex. All democracies are disaggregated, some dramatically so. Even nominally centralized systems cede some authority to local decision-makers, and the United States cedes a substantial amount. More importantly, these institutions rarely mirror the national polity. While our ideal for unitary institutions is statistical mirroring, what I've called "first-order diversity," our disaggregated system facilitates "second-order diversity," a regime in which national minorities can constitute local majorities and decision-making bodies vary in their composition.[5] Once we recognize the democratic possibilities associated with second-order diversity, it becomes clear that it's a mistake to extend theories of equality derived from unitary institutions to decentralized ones. We should be attentive, in short, to the unique benefits associated with second-order diversity.

The moment one mentions federalism and localism in equality debates is the moment when some stop reading.[6] Federalism calls to mind the Alabamas of the past and the Fergusons of the present. Add to that a healthy skepticism as to whether the equality project should ever be left in the hands of democracy, let alone *local* democracy, and you might not even need a theoretical account to explain why decentralization has long been in political theory's blind spot. It is precisely to combat the evils of decentralization that equality scholars emphasize the need for nationally enforced constitutional rights in in the first place.

These arguments, while common, rest on two mistakes. The first is an outdated factual premise. Ours is not our fathers' federalism. Today's federalism is sheared of sovereignty. Despite the best efforts of its conservative majority, the Supreme Court has failed to curb federal power. As a result, states cannot shield their discrimination from national norms as they did during the days of Jim Crow. If the national government wants to enforce equality norms, it can, provided it's willing to spend the political capital to do so.

But a deeper mistake undergirds the view that the key to equality is rights, not politics (and certainly not local politics): namely, a static, almost apolitical conception of rights. The static view ignores a fundamental point: rights—like families—are built, not born. As legal scholars will tell you,[7] constitutional rights don't descend from on high. They are built through social movements, which are essential to make norms stick and thereby convert the rights guarantees that lawyers dismiss as "parchment barriers"[8] into robust shields. And social movements are almost always built from the ground up, moving through local and state sites before hitting the national stage. It would certainly be easier if those who believed in equality norms didn't have to fight for them. But there is a profound difference between calling for a national rights regime and achieving one.

Note that I am framing the conversation about decentralization quite differently from most. Academics often unthinkingly blame decentralization for shortfalls in our equality norms. This simplistic formulation ignores the fact that the turn to decentralization is a sign of weakness in the norms themselves. We adopt a decentralized solution only when our national norm is to tolerate shortfalls. Rather than condemning federalism for weak national norms, we should focus on whether federalism makes it easier or harder to change those norms. We should focus, in short, on whether decentralization helps us get from "here to there" with the equality project.[9] It is a fiendishly complex inquiry because local and national politics constitute each other. But it's the right inquiry nonetheless.

Reframing the conversation raises the correct questions, but it does not make them easier to answer. There are clearly sophisticated grounds for thinking that decentralization undermines the creation of national equality norms. What is less appreciated is that it also plays a crucial role in building those norms. Once you turn your focus from enunciating national norms to bringing them about, it becomes clear that a disaggregated democracy offers a far more interesting set of opportunities for minority empowerment than we've imagined. That's because decentralization plays a central role in the process by which equality norms are constructed. The most remarkable example in recent years has been the same-sex marriage movement, which depended heavily on state and local sites as staging grounds for organizing and debate. But we see the same phenomenon with other core parts of the equality project, including immigration reform, policing, sentencing, and the living-wage movement, just to name a few.

Decentralization fuels the process by which equality norms are constructed for the simplest of reasons: it enables national minorities to constitute local majorities. When decision-making bodies are second-order diverse, minorities can rule and not just be ruled. They can speak truth with power, not just to it. Those who push for change aren't limited to speech; they can also engage in what I've termed as "dissenting by deciding," putting their principles into policy.[10] Racial minorities can turn the tables and stand in the shoes of the majority; they can vote the bums out and their own representatives in. Advocates of equality can act as well as speak and thereby leverage a vast policymaking apparatus in the service of changing national norms. When democratic institutions are second-order diverse, an individual can experience a variety of participatory opportunities over the course of her civic life, with different parts of her identity coming to the surface at different moments. The fact that minorities can *rule* at the local level matters, then, whether you care most about participation or power. It means that when we engage with the project of equality, we can think about governance and not just rights, votes and not just voice, insiders and not just outsiders, minority rule and not just minority rights.

The disaggregated nature of our democracy also supplies resources of a more critical sort, as it reveals how strangely anemic most theoretical accounts of minority empowerment are. Diversity — the notion that decision-making bodies should mirror the polity from which they are drawn — has become the touchstone for democratic legitimacy. While diversity is a lofty ideal, it is also a statistical guarantee of the majority's power. The conventional strategy for minority "empowerment" thus relentlessly reproduces the same inequalities in governance that racial and political minorities experience everywhere else. On the issues that divide us, it consigns minorities to the status of perpetual losers. Statistical mirroring should not be seen as the sole means for measuring our progress toward equality.

Decentralization, in short, offers a wide range of resources for exploring questions of equality, diversity, and dissent — resources that theorists have largely neglected. By the end of this paper, I hope to convince you that it would be a shame to discard some of the most important weapons in this fight — namely, the many sites of power currently controlled by coalitions that favor equality. I even hope to convince you that Ferguson, which is often held up as the epitome of decentralization's failures, takes on a quite different cast when viewed against the backdrop of decentralization's virtues. Even if you buy none of my arguments, at the very least you should wonder whether those who believe in equality can afford to lose track of the local.

A short book chapter like this one cannot fully canvass the costs and benefits associated with what constitutional theorists call *structure* — federalism, localism, and other institutional strategies for dividing governmental power. Instead I'll simply identify the many ways structure can further the aims of equality. While I'll focus on the question of racial equality, I'll often touch upon the role structure plays in promoting dissent. That's not to equate racial minorities with dissenters but to acknowledge that the push for equality often requires robust forms of oppositional politics.

This paper focuses on the two primary ways decentralization helps us construct more robust equality norms: First, decentralization facilitates different forms of advocacy, offers different platforms for mobilizing, and provides different levers of change, all of which may be especially important for those in the minority. Indeed, if anything, decentralization has taken on an even more salient role in the equality fight due to the inherent limits of the rights paradigm and the salience of local institutions to people's lived experiences. Second, decentralization allows racial minorities to turn the tables. It thus facilitates democratic arrangements that may promote respect and destabilize existing racial categories.

In canvassing these arguments, I will dwell largely on the affirmative case for decentralization. That's not because I am naive about decentralization's costs. It's because those costs are so familiar. If there's work to do, it is in understanding decentralization's virtues. Put differently, equality scholars often write as if the relationship between federalism and equality were a simple story—and a depressing one at that. My hope isn't to recast that story as an optimistic one but simply to convince you that it's a great deal more complex than most believe.

1. Why Decentralization's Virtues Are Overlooked

When one discovers a gap in the literature this pronounced, it is useful to ask why the gap exists in the first place lest doubting Thomasinas read no further. So why has democratic theory largely neglected[11] the virtues of decentralization when it comes to equality? To be sure, scholars sometimes wax eloquent about the use of territorial enclaves as a solution to intractable ethnic and racial divides, but those solutions are not realistic for the United States, let alone attractive for the reasons I discuss below.[12] Democratic theory also offers occasional paeans to the values of local participation, some of which are atmospheric enough to make one's skin crawl. As a general matter, however, scholars neglect state and local institutions when it comes to the groups about which we worry the most: political and racial minorities.

a. Too Abstract?

The reason for this neglect may be that democratic theorists often shear away a fair amount of institutional detail in order to lay bare core problems. They tend to write in fairly abstract terms about "the" decision-making body, be it a legislature, an electorate, or a jury. That strategy has many virtues and generates important insights, but it has led theorists to overlook a key fact about the United States and most other democracies: there isn't one decision-making body in a democracy; there are many. "Our federalism" is made up of state legislatures and local school boards, federal and state juries, city councils and local zoning commissions, state administrative agencies, and regional boards. We term this system "federalism" because of the power we cede to the states, but when one looks to the many substate, local, and sublocal decision-makers involved in policymaking, "federalism all the way down"[13] better captures how governance works in this country.

You might think that at the very least we can identify unitary bodies at the national level. But our disaggregated democracy extends even to "the" federal government. Congress and the executive—institutions that are themselves better classified as theys rather than its[14]—are inevitably dependent on many other institutions to carry out their mandates. Many of our most important national policies—those having to do with the environment, healthcare, Medicaid, transportation, energy, and the workplace—are implemented by elected state officials and appointed state administrators, not to mention myriad local institutions.[15] Even in areas without formally delineated cooperative federal regimes, federal policy depends heavily on state and local institutions.[16] Federal drug policy can't be enforced without the help of local police officers, local prosecutors, and locally drawn juries. Federal education policy requires the assistance of state and local agencies, school boards, and teachers. Federal dependence on state and local officials is so pronounced that one scholar has argued that states can even "nullify" federal law merely by choosing not to carry it out, as did Washington and Colorado with regard to federal marijuana laws.[17] In addition, state and local officials routinely tread on areas thought to be reserved to the federal government alone, including immigration, labor, securities regulation, national security, foreign policy, and intellectual property.[18]

Across the policymaking spectrum, then, the states and the federal government regulate shoulder to shoulder. Integration, vertical overlap, and mutual dependence are the rule, not the exception. And those at the top of the political hierarchy depend heavily on others to carry out national policy. It's hard to control Washington, but it's even harder for Washington to control the rest of us. The power of the "street-level bureaucrat"[19] is rarely confined to the street.

Even "the" national government, in short, presides over a Tocquevillian bureaucracy, not a Weberian one.[20] Communities whose populations depart markedly from the national polity are constantly implementing, even editing, the law they lack the power to authorize.[21]

Our politics mirror these institutional arrangements; they are integrated from top to bottom.[22] States and localities are not separate and autonomous enclaves that facilitate a retreat from national norms. Instead they are at the center of the fight over what our national norms should be, with social movements using these sites to tee up national debates and war over national commitments.[23] All of these state, local, substate, and sublocal institutions that make up "federalism all the way down" provide a rich and evocative array of policymaking sites, political benefits, and participatory opportunities that have not been fully limned by democratic theorists.

b. Not Abstract Enough?

While it's possible that political theorists have sheared away too many details to spot decentralization's egalitarian possibilities, my suspicion is that the real problem is that theorists haven't sheared away enough. Those interested in equality and dissent often overlook federalism and its homely cousin localism because both are steeped in such an ugly history. We have long cast decentralization in opposition to the interests of racial minorities. Jim Crow, after all, was one of federalism's ugliest moments, with states' rights routinely invoked to deprive individuals of their rights. Our collective skepticism of decentralization thus grew out of the intuition that, as William Riker put it, "if one disapproves of racism, one should disapprove of federalism." [24] Unsurprisingly given the treatment of civil-rights protestors, religious minorities, and other dissenters during that period, racism isn't the only ism linked to federalism and localism. We also associate these institutional arrangements with other dreaded isms, like parochialism and cronyism. Like Ferris Bueller, many of us "don't believe in isms." As a result, in the United States democratic theory tends to look to rights, not structure, when it comes to the groups that we most want to protect: dissenters and racial minorities.

That is a mistake. In the past, state sovereignty loomed large and was invoked as a shield against the enforcement of national norms. Today, however, federalism is little different from what those in other countries would call decentralization despite the Supreme Court's efforts to shore up state sovereignty. [25] For every limit the court has tried to impose on the national government, there is a ready workaround. [26] The nationalists have lost battles, to be sure — *Shelby County* [27] being the most heartbreaking defeat — but they are undoubtedly winning the war. If the national government wants to enforce equality norms, it can, provided it's willing to spend the political capital to do so. [28] The central barrier to a robust, nationally enforced equality regime isn't law; it's our politics. [29] Or, put more precisely, the central barrier to a robust, nationally enforced equality regime is a politics that has been infected by racism from the start.

c. An Argument Misframed?

The arguments above answer the conventional challenges to decentralization on their own terms, but in my view those challenges are misframed.
The preference for rights over structures—for law over politics—runs
deep in the democratic theory generally and political philosophy in particular. We often blame decentralization for shortcomings in our equality
norms, and many insist that we should depend on rights, not politics,
when it comes to equality guarantees. As I noted in the first section of this
paper, while there is a sophisticated argument for blaming federalism for
shortfalls in our equality norms, that's not the argument most are making.
Most instead blame decentralization for the shortfalls themselves, equat-
ing federalism with racism, just as Riker did. For this purpose, however,
federalism is the symptom, not the cause, of what ails us. We turn to federalism precisely when national norms are too weak to insist upon uni-
formity. We shouldn't condemn decentralization as antiegalitarian without asking whether the real problem is that our norms aren't sufficiently
egalitarian. At the very least, we shouldn't naturalize decentralization as
if it were unchanging. Decentralization is a choice. It's a choice that affects our choices going forward, as I discuss below,[30] but it's still a choice.

The deeper mistake, however, is to equate equality talk with "rights
talk."[31] It's not surprising that many are uncomfortable with leaving
something as sacred as equality to the vagaries of politics. But this pain-
fully static conception of rights ignores that rights do not descend from
what lawyers derisively call the "brooding omnipresence in the sky."[32]
As an enormous range of legal scholarship has shown, rights are forged
through social movements and instantiated through policy.[33]

That's why it's not enough simply to call for a robust equality regime.
It is not even enough to write one into the Constitution, as is made clear
by the fate of the Reconstruction Amendments, which could not overcome deep-seated and pervasive racism. If you care about equality, you
must build national norms robust enough to convert parchment barriers
into robust shields. That's an uncomfortable truth for those who think
that rights should lie outside of politics. But it's a truth nonetheless, one
faced by Rogers, Sethi, and Banaji and Lai in their articles in this volume.
The way to push something outside of politics is to politic about it in the
first place. Rights supporters should thus heed Louis Menand's wry observation about the abolitionists: "The renunciation of politics was the
secret of their politics."[34] When a right is viewed as fundamental and outside of politics, that consensus is almost always forged through decades
of debate rather than established by fiat. That's why robustly enforced

rights usually mark the end of a debate, not the beginning. Their success depends heavily on equality norms being settled.[35] Here, as with other parts of democracy-focused scholarship, we need to put more politics into political theory.[36]

None of these truths has been lost on social movements. Indeed one wonders whether political philosophy's discomfort with politics stems in part from the same problem Melvin Rogers's chapter in this volume identifies—that theorists, focused as they often are on the grand narrative of the elite, often miss the insights and lived experiences of the people who have done the work of generating and instantiating equality's ideals.[37] It took decades of civil rights work to breathe life into the Reconstruction Amendments. Or think about the same-sex marriage movement. Not a single word in the Constitution changed[38] between the Supreme Court's 1986 decision in *Bowers v. Hardwick* (which blessed as constitutional a decision to jail those who engaged in same-sex sodomy) and *Obergefell v. Hodges* (where the Supreme Court insisted in 2015 that same-sex marriage is constitutionally required). The law didn't change; our politics changed. That process may also explain why those equality norms now run deep enough that *Obergefell*—a decision that would surely have caused intense controversy not so long ago—was greeted with enormous enthusiasm in many quarters and opposed in precious few.

I won't address the foolish question these arguments naturally raise—if decentralization is so great, why aren't our equality norms stronger? Overcoming discrimination is difficult no matter what the group, and racism has proved to be dishearteningly powerful, as both our local and national politics make clear. Moreover, the hydraulics of inequality are powerful and complex. Given how deep racism runs in our history, it's hard to know what the baseline is for measuring progress. Wu's chapter does a wonderful job of probing the problem. As if that weren't enough, we are all trapped in the same predictive dilemma. National and local politics constitute each other. We could no more decide whether things would be different without states and localities than we could decide whether things would be different without the First Amendment. We are rightly angered when states and localities fall short of equality norms today, but it's not clear why we assume that a national norm would embody perfection when the best evidence we have—existing practice—is that the national norm *is* to tolerate those shortfalls. We tend to naturalize decentralization. But institutions no more descend from the "brooding omnipresence" than rights do. Decentralized decisions and institutions can be centralized if the center chooses to do so (and those choices are also mediated through politics).

While we should resist the simple conflation of decentralization with inequality, we should also acknowledge the complex relationship between the two. While national norms are responsible for shortfalls in our equality regime, decentralization surely makes it easier to tolerate these shortfalls. And embedding a weak national norm through decentralization can make change harder going forward. That's not because sovereignty poses a barrier to enforcing equality norms any more, as noted above, but because institutional arrangements are sticky. Think, for instance, about our collective decision continuing to leave school funding or public housing to state and local authorities—a decision that makes it more difficult to change our minds going forward. Given the overlay of residential segregation and economic inequality, decentralization can preserve, even compound, the deep and persistent effects of discrimination, something that makes it that much harder to pursue a centralized solution in the future.

These costs are quite familiar, and they would be enough to condemn decentralization but for the fact that, as I explain in the next part, decentralization also plays a central role in the creation of national norms. Counterintuitively enough, decentralization can beget centralization, and localism can beget national norms. Precisely because local and national politics constitute one another, decentralization can be as much a tool for change as it is a tool for preservation. This complex pairing may irritate us, but it at least frames the question correctly.

2. Why Decentralization's Virtues Ought Not Be Overlooked

If we frame the question correctly—if we focus on building norms rather than willing them into existence—then it becomes clear that decentralization can be an underappreciated weapon in the fight for equality. As noted above, in thinking about what a democracy owes its minorities, political theorists typically extend accounts of minority empowerment built around unitary institutions to our disaggregated democracy. The baseline assumption is that minorities should have the right to speak and to vote in proportion to their numbers. That's precisely why "first-order diversity"—the idea that decision-making bodies should mirror the polity—has become the touchstone for democratic fairness.[39] The notion has such a powerful hold on our imagination that one theorist has even gone so far as to suggest that we assign Americans to randomly drawn, nonterritorial congressional districts, thereby guaranteeing that each mirrors the national polity.[40]

Under certain circumstances this could be an excellent model. Depending on the dynamics of the decision-making process, members of the group could take part in, perhaps even influence, every decision made. But voice is different from political muscle, and influence is different from control. Indeed if you peer through the lens of power relations, you'll quickly see that first-order diversity is also a statistical guarantee of the majority's power., a point that Wu's chapter also probes. If all of our decision-making bodies were first-order diverse — mirroring the polity as a whole — then our strategy for minority "empowerment" would relentlessly reproduce the same inequalities in governance that minorities experience everywhere else.[41] You don't have to be a cynic to think that it's an odd theory of empowerment.

Nor does a Dahlian account alleviate these concerns. Dahl famously argued that "minorities rule" in a democracy, with shifting coalitions of minorities wielding majority power over time.[42] But, of course, we worry about racial minorities precisely because they aren't full partners in Dahlian coalitions.[43]

Even where race does not divide voters, first-order diversity would ensure that the same decision-making process is reproduced again and again. Every decision would reflect the views of the median decision-maker, the institutional equivalent of the swing voter. Democratic outcomes would be roughly the same. In short, with a system that is first-order diverse, we would see one form of democratic compromise, not many.[44]

Decentralization offers an intriguing alternative. At least where residential housing patterns are lumpy or institutions are composed through a random draw, decision-making bodies will be "second-order diverse";[45] they will reflect a wide variety of compositions. Some will be majority black or majority Latino; others will allow for robust multiracial coalitions. Rather than giving racial minorities the same level of influence over each decision, this institutional design choice grants some racial group members the power to decide, a power that would otherwise be enjoyed only by members of the white majority. The second-order diversity that emerges naturally in our disaggregated system enables racial minorities to turn the tables, exercising majoritarian power even in a system in which they are the minority. They have the chance to wield the same power that members of the majority wield unthinkingly: the power to elect a champion of their own. Even when racial minorities are not in the majority, second-order diversity makes possible a much more varied range of coalitional politics precisely because decision-making bodies vary along political as well as racial lines. Even in the presence of weak national norms, robust egalitarian politics will be possible in at least some places.

Decentralization, then, offers a range of benefits that have not been fully explored by those engaged with the equality project. These benefits matter for purely intrinsic reasons, but they should also matter to anyone who seeks change. First, decentralization provides a crucial complement to the First Amendment, lending minorities different platforms for mobilizing and different levers of change. Indeed, if anything, local institutions are becoming more important in the fight for equality, both because of the inherent limits of the rights paradigm and because local institutions are so salient to people's lived experiences. Second, by turning the tables, decentralization facilitates democratic arrangements that may help destabilize existing racial categories.

a. The Discursive Benefits of Structure

If your aim is to build equality norms, you might believe that the First Amendment is all that minorities require. It isn't.[46] In the abstract, the opportunity to voice one's concerns and vote one's conscience seems like it ought to be enough. The moment power enters the equation, however, these democratic gestures seem less grand. The iconoclastic dissenter is an archetype in constitutional theory. But he exercises his First Amendment rights as an outsider, not an insider. He is licensed to speak truth to power, not with it. He may object to power's exercise, but he's rarely able to influence it. The First Amendment confers a right to speak against a decision. Not to change it. Not even to influence it. That state of affairs may seem perfectly natural if you imagine there being only *one* decision. It takes on a different cast if you recognize that there are many.

The real problem for those who seek change isn't getting their message out; it's getting their message *across*.[47] There are plenty of fora for speech these days. But what social movements need is varied forms of advocacy, varied platforms for mobilizing, and varied levers of change. It's hard to imagine what those sites look like in a unitary institution. It's far easier to see them when you recognize the wild array of decision-making bodies that make up "federalism all the way down." Decentralization dramatically expands the leverage points for change and gives social movements the chance to use state and local policymaking as an organizing tool, a rallying cry, a testing ground for their ideas. It creates opportunities not just for dissent but for dissenting by deciding, which can often be a far more powerful tool for change.

The marriage-equality movement is but the latest example of how equality debates are pushed forward not just through speech but through

state and local governance. DREAMers have fought for educational benefits at the state and local level. Cities like New Haven and New York have
offered government-issued IDs to undocumented residents, with California following suit with driver licenses. States and localities have long
been ground zero for many of the fights over racial equality, with fights
over abolition waged in the North and early efforts at desegregation run
through the border states. Today a host of issues salient to racial equality
are pushed through states and localities, from university admissions to
public school districting, from police practices to the living wage, from
environmental justice to sentencing reform. Successes on these fronts are
often the product of coalitional politics, but these were easier coalitions
to build precisely because they were drawn from communities that didn't
mirror the national polity.

It's clear why social movements turn to state and local sites in pushing for change.[48] Decentralization allows for different political coalitions
to prevail at the state and local levels than obtain at the national level.
It thus makes it possible for those seeking change to embed a principle
into policy.[49] That option is unavailable to dissenters in a system that is
first-order diverse, as their only choice set is to influence a decision or
speak out against it. And "dissenting by deciding" offers benefits that free
speech cannot supply, benefits that matter a great deal to those who seek
to change our equality norms.

The platform alone matters. Decisions made by state and local governments are highly visible, as they typically garner more publicity than
protests or blogs or editorials. Think, for instance, about the sea change
that occurred in the marriage debate when Massachusetts and San Francisco began issuing marriage licenses to same-sex couples. Supporters of
marriage equality spent years writing editorials, marching in parades, and
arguing with their neighbors. The movement received a much-needed
boost when state and local governments put those ideas into practice.
Or consider immigration reform, another perennial subject of debate.
What has moved that debate from the editorial page to the front page in
recent years? Arizona's anti-immigrant initiatives and the efforts of cities
like New Haven and New York to provide municipal IDs to individuals regardless of their immigration status. You can play this parlor game
with almost any topic. Disputes over vote fraud garnered a lot more attention once state legislatures started passing voter ID laws. The movement for universal health care was given a lift when Massachusetts put
Obamacare's predecessor into place. Marijuana policy now dominates
the airwaves in the wake of the Colorado and Washington initiatives.

These shifts did not come about because advocates had more opportunities to speak. They came about because advocacy was run through a different platform and took a different form.

Decentralization also facilitates agenda setting.[50] When those seeking change put in place a real-life instantiation of their ideas, the majority can't ignore them as majorities are wont to do. The iconic image associated with free speech is someone standing on a soapbox. And we all know what those in the majority do when they see someone standing on a soapbox: they walk right on by. Radio silence is the tool of the powerful. It's often safer to ignore those who advocate change than to engage with them. But those in power can't afford to be passive when social movements disturb the status quo by embedding change into state and local policy. Instead the majority must *do* something to get the policy overturned. Decentralization thus helps social movements shift the burden of inertia and force the majority to engage.[51]

The advantages of decentralization go beyond making dissent visible and setting the agenda. "Dissenting by deciding" also gives dissenters a chance to move from the abstract to the concrete. They don't have to talk about how a policy would work in theory. They can show how it does work in practice. They can show it *will* work in practice. New Haven's "Elm City ID" made it possible for cities in eight different states to create a government ID for all of their residents regardless of their immigration status.[52] That effort, in turn, made it possible for states like California to do the same through driver's licenses.[53] The fifteen-dollar minimum-wage movement has moved from cities to states in a similar fashion. Following Baltimore's lead in the 1990s, 140 cities had passed living-wage ordinances by 2009.[54] Grassroots efforts continue among cities, and now two states—New York and California—have followed their lead in the "Fight for 15."[55] So too the movement to place body cameras on police officers has moved from cities to eleven states[56] and now even has garnered the support of the president and the Department of Justice.[57]

Decentralization also allows advocates of change to build their movement one step at a time. It is hard to jumpstart a national movement. That's why virtually every national movement began as a local one.[58] Equality movements of all sorts began small and grew into something bigger. These state and local platforms aren't just sites for early mobilization efforts; they also connect social movements to the large and powerful networks that fuel policymaking in the United States.[59]

Just as our deeply integrated politics have enabled cities and states to push for change, so too our imbricated policymaking apparatus has turned decentralization into a tool for change. Precisely because the federal government depends so heavily on states to carry out its policies, the states can exercise unexpected sway over national policymaking. Needless to say, this high level of policymaking overlap confers an important advantage on would-be dissenters, one that the First Amendment cannot supply. For instance, when states like Colorado and Washington legalized marijuana, they effectively changed federal policy as well because the federal government depends almost entirely on states to enforce its marijuana prohibition.[60] Similarly, in the wake of *Windsor v. United States*, states could force the federal government to recognize same-sex marriages simply by legalizing those marriages within the state.[61] Note that this argument is the flip side of arguments often cast against decentralization—namely, that state and local control over policy slows the spread of national norms. While that is surely true, we must also acknowledge the abilities of states and localities to tug a reluctant federal government along that path to equality.

In sum, while rights and structure have long been cast in opposition to one another, in fact rights and structure serve as interlocking gears in a disaggregated democracy—the First Amendment and federalism working in tandem to move debates forward. Debate leads to policy, which in turn provides a rallying point for still more debate. Social movements include pragmatic insiders forging bargains from within and principled outsiders demanding more and better from without.

There is, of course, no guarantee that the interlocking gears of rights and structure will always move us forward on the equality project (though that is true of a centralized system as well). Decentralization itself doesn't have a political valence, and nothing excuses those who believe in equality from engaging in the hard work of politicking. The key questions are *how* one wants to politic and what tools will be available. Decentralization makes it possible for majority-minority decision-making bodies to be part of that fight, and it ensures that cities and states with robust equality coalitions can use their policymaking power to move debates forward. Those sites constitute powerful tools for change no matter what your views. The question is whether those engaged with the equality project will take advantage of them. Put differently, while decentralization isn't a sufficient condition for change, it may be a necessary one.

None of this is to say that decentralization is an unmitigated good for those who seek change. If a polity is too fragmented, it will be hard to build national equality norms in the first place. Moreover, decentralization can make it too easy to compromise on equality norms, thus excusing us from having the fights we need to have. And as I noted above, institutional arrangements are sticky, which makes it harder to enforce national norms once they've been crystallized. That's intensely frustrating, because the overlay of residential segregation and economic inequality makes it especially important to centralize some decisions in order to move the equality project forward.[62] The point here is simply that those who blithely call for having a "national conversation" on equality often forget how hard a national conversation is to gin up.[63] National policy is a giant gear to move forward. We should remember that localism and federalism provide the smaller gears that make that movement possible.

If anything, state and local politics have become only more salient in the push for national equality norms in recent years. First, as noted above, our politics are now deeply integrated.[64] While states and localities were once cast in Westphalian terms,[65] they are no longer red and blue enclaves that allow us to live and let live, separate and apart from one another. Instead state and local platforms are at the center of fights over national values. There aren't fifty "laboratories of democracy."[66] There are basically two. One is red and one is blue, and they are composed of highly networked national interest groups running their battles through any state (or local) system where they have political leverage.[67]

The second reason that states and localities matter so much is that we may have reached the point where rights have run their course as tools for promoting equality.[68] It takes more than litigation to keep up with the hydraulics of inequality or domination. A rights framework can guarantee the right to vote; it's much less helpful in raising voter turnout. Constitutional rights do a better job of combating state-mandated school segregation[69] than preventing the private choices that lead to residential segregation. Courts can ensure that vulnerable populations have a right to counsel, but they are poorly suited to monitoring prosecutorial discretion, instantiating community policing, or improving police training. Rights can deter the most obvious forms of employment discrimination, but they cannot guarantee a robust minimum wage or eliminate the effects of implicit bias or structural discrimination. Courts may drive efforts to equalize sentences, but it's legislatures that need to do the work to reduce sentence lengths. Banning discrimination in university admissions is not the same as licensing admissions officers to take into account discrimination's effects. Litigating equality suits against private industry is tougher than conditioning government contracts on the inclusion of minority-owned businesses. Immigrants are afforded limited constitutional protections, but much of the work of integration is being done at the state and local level.[70] It is thus unsurprising that a great deal of equality work is done through state and local policymaking these days.

To be sure, policymaking can be pursued at the national level as well as at the state and local levels. But the leverage points for egalitarian policymaking these days are far easier to find at the state and local levels. That's where the fight is.

States and localities aren't just where the fight is. As Guy Charles has noted, it is also "where the action is."[71] If you care about racial equality, you can't ignore the local. It's the center of people's lived experience, including their lived experience of race. Little wonder that it's also where the most powerful efforts to frame inequality and domination are occurring, most notably the Black Lives Matter movement. Schools, housing, policing, transportation—the institutions most salient to everyday people's lives—all are controlled at the state and local levels, where quality cannot be had without changing these institutions.

b. Promoting Respect and Destabilizing Hierarchy

If you care about the equality project, you should also care not just about purely instrumental concerns, like empowering social movements and driving change through policy, but also the expressive and constitutive dimensions of equality politics.[72] The quotidian dimensions of participation are admittedly more nuanced, even atmospheric, but there's little doubt that the micro affects the macro—that these microinteractions shape our equality norms.[73] Note, however, the relationship between the ideas I canvass in this section and the ones described above. Political theorists have long argued that participation helps constitute one's civic identity and that rules about participation convey an expressive message (Rogers discusses this strand of republican political thought in his chapter).[74] But those arguments are almost always cast in anodyne, individualistic terms. Little attention is paid to context, let alone crass categories like winners and losers. If we pay attention to power dynamics, however, the first-order diversity so often lauded in these debates means that racial minorities will be the perpetual losers on any issue where people divide along racial lines. The only political "script"[75] available to racial minorities is to be the junior partner or dissenting gadfly, something that might affect how racial minorities understand their civic identity or at least influence their sense of political ownership. We should take into account the possibility that membership in a group routinely defeated in politics might affect an individual's relationship with the polity as a whole.[76] Again, Rogers's chapter provides compelling examples of precisely that phenomenon in the writings of Martin Delany. Put simply, in the presence of salient and persistent group identities, instrumental notions like "winner," "loser," and "swing voter" may carry symbolic baggage with them.

Decentralization is useful for promoting equality norms because it doesn't reproduce the same democratic dynamics in every decision-making body, nor does it condemn racial minorities to the permanent status of influencer or dissenter. Instead the tables are sometimes turned. Decentralization thus allows racial minorities to exercise the same power that the majority unthinkingly wields.[77] They get a chance to enjoy the same type of participatory experience—the sense of agency associated with being in charge—that is usually reserved for members of the majority. Instead of being the junior partners to *every* decision, racial minorities occasionally enjoy the power of seniority. Minority group members will thus have a chance to elect a champion, forge an affirmative agenda, spearhead a compromise, deal with dissenters, and enjoy the sense of efficacy (and discomfort) that accompanies the power to make a decision.[78] The traditional power dynamics associated with whites' majority status will be denaturalized.

Second-order diversity also makes it more likely that the people who represent us will be racial minorities, something that has symbolic effects of its own.[79] You can read Melissa Williams[80] or just notice the outpouring of emotion over the picture of a young African American boy rubbing President Obama's head[81] to understand why.

Turning the tables doesn't help us merely shed crude but important political scripts like winner and loser; it also gives racial minorities a chance to take their turn "stand[ing] for the whole," which George Kateb has argued is a key feature of representative democracy.[82] Everyone has a chance to rule and to be ruled in a decentralized system. If, as Ajume Wingo argues in this volume, "speaking and acting for oneself is at the heart of human dignity,"[83] then it is essential that participatory opportunities be distributed fairly.[84]

Moreover, there is a dignity associated with privileging structure over rights. When racial minorities depend upon rights rather than structure, they must look to the courts or the Department of Justice for solace, as if those institutions were "white knights" rescuing the community. Structure enables racial minorities to do what other groups routinely do—protect themselves using the policymaking tools available to them. They can enact a contracting set-aside or give jobs to people in their community or create a magnet school or mandate community policing or pass a minimum wage law or provide ID to people regardless of their citizenship status. Decentralization thus reduces the chance that we will treat racial minorities as what Pam Karlan calls "objects of judicial solicitude," rather than as "efficacious political actors in their own right."[85]

So too decentralization can temporarily deprive whites of the comfort—and power—associated with their majority status. Some members of the majority will feel the sting of defeat, the bitter aftertaste that comes from compromising too much, or the frustration of not being heard.[86] Second-order diversity thus destabilizes the power dynamics associated with a "normal" participatory experience. One might even hope that such experiences deepen majority members' awareness of the costs their decisions impose on those who cannot muster more than half of the votes, and thus reduce their incentive to ride roughshod over minority interests.[87]

c. Destabilizing Political Hierarchies and Identity Categories

Even setting aside categories like "majority and minority" and "winners and losers," second-order diversity generates a wide range of participatory experiences for *all* individuals over the course of a civic life.[88] In a system that is second-order diverse, some decision-making bodies will be dominated by women, some by Latinos, some by the poor. The composition of some will be conducive to measured deliberation; others will promote old-fashioned foot-stamping. Some decision-making bodies will be the type one would design if cross-racial coalitions were the overriding goal; others will fuel racial division.

If we believe that personal identity is or ought to be fluid,[89] decentralization may also be attractive because it creates conditions in which *civic* identity can be fluid as well. Variation in the composition of disaggregated bodies creates the opportunity for the unexpected to happen. It places individuals in a political dynamic that may differ markedly from the dynamic they routinely experience, which may in turn lead them to privilege different parts of their identity at different times.[90] Here again, decentralization offers individuals more "scripts,"[91] to use Anthony Appiah's term, for defining their civic identity.

The second-order diversity that decentralization naturally begets also makes those varied scripts more visible than does a system that is first-order diverse. A jury system that is second-order diverse, for instance, will produce a wide variety of verdicts rendered by majority-minority juries. James Forman's important work explores how the majority-black city of DC led the way in the "tough on crime" movement—now almost universally attributed to a white-dominated power structure—for reasons that had to do with class divisions as well as race; his work has thereby added a layer of complexity to contemporary debates over race and crime.[92] So too a districting system that is second-order diverse might produce districts that elect figures ranging from Mel Watt to John Lewis, from Barack Obama to Cynthia McKinney, thereby ensuring that blacks are represented by as varied a group of elected officials as whites are.

As the preceding examples make clear, disaggregated democracy can reveal not only lines of division and connection that first-order diversity conceals, but the ways in which known group divisions manifest themselves — or fail to emerge — when internal power dynamics vary. And we can see lines of division — subtle fractures in groups that seem unified in the "normal" political process — as well as unexpected connections among groups. Second-order diversity thus offers us a kaleidoscopic view of the polity, a view that is constantly shifting and composed of many distinct parts.

A decentralized democracy can also complement the expressive dimensions of the right to vote. Politics of recognition theorists[93] have argued that first-order diversity is a symbol of equal status because it recognizes minorities' right to participate. Many have argued that it is important for members of traditionally subordinated groups to participate in the political process, as such inclusion represents a symbol of equality. This "politics of presence"[94] signifies "a public acknowledgment of equal value"[95] and offers racial minorities the dignity of "voice."[96]

The second-order diversity that decentralization engenders also offers an acknowledgment of equal status, albeit of a quite different sort. Racial minorities don't just participate but rule. In place of the politics of presence, we have the politics of power. Decentralization confirms the majority's willingness not only to allow racial minorities to win but to allow its own members to lose. First-order diversity offers racial minorities the dignity of voice. Second-order diversity offers them the dignity of deciding. Both elements contribute to being free from domination, but the latter is the decisive element.

Decentralization also represents an interesting competitor to institutional strategies deployed by other democracies, which create separate racial or ethnic enclaves for their minorities and protect them with sovereignty, veto rules, and the like. There are obviously advantages associated with homogenous enclaves, especially where cleavages are deep, politics are divisive, and violence is a lingering threat. But sovereignty and separation carry with them the risk of isolation and distance.

Second-order diversity, in contrast, involves *heterogeneous* institutions, albeit ones where the usual power dynamics are upended. They thus facilitate bridging rather than bonding and may contribute to what Danielle Allen has called a "connected society."[97] That means racial minorities exercise control *without* being shielded from everyday politics. They have an opportunity to rule, but inside heterogeneous polities and a party system that is linked top to bottom. Like any other group, they must "pull, haul, and trade"[98] inside their community and inside their party, at the local level and at the national level. Our system thus provides opportunities for racial empowerment while allowing cross-cutting cleavages to develop. And it eliminates any inference that minority group members require protection from the rough-and-tumble of politics.

Finally, second-order diversity avoids the problems associated with freezing into place a permanent solution to intergroup conflict.[99] By constituting and reconstituting debates in an endless cycle, second-order diversity allows members of opposing groups a chance to revisit an issue in different contexts and at different times. It does not ossify a particular set of power relations but instead ensures that political dynamics vary over time. In a jury system, for instance, African Americans and whites will encounter each other on juries where whites are sometimes in the majority and where sometimes blacks are. They will come together to resolve cases that stem from shared problems, conflicts that polarize the polity, issues that divide each group internally, and questions that neither group cares much about. They will come together when the broader political context is polarized along group lines and when it is relatively harmonious. And precisely because the political environment—whether it is defined in terms of power, issues, or political atmospherics—is temporary, there may be greater freedom for participants to experiment with their own identity choices, as well as with different strategies for addressing the conflict.[100]

Decentralization, in sum, offers a range of opportunities for changing equality norms that hinge on the expressive and constitutive dimensions of politics, many of which are explored in other papers in this volume. Decentralization can help create opportunities for political ownership, equalize participatory chances over time, and proliferate bridging opportunities. Such opportunities thus reinforce—and are buttressed by—the more instrumental benefits that decentralization makes available to those seeking change.

Note, however, that none of these arguments favors a "one-way ratchet" in favor of decentralization. Instead we should think about policy just as lawyers think of property—as a bundle of "sticks," distinct powers that can be separated. Even if you own a piece of property, the tax collector can put a lien on it, zoning laws can prevent you from building on it, and you can lease grazing rights or rent your house without giving up your title. Policy works the same way; it can be split apart. Just to give a rudimentary but familiar example, it makes a good deal of sense to centralize funding sources for schools and housing in order to overcome the effects of economic inequality and residential segregation.[101] But centralized funding does not preclude the existence of city councils or local school boards. Here again, the key isn't to put a thumb on the scale of decentralization; it's to denaturalize it and recognize both its productive and its pernicious features.

3. Conclusion: A Tale of Three Cities

Let me close with a tale of three cities: Richmond, Virginia, in 1983; Omaha, Nebraska, in 2006; and Ferguson, Missouri, in 2016. I introduce these stories not by way of proof but simply to ground the somewhat abstract arguments I've made here.

Richmond in 1983 was a story about the interlocking gears of rights and structure. Thanks to the Voting Rights Act, the former capital of the Confederacy was able to elect a black-majority city council for the first time. One of the early initiatives the city council undertook was to create a minority set-aside program to combat discrimination in the contracting industry, where 99.33 percent of the contractors in the majority-black city were white.[102] The legislation was challenged in a suit that eventually reached the Supreme Court. The court struck down the set-aside program as violating the Fourteenth Amendment. In doing so, it insisted—relying on the great John Hart Ely—that the program was more constitutionally suspect because it had been adopted by a black-majority city council.[103] The court had unthinkingly blessed the legislative products of white-majority city councils and legislatures many times, but in Richmond's actions the Supreme Court saw only racial self-dealing.

Or turn to Omaha, Nebraska, in 2006. The state legislature attempted to address school failures in Omaha by dividing the city into three "racially identifiable" but heterogeneous school districts: one predominantly white, one predominantly black, and one predominantly Latino. What made the story unusual was that the plan's author was Ernie Chambers, the only African American in Nebraska's legislature. He wanted black and Latino parents to exercise the same level of control over their kids' schools that is routinely exercised by white parents across the country.[104] And what was the headline the *New York Times* paired with its story on Chambers's efforts? "Law to Segregate Omaha Schools Divides Nebraska."[105]

Both of these examples point up the limits of our vocabulary in thinking about the equality project. We unthinkingly classify institutions as *diverse* or *segregated*. "Diverse" institutions mirror the polity. "Segregated" institutions are those where racial minorities dominate. We have no laudatory term—let alone a full-blown theory—for heterogeneous institutions where racial minorities are in the majority and whites are in the minority; those get lumped together with "segregated" institutions. As a result, we have no means of distinguishing between the racially homogenous enclaves of Jim Crow and the heterogeneous institutions where racial minorities wield majority power. Ours is a world in which decision-making bodies of every sort (school committees and city councils and juries) are dominated by groups of every sort (Italians and Irish, Catholics and Jews, Greens and libertarians). We don't worry about this representational kaleidoscope—let alone term it "segregated"—merely because one group or another is taking its turn standing in for the whole. True integration would mean that the same is true when racial minorities form part of that kaleidoscope.

You don't have to favor either Richmond's set-aside or Omaha's districting plan to recognize that it might be useful to have some institutions where racial minorities—by themselves or in coalition with others—can control policy outcomes, can set the agenda, can elect a champion of their own. It might even be necessary. Richmond was far more likely to integrate its contracting industry through a set-aside than by passing yet another ban on racial discrimination. And education, now largely controlled at the state and local levels, is an essential part of the equality project. If you don't use these sites to push forward the equality debate, you aren't taking advantage of genuine opportunities for change.

Now turn to Ferguson in 2016. If William Riker were still around, he might well say that if you are against racism, you must be against localism too. But communities plagued by discrimination, poverty, and a vicious power structure exist in many places. The difference between Ferguson and those other places is that in Ferguson, African Americans are in the majority and thus posses the voting power to vote the bums out. That is in fact precisely what the residents of Ferguson have done in the wake of Michael Brown's death, voting in record numbers and tripling the number of African Americans on the city council, thereby ensuring that half of its seats are now held by blacks.[106] The city council has in turn appointed African Americans to key positions, including city manager, head of human resources, and chief of police.[107]

Again, decentralization plainly has much to do with Ferguson's problems. Our decentralized system for funding taxes and public housing, standing alone, has done a great deal to perpetuate the sort of inequality we witnessed in Ferguson.[108] But of course that's because our national norm *is* to decentralize funding, and you don't have to be a cynic to suspect that discrimination has something to do with that choice. Decentralization will make that weak national norm harder to overcome in some ways due to institutional inertia and the many ways in which the overlay of inequality makes change harder to come by. But the black community in Ferguson now at least has more political muscle than many other black communities facing similar problems but lacking the electoral muscle to do anything.

I don't want to be unduly sunny. A city controlled by African Americans is not a panacea for the deep structural inequalities that exist in American society, as Flint makes absolutely clear. The question isn't whether decentralization is a cause or a cure for inequality. It is both. But we've made a mistake in damning it as cause without considering its possibilities as cure. You can aim for strong national norms and centralized solutions and still think that decentralization is one of the tools we need to achieve them.

That's why this paper poses several simple questions. In the fight to change equality norms, is it useful to have majority-black city councils and Latino-majority school boards and states with robust equality coalitions in the mix? Is it useful for Richmond, Virginia, to be able to use its policymaking muscle to desegregate its contracting industry? Is it useful for black and Latino parents to enjoy the dignity associated with making decisions about their children's futures in Omaha? Is it useful for African Americans caught up in policies like Ferguson to have enough votes to change those policies? Is it useful to have states like New York and California and Massachusetts in the policymaking mix? Your answer to those questions may well be no, but at least you ought to be asking them.

Notes

1. Consociationalism is a power-sharing arrangement often used by countries with deep ethnic or religious divides. Consociationalist democracies are not purely majoritarian; instead they provide a variety of protections for certain minorities through voting arrangements, veto rights, and the like. See generally Lijphart, *Democracy in Plural Societies*.

2. Kymlicka, *Multicultural Citizenship*, 109.

3. Guinier, *Tyranny of the Majority*, 5, 73, 107.

4. Clinton used this phrase in 1992 to describe his cabinet; Balz and Marcus, "Clinton Said to Fill Last 4 Cabinet Jobs," *Washington Post*, December 24, 1992, A1. Ellen Wu's paper in this volume makes clear the deep hold that the statistical-mirroring model exercises on our collective imagination.

5. For further refinement of this term, see Gerken, "Second-Order Diversity."

6. Throughout this paper I will use a set of terms interchangeably: decentralization, federalism, localism, and "federalism all the way down." For an explanation of the last term, see Gerken, "Supreme Court 2009 Term."

7. Many law professors have abandoned this formalist conception of rights and acknowledged the crucial role that politics plays in forging robustly enforced rights regimes. The work on "democratic constitutionalism" is extensive. For an excellent overview of these question, see Levinson, "Rights v. Votes."

8. The term was first coined by James Madison; Hamilton, Madison, and Jay, *Federalist Papers*, no. 48, at 305. For an exploration of how parchment barriers become constitutional commitments, see Levinson, "Parchment and Politics."

9. For an analysis of why scholars should pay more attention to the "here to there" on the context of reform, see Gerken, *Democracy Index*.

10. Gerken, "Dissenting by Deciding."

11. I have been writing about these issues since 2004 for a law audience, and some of this essay draws upon ideas explored in greater depth elsewhere. Gerken, "Dissenting by Deciding"; Gerken, "Exit, Voice, and Disloyalty"; Gerken, "Second-Order Diversity"; Gerken, "Supreme Court 2009 Term"; Gerken, "Loyal Opposition." For those writing in a similar vein in political theory, see, e.g., Young, *Justice and the Politics of Difference*; Waldron, *Political Theory*, chap. 5.

12. See below, text accompanying notes 96 and 97.

13. Gerken, "Supreme Court 2009 Term."

14. Shepsle, "Congress Is a 'They,' Not an 'It.'" See also Vermeule, "The Judiciary Is a They, Not an It."

15. See, e.g., Gerken, "Federalism and Nationalism."

16. Gerken, "Federalism and Nationalism."

17. Mikos, "On the Limits of Supremacy"; Young, "Modern-Day Nullification."

18. Gerken, "Federalism and Nationalism."

19. Lipsky, *Street Level Bureaucracy*.

20. For an in-depth treatment of these issues, see Gerken, "Supreme Court 2009 Term"; Gerken, "Federalism and Nationalism."

21. I borrow this phrase from Pettit, "Republican Freedom and Contestatory Democratization" (183–84), though he refers only to the ability of electoral minorities to challenge the law in an acceptably neutral process.

22. See Bulman-Pozen, "Partisan Federalism."

23. Bulman-Pozen, "Partisan Federalism"; Rodríguez, "Negotiating Conflict through Federalism."

24. Riker, *Federalism*, 155.

25. For further explanation, see Gerken, "Supreme Court 2009 Term"; Gerken, "Slipping the Bonds of Federalism." For the seminal work on these questions, see Rubin and Feeley, "Federalism."

26. As I have detailed elsewhere, "Congress has a readymade workaround to bypass the anti-commandeering doctrine, it can usually write in a jurisdictional element to satisfy *Lopez*, it can borrow a page from Justice O'Connor's 'drafting guide' to fit its regulations within the ambit of *Raich*, it can turn to its taxing power when the Commerce Clause won't do, and it will presumably have no trouble evading the dictates of *Sebelius* (unless the Court lends some oomph to its Spending Clause ruling)." Gerken, "Slipping the Bonds of Federalism."

27. *Shelby County v. Holder*, 570 US 529 (2013), invalidated a key provision of the Voting Rights Act.

28. That is even true of *Shelby County*. There were plenty of constitutionally viable strategies for reviving Section 5; the problem is they weren't *politically* viable due to weak national norms.

29. For further explanation and a discussion of why this fact makes it difficult for law professors to engage with contemporary federalism debates, see Gerken, "Federalism and Nationalism."

30. See text accompanying notes 38 and 39.

31. I borrow the formulation from Mary Ann Glendon (*Rights Talk*).

32. The term comes from Justice Holmes, in *Southern Pacific Company v. Jensen*, 244 US 205 (1917), p. 222.

33. The work on the relationship between politics and constitutional change is legion. For just a sampling, see, e.g., Ackerman, *Foundations*; Ackerman, *Transformations*; Ackerman, *Civil Rights Revolution*; Eskridge and Ferejohn, *Republic of Statutes*; Kramer, *The People Themselves*; Devins and Fisher, *Democratic Constitution*; Griffin, *American Constitutionalism*; Tushnet, *Taking the Constitution Away from the Courts*; Tushnet, *New Constitutional Order*; Strauss, "Common Law Constitutional Interpretation"; Strauss, "Irrelevance of Constitutional Amendments"; Balkin and Siegel, "Principles, Practices, and Social Movements"; Kramer, "Popular Constitutionalism, circa 2004"; Post and Siegel, "Legislative Constitutionalism and Section Five Power"; Post and Siegel, "Protecting the Constitution from the People"; Post and Siegel, "Roe Rage"; Post, "The Supreme Court 2000 Term"; Siegel, "Constitutional Culture, Social Movement Conflict, and Constitutional Change"; Balkin, "Populism and Progressivism as Constitutional Categories"; Balkin and Levinson, "Processes of Constitutional Change"; Balkin, "Respect-Worthy"; Balkin and Levinson, "Understanding the Constitutional Revolution"; Friedman, "Mediated Popular Constitutionalism"; Friedman and Smith, "Sedimentary Constitution."

34. Menand, *Metaphysical Club*, 13.

35. For a deep and thoughtful exploration of these ideas in the context of constitutional rights, see Levinson, "Parchment and Politics."

36. For efforts to put the political back into political theory, see Galston, "Realism in Political Theory"; Waldron, *Political Political Theory*; Rosenblum, *On the Side of the Angels*.

37. Melvin Rogers's paper in this volume; Shklar, *American Citizenship*, 25–62.

38. At least no relevant word of the Constitution has changed. The Twenty-Seventh Amendment was passed during this period, but its relevance to gay rights is limited to Pam Karlan's observation that "you could rearrange the letters in the amendment's key words—about 'varying the compensation'—into 'ten gay companions thrive.'" Karlan, "Karlan Speaks at the 2014 LGBT Pride Month Celebration."

39. For an analysis, see Gerken, "Second-Order Diversity."

40. Rehfeld, *Concept of Constituency*.

41. For a more in-depth exploration of these themes, see Gerken, "Second-Order Diversity."

42. Dahl, *Preface to Democratic Theory*, 133.

43. Thomas Christiano terms this "the problem of persistent minorities": Christiano, *Constitution of Equality*, 288. See also 226–28, 288–99 in that same book; Gerken, "Second-Order Diversity," 1110.

44. For additional analysis, see Gerken, "Making Representative Democracy Work."

45. For a full development of this term, see Gerken, "Second-Order Diversity."

46. For a more in-depth exploration of the First Amendment's shortcomings, see Gerken, *Loyal Opposition*.

47. See Allen, "Reconceiving Public Spheres"; Zuckerman, "Cute Cats to the Rescue?"

48. The next few paragraphs are loosely adapted from Gerken, *Loyal Opposition*.

49. For a more in-depth exploration of this term, see Gerken, "Dissenting by Deciding."

50. Agenda setting may be the most powerful tool minorities wield in a majoritarian system. See Vermeule, "Submajority Rules," 74, 80–83.

51. For a fuller account, see Gerken, "Dissenting by Deciding," 1763–65.

52. Bass, "ID Idea Catches On."

53. Sanchez, "There's a Boom in Driver's Licenses Issued to Immigrants Here Illegally."

54. Living Wage Resource Center, "Living Wage Successes."

55. Victor, "California Enacts $15 Minimum Wage"; McGeehan, "New York's Path to $15 Minimum Wage: Uneven and Bumpy."

56. See La Vigne et al., "Police Body-Worn Cameras."

57. Epstein and Brown, "Obama Considered Trip to Ferguson"; Dept. of Justice, "Justice Department Announces $20 Million in Funding to Support Body-Worn Camera Pilot Program."

58. This idea may even undergird *Romer v. Evans*, 517 US 620 (1996), the first gay-rights victory at the Supreme Court. See, e.g., Zeppos, "Dynamics of Democracy," 445, 452–55.

59. For a description of these networks, see Bulman-Pozen, "Partisan Federalism"; Resnik, "Law's Migration"; and Gerken and Tyler, "Myth of the Laboratories of Democracy."

60. Mikos, "On the Limits of Supremacy," 1421, 1425.

61. For an analysis, see Gerken, "*Windsor*'s Mad Genius."

62. Cf. National Commission on Fair Housing and Equal Opportunity, "The Future of Fair Housing"; Orfield, "Reviving the Goal of an Integrated Society."

63. For an argument that a national conversation may not be possible without a series of local ones first, see Rodríguez, "Federalism and National Consensus," 5.

64. For the best work on the subject, see Bulman-Pozen, "Partisan Federalism."

65. For a thoughtful analysis, see Hills, "Federalism as Westphalian Liberalism."

66. *New State Ice Co. v. Liebmann*, 285 US 262, 311 (1932) (Brandeis, J., dissenting).

67. Gerken and Tyler, "Myth of the Laboratories of Democracy."

68. For one of the best analyses of the shortcomings of rights as compared to governance, see Levinson, "Rights and Votes."

69. Even here, the evidence suggests that the policymaking apparatus—legislatively created and administratively implemented—matters more. See Ackerman, *Civil Rights Revolution*.

70. Rodríguez, "Significance of the Local in Immigration Regulation."

71. Email from Guy Charles to Heather Gerken, August 24, 2016. I'm deeply indebted to Guy Charles for encouraging me to work through these arguments.

72. For an earlier exploration of the ideas in this section, see Gerken, "Second-Order Diversity."

73. Some of the best work on the ways in which the micro shapes the macro comes

from one of this volume's editors. See Allen, *Talking to Strangers*; Allen and Light, *From Voice to Influence*. In law, Marc Poirier has led the way. See, e.g., Poirier, "Whiffs of Federalism in *Windsor v. United States*"; Poirier, "Same-Sex Marriage, Identity Processes, and the Kulturkampf"; Poirier, "Microperformances of Identity." Two of the papers in this volume elegantly explore how the macro shapes the micro. See Lai and Banaji, "If Bias Is Implicit, Can It Be Changed?"; Sethi, "Crime and Punishment in Divided Society."

74. See, e.g., Barber, *Strong Democracy*, 119–20, 152; Pateman, *Participation and Democratic Theory*, 23–33; Young, *Justice and the Politics of Difference*, 92; Katz, "Race and the Right to Vote after *Rice v. Cayetano*," 491, 512–14; Michelman, "Conceptions of Democracy in American Constitutional Argument," 443, 478–79.

75. I borrow the term from Appiah, "Race, Culture, Identity," 30, 97.

76. In arguing that constitutive experiences are refracted through group identity, I do not mean to suggest that a group is somehow a monolithic entity whose sense of identity is easily defined or that automatically absorbs each experience of its members. I envision something much less systematic: the simple possibility that members of a group interact with one another and, in doing so, convey information about their democratic experiences, which gradually helps shape each other's sense of themselves and their group identity. My assumption is that these interactions eventually take on a common shape within the group as a whole; they eventually become part of the story that serves as a narrative for members of the group to explain themselves and their relationship to the world. Group narratives, in my view, thus bear some resemblance to the conversations that Jane Mansbridge terms "everyday talk." In Mansbridge's words, "Everyday talk produces results collectively, but not in concert . . . through the combined and interactive effects of relatively isolated individual actions": Mansbridge, "Everyday Talk in the Deliberative System," 211, 212. See also Allen and Light, *From Voice to Influence*, 294 ("the formation of subjectivity, identity, and culture, all of which are direct products of linguistic exchange, have consequences at the level of structure, and therefore, for politics").

77. For a deeper examination of these ideas, see Gerken, "Second-Order Diversity," 1156–58.

78. For a similar take, see Allen, "Difference without Domination," in this volume ("the goal instead is to establish practices that result in political losses circulating through the citizenry over time").

79. Thanks to James Forman for encouraging me to discuss this point.

80. Williams, *Voice, Trust, and Memory*.

81. See Calmes, "When a Boy Found a Familiar Feel in a Pat on a Head of State."

82. Kateb, "Moral Distinctiveness of Representative Democracy," 357, 360.

83. Wingo, "Human Dignity and Modern Democracies," in this volume.

84. These ideas thus resonate with those offered by Danielle Allen in her contribution to this volume. See also Ackerman, *Social Justice in the Liberal State*, 298 (concluding that one argument that favors a "responsive lottery"—a weighted lottery for resolving disputes—is that "it gives the egalitarian minority at least *some* chance of determining the political outcome"); Katz, *Democracy and Elections*, 44 ("would not a better notion of popular sovereignty assure that each individual or group saw its view prevail a fair proportion of the time?").

85. Karlan, "John Hart Ely and the Problem of Gerrymandering," 1329, 1332.

86. To be sure, sometimes a social movement can go too far too fast and prompt backlash. *Brown v. Board of Education*, for instance, prompted intense backlash from white southerners. But it's essential to take a long view on whether the backlash game is worth

the candle. Notice, for instance, that there was backlash to the *Brown* backlash, as the brutal resistance in the South reshaped the debate over race and prompted the passage of the country's most important civil rights legislation. I don't mean to suggest a Whiggish view. But backlash is an intensely complex phenomenon and not one subject to easy generalizations.

87. Cf. Allen, *Talking to Strangers*, 117–18 ("the problem is . . . how to move beyond the idea of the zero-sum political game to a conception of reciprocity so fluid that even a winner doesn't expect to stay a winner for long"). Although Madison hoped that our constitutional structure would refine and enlarge public opinion to focus on the common good, strands of his argument focus on a set of arguments similar to those offered here. See Hamilton, Madison, and Jay, *Federalist Papers*, no. 10, pp. 82–84. See also Guinier, *Tyranny of the Majority*, 4, 17 (arguing that the Madisonian ideal is possible only when voter groupings are fluid and temporary); Mansbridge, "Living with Conflict," 466, 471 (arguing that majority rule precludes optimal equality unless "citizens' interests so crosscut one another that minorities can hope 'that one day they will not lose out and will be deferred to in turn'" (quoting Michael Walzer, *Obligations: Essays on Disobedience, War, and Citizenship* [Cambridge, MA: Harvard University Press, 1970], 47).

88. This argument bears some connection to those made by Nancy Rosenblum in lauding "the possibility of shifting involvements among associations—the *experience of pluralism* by men and women personally and individually": Rosenblum, *Membership and Morals*, 17.

89. Although a formal, stable conception of racial categories permeates most legal debates (see Minow, *Not Only for Myself*, 59), I subscribe to the view that race is a semifluid category, one that can be shaped by individuals as they participate in the political process. See, e.g., Appiah, "Race, Culture, Identity," 78–80 (arguing that although "racial identification is [hard] to resist" in part because racial ascription by others is so insistent, one "*can* choose how central [one's] identification with it will be—choose, that is, how much [one] will organize [one's] life around that identity"); Ford, "Beyond 'Difference,'" 38, 48 (arguing in favor of a concept of racial identity "not as monolithic" but "as fluid and kaleidoscopic," and arguing that "American racial hierarchy creates a mix of racial identities"). See also Appiah, *Ethics of Identity*, chap. 3; Minow, *Not Only for Myself*, 50–51; Young, *Justice and the Politics of Difference*; Shelby, *We Who Are Dark* (exploring the connection between racial identity and other cross-cutting identities).

90. Cf. Parikh, *New Politics of Identity*.

91. Appiah, *Race, Culture, Identity*, 97.

92. Forman, *Locking Up Our Own*.

93. There are as many different versions of this theory as there are theorists, and their views of identity and the role it ought to play vary dramatically. Some find group identity to be a meaningful category; others focus simply on the experience or social status shared by group members; others posit that shared experiences will lead to common interests or perspectives; and still others question the very usefulness of such categories. For a helpful introduction to identity theory and the history of its development, see Taylor, "Politics of Recognition." For additional reflections on the politics of recognition, both supportive and critical, see Minow, *Not Only for Myself*, 30–58; Gutmann, *Multiculturalism*; Phillips, *Politics of Presence*; Rosenblum, *Membership and Morals*, 319–48; Williams, *Voice, Trust, and Memory*; Young, *Justice and the Politics of Difference*, 121–53; and Mansbridge, "Should Blacks Represent Blacks and Women Represent Women? A Contingent 'Yes.'"

94. Phillips, *Politics of Presence*.

95. Phillips, *Politics of Presence*, 40. See also Barber, *Strong Democracy*, 120 ("where democracy is end as well as means, its politics take on the sense of a journey in which ... the relations among travelers are as vital as the destinations they ... are seeking"). For a general defense of the right to vote as a symbol of inclusion, see Shklar, *Amerian Citizenship*.

96. See, e.g., Mansbridge, "Should Blacks Represent Blacks and Women Represent Women? A Contingent 'Yes,'" 651.

97. Allen, "Toward a Connected Society."

98. I borrow the phrase from Justice Souter, *Johnson v. De Grandy*, 512 US 997, 1020 (1994).

99. This solution bears some resemblance to the model put forward by Anne Phillips in *Multiculturalism without Culture*, though she is more skeptical of the role played by political institutions than I am. For an exploration of the virtues of cycling in institutional design, see Calabresi and Bobbitt, *Tragic Choices*.

100. Indeed while the temporary nature of the interaction may undermine chances that participation will create long-term affective ties, as Nancy Rosenblum points out in discussing voluntary associations, "precisely because [such associations] are *not* mini-communities and involve only weak ties, small groups may be a training ground for ordinary interactions": Rosenblum, *Membership and Morals*, 361.

101. See generally National Commission on Fair Housing and Equal Opportunity, *Future of Fair Housing*; Orfield, "Reviving the Goal of an Integrated Society."

102. *City of Richmond v. J. A. Croson*, 488 US 469 (1989).

103. *City of Richmond v. J .A. Croson*, 488 US 469 (1989).

104. "Plan for Omaha Schools Raises Segregation Concerns" (quoting Ernie Chambers: "The real issue is one of power. We believe that the people whose children attend schools ought to have local control over those schools, a concept very familiar with white people.... Whenever you give adults, parents, members of the community a stake in the education of the children who represent the future, they take an interest, they participate in making sure that the schools do as they should").

105. Dillon, "Law to Segregate Omaha Schools Divides Nebraska."

106. Basu, "Ferguson Election Makes History, Adds More Blacks to City Council."

107. Pierre and Jackson, "In Ferguson, City Increases African American Representation."

108. Cf. Rothstein, "Making of Ferguson." And see generally National Commission on Fair Housing and Equal Opportunity, *Future of Fair Housing*; Orfield, "Reviving the Goal of an Integrated Society."

Works Cited

Ackerman, Bruce. *The Civil Rights Revolution*, vol. 3 of *We the People*. Cambridge, MA: Belknap, 2014.

Ackerman, Bruce. *Foundations*, vol. 1 of *We the People*. Cambridge, MA: Belknap, 1991.

Ackerman, Bruce. *Social Justice in the Liberal State*. New Haven, CT: Yale University Press, 1980.

Ackerman, Bruce. *Transformations*, vol. 2 of *We the People*. Cambridge, MA: Belknap, 1998.

Allen, Danielle. "Reconceiving Public Spheres: The Flow Dynamics Model." In Allen and Light, *From Voice to Influence*, 178–210.

Allen, Danielle. *Talking to Strangers: Anxieties of Citizenship since "Brown v. Board of Education."* Chicago: University of Chicago Press, 2004.

Allen, Danielle. "Toward a Connected Society." In *Our Compelling Interests: The Value of Diversity for Democracy and a Prosperous Society*, edited by Earl Lewis and Nancy Cantors, 71–105. Our Compelling Interests 1. Princeton, NJ: Princeton University Press, 2016.

Allen, Danielle, and Jennifer S. Light. *From Voice to Influence: Understanding Citizenship in a Digital Age*. Chicago: University of Chicago Press, 2015.

Appiah, Kwame Anthony. "Race, Culture, Identity: Misunderstood Connections." In K. Anthony Appiah and Amy Gutmann, *Color Conscious: The Political Morality of Race*, by 30–105. Princeton, NJ: Princeton University Press, 1996.

Appiah, Kwame Anthony. *The Ethics of Identity*. Princeton, NJ: Princeton University Press, 2005.

Balkin, Jack M. "Populism and Progressivism as Constitutional Categories." Review of Cass R. Sunstein, *Democracy and the Problem of Free Speech* (New York: Free Press, 1995). *Yale Law Review* 104, no. 7 (1995): 1935–90.

Balkin, Jack M. "Respect-Worthy: Frank Michelman and the Legitimate Constitution." *Tulsa Law Review* 39, no. 3 (2013): 485–510.

Balkin, Jack M., and Sanford V. Levinson. "The Processes of Constitutional Change: From Partisan Entrenchment to the National Surveillance State." *Fordham Law Review* 75, no. 2 (2006): 489–535.

Balkin, Jack M., and Sanford V. Levinson. "Understanding the Constitutional Revolution." *Virginia Law Review* 87, no. 6 (2001): 1045–110.

Balkin, Jack M., and Reva B. Siegel. "Principles, Practices, and Social Movements." *University of Pennsylvania Law Review* 154, no. 4 (2006): 927–50.

Balz, Dan, and Ruth Marcus. "Clinton Said to Fill Last 4 Cabinet Jobs: Baird, Babbitt, Espy, Peña Chosen." *Washington Post*, December 24, 1992, A1.

Barber, Benjamin R. *Strong Democracy: Participatory Politics for a New Age*. Berkeley: University of California Press, 1984.

Bass, Paul. "ID Idea Catches On." *New Haven Independent*, August 15, 2007.

Basu, Moni. "Ferguson Election Makes History, Adds More Blacks to City Council." *CNN.com*, April 8, 2015.

Bulman-Pozen, Jessica. "Partisan Federalism." *Harvard Law Review* 127, no. 4 (2014): 1077–146.

Calabresi, Guido, and Philip Bobbitt. *Tragic Choices: The Conflicts Society Confronts in the Allocation of Tragically Scarce Resources*. Fels Lectures on Public Policy Analysis. New York: W. W. Norton, 1978.

Calmes, Jackie. "When a Boy Found a Familiar Feel in a Pat on a Head of State." *New York Times*, May 23, 2012.

Christiano, Thomas. *The Constitution of Equality: Democratic Authority and Its Limits*. New York: Oxford University Press, 2008.

City of Richmond v. J. A. Croson, 488 US 469 (1989).

Dahl, Robert A. *A Preface to Democratic Theory*. Chicago: University of Chicago Press, 1956.

Department of Justice Office of Public Affairs. "Justice Department Announces $20 Million in Funding to Support Body-Worn Camera Pilot Program," Press release.

May 1, 2015. http://www.justice.gov/opa/pr/justice-department-announces-20
-million-funding-support-body-worn-camera-pilot-program.

Devins, Neal, and Louis Fisher. *The Democratic Constitution*. New York: Oxford University Press, 2004.

Dillon, Sam. "Law to Segregate Omaha Schools Divides Nebraska." *New York Times*, April 15, 2006, A9.

Epstein, Jennifer, and Carrie Budoff Brown. "Obama Considered Trip to Ferguson: White House Decided Presidential Visit Would Be Too Disruptive." *Politico*, December 1, 2014.

Eskridge, William N., Jr., and John Ferejohn. *A Republic of Statutes: The New American Constitution*. New Haven, CT: Yale University Press, 2010.

Ford, Richard T. "Beyond 'Difference': A Reluctant Critique of Legal Identity Politics." In *Left Legalism / Left Critique*, edited by Wendy Brown and Janet Halley, 38–79. Durham, NC: Duke University Press, 2002.

Forman, James, Jr. *Locking Up Our Own: Crime and Punishment in Black America*. New York: Farrar, Strauss and Giroux, 2017.

Friedman, Barry. "Mediated Popular Constitutionalism." *Michigan Law Review* 101, no. 8 (2003): 2596–636.

Friedman, Barry, and Scott B. Smith. "The Sedimentary Constitution." *University of Pennsylvania Law Review* 147, no. 1 (1998): 1–90.

Galston, William A. "Realism in Political Theory." *European Journal of Political Theory* 9, no. 4 (2010): 385–411.

Gerken, Heather K. *The Democracy Index: Why Our Election System Is Failing and How to Fix It*. Princeton, NJ: Princeton University Press, 2009.

Gerken, Heather K. "Dissenting by Deciding." *Stanford Law Review* 57, no. 6 (2005): 1745–805.

Gerken, Heather K. "Exit, Voice, and Disloyalty." *Duke Law Journal* 62, no. 7 (2013): 1349–86.

Gerken, Heather K. "Federalism and Nationalism: Time for a Détente?" *St. Louis University Law Review* 59, no. 4 (2015): 997–1044.

Gerken, Heather K. "The Loyal Opposition." *Yale Law Journal* 123, no. 6 (2014): 1958–94.

Gerken, Heather K. "Making Representative Democracy Work." Review of *The Concept of Constituency: Political Representation, Democratic Legitimacy, and Institutional Design*, by Andrew Rehfeld (Cambridge: Cambridge University Press, 2005), and *Saving Democracy: A Plan for Real Representation in America*, by Kevin O'Leary (Stanford, CT: Stanford University Press, 2006). *Political Theory* 37, no. 6 (2009): 838–44.

Gerken, Heather K. "Second-Order Diversity." *Harvard Law Review* 118, no. 4 (2005): 1101–96.

Gerken, Heather K. "Slipping the Bonds of Federalism." *Harvard Law Review* 128, no. 1 (2014): 85–123.

Gerken, Heather K. "The Supreme Court 2009 Term—Foreword: Federalism All the Way Down." *Harvard Law Review* 124, no. 1 (2010): 4–74.

Gerken, Heather K. "*Windsor*'s Mad Genius: The Interlocking Gears of Rights and Structure." *Boston University Law Review* 95, no. 2 (2015): 587–613.

Gerken, Heather K., and Charles Tyler. "The Myth of the Laboratories of Democracy." Unpublished manuscript, 2013 (on file with author).

Glendon, Mary Ann. *Rights Talk: The Impoverishment of Political Discourse*. New York: Free Press, 1991.

Griffin, Stephen M. *American Constitutionalism: From Theory to Politics*. Princeton, NJ: Princeton University Press, 1996.

Guinier, Lani. *The Tyranny of the Majority: Fundamental Fairness in Representational Democracy*. New York: Free Press, 1994.

Gutmann, Amy, ed. *Multiculturalism: Examining the Politics of Recognition*. Princeton, NJ: Princeton University Press, 1994.

Hamilton, Alexander, James Madison, and John Jay. *The Federalist Papers*. Edited by Clinton Rossiter. New York: Penguin, 2003.

Hills, Roderick M., Jr. "Federalism as Westphalian Liberalism." *Fordham Law Review* 75, no. 2 (2006): 769–98.

Johnson v. De Grandy, 512 US 997 (1994). Justice Souter.

Karlan, Pamela. "Deputy Assistant Attorney General for the Civil Rights Division Pamela Karlan Speaks at the 2014 LGBT Pride Month Celebration." Washington, DC, June 10, 2014. https://www.justice.gov/opa/speech/deputy-assistant-attorney-general-civil-rights-division-pamela-karlan-speaks-2014-lgbt.

Karlan, Pamela S. "John Hart Ely and the Problem of Gerrymandering: The Lion in Winter." *Yale Law Journal* 114, no. 6 (2005): 1329–51.

Kateb, George. "The Moral Distinctiveness of Representative Democracy." *Ethics* 91, no. 3 (1981): 357–74.

Katz, Ellen D. "Race and the Right to Vote after *Rice v. Cayetano*." *Michigan Law Review* 99, no. 3 (2000): 481–531.

Katz, Richard S. *Democracy and Elections*. New York: Oxford University Press, 1997.

Kramer, Larry D. *The People Themselves: Popular Constitutionalism and Judicial Review*. New York: Oxford University Press, 2004.

Kramer, Larry D. "Popular Constitutionalism, circa 2004." *California Law Review* 92, no. 4 (2004): 959–1011.

Kymlicka, Will. *Multicultural Citizenship: A Liberal Theory of Minority Rights*. New York: Oxford University Press, 1995.

La Vigne, Nancy G., et al. "Police Body-Worn Cameras: Where Your State Stands." *Urban Institute*. http://apps.urban.org/features/body-camera/.

Levinson, Daryl T. "Parchment and Politics: The Positive Puzzle of Constitutional Commitment." *Harvard Law Review* 124, no. 3 (2011): 657–746.

Levinson, Daryl T. "Rights and Votes." *Yale Law Journal* 121, no. 6 (2012): 1286–363.

Lijphart, Arend. *Democracy in Plural Societies: A Comparative Exploration*. New Haven, CT: Yale University Press, 1977.

Lipsky, Michael. *Street Level Bureaucracy: Dilemmas of the Individual in Public Services*. New York: Russell Sage Foundation, 1980.

Living Wage Resource Center. "Living Wage Successes." 2009. http://bit.ly/2btwj9K.

Mansbridge, Jane. "Everyday Talk in the Deliberative System." In *Deliberative Politics: Essays on Democracy and Disagreement*, edited by Stephen Macedo, 211–42. New York: Oxford University Press, 1999.

Mansbridge, Jane J. "Living with Conflict: Representation in the Theory of Adversary Democracy." *Ethics* 91, no. 3 (1981): 466–76.

Mansbridge, Jane. "Should Blacks Represent Blacks and Women Represent Women? A Contingent 'Yes.'" *Journal of Politics* 61, no. 3 (1999): 628–57.

McGeehan, Patrick. "New York's Path to $15 Minimum Wage: Uneven and Bumpy." *New York Times*, April 1, 2016.

Menand, Louis. *The Metaphysical Club: A Story of Ideas in America*. New York: Farrar, Straus, and Giroux, 2001.

Michelman, Frank I. "Conceptions of Democracy in American Constitutional Argument: Voting Rights." *Florida Law Review* 41 (1989): 443–90.

Mikos, Robert A. "On the Limits of Supremacy: Medical Marijuana and the States' Overlooked Power to Legalize Federal Crime." *Vanderbilt Law Review* 62, no. 5 (2009): 1421–82.

Minow, Martha. *Not Only for Myself: Identity, Politics, and the Law*. New York: New Press, 1999.

National Commission on Fair Housing and Equal Opportunity. "The Future of Fair Housing." 2008.

New State Ice Co. v. Liebmann, 285 US 262 (1932). Justice Brandeis, dissenting.

Orfield, Gary. "Reviving the Goal of an Integrated Society: A 21st Century Challenge." Los Angeles: Civil Rights Project / UCLA, January 2009.

Parikh, Bhikhu. *A New Politics of Identity: Political Principles for an Interdependent World*. New York: Palgrave, 2008.

Pateman, Carole. *Participation and Democratic Theory*. Cambridge: Cambridge University Press, 1970.

Pettit, Philip. "Republican Freedom and Contestatory Democratization." In *Democracy's Value*, edited by Ian Shapiro and Casiano Hacker-Cordón, 163–90. Cambridge: Cambridge University Press, 1999.

Phillips, Anne. *Multiculturalism without Culture*. Princeton, NJ: Princeton University Press, 2007.

Phillips, Anne. *The Politics of Presence*. Oxford: Clarendon, 1995.

Pierre, Jeffrey, and Phillip Jackson. "In Ferguson, City Increases African American Representation." *Voting Wars, News12*, August 20, 2016. https://votingwars.news21.com/in-ferguson-city-increases-african-american-representation/.

"Plan for Omaha Schools Raises Segregation Concerns." *PBS NewsHour*, May 31, 2006. Transcript available at https://www.pbs.org/newshour/show/plan-for-omaha-schools-raises-segregation-concerns.

Poirier, Marc R. "Microperformances of Identity: Visible Same-Sex Couples and the Marriage Controversy." *Washington and Lee Journal of Civil Rights and Social Justice* 15, no. 1 (2008): 3–84.

Poirier, Marc. "Same-Sex Marriage, Identity Processes, and the Kulturkampf: Why Federalism Is Not the Main Event." *Temple Political and Civil Rights Law Review* 17, no. 2 (2008): 387–420.

Poirier, Marc. "Whiffs of Federalism in *Windsor v. United States*: Power, Localism, and Kulturkampf." *Colorado Law Review* 85, no. 4 (2014): 935–1001.

Post, Robert C. "The Supreme Court 2000 Term—Foreword: Fashioning the Legal Constitution: Culture, Courts, and Law." *Harvard Law Review* 117 (2002).

Post, Robert C., and Reva B. Siegel. "Legislative Constitutionalism and Section Five Power: Policentric Interpretation of the Family and Medical Leave Act." *Yale Law Journal* 112, no. 8 (2003): 1943–2059.

Post, Robert C., and Reva B. Siegel. "Protecting the Constitution from the People: Juricentric Restrictions on Section Five Power." *Indiana Law Journal* 78, no. 1 (2003): 1–45.

Post, Robert, and Reva Siegel. "Roe Rage: Democratic Constitutionalism and Back-lash." *Harvard Civil Rights-Civil Liberties Law Review* 42, no. 2 (2007): 373–433.

Rehfeld, Andrew. *The Concept of Constituency: Political Representation, Democratic Legitimacy, and Institutional Design.* Cambridge: Cambridge University Press, 2005.

Resnik, Judith. "Law's Migration: American Exceptionalism, Silent Dialogues, and Federalism's Multiple Ports of Entry." *Yale Law Journal* 115, no. 7 (2006): 1564–670.

Riker, William H. *Federalism: Origin, Operation, Significance.* New York: Little, Brown, 1964.

Rodríguez, Cristina M. "Federalism and National Consensus." Unpublished paper, October 2010 draft.

Rodríguez, Cristina M. "Negotiating Conflict through Federalism: Institutional and Popular Perspectives." *Yale Law Journal* 123, no. 6 (2014): 1626–2133.

Rodríguez, Cristina M. "The Significance of the Local in Immigration Regulation." *Michigan Law Review* 106, no. 4 (2008): 567–642.

Rosenblum, Nancy. *Membership and Morals: The Personal Uses of Pluralism in America.* Princeton, NJ: Princeton University Press, 1998.

Rosenblum, Nancy. *On the Side of the Angels: An Appreciation of Parties and Partisanship.* Princeton, NJ: Princeton University Press, 2008.

Rothstein, Richard. "The Making of Ferguson: Public Policies at the Root of Its Troubles." Economic Policy Institute, October 15, 2014. https://www.epi.org/publication/making-ferguson/.

Rubin, Edward L., and Malcolm Feeley. "Federalism: Some Notes on a National Neurosis." *UCLA Law Review* 41 (1994): 903–52.

Sanchez, Tatiana. "There's a Boom in Driver's Licenses Issued to Immigrants Here Illegally." *Los Angeles Times*, February 8, 2016.

Shelby, Tommie. *We Who Are Dark: The Philosophical Foundations of Black Solidarity.* Cambridge, MA: Harvard University Press, 2005.

Shelby County v. Holder, 570 US 529 (2013).

Shepsle, Kenneth A. "Congress Is a 'They,' Not an 'It': Legislative Intent as Oxymoron." *International Review of Law and Economics* 12, no. 2 (1992): 239–56.

Shklar, Judith N. *American Citizenship: The Quest for Inclusion.* Tanner Lectures on Human Values. Cambridge, MA: Harvard University Press, 1991.

Siegel, Reva B. "Constitutional Culture, Social Movement Conflict, and Constitutional Change: The Case of the De Facto Era." *California Law Review* 94, no. 5 (2006): 1323–419.

Southern Pacific Company v. Jensen, 244 US 205 (1917). Justice Holmes.

Strauss, David A. "Common Law Constitutional Interpretation." *University of Chicago Law Review* 63, no. 3 (1996): 877–935.

Strauss, David A. "The Irrelevance of Constitutional Amendments." *Harvard Law Review* 114, no. 5 (2001): 1457–1505.

Taylor, Charles. "The Politics of Recognition." In *Multiculturalism: Examining the Politics of Recognition*, edited and introduced by Amy Gutmann, 25–73. Princeton, NJ: Princeton University Press, 1994.

Tushnet, Mark. *The New Constitutional Order.* Princeton, NJ: Princeton University Press, 2004.

Tushnet, Mark. *Taking the Constitution Away from the Courts.* Princeton, NJ: Princeton University Press, 2000.

Vermeule, Adrian. "The Judiciary Is a They, Not an It: Interpretive Theory and the Fallacy of Division." *Journal of Contemporary Legal Issues* 14, no. 2 (2005).

Vermeule, Adrian. "Submajority Rules: Forcing Accountability upon Majorities." *Journal of Political Philosophy* 13, no. 1 (2005): 74–98.

Victor, Daniel. "California Enacts $15 Minimum Wage." *New York Times*, April 4, 2016.

Waldron, Jeremy. *Political Political Theory, Essays on Institutions.* Cambridge, MA: Harvard University Press, 2016.

Williams, Melissa S. *Voice, Trust, and Memory: Marginalized Groups and the Failings of Liberal Representation.* Princeton, NJ: Princeton University Press, 1998.

Young, Ernest A. "Modern-Day Nullification: Marijuana and the Persistence of Federalism in an Age of Overlapping Regulatory Jurisdiction." *Case Western Law Review* 65, no. 3 (2015): 769–94.

Young, Iris Marion. *Justice and the Politics of Difference.* Princeton, NJ: Princeton University Press, 1990.

Zeppos, Nicholas S. "The Dynamics of Democracy: Travel, Premature Predation, and the Components of Political Identity." *Vanderbilt Law Review* 50 (1997).

Zuckerman, Ethan. "Cute Cats to the Rescue? Participatory Media and Political Expression." In *From Voice to Influence: Understanding Citizenship in a Digital Age,* edited by Danielle Allen and Jennifer Light. Chicago: University of Chicago Press, 2015.

9

Contributing to a Society of Equals

AFFIRMATIVE ACTION BEYOND THE "DISTRIBUTIVE PARADIGM"

Urs Lindner

Affirmative action is one of the most famous and commonly adopted measures of "the politics of difference" (Young 1990/2011). Addressing disadvantages people suffer because of race, caste, gender, sexuality, or able-bodiedness, affirmative action policies emerged at different times and places around the globe. The United States, which developed affirmative action measures in the second half of the 1960s (Skrentny 1996), was by no means the first country to do so. India prominently preceded the United States, implementing public service quotas for lower-caste people already at the dawn of the twentieth century (Jaffrelot 2006). Today, with Brazil, South Africa, and the European Union at the forefront, affirmative action has become a global policy (Kennedy-Dubourdieu 2006; Brown, Langer, and Stewart 2012; Dupper and Sankaran 2014).

At the same time, affirmative action is also one of the most controversial and contested public policies. The contestation pertains to its aims, its means, and its range, implicating both normative and pragmatic criteria of evaluation. In rough terms, conservatives charge affirmative action with being socially divisive, dismantling meritocratic reward systems, and perpetuating heinous classifications. They criticize policies that seem to turn away from ensuring that an atomistic individual gets what he or she deserves on the basis of effort and talent. Leftists, on the other hand, typically argue that affirmative action fails to attack the structural roots of social inequality and does not reach the truly needy. Following political theorist Nancy Fraser, they distinguish transformative policies of redistribution from those that affirm the status quo and assign affirmative action to the latter category.[1]

Both groups of critics and many supporters of affirmative action share some common ground: they frame affirmative action policies according to the "distributive paradigm" (Young 1990). In this paradigm, justice and equality are treated as having primarily to do with what people get in terms of goods and resources. Yet a plausible justification of affirmative action, I will argue in this paper, requires leaving the terrain of distributive justice and focusing on relational or social equality instead. I do not deny that affirmative action in a certain sense can be seen as a (re)-distributive strategy, nor should the importance of (re)distributions in general be disputed. Yet by shifting to a framework of relational equality for thinking about affirmative action measures, we can not only offer a stronger justification for such policies but also show how they can have a transformative impact at a structural level, spurring change toward development of a "society of equals" (Rosanvallon 2013). The first claim falls within the domain of normative political theory; the second is based on a sociological account of how social inequality works.

In what follows, I begin by distinguishing several kinds of affirmative action; I also briefly discuss the one-sidedness of the US debate. Then I introduce the pursuit of social equality as a potential rationale for affirmative action, and argue that this is a far stronger justification than those resting on claims of distributive egalitarianism, rectificatory compensation, or diversity. Third, I turn to sociological work on inequality in order to clarify the project of transforming inegalitarian into egalitarian social relations. In doing so, I draw in particular on the work of Pierre Bourdieu and Charles Tilly. In a fourth and final section, I discuss to what extent different affirmative action measures may have a transformative impact on social structures and thereby contribute to achieving more equal social relations, as opposed to merely mitigating distributive imbalances. In focusing on more equal social relations, I offer one approach to fleshing out the principle of "difference without domination."

1. Debating Affirmative Action

Even if affirmative action policies are highly contested, there may be — at least in a comparative perspective — agreement that they share some general features. Depending on geographical context and timing, affirmative action addresses disadvantages that people are suffering because of race, caste, gender, sexuality, or able-bodiedness. It is normally implemented in one or several of the following domains: political representation, employment, public procurement, and college admission. Furthermore, it has a juridical anchorage, which varies with the spectrum of constitutions, specific codes, or the invention of traditions by courts. Finally, the functioning of the concrete policies deployed under the heading of "affirmative action" can be clarified by distinguishing three kinds of them: facilitative, preferential, and indirect affirmative action.[2]

Facilitative affirmative action policies cover an array of measures that in both their means and their ends are oriented toward difference and pick out members of disadvantaged groups. Among them one can further distinguish "outreach" and "empowerment schemes." Outreach primarily consists of recruiting methods that specifically target members of those groups. Their aim is to broaden the pool of qualified job or admission candidates to such an extent that existing talent becomes eligible. When the term "affirmative action" became prominent in the United States in the first half of the 1960s, its meaning was initially restricted to nondiscrimination and special efforts in this sense of outreach (Skrentny 1996). In its empowering dimension, facilitative affirmative action provides training programs for disadvantaged individuals that help them acquire capacities, in the sense of either qualifications required for a certain task or techniques of self-assertion in a discriminatory environment. Whereas outreach is typically restricted to the recruitment process, empowering capacity building is relevant before and after this stage. In Germany, affirmative action for a long time mainly implied this empowerment aspect by providing programs for "women's promotion" (*Frauenförderung*).

By contrast to facilitative affirmative action policies, preferential affirmative action does not regulate the environment of the competition for jobs, mandates, admissions, or public spending, but deploys group disadvantage as a factor that influences the outcome of the selection process itself. Whereas recruitment strategies affect who shows up at the starting line, preferential affirmative action reorganizes the criteria for awarding the goods or benefits of a competition, in a context of scarcity. There are basically four forms of preferential treatment: (1) quotas in the sense of reserved seats or set-asides; (2) tiebreaker rules; (3) numerical advantages such as adding points to a standardized test score; and (4) individualized procedures that treat group membership as one factor among others. India, the country that invented preferential affirmative action, has so far the most elaborate quota scheme on the globe.[3] In the United States, right from the start of affirmative action policies, talking about quotas was a taboo. The Supreme Court explicitly declared racial quotas in higher education to be unconstitutional in *Bakke* and allowed only individualized admission preferences (like the Harvard system, as Wu discusses in this volume). This approach resulted in actors' using a euphemistic terminology of "goals, targets, and timetables." In Germany and the European Union, preferential treatment existed for a long time primarily in the form of tiebreaker rules. Recently, however, employment quotas for women have been introduced, primarily at the level of corporate management.[4]

I understand "indirect affirmative action" to refer to policies that are neutral in their means but aim at particularly enhancing the prospects of members of disadvantaged groups. These policies, again, can be differentiated according to the facilitative-preferential distinction. The preferential strand of indirect affirmative action typically takes geography as a proxy for race when scarce goods are allocated. The most prominent examples for this are University of Texas's admission rules enabling access to the top 10 percent from all Texas high schools and the special admission track for students from "educational priority areas" that has been introduced at Sciences Po, one of France's elite universities (Sabbagh 2011b). By contrast, the facilitative strand of indirect affirmative action relates to the conditions of inclusion by designing measures that may be to the benefit of everyone. One case is accessibility: all people benefit from architectural reconstructions that, for example, flatten entrances, although such a reconstruction is particularly undertaken for the sake of people with special needs. Yet another example is parental leave and allowance: such policies are formally gender neutral because they can be claimed by men as well as women, but their purpose is gender conscious. These policies aim to enable women to continue their careers—not least by giving men incentives to engage in early childhood care.

Among the three types of affirmative action, preferential affirmative action is particularly contested as it introduces group membership as a criterion within the competition for jobs, mandates, admissions, or public spending. The contestation has many twists, but in the United States it developed particularly around two related problems: first, the challenge from conservatives that preferential treatment eviscerates merit, a valuable concept in its own right; and second, a question based on the equal protection clause of the US Constitution about whether people have a right to equal treatment as regards the distribution of scarce goods. Proponents of affirmative action have replied to conservative critics by noting that all affirmative action regimes employ basic thresholds of qualification. They have further pointed to the ambiguities of the merit principle. According to them, this principle usually confounds past achievement, future potential (as indicated by qualifications), and desert, that is, issues of efficiency with those of moral entitlements. They also point out that qualifications are not objectively measurable but a subject of reasonable disagreement (Gutmann 1996, 120), and thus, in the last instance, a matter of politics.[5] As for the alleged requirement of equal treatment, defenders of affirmative action have argued, following Dworkin (1976), that people basically have a right to treatment as equals, to equal respect and concern in the sense of not being treated as inferiors or subjected to arbitrary procedures. In certain contexts this treatment as equals may necessitate equal treatment (equality *before* the law) and in others differential treatment in favor of the disadvantaged (equality *through* the law). Therefore, constitutional equality clauses should not be interpreted according to the formalistic principle of "anticlassification" or "antidifferentiation," but in consistence with the substantive ideals of "antisubordination" or "antihierarchization."[6]

Importantly, this contestation around preferential affirmative action policies has focused the discussion not on the broader egalitarian goals of affirmative action but on the narrow grounds of distributive principles for the allocation of jobs, seats in college, and contracts. The same is true about one final point made by critics: the so-called creamy layer problem. According to this critique, affirmative action (in both its preferential and facilitative forms) produces new distributive injustices by systematically privileging the economically privileged within the disadvantaged, thus not reaching the "truly needy."[7] Again, this challenge to affirmative action policies, which reduces the complexities of inequality to economic inequality or — as most critics are not egalitarians at all — to poverty, may appear in a different light as soon as the framework of justification is no longer dominated by the distributive paradigm.

Proponents of affirmative action have been aware of this and have, in order to justify their favored policy, often switched from distributive justice to two other rationales: an argument for corrective compensation and/or the diversity model. According to the compensation rationale, affirmative action is not a matter of distributive but of corrective justice, repairing past wrongs. Now there are several difficulties with this justification, but one in particular ties it to questions of distributive justice: why should, of all possible policies, affirmative action measures be adequate means for reparations and not, for example, generous cash transfers or property redistributions, which ensure that the most severely injured or their descendants are reached? Thus the corrective compensation rationale does not specifically justify affirmative action policies. The diversity rationale, which justifies affirmative action in reference to the needs of culturally heterogeneous customers, the educational necessity of embracing difference, or the open-mindedness of governance, is haunted by a similar question: it presupposes a distributive standard that is all but innocuous, that is, "equal representation" or "exact mirroring." Within the diversity framework, this standard introduces de facto quotas in favor of the already privileged, as too many members of disadvantaged groups would amount to overrepresentation, as Ellen Wu details in her chapter. The diversity rationale, its implicit expectation of mirroring, and related tacit use of quotas may reify minority status.[8] Here we hit the problems of measurement and categorization that plague this space, as the chapters in this section of the volume argue.

2. The Social Egalitarian Justification of Affirmative Action

Is there yet another justification for affirmative action policies — a ratio-nale that takes the ideal of political equality seriously, as in the chapter by Allen in this volume, without getting caught up in self-defeating contra-dictions? Surprisingly, advocates of affirmative action have rarely even posed this question. Usually when confronted with the issue of equality, they retreat to a (substantialized) principle of equal opportunity, thus presenting affirmative action as a simple prolongation of antidiscrimina-tion policies.[9] One reason for this anxious stance on equality may have to do with the philosophical debate following the publication of John Rawls's pathbreaking *A Theory of Justice* (1971).

Rawls's theory of egalitarian justice connected the distribution of "pri-mary goods" (liberty and opportunity, income and wealth, and the "social bases of self-respect") to the main institutional features of society (the "basic structure," the "system of social cooperation"). If people contrib-ute as moral equals to a common cooperative framework, then, the ar-gument runs, there is a presumption of equality (Gosepath 2015) in the distribution of benefits produced by this system, meaning that people are entitled to equal shares in wealth and income, where inequalities are limited by the difference principle.[10] The discussion following Rawls fo-cused initially on the distributive part of his argument and the metric of egalitarian justice (Cohen 1989), the "equality of what" question (Sen 1979), and paid relatively little attention to the relational elements of the contractarian framework of cooperation.[11] Beginning in the late 1980s this kind of distributive egalitarianism came under heavy attack, among others from proponents of the "sufficiency principle." Philosophers like Harry Frankfurt argued that an equal distribution is of no intrinsic value. People do not need an equal amount of goods but enough to pursue a decent life (Frankfurt 1987).[12]

Only in the late 1990s would the pendulum swing again in the direc-tion of egalitarianism. This time, however, it sparked a reorientation away from distributive questions and toward the topic of social equality. For social egalitarians the primary question of justice is not what people get but whether they can relate to and encounter each other as equals. How certain goods are to be distributed depends on the characteristics of the

relations in which people stand, and cannot be decided on a purely distributive basis.[13] This also enabled a rereading of Rawls, who already in
A Theory of Justice had distinguished between "distributive justice" and
"allocative justice" (1971, 88). The former connects distributive claims
to a "fair system of social cooperation" whereas the latter cuts this connection and treats the distributive level in isolation, thus becoming inde-
fensible. For social egalitarians this implies, already within Rawls, a clear
commitment to view relationships as prior to distributions, or relations
as prior to transactions, as Loury argues in this volume.

To the extent that social egalitarians share Rawls's contractarian framework of cooperation, they may agree that an egalitarian distribution of
wealth and income is intrinsically just, that is, of moral worth in itself, as a
logical consequence of the contractarian position (Schemmel 2011b). But
this is not their main concern with distributions. Instead they consider
them primarily from an instrumental perspective. Thus they argue that
equalizations of resources can prevent the development of durable power
differentials (domination) and hierarchical status orders—structural features, which clearly do not allow people to relate to each other as equals
or to be treated as such by institutions (Scanlon 1996).[14] Social egalitarians subscribe to what critical legal theory calls the "antisubordination
principle": distributive inequalities may be tolerable as long as they do
not imply or lead to social relations of superiority and inferiority. This
bears an affinity to the nondomination principle articulated in the volume by Allen and Rogers.

To adopt an argument for the pursuit of social equality as a justification for affirmation action is to propose that we need policies that ensure
that members of a society relate to and encounter each other as equals,
and that affirmative action policies fit that bill. On the basis of such a justification, the aim of affirmative action policies would be to fully include
people and enable their participation as equals in social life. That people
can relate to each other as equals presupposes institutional contexts in
which they are treated on the basis of equal concern and respect. According to the social equality rationale, affirmative action measures have
the function of removing barriers to this kind of inclusion and participation and allowing people to use their new opportunities with self-respect.
Whether those policies successfully fulfill this function is the main standard for evaluating their practical adequacy.

The social equality rationale does not consider affirmative action's
(re)distributions to be intrinsically just. Instead the question is whether
the redistributions of affirmative action policies are *instrumentally* just.

Do they help establish cooperative relations of equality within a population? Interestingly, social egalitarianism may also redirect the semantics of "equal representation" and "statistical mirroring": for example, a 50 percent quota for women may turn out to be an important vehicle of recognition, signalizing that women are welcome as an equal part of society. As tools to advance social equality, affirmative action's distributive standards are highly context-dependent. This means it is not predetermined how the barriers to full inclusion and participation as equals are best removed, whether we need, for example, quotas or not, quotas of which percentage, etc.[15]

This social egalitarian justification of affirmative action is heavily indebted to Elizabeth Anderson's work on democratic equality in general (1999 and 2012) and on affirmative action in particular (2002 and 2010). Where we part company, however, is Anderson's elaboration of the social egalitarian justification according to a paradigm of integration. I consider this elaboration an unnecessary limitation of the quest for relational equality for two main reasons. First, it clearly builds on the workings of racial inequality (and, by analogy, those of caste). Yet one may wonder whether affirmative action for women or people with special needs can be convincingly justified in terms of integration; after all, women especially are not segregated, or not systematically segregated, so a goal of integration would not support the pursuit of equality for these groups.[16] Second, the integration rationale also rules out the use by disadvantaged groups of an emancipatory politics of self-segregation. With this feature of her argument Anderson has severed affirmative action from the richness of black liberation thinking (as described for the nineteenth century by Rogers in this volume) or politics in the Ambedkarite tradition.[17] Thus one of the central arguments of this paper is that the social egalitarian justification of affirmative action by no means automatically implies an imperative of integration.

Generally, affirmative action's instrumentally just distributive standards depend on the kinds of barriers that have to be removed. These barriers, one can reasonably assume, are at the same time sources of group inequality. But how are those sources of inequality to be understood? If affirmative action is justified as an instrument for advancing social equality, then we need an empirical understanding of how it works as a tool. This is the point where the social equality rationale has to develop a connection to social theory. The work of justifying affirmative action policies on the basis of the pursuit of social equality is complete only if and when sociological accounts about the workings of social inequalities give us reasons to believe that affirmative action measures intervene effectively in their processes. The next section reviews social theories of inequality to make the argument that they support the view that affirmative action policies may be efficacious tools for advancing the cause of social equality.

3. The Ladder and the Maze: Two Sociologies of Inequality

According to the social equality rationale, affirmative action policies do not merely redistribute some jobs and assets but may also tackle the structural roots of inequality. This claim clearly depends on how we explain social inequality. According to the commonsense view, inequality is primarily a distributive question of how much people have and, at best, only secondarily a matter of how people relate to each other. In other words, the tendency to justify or reject affirmative action on distributive grounds connects to underlying common understandings of inequality as primarily a distributive question.

Work in sociology has, however, already provided an alternative relationally focused account of the sources of inequality. Within the constellation of work emerging on this relational terrain, there are two basic approaches: a "resourceist" and a "mechanism-based" account of social inequality. As we shall see, the latter, mechanism-based view is more useful for understanding how affirmative action policies can tackle inequality. (In fact, this distinction tracks Sethi's contrast of his own mechanism-based view of inequality, where the relevant mechanisms are stereotypes, and an environmental determinism that focuses on the resources at an individual's disposal.)

The resourceist approach to social inequality builds on the imaginary of the ladder, "on which individuals or groups occupy rungs higher or lower than all the rest" (Tilly 2005, 71). This underlying metaphor characterizes most stratification theories. According to this view, there is one social (class) structure consisting of relations among hierarchically ordered positions in which people are placed. Traditionally this placement may have been an effect of status hierarchies and ascriptive identities that define social positions in a hereditary and enclosed way. Yet today, with capitalist modernity, formal liberty and (some) social mobility prevail, and the occupancy of social positions is no longer congealed but rather dependent on the resources people possess. An elaborate version of this view can be found in Pierre Bourdieu's concept of social space that includes three dimensions: (1) a vertical dimension defined by capital volume, which takes up the imaginary of the ladder; (2) a horizontal dimension concerning the forms of capital ranging from a preponderance of cultural capital to a preponderance of economic capital;[18] (3) a temporal dimension representing the social career of individuals (Bourdieu 1984). According to Bourdieu's perspective, social inequality is a matter of how much capital individuals can accumulate within the social space, thus defining the distance in which people stand to each other.

This resourceist view equates social relations from the start with distributive relations. An account, in other words, that begins with a relational focus reverts to being fundamentally a distributive view of inequality. This approach is then often connected to policy strategies that focus not on changing social structures but on enabling people to climb the ladder, often through the provision of "services," another word for "resources." In doing so, the resourceist view of inequality does not answer the question of what policy frameworks could impact social relations themselves to achieve egalitarian social realities. This resourceist sociological view provides support to narrow philosophical accounts of distributive justice, to "allocative justice" in Rawls's terms, and thus to a view of affirmative action that remains within the distributive paradigm.

The mechanism-based approach to social inequality sharply diverges from the resourceist perspective. Prominently developed by sociologist Charles Tilly, the underlying metaphor of the mechanism-based view is an image not of a ladder but of a maze. Tilly writes, "Most vivid accounts of inequality employ the image of a giant ladder on which individuals or groups occupy rungs higher or lower than all the rest. Let me make the case for inequality as a maze in which clusters of people wander separated by walls they have built themselves, not always knowingly" (Tilly 2005, 71). Gated communities and status hierarchies would be examples of such walls.

On this argument, there is not one hierarchical distributive structure but a variety of social structures in which inequalities are produced and spread.[19] And there is not social inequality (singular) but inequalities (plural) — that is, unequal relations, even within a single social structure. Thus structural inequalities are much more complex and entwined than the resourceist view of the ladder suggests; they are more, as Tilly states, like a maze where people navigate in clusters — working their way through pathways and around walls and obstacles that are constantly building and appearing in new places, as they sometimes open loopholes, passages, and tunnels and sometimes undertake major reconstructions of the landscape.[20]

According to Tilly, it is exactly four major social mechanisms—

"recurrent causal sequences of general scope" (1999, 7) — that produce "durable inequalities": exploitation (the one-sided appropriation of surplus labor in the sense of Marx), opportunity hoarding (the monopolization of resources, which is the front side of what Weber called "social closure"), emulation (the copying of organization schemes), and adaptation (their accommodation to specific social contexts). The first two mechanisms actually *cause* social inequality, whereas the latter two are primarily responsible for its diffusion and thus its systemic character. On this basis, classifications — Tilly focuses on paired categories like female-male, black-white, able-bodied-disabled, and citizen-foreigner — define memberships and regulate boundary work. Such classifications may promote the construction of identities, but they do not have the causal power to produce or spread social inequalities. One can't read straight from an identity to a property of social structures. One needs instead to unpack the mechanisms of relational inequality that interfere with particular people's life courses.

This mechanism-based account of social inequalities changes our perspective on affirmative action in several respects. First, by replacing the image of a single unified hierarchical/distributive structure with that of entwined and labyrinthine social structures/relations of inequality, the account guides us away from framing affirmative action as an all-or-nothing question, as either needing to equalize the overall distribution of resources or not being worth undertaking. On the maze model of inequality, affirmative action measures may remove some very specific walls (for instance, certain hegemonic norms), while other egalitarian policies may address other features of the maze of unequal relationships. Second, by naming concrete mechanisms that produce social inequality, for instance opportunity hoarding, this approach identifies the targets that affirmative action measures must be able to strike if they are to be considered effective. Third, by stressing the necessity of institutional change and innovation, Tilly bypasses the idealistic view that changes in culture and mentality alone can move us toward a more equal society. (He starts, in other words, by presuming limitations to the methods described in this volume by Banaji and Lai.) Fourth, by assigning to identity classifications a precise but limited causal role, the mechanism-based account avoids a conflation of identity with unequal structural standing. (Sethi called such conflations "essentialist causal misattributions.") This treatment of identity forces us to see what is happening in unequal relationships. By taking this approach, the mechanism view may attenuate the fears of some critics of affirmative action that benign governmental engagement with classification systems becomes a source of group inequality.

4. Affirmative Action's Transformative Potential

The mechanism-based understanding of social inequality may give us a clear account of the barriers to full inclusion and participation among equals, barriers that egalitarian public policies have to remove. The focus is on inequality-generating mechanisms that may be at work even when formal antidiscrimination measures are in place. In the version introduced by Tilly, however, I consider the mechanism-based approach to be still too simplistic. Thus I would add to Tilly's Marxo-Weberian synthesis of exploitation and opportunity hoarding / social closure two further inequality-generating mechanisms: hierarchization (of both organizational structures and status orders) and normalization (in the sense of hegemonizing and enforcing inegalitarian or inequality-inducing norms).[21] One question that is of particular importance from the perspective of affirmative action relates to the role that discrimination may play within this quadriga of mechanisms. My view on this is that direct discrimination should be understood as one way that opportunity hoarding and status hierarchization work at the micro level of interaction, whereas indirect discrimination, the application of norms with disparate impact, clearly is an aspect of normalization. From the perspective of affirmative action, it is of further importance to pay attention not only to social mechanisms but also to cognitive mechanisms like stereotyping and implicit bias. (Again, these are the themes addressed by Sethi and by Banaji and Lai in this volume.)

Before discussing how affirmative action policies may tackle inequality-generating mechanisms, I'll make one further remark on how the social equality rationale in combination with the mechanism-based approach to social inequality can broaden our thinking about affirmative action. Most affirmative action regimes exclude class from their range. The reason for this may be that class inequalities are seen as purely economic and thus produced by exploitation, a mechanism that—in most of its forms—cannot be addressed by affirmative action measures; or they may be seen as the result of individual achievement and effort and thereby assigned to the category of difference where domination does not operate, therefore requiring no remedy. Yet class inequalities continue to have an ascriptive character in the modern world. They also function via markers like names, bodily appearance, and habitus and are reproduced by mechanisms like opportunity hoarding, status hierarchization, and normalization.[22] If this is an adequate description, then there is no principled reason to exclude class from affirmative action devices. Indeed if these policies are to truly fulfill their egalitarian mission, then class has to be included within their ambit. This suggestion departs sharply from two common criticisms. It does not aim at *replacing* race or other categories by class, as proponents of class-based affirmative action usually demand, but at broadening the scope of this policy in an egalitarian way. Second, it is strictly opposed to every view of affirmative action as an all-or-nothing matter. Even if class inequalities were included, the range of affirmative action would still be limited. There are mechanisms of inequality, first and foremost exploitation as capitalism's basic injustice, which are—in most cases—beyond its reach but should be tackled by other policy tools. As policies addressing these mechanisms and those addressed by affirmative action mutually reinforce each other, we achieve a suite of egalitarian policies that work best in tandem with one another.

Such a broadened version of the mechanism-based account supports a differentiated discussion of the transformative potential of affirmative action. At the beginning of this paper I distinguished between three kinds of affirmative action—facilitative, preferential, and indirect—and further differentiated indirect affirmative action into a preferential and facilitative strand. We can now ask: What role do these kinds of affirmative action play in combating the mechanisms that cause and reproduce social inequality?

Let's begin with "facilitative affirmative action." Policies of outreach may have a weak impact on organizational culture by modifying recruiting schemes and procedures. Such a weak impact on the culture of organizations may also be observable with respect to empowerment schemes. Special programs for women and minorities may leave some traces on organizational rules in general. But commonly facilitative measures are oriented not toward social structures and toward dismantling the mechanisms that produce inequality but toward recipients who benefit from getting (information about) a certain good. In this focus on recipients, the empowerment form of facilitative affirmative action does at least touch on a "good" that is of particular importance from the perspective of social egalitarianism: social self-assertiveness or—as Rawls has called it—the "social bases of self-respect." This good is a necessary condition for functioning relations among equals. By empowering people, facilitative affirmative action equips agents to make use of opportunities that open up as structural barriers to inclusion and participation are removed.

Let us turn, then, to address whether preferential affirmative action successfully meets the requirements of a social equality rationale for affirmative action. Indeed preferential affirmative action not only redistributes some roles and offices but may also have a transformative structural impact—not directly on macro social structures but on organizations and thus on the meso level. Preferential treatment, the strongest form being quotas, tackles one of the main organizational mechanisms of group inequalities—in other words, opportunity hoarding. By removing the monopolization of resources and chances and creating entry points into jobs and education for the disadvantaged, this kind of affirmative action directly changes the way people relate to each other. Preferential affirmative action may thus also be seen as one of the most promising ways to prevent discrimination. If implicit bias and stereotyping as cognitive drivers of discrimination are ubiquitous and even work underneath an explicit value orientation toward equality, then measures like quotas may serve as an organizational blocker, as a structural surrogate, ensuring that members of certain groups and their concerns are not ignored (Alfinito Viera and Graser 2014). The materialist hope is that mentalities may—over time—adapt to transformed organizational structures.

Preferential affirmative action, however, not only has the potential to transform organizational structures but may also help bringing about further structural change. In political science this potential to initiate change is discussed under the heading "substantive representation," examining the assumption that an increased presence of members of disadvantaged groups within legislative bodies may lead to decisions that transform structures according to the interests of these groups (Phillips 1995; Mansbridge 1999). Now this has two implications that are commonly not taken into consideration. First, the presence of members of disadvantaged groups may have a strong impact on power relations not only within legislative bodies but also within organizations and on their culture in general. Affirmative action measures thus are of particular importance to restructuring organizations at the managerial level, since they affect decision-making processes. Second, organizational entry points for the disadvantaged opened up by quotas may also translate into (broader) political processes that effectively challenge social inequalities at the macro level. This is exactly what happened with public service quotas for the former "untouchables" in India. They became the nucleus for political mobilizations that successfully spread a sense of self-assertiveness among Dalit communities, thus making caste inequalities a fiercely contested terrain. This may not be the great macro transformation some proponents of affirmative action have dreamed of, but on the meso and micro levels the transformative impact on social structures seems undeniable.[23]

The most interesting case for this discussion, however, is indirect affirmative action. As was suggested in the first part of this paper, this kind of affirmative action should be further differentiated into a preferential and a facilitative variant. Let's begin with its preferential strand. When geographic location is used as a proxy for race, as in the case of admissions at University of Texas and Science Po, then indirect affirmative action may have an effect on organizational structures similar to that of direct preferential treatment, provided that spatial segregation is sharply developed.[24] In comparison to direct preferential treatment, however, indirect measures bear a heavy load of opacity, as the difference-sensitive goals of the policy are systematically concealed. For this reason they are in conflict with the democratic principle of publicity and transparency (cf. Sabbagh 2011b). Proponents of indirect affirmative action, in turn, argue that these "opportunity costs" are outweighed by the fact that indirect measures do not reinforce invidious classifications and for this reason have no stigmatizing effect on its recipients. To reach a conclusion, the following conditionals seem to apply: any assessment of indirect preferential treatment depends on (1) what role is assigned to classification schemes within the (re)production of social inequality, and (2) the extent to which direct preferential treatment is considered to have stigmatizing effects damaging the self-esteem of its recipients.[25]

In contrast to its preferential form, the facilitative variant of indirect affirmative action turns out to be a very different case. As it is not a mere proxy but does involve benefits for everyone, this form of indirect affirmative action is not in conflict with the democratic transparency principle. The most exciting thing, however, is its egalitarian structure-changing potential in comparison with direct facilitative affirmative action. For example, accessibility measures, like the introduction of ramps, intervene in the process of normalization by which hegemonic norms are imposed on people, in this case norms of able-bodiedness. The sheer materiality of alternative approaches to construction undermines the mechanism of normalization that introduces inequality to the experience of special needs. These policies subvert the material environment that is necessary for norms of "abledness" to become dominant. In so doing they may also erode status hierarchies and force "abled" people to see the world with different eyes (Silvers 2013).

Similar effects may be attributed to parental leave and allowance. In giving an incentive to men to engage in care work, these measures may change the gendered division of labor. In doing so they intervene into three inequality-generating mechanisms: (1) by severing the tie between care work and femininity, they shift hegemonic norms concerning gender behavior and help; by generalizing the engagement in care work, they (2) enhance the status of these tasks and (3) may remove domestic exploitation. This short discussion shows that indirect facilitative affirmative action measures may have a considerable transformative structural impact — effects that apply both to the power of cultural norms and the division of labor. And they hold an important lesson: neutrality of means may sometimes be crucial for combating group inequalities. Were parental leave and allowance limited to women, this would reproduce patriarchal role divisions by linking caring tasks to a female role.

As this short discussion shows, affirmative action, under certain conditions, may transcend mere distribution and have a transformative structural impact. Yet there is still another aspect of this policy that may not be well understood within the distributive paradigm. Social egalitarians are concerned not only with relational standings among people, the mechanisms they are confronted with, and therefore how they are treated, but also with the institutional attitudes that motivate these treatments — that is, with the "expressive value" of social practices (Anderson and Pildes 2000). On the social equality rationale, institutions themselves need to convey affirmation of the principle of equal worth of all people. Yet institutions often treat members of certain groups with outright hostility or openly engage in exploitation, opportunity hoarding, status hierarchization, and normalization. They may express contempt by allowing others to engage openly in oppressive practices. Or the attitude behind institutional policies may be neglect or indifference to disadvantage and debasement (Schemmel 2011a). Yet an alternative attitude might be expressed in institutional practices, and this is concern. Institutions convey concern when they do not shy away from undertaking special efforts to fight inequalities and improve the lot of the disadvantaged. A demand for such an attitude of concern is implied in the slogan "Black lives matter" (cf. Lebron 2017). And it is this attitude that is expressed in affirmative action policies. Indeed one may wonder whether such an attitude of concern, when confronted with opportunity hoarding, can be expressed other than through direct preferential treatment and quotas. According to the social egalitarian justification of affirmative action, it may be precisely such differential treatment that, under conditions of inequality, does express equal concern and respect.[26] Organizations pursuing an affirmative action policy, then, may be evaluated as more just than those lacking such measures for the simple reason that they display an attitude of concern for the disadvantaged. They tackle the mechanisms that produce inequality at least symbolically, by affirming an intent to undermine them.

5. Conclusion: Affirmative Action and Egalitarian Politics

In this paper I have explored the terrain of what affirmative action policies amount to as soon as we leave behind the requirement that they embody a distributive paradigm of justice and equality. I have combined a sociological and a philosophical perspective. The philosophical debate on social equality suggested where to look: not only at distributive patterns but also at relational standings, institutional treatments, and the attitudes expressed in social practices. The mechanism-based approach to social inequality, in turn, helped us to clarify what concrete things affirmative action policies ought to do: affirmative action policies ought to intervene in particular inequality-generating mechanisms. The result can be summarized as follows: The social egalitarian justification of affirmative action provides a normative framework for this policy that is much more robust than conventional views that affirmative action redistributes goods, provides corrective justice for past wrongs, or facilitates diversification. Instead the social equality rationale justifies affirmative action policies to the extent that they undo inequality-producing mechanisms and enable people to participate as equals in social life. According to this view, affirmative action should have a transformative impact on social structures and, in doing so, contribute to forming a society of equals. Furthermore, this rationale provides a framework for analyzing the full range of affirmative action's measures: facilitative, preferential, and indirect affirmative action.

If the social equality rationale implies a justification of all kinds of affirmative action, this does not mean that it justifies all actually existing affirmative action programs. Quite the contrary: the social equality rationale formulates a clear standard according to which these programs can be evaluated. If they do not remove barriers to full inclusion and equal participation opportunities or if they produce costs that are in other respects unacceptable, then they have to be either replaced or modified. Thus, to take an example from the Indian context, one may wonder whether the OBC (Other Backward Castes) quota in higher education meets this standard or whether it should be replaced by a flexible preference scheme that better provides for the complexities of the Indian subcontinent.[27] Another case that has already been discussed is parental leave and allowance. Sometimes a policy that is difference-neutral in its means may best serve the politics of difference, at least if it is equality oriented, as Iris Marion Young (2009) has suggested it should be.

Importantly, the social equality rationale does not generate a policy blueprint. Instead it constitutes a plea to creatively combine the different possible kinds of affirmative action into a suite of policies neatly tailored to the specificities of context and structured to pursue a clearly defined goal of undoing the mechanisms that cause inequality. The ability to pursue difference without domination requires seeing that many mechanisms work together—and will have to change as society changes—to undermine or reverse forms of domination that may even emerge from free social relations.

Notes

1. To be fair, Fraser has launched this challenge only once, in her Tanner Lectures (Fraser 1996), and cut it in her subsequent exchange with Honneth on redistribution and recognition (Fraser and Honneth 2003). Fraser is mentioned here only as a placeholder, as her critique has been widely adopted within the affirmative action debate.

2. This is an elaboration of Daniel Sabbagh's (2011a) distinction between "outreach," "direct," and "indirect affirmative action." Sabbagh's terminology is unfortunate, as an either-or distinction (direct vs. indirect) cannot be used within a tripartite structure. In fact, indirect affirmative action, as we will see, can itself be differentiated into facilitative and preferential variants, with the result that "direct vs. indirect" turns out to be the generic distinction.

3. After independence India introduced at the federal level—diverging provisions at the state level continue to exist to the present day—quotas for Scheduled Castes (*dalits* / former untouchables) and Scheduled Tribes (*adivasis* / indigenous populations) in parliament, public service, and higher education. In the early 1990s a women's quota in local parliaments was implemented, and public service quotas were extended to "Other Backward Classes" or OBCs (i.e., primarily lower-caste Hindus), followed up by an OBC quota in higher education in 2006. Additionally, there are at the moment discussions about quotas for Muslims, a women's quota in national parliament, and the implementation of affirmative action in the private sector (both "preferential" and "facilitative"). On affirmative action in India, see Galanter 1984; Hasan 2009; Deshpande 2013.

4. Besides this, in contemporary Germany there is a 5 percent job quota for severely handicapped people.

5. For an excellent overview on different "merit principles," see McCrudden 1998.

6. Following Owen Fiss's seminal intervention (1976), these terms have been coined by Balkin and Siegel (2003) and German law scholar Ute Sacksofsky (2015).

7. Of course, whether a "creamy layer problem" exists at all is first and foremost an empirical question. For an evidence-based defense of (parts of) the Indian "Reservation System" against such a critique; Thorat, Tagede, and Naik 2016.

8. The other main problem of the diversity rationale is that it subjects its recipients to an essentializing process of othering: they have to present themselves as being as different as possible in order to meaningfully contribute to the multiplicity of cultural items that is favored by diversity.

9. Paradigmatically for this: Fullinwider 1986.

10. According to the "difference principle" inequalities in wealth and income are justified only if they are to the benefit of the worst off (Rawls 1971, §13).

11. For instance, luck egalitarians (e.g., Ronald Dworkin, G. A. Cohen, Richard Arneson) debated how to distinguish between "choice" and "circumstance," "option luck" and "brute luck," with the idea that such distinctions clarify what is required of just distribution. Their argument is that the effects of brute luck should be equalized, while individuals are responsible for the outcomes that flow from their choices for option luck. Capability theorists like Amartya Sen and Martha Nussbaum take a different tack but

still focus on distribution. They scrutinize how material resources may be converted into effective freedoms ("capabilities"), allowing individuals to pursue their life-plans in the doings and beings ("functionings") they consider important. The ability to secure capabilities should be equalized for all, they argue.

12. A reconstruction of sufficientarianism's arguments can be found in Casal 2007.

13. Within this debate, "social equality," "relational equality," "status equality," and "democratic equality" are used more or less interchangeably. Main contributions include Scanlon 1996; Miller 1997; Wolff 1998; Anderson 1999 and 2012; Scheffler 2003 and 2010; O'Neill 2008; Rosanvallon 2013; Schemmel 2011a and 2011b; Fourie 2012; Kolodny 2014; Fourie, Schuppert, and Wallimann-Helmer 2015a and 2015b; Schuppert 2015.

14. Under the heading "the fair value of political liberties," one can find a similar argument in Rawls.

15. "Critical mass" as a quantitative measure has turned out to be highly contextual, often dependent on qualitatively engaged "critical actors" (Childs and Krook 2009).

16. To be fair, this is not Anderson's aim.

17. Such a critique has been raised by Shelby (2014). In the 1950s Ambedkar, the "father of the Indian Constitution," considered conversion to Buddhism and thus self-segregation the only viable option for Dalits in order to escape the atrocities of the caste system.

18. The two other forms of capital that are critical to Bourdieu's theory of social inequality—social and symbolic capital—are not represented in his standard account of the social space. If I label this concept "resourceist" this does, of course, not mean that Bourdieu's entire approach should be seen this way.

19. These social structures may be specified by the macro, meso, and micro distinction. Tilly himself—at least from the 1990s onward—has tried to avoid the term *structure*, talking instead of "relations" and "transactions." Yet as soon as one asks for the mode of existence of these relations and transactions, one may come to the conclusion that they exist within or between social entities. And these entities may be called "structures" (Elder-Vass 2010), "systems" (Bunge 1996; Wan 2011), or "assemblages" (DeLanda 2006). What Tilly shares with these authors is not only a focus on causal mechanisms but also a denial of the view that there is one social macro system/structure more or less integrating the rest of society.

20. "From a relational perspective," says Tilly, reciting the famous Foucaultian description of power, "inequality appears everywhere, but it rarely crystallizes into neat, continuous hierarchies somehow arraying whole populations into strata" (2005, 100).

21. On hierarchization as a further inequality-generating mechanism, see Therborn 2013; normalization is the point where poststructuralist approaches become relevant for the thinking about social inequality.

22. Marx has given us an account of the capitalist mode of production that deliberately abstracts from the ascriptive dimensions of class inequality. Many of his critics as well as of his followers have mistaken this theoretical abstraction for an ontological reduction.

23. Already the quotas for Dalits in India show how complex the question of transformative impacts of affirmative action is. In contrast to public service quotas, the reservation of parliamentary seats for dalits had virtually no transformative effect, as political parties were able to manipulate the holders of reserved seats, thus cultivating a submissive class of dalit politicians. Quotas in higher education, again, primarily tell a history of nonimplementation. These obstructions to affirmative action's goals of deactivating

mechanisms of inequality production, however, should not be taken as an argument against the policy itself. In my eyes, the situation runs the other way round: what these obstructions demonstrate is a necessity to counter the countermeasures so that preferential affirmative action can do its job to prevent opportunity hoarding and equalize power relations.

24. Segregation, to my understanding, is one dimension and effect of opportunity hoarding / social closure.

25. For evidence-based arguments against stigmatizing effects of direct preferential treatment: Onwuachi-Willig, Houh, and Campbell 2008; Deshpande 2017. As emphasized by Stanley Fish, one should also keep in mind that the conservative discourse on the stigmatizing impact of affirmative action has its own performative effects: "At any rate, low self-esteem is at least in part the product of speculation about it. People who never would have thought of questioning their accomplishments might begin to do so if the question was raised every night on the evening news" (2000, 81).

26. "Equal consideration for all may demand very unequal treatment in favor of the disadvantaged" (Sen 1992, 1).

27. I have in mind Satish Deshpande and Yogendra Yadav's suggestion to replace the OBC quota in higher education with a more fine-tuned device of preferential treatment that takes into consideration not only caste but also gender, region, and the urban-rural divide, as well as individual class position as identifiable by parents' income and educational attainment (2006).

Works Cited

Alfinito Viera, Ana Carolina, and Alex Graser. 2014. "The Case against the Case against Affirmative Action." In *Affirmative Action: A View from the Global South*, edited by Ockert Stellenbosch Dupper and Kamala Sankaran, 63–87. Stellenbach, South Africa: Sun Press.

Anderson, Elizabeth S. 1999. "What Is the Point of Equality?" *Ethics* 109 (2): 287–337.

Anderson, Elizabeth S. 2002. "Integration, Affirmative Action, and Strict Scrutiny." *New York University Law Review* 77 (5): 1195–271.

Anderson, Elizabeth S. 2010. *The Imperative of Integration*. Princeton, NJ: Princeton University Press.

Anderson, Elizabeth S. 2012. "Equality." In *The Oxford Handbook of Political Philosophy*, edited by David Estlund, 40–57. Oxford: Oxford University Press.

Anderson, Elizabeth S, and Richard R. Pildes. 2000. "Expressive Theories of Law: A Restatement." *University of Pennsylvania Law Review* 148 (5): 1503–75.

Balkin, Jack M., and Reva B. Siegel. 2003. "The American Civil Rights Tradition: Anti-classification or Antisubordination?" *University of Miami Law Review* 58 (1): 9–33.

Bourdieu, Pierre. 1984. *Distinction: A Social Critique of the Judgment of Taste*. Translation of *La distinction: Critique sociale du judgement* (Paris, 1979). New York: Routledge, 2010.

Brown, Graham K., Arnim Langer, and Frances Stewart, eds. 2012. *Affirmative Action in Plural Societies: International Experiences*. Basingstoke, UK: Palgrave Macmillan.

Bunge, Mario. 1996. *Finding Philosophy in Social Science*. New Haven, CT: Yale University Press.

Casal, Paula. 2007. "Why Sufficiency Is Not Enough." *Ethics* 117 (2): 296–326.

Childs, Sarah, and Mona Lena Krook. 2009. "Analysing Women's Substantive Representation: From Critical Mass to Critical Actors." *Government and Opposition* 44 (2): 125–45.

Cohen, G. A. 1989. "On the Currency of Egalitarian Justice." *Ethics* 99 (4): 906–44.

DeLanda, Manuel. 2006. *A New Philosophy of Society: Assemblage Theory and Social Complexity*. London: Continuum.

Deshpande, Ashwini. 2013. *Affirmative Action in India*. New Delhi: Oxford University Press.

Deshpande, Ashwini. 2017. "Stigma or Red Tape? Roadblocks in the Use of Affirmative Action." Working Paper 208. Delhi: Centre for Development Economics, Delhi School of Economics.

Deshpande, Satish, and Yogendra Yadav. 2006. "Redesigning Affirmative Action: Caste and Benefits in Higher Education." *Economic and Political Weekly* 41, no. 24 (June 17, 2006): 2419–24.

Dupper, Ockert, and Kamala Sankaran, eds. 2014. *Affirmative Action: A View from the Global South*. Stellenbosch, South Africa: Sun Press.

Dworkin, Ronald. 1976. "Reverse Discrimination." In his *Taking Rights Seriously*, 223–39. Cambridge, MA: Harvard University Press, 1977.

Elder-Vass, Dave. 2010. *The Causal Power of Social Structures: Emergence, Structure and Agency*. Cambridge: Cambridge University Press.

Fish, Stanley. 2000. "The Nifty Nine Arguments against Affirmative Action in Higher Education." *Journal of Blacks in Higher Education* 27 (Spring): 79–81.

Fiss, Owen M. 1976. "Groups and the Equal Protection Clause." *Philosophy and Public Affairs* 5 (2): 107–77.

Fourie, Carina. 2012. "What Is Social Equality? An Analysis of Status Equality as a Strongly Egalitarian Ideal." *Res Publica* 18, no. 2: 107–26.

Fourie, Carina, Fabian Schuppert, and Ivo Wallimann-Helmer. 2015a. "The Nature and Distinctiveness of Social Equality: An Introduction." In *Social Equality: On What It Means to Be Equals*, edited by Carina Fourie, Fabian Schuppert, and Ivo Wallimann-Helmer, 1–17. Oxford: Oxford University Press.

Fourie, Carina, Fabian Schuppert, and Ivo Wallimann-Helmer, eds. 2015b. *Social Equality: On What It Means to Be Equals*. Oxford: Oxford University Press.

Frankfurt, Harry. 1987. "Equality as a Moral Ideal." In his *The Importance of What We Care About: Philosophical Essays*, 134–58. Cambridge: Cambridge University Press, 1998.

Fraser, Nancy. 1996. "Social Justice in the Age of Identity Politics: Redistribution, Recognition, and Participation." Tanner Lectures on Human Values, Stanford University, April 30–May 2, 1996.

Fraser, Nancy, and Axel Honneth. 2003. *Redistribution or Recognition? A Political-Philosophical Exchange*. London: Verso.

Fullinwider, Robert. 1986. "Reverse Discrimination and Equal Opportunity." In *New Directions in Ethics: The Challenge of Applied Ethics*, edited by John P. DeMarco and Richard M. Fox, 173–89. New York: Routledge.

Galanter, Marc. 1984. *Competing Equalities: Law and the Backward Classes in India*. Berkeley: University of California Press.

Gosepath, Stefan. 2015. "The Principles and the Presumption of Equality." In *Social Equality: On What It Means to Be Equals*, edited by Carina Fourie, Fabian Schuppert, and Ivo Wallimann-Helmer, 167–85. Oxford: Oxford University Press.

Gutmann, Amy. 1996. "Responding to Racial Injustice." In *Color Conscious: The Political Morality of Race*, edited by K. Anthony Appiah and Amy Gutmann, 106–78. Princeton, NJ: Princeton University Press.

Hasan, Zoya. 2009. *Politics of Inclusion: Castes, Minorities, and Affirmative Action.* New Delhi: Oxford University Press.

Jaffrelot, Christophe. 2006. "The Impact of Affirmative Action in India: More Political Than Socioeconomic." *India Review* 5, no. 2: 173–89.

Kennedy-Dubourdieu, Elaine, ed. 2006. *Race and Inequality: World Perspectives on Affirmative Action.* Aldershot, UK: Ashgate.

Kolodny, Niko. 2014. "Rule over None II: Social Equality and the Justification of Democracy." *Philosophy and Public Affairs* 42, no. 4: 287–336.

Lebron, Christopher J. 2017. *The Making of Black Lives Matter: A Brief History of an Idea.* Oxford: Oxford University Press.

Mansbridge, Jane. 1999. "Should Blacks Represent Blacks and Women Represent Women? A Contingent 'Yes.'" *Journal of Politics* 61, no. 3: 628–57.

McCrudden, Cristopher. 1998. "Merit Principles." *Oxford Journal of Legal Studies* 18, no. 4: 543–79.

Miller, David. 1997. "Equality and Justice." *Ratio* 10, no. 3: 222–37.

O'Neill, Martin. 2008. "What Should Egalitarians Believe?" *Philosophy and Public Affairs* 36, no. 2: 119–56.

Onwuachi-Willig, Angela, Emily Houh, and Mary Campbell. 2008. "Cracking the Egg: Which Came First—Stigma or Affirmative Action?" *California Law Review* 96, no. 5: 1299–352.

Phillips, Anne. 1995. *The Politics of Presence.* Oxford: Oxford University Press.

Rawls, John. 1971. *A Theory of Justice.* Cambridge, MA: Belknap.

Rosanvallon, Pierre. 2013. *The Society of Equals.* Translated by Arthur Goldhammer from *La société des égaux* (Paris, 2011). Cambridge, MA: Harvard University Press.

Sabbagh, Daniel. 2011a. "Affirmative Action: The U.S. Experience in Comparative Perspective." *Daedalus* 140, no. 2: 109–20.

Sabbagh, Daniel. 2011b. "The Rise of Indirect Affirmative Action: Converging Strategies for Promoting 'Diversity' in Selective Institutions of Higher Education in the United States and France." *World Politics* 63, no. 3: 470–508.

Sacksofsky, Ute. 2015. "Frauenquoten—Weg zur Gleichheit der Geschlechter oder 'umgekehrte Diskriminierung' von Männern?" In *(Un-)Gerechte (Un-)Gleichheiten*, edited by Steffen Mau and Nadine M. Schöneck, 134–41. Berlin: Suhrkamp.

Scanlon, T. M. 1996. "The Diversity of Objections to Inequality." In his 2003 *The Difficulty of Tolerance*, 202–18. Cambridge: Cambridge University Press.

Scheffler, Samuel. 2003. "What Is Egalitarianism?" *Philosophy and Public Affairs* 31 (1): 5–39.

Scheffler, Samuel. 2010. *Equality and Tradition: Questions of Value in Moral and Political Theory.* Oxford: Oxford University Press.

Schemmel, Christian. 2011a. "Distributive and Relational Equality." *Politics, Philosophy and Economics* 11, no. 2: 123–48.

Schemmel, Christian. 2011b. "Why Relational Egalitarians Should Care about Distributions." *Social Theory and Practice* 37, no. 3: 365–90.

Schuppert, Fabian. 2015. "Non-domination, Non-alienation and Social Equality: Towards a Republican Understanding of Equality." *Critical Review of International Social and Political Philosophy* 18, no. 4: 440–55.

Sen, Amartya. 1979. "Equality of What?" Tanner Lectures on Human Values, Stanford University, May 22, 1979.

Sen, Amartya. 1992. *Inequality Reexamined*. Cambridge, MA: Harvard University Press.

Shelby, Tommie. 2014. "Integration, Inequality, and Imperatives of Justice: A Review Essay." *Philosophy and Public Affairs* 42, no. 3: 253–85.

Silvers, Anita. 2013. "Feminist Perspectives on Disability." In *Stanford Encyclopedia of Philosophy*, edited by Edward N. Zalta. Stanford, CA: Metaphysics Research Lab. http://plato.stanford.edu/entries/feminism-disability/.

Skrentny, John David. 1996. *The Ironies of Affirmative Action: Politics, Culture, and Justice in America*. Chicago: University of Chicago Press.

Therborn, Göran. 2013. *The Killing Fields of Inequality*. Cambridge: Polity.

Thorat, Sukhadeo, Nitin Tagede, and Ajaya N. Naik. 2016. "Prejudices against Reservation Policies: How and Why?" *Economic and Political Weekly* 51, no. 8 (February 20): 61–69.

Tilly, Charles. 1999. *Durable Inequality*. Berkeley: University of California Press.

Tilly, Charles. 2005. *Identities, Boundaries, and Social Ties*. Boulder, CO: Paradigm.

Wan, Poe Yu-Ze. 2011. *Reframing the Social: Emergentist Systemism and Social Theory*. Farnham, UK: Ashgate.

Wolff, Jonathan. 1998. "Fairness, Respect, and the Egalitarian Ethos." *Philosophy and Public Affairs* 27, no. 2: 97–122.

Young, Iris Marion. 1990/2011. *Justice and the Politics of Difference*. Rev. ed. Princeton, NJ: Princeton University Press.

Young, Iris Marion. 2009. "Structural Injustice and the Politics of Difference." In *Contemporary Debates in Political Philosophy*, edited by Thomas Christiano and John Christman, 362–83. Oxford: Blackwell.

10

The Measurement and Mismeasurement of Social Difference

ROHINI SOMANATHAN

1. Introduction

Measures of social difference are commonplace in mainstream research in the quantitative social sciences. They are used to "explain" collective outcomes ranging from voluntary contributions in elementary schools to civil wars. Heterogeneous communities appear to experience lower rates of investment and economic growth, restrict spending on public goods, limit income redistribution, exhibit less interpersonal trust, and suffer higher rates of crime and environmental degradation.[1]

Several mechanisms are proposed to link heterogeneity and under-performance. Citizens vote for lower taxes if public spending choices are made by leaders who do not share their preferences (Alesina, Baqir, and Easterly 1999). Cooperation is more difficult to achieve because social sanctions operate most effectively within groups (Miguel and Gugerty 2005). Communities may waste their collective resources in struggles for power rather than in the production of public goods, and it is easier to organize conflict around ethnic lines than around class lines (Esteban and Ray 2008; Caselli and Coleman 2013). There may be active discrimi-nation against ethnic minorities due to fears of cultural contamination (Adida, Laitin, and Valfort 2016). Or those in mixed societies may simply feel socially isolated, "hunker down," and disengage from the collective enterprise (Putnam 2007).

These theories have been tested using data gathered by national statis-tical agencies and independent teams of researchers. The standard source for within-country data is the national census. Multicountry studies have additionally used ethnographic studies and language trees to construct datasets that include many hundreds of ethnic, linguistic, and religious groups (Alesina et al. 2003; Fearon 2003; Montalvo and Reynal-Querol 2005). The distribution of the population across groups is used to gen-erate community-level indices of heterogeneity such as Polarization and Ethnolinguistic Fractionalization (ELF). Armed with a large number of data points on these measures and collective outcomes related to co-operation and conflict, innumerable papers have tested the hypothesis that heterogeneity hurts.[2]

This body of research on the effects of social identity is based on two premises. First, the categories of classification that we use are individually and socially relevant. Second, group membership determines our preferences and proclivities, and groups cannot easily cooperate to further common goals. These assumptions have resulted in a dangerously simplistic view of successful communities as particular types of demographic maps. They have hampered our understanding of when and how diverse societies flourish, because we have not adequately distinguished between the chosen and inherited aspects of identity and have come to view diversity as a disadvantage that must be managed. Instances of successful integration in firms, neighborhoods, and schools are analyzed as aberrations with no general lessons for institutional design or public policy.

I draw upon recent research in the social sciences to challenge these assumptions. The historiography of social classification reveals many influences on identity labels. Census data reflect both demographics and political ideas about which differences should be recorded. We have counts by race and Hispanic origin in the United States, nationalities and languages in Europe, castes and religions in India, and color in Central and South America. Taxonomies have also changed over time, and many countries now allow their residents to self-classify. The United States has introduced mixed-race options, and several South American states have new questions on African descent. Studies that compare responses for individuals across years and alternative survey formats find that those of mixed race are most likely to shift among available alternatives. Responses to questions on race and ethnicity are also influenced by the order in which they are asked. It is therefore unclear what measures of community heterogeneity based on these data represent.

Lieberman and Singh (2017) classify census procedures in around 150 countries since the eighteenth century. They show that ethnic counting significantly increased in the nineteenth century with the spread of colonialism, and this institutionalization of social cleavages provided "ethnic entrepreneurs" an opportunity to mobilize civil conflict along these lines. The act of ethnic classification seems to directly influence intergroup conflict by making specific identities salient.

New longitudinal data sets that link census tracts with income and employment outcomes also challenge the heterogeneity hypothesis by identifying poverty rather than demography as the critical determinant of well-being. When racial and ethnic groups face very different opportunities, racially homogenous minority neighborhoods also tend to have high poverty rates. Tax data show that those who start their working lives in segregated neighborhoods have lower relative earnings if they are black, Hispanic, or American Indian. This helps explain the more limited mobility of black workers in the income distribution. They have smaller probabilities of moving out of the bottom of the income distribution and higher chances of sliding back when they are in upper-income classes (Akee, Jones, and Porter 2017).

The main policy response to ghettos has been to help some families exit to safer neighborhoods via better-functioning school systems. The Moving to Opportunity (MTO) program of the US Department of Housing and Urban Development in the 1990s is the best-known example of this kind. While the program did not target race, the intersection of race and poverty resulted in a high fraction of vouchers going to African American or Hispanic females, many of whom signed up to get their children away from gangs and drugs. The program resulted in sizable gains in the health and employment prospects of young children but had negative effects on adolescents who were disrupted at a critical age (Chetty, Hendren, and Katz 2016; Ludwig et al. 2012). Tommie Shelby's 2016 book *Dark Ghettos: Injustice, Dissent, and Reform* sharply criticizes this approach because rather than addressing grossly unequal social structures and the stereotypes that go with them, it blames their victims and deprives them of dignity and agency.

Chetty et al. (2018) directly provide evidence on the importance of racial bias in determining black-white income gaps. They use longitudinal data for almost the entire US population from 1989 to 2015 and show that wage gaps exist even within neighborhoods and after controlling for parental income. Most importantly from the perspective of this volume, areas with relative racial equality are those where there is little racial bias among whites as measured by the Implicit Association Tests discussed in detail in Lai and Banaji's chapter.

When Alesina, Baqir, and Easterly (1999) studied public goods and social divisions in the United States two decades ago and set the tone for much of the literature on the negative effects of community heterogeneity, these types of data and the related evidence were not available. The correlation between heterogeneity and public spending did not seriously account for neighborhood poverty and all that went with it. Housing markets had priced many minority communities out of attractive neighborhoods into racially mixed urban counties that were also poor, and it was difficult to disentangle the effects of poverty and heterogeneity in the cross-sectional datasets that were available.

Laboratory and field experiments have also provided new insights into collective decision-making. We see, both with undergraduates in the US universities and with community groups in postconflict societies in Africa that deliberation in the democratic process matters. Groups that actively choose policies are more likely to cooperate with each other (Dal Bó, Foster, and Putterman 2010). Mixed groups find it harder to agree, but if they are supported in this process, they choose more effective leaders because they cannot rely on traditional social networks and have to find new ways of communicating and aggregating information (Fearon, Humphreys, and Weinstein 2015).

Reexamining the literature on identity and community performance in the light of these new findings can help us better understand the links between social difference and domination, the theme of this volume.

The remainder of this chapter is in five parts. The next section provides a comparative account of the collection of social data, highlighting differences in classification across countries and over time. Section 3 is a case study of India, where contests over classification have been both violent and political because they determine access to the world's largest affirmative action program. Section 4 discusses how commonly used measures of heterogeneity convert demographics into indices of difference. Section 5 deals with the problem of mismeasurement. Mismeasurement arises on multiple fronts: the collection of identity data, the indices based on these data, and specification of models that link demographics and community performance. I conclude with some implications of my analysis for the collection and use of social data.

2. Categories of Difference

Most countries collect some form of social data. Race, religion, caste, ancestry, nationality, language, and color are all used in different combinations. The types of data collected, the coarseness of categories used for tabulation, and how citizens respond to questions on social background all vary. In some countries, census questionnaires allow individuals to self-report their group in response to open-ended questions about identity, while in others, enumerators are given strict instructions on how to classify ambiguous responses. There have also been changes in format and content over time. When waves of immigration have brought in new ethnicities and nationalities, statistical agencies have often incorporated them into their questionnaires.

The United Nations Statistical Division has an archive of forms and data for countries that conduct census operations. Morning (2008) examined 138 questionnaires around the year 2000 and finds that 87 of them collect some type of ethnic information. This excludes those with questions on religion, language, and legal citizenship that are also common markers of group identity. Over half of the 138 questionnaires explicitly use the term *ethnicity*, 20 percent (mainly in Europe) use *nationality*, and 15 percent (mainly in South America) record indigenous origins. *Race* is used mostly in former slaveholding societies.

Lieberman and Singh (2017) examine over a thousand census questionnaires administered by 156 countries between 1800 and 2005. They find a steady increase in ethnic enumeration throughout the nineteenth century and in the decades leading up to the Second World War. In this period over 85 percent of censuses enumerated ethnicity. After the war there was resistance to ethnic classification, particularly in Europe, and by the 1990s only two out of three countries asked about ethnicity. Since then the trend has been upward once again.

Enumeration histories within continents also reveal interesting contrasts. The United States and Canada are a good example. The first US census, in 1790, distinguished white males and females, all other free persons, and enslaved people. Its main purpose was to determine representation in the legislature and taxation. Native Americans, who were not taxed, were excluded. *Color* appeared in 1850, when whites, blacks, and mulattoes were enumerated. *Race* appeared as an explicit question in 1870. In the years that followed, under pressure from race scientists, many terms were introduced to denote mixtures.[3] The arrival of large numbers of Asian and Latino immigrants led to new categories. Chinese, Japanese, Korean, Mexican, Hindu, Cuban, Vietnamese, and Asian Indian were added as options in the race question after these groups entered the country. These labels would typically come under the heads of language or nationality in other countries.

Starting in 1970, race and ethnicity in the United States have been self-reported and the methodology and results of the census have been challenged in and out of court. There have been allegations of systematically undercounting poor and minority households, with implications for the funding and representation of these groups (Anderson and Fienberg 2000). In both 1980 and 1990, millions of Americans reported themselves as *Other* under the race question, and multiracial populations complained about being unable to properly self-classify. These challenges led to a 1997 federal directive that expanded the number of categories and allowed multiple responses to the race question in the following census.[4]

Canada has a similar history of immigration and has also been collecting census data since the late eighteenth century, but statistical agencies have been more open-minded on what constitutes identity. Until the middle of the twentieth century, the census asked about race. In 1951 this was replaced with a question on *ethnic origin*, with options for race, religion, and country of origin. This was unlike the United States, where race and ethnicity continued to be asked as separate questions. Canadian was a possible option, although it was discouraged by enumerators until 1971 and these responses were not tabulated. Starting in 1986, counts for Canadian were made available, and in that year 0.5 percent of the population chose this ethnicity. By 1996 about a third of the population had decided that this was their main ethnicity (Boyd 1999).

The Canadian census has also experimented with changing the order in which respondents see options for the ethnic origin question. French appears before English in some years and not others. In 2011, in the face of much protest by academic bodies, the long form of the census with ethnicity questions was made voluntary. If nonresponse bias varies by ethnicity, these data will no longer provide unbiased estimates of the ethnic distribution of the population.[5]

Europe's attitude to collecting social statistics after the Second World War was shaped by its experience with ethnic conflict in the interwar period. Anti-Semitism and its disastrous effects in the 1930s led European countries to prohibit collection of ethnic data. Today most countries in Western Europe restrict themselves to collection of data on country of birth for individuals and their parents. In some countries, mostly in central and eastern Europe, questions on language, religion, and ethnicity are asked but are considered sensitive and remain optional. Russia made the entire census optional in 2002.[6]

For Latin America, *National Colors* by Mara Loveman (2014) traces the history of population enumeration in nineteen countries. In the colonial period, ethnic counts were used for conscription to forced labor and taxation. After independence from Spain and Portugal, racial distinctions were condemned by most national leaders. Yet when census operations began, the four categories of white, black, Indian, and mixed were recorded in most countries. Racial mixing and the presence of indigenous populations distinguished these nations from their colonizers, and recording these categories in the census asserted the new nationhood. In fact, after the Mexican Revolution of 1910, the order in which racial data was tabulated also changed to emphasize the new balance of power. Indigenous populations were listed first, followed by mixed and then white. After 1950 most censuses on the continent stopped recording race, and some replaced this with language. By 1970 no country other than Cuba recorded race. Since then, however, race has once again appeared on census forms, largely in response to local and international pressures to actively bridge racial gaps in opportunities. Almost all countries now have questions on indigenous and African descent.[7]

Brazil has been especially well studied because its political movement Movimento Negro succeeded in creating a new Afro-Brazilian consciousness. This led to the adoption of race-based affirmative action programs in prestigious public universities, starting around the turn of the twenty-first century. The Brazilian census historically used a classification of social groups based on color: white, brown/mulatto, black, and yellow. In 1991 it added a fifth category of indigenous.

Several recent studies have compared respondent responses in different formats to ask how well these categories capture present-day social identities. I return to these in section 5.

This account of the many approaches to gathering social data could go on. Israel records religion and birthplace but not ethnicities such as Arab, although this is the most salient contemporary divide in the region. Rwanda, in its attempt at nation-building after the genocide in 1994, outlawed the use of ethnic labels like Hutu and Tutsi. These were occupations in the precolonial period and classified as ethnicities by Belgian colonizers.[8] The main takeaway from this historical account of enumeration is that the categories in which social data are recorded are subjective, idiosyncratic, and determined by many of the same forces that shape other indicators of community success. It is hard to justify their treatment as exogenous determinants of community outcomes.

Several countries have recently changed their policies on collecting social data in attempts to balance privacy concerns, rising costs of the census, and a commitment to address discrimination. There has been some convergence across countries. Those with a long history of recording identity are making these questions optional and open-ended, while European nations have started tracking group inequalities. One-third of respondents in New Zealand and two-thirds in Poland completed their most recent census forms online, and Canada has made the long form of the census voluntary. On the other hand, the Diversity Barometer has been introduced in Belgium, the Integration Barometer in Denmark, and the Trajectories and Origins Survey on Living Conditions in France. The most recent Eurobarometer survey on discrimination took place in 2015 and covered twenty-eight member states and 27,718 respondents from across the social spectrum (Kukutai, Thompson, and McMillan 2015; Farkas 2017).

3. Caste, Identity, and the Indian Census: A Case Study

Nowhere is the official classification of social groups more contentious than in India. Over the years, hundreds of caste groups have petitioned the government for a change in status, and promises of recategorization appear in most political manifestos. Current controversies are the combined result of colonial and precolonial attempts at enumeration and the commitment to large-scale affirmative action after political independence.

Census operations first started in India under British rule in the 1860s and were carried out at ten-year intervals starting in 1881.[9] There were elaborate listings by occupation and caste as early as 1600, under the Mughals, but these were primarily for taxation since taxes varied by occupation and local influence (Guha 2003).[10]

With British rule, enumeration became a means to understand Indian society in order to govern and control it more effectively. British officials wrote obsessively about caste, turning British India into what Nicholas Dirks (2001, 6) has termed an "ethnographic state." There was much confusion about the meaning of caste, however, about whether it should be self-reported and how one should reconcile small differences in spelling and big swings in numbers across census years.

In 1885 Eustace Kitts published *Compendium of the Castes and Tribes Found in India* from the census reports of the British Provinces for 1881. Enumerators for that census were given instructions to count the number of each caste in order to lay "a foundation for further research into the little-known subject of Caste," but Kitts admits that they encountered a "mighty maze without a plan" (Kitts 1895, v). In the years that followed, caste statistics became more elaborate and administrators continued to grapple with the relationship between caste names, language, religion, and occupation. In some provinces and for some years, all religions were subdivided by caste; in other cases, caste was admissible only for Hindus.

In 1881, enumerators were asked to report numbers of all castes above 100,000 people in their province and to use their local knowledge to determine whether some of the reported names were synonyms. Castes were listed alphabetically. In 1891, castes were grouped under what was believed to be their traditional occupations, so for example the census listed martial castes, pastoral castes, and major landowners, irrespective of the fractions of these groups then pursuing those occupations.

The 1901 enumeration went back to an alphabetical listing and was far more elaborate than any of the other censuses. Herbert Risley, an ethnographer, was in charge and used the opportunity provided by endogamous caste groups to examine his theories on the physical basis for race. Descriptions of the skulls and noses of different castes add considerably to the bulk of the 1901 census report. The number of castes recorded in the Census of India, General Report, went up from 204 in 1881 to 718 in 1901, and back down to 256 in 1931. These were only those castes that were considered significant for the country as a whole. Provincial reports recorded many more. In 1911 and 1921, castes continued to be alphabetically listed, but attention was once again restricted to larger caste groups to avoid "an undue expenditure of time and labor."[11]

In 1931 caste was once again grouped by occupation to "avoid the dispersion of closely connected castes involved in an alphabetical arrangement," and all provinces were asked to compile figures only for those castes that the "local government considered of sufficient importance." The 1931 census also mentions a campaign against caste returns based on their role in perpetuating an oppressive system. A response of *caste nil* was accepted for the first time in this year and was chosen by two million people. Nearly all of them were from Bengal, where social reform movements, such as the Brahmo Samaj, were taking root.

In spite of the confusion surrounding social classification in the colonial period, the statistics collected had profound effects on state policy after independence in 1947.

At the time, no household data was available on assets, income, or consumption, but a caste enumeration was available from the 1931 census. Census reports also had elaborate descriptions of the lifestyle of various castes, their relative position in society, the clothes they wore, the food they ate, and their role in village society. These were the basis for drawing boundaries between privilege and disadvantage in India. The most significant legacy of the 1931 census is its list of "exterior castes." Census officials in each province had been asked to list castes who "suffered disability on account of being debarred from temples, schools or wells" (*Census of India, 1931*, app. 1, 471).

Based on these "data," the new constitution in 1950 created schedules for two categories of disadvantaged groups: the Scheduled Castes (SCs) and the Scheduled Tribes (STs). The constitution mandated quotas in parliament, and later education and employment, in proportion to their population shares. For each census year following this, enumerators would ask households their caste if they claimed to be either an SC or an ST. They would enter them as such only if their caste name appeared on the list and if their religion was Hindu, Buddhist, or Sikh. All other religious groups were ineligible, irrespective of their caste or tribe. In particular Muslims, who are currently 14 percent of the Indian population, or Christians, who are 2 percent, were kept outside these schedules and the ambit of affirmative action.

In addition to the SC and ST classification, a new category of Other Backward Classes (OBCs) was created in 1955, with two thousand caste groups. These are not enumerated by the census, but survey data do record membership. They are also eligible for affirmative action, with a quota of 27 percent in all federal employment and seats in public universities. Some Muslim groups are now included among the OBCs.

Through this categorization, the state created a new layer of identities that sat above the more complex and tangled layer of caste. There are over eight hundred groups in the SC and ST lists.[12] They are typically endogamous and have very different levels of education and access to the modern sector of the Indian economy. I return to these differences and their implications for justice in section 5.

4. Measures of Difference

The two previous sections have illustrated the historically contingent nature of identity as recorded in census data. In this section I abstract from the difficulties of drawing social boundaries and discuss two commonly used measures of community cohesion, given a distribution of the population across well-defined groups.

The Ethnolinguistic Fractionalization (ELF) Index is most frequently used as a proxy for the ability of communities to cooperate on policies that jointly affect them. It is defined as the sum of squares of all groups subtracted from unity. With n groups and s_i denoting the fraction of group i in the population of interest, the ELF is computed as follows:

$$\text{ELF} = 1 - \Sigma_{i=1}^{n} s_i^2$$

This measure takes the value of zero with a single large group, and increases in the total number of equal-sized groups in the population. The ELF happens to be the probability that two randomly chosen people in a population will be of the same group. If we view collective action as emerging from sharing of ideas in chance meetings between group members, this seems a reasonable measure.

The fractionalization measure is highest for populations with a large number of very small groups, while group conflict is usually associated with clashing identities and competing interests of salient groups. Polarization measures place higher weights on larger groups and are maximized in a population with two equally sized groups. Joan Esteban and

Debraj Ray have proposed a family of polarization measures to measure the propensity for conflict in a society. Empirical work on conflict based on these measures commonly uses the following variant, found in Esteban and Ray (2011, equation 5, p. 1348).

$$P = \sum_{i=1}^{n} s_i^2 (1 - s_i)$$

Since within-group inequality in outcomes does not enter either the fractionalization or polarization indices, and all groups enter symmetrically, both measures implicitly assume that groups are unitary and equidistant from each other in some social space.

Country studies on the effects of ethnic diversity use census classifications to construct these measures. For example, Alesina and coauthors (2003) in their study of US counties use the three race categories of white, black, and other for 1960 and the fivefold classification with two additional categories of American Indian and Asian / Pacific Islander for 1990. Banerjee, Iyer, and Somanathan (2008) combine census data from 1931 to 1991 to generate caste and religious fractionalization measures for districts in India. Many localized studies also collect primary data from their respondents. Miguel and Gugerty (2005) administered questionnaires in two districts of Kenya to examine whether ethnically heterogeneous primary schools receive lower parental contributions.

Cross-country research relies on ethnic and linguistic graphs constructed by teams of researchers. The *Atlas Narodov Mira* was one of the earliest attempts at a multicountry listing of ethnicity. It was created by Soviet ethnographers in the 1960s and lists 910 ethnolinguistic groups across the world. Alternative datasets have now been provided by Alesina et al. (2003), Fearon (2003), and Montalvo and Reynal-Querol (2005), among others. Each of these differs in its classification criteria and coverage. Major sources used are the *Encyclopaedia Britannica*, the CIA *World Factbook*, Library of Congress Country Studies, and the *World Christian Encyclopedia*.

5. The Problem of Mismeasurement

With the necessary background in place, I now turn to my main arguments for why research across multiple disciplines calls for a reexamination of how we collect and use social data.

I consider the problem of mismeasurement at three levels. First, in the drawing of social boundaries, I consider examples from the United States, Brazil, and India that illustrate fluidity of reported identities and their response to economic incentives. The second source of mismeasurement is in the indices discussed in the previous section that collapse data on identity into proxies for the likelihood of cooperation. Finally, I argue that the models used to predict the effects of heterogeneity on community performance are misleading in that they ignore the type of evidence that is most useful in building cooperation in diverse social environments.

a. Fluid Identities

There has already been excellent scholarship on the contingent nature of social boundaries. Over a number of years, Rogers Brubaker, Charles Tilly, Andreas Wimmer, and many others have provided theoretical principles and historical accounts of boundary-making and its effects.[13] I restrict myself here to quantitative examples from three of the world's largest democracies: the United States, Brazil, and India.

In the United States, the federal directive of 1997 allowed respondents to list two or more races in addition to the five categories that were previously available. The data from the following two census years are comparable in that the format of the race question remained the same. In the 2000 census 2.4 percent of the population listed two or more races, and the bulk of these respondents were in three states: California, Texas, and New York. In 2010 this number went up by over two million or 32 percent, with the largest increase in the *White and Black* category (Jones and Bullock 2013).

Liebler et al. (2017) link individual responses for about half the population in the two census years. Their study, aptly named "America's Churning Races," reveals the fluidity of identity among sizable sections of the population. They find about 6 percent switched racial categories, and Hispanics, American Indians, younger populations, and those reporting two or more races in either year were disproportionately represented in this group.

The above findings caution us against the use of identity measures in statistical analyses of the type common in the heterogeneity and public goods literature. Considering the distribution of mixed-race responses by age and geography, it is certainly plausible that individuals are more likely to report themselves of mixed race in environments where these responses are most socially acceptable. The fraction doing so, while rising fast, is still small enough to be swamped in a study of US counties or school districts. In other words, it may well be that the most progressive and dynamic localities in terms of racial integration are ignored as outliers in studies of heterogeneity using large datasets.[14]

My second example is Brazil. As described in section 2, Brazil has historically used a classification of race based on color, and 99 percent of the population classify as white, brown, or black in all census years. The Brazilian Statistical Agency responsible for the census periodically conducts household surveys that have an open-ended question asking the respondent to identify their color and another question (later in the survey) asking them to identify themselves using the census classification. A comparison of responses across formats shows many Brazilians using noncensus categories and for skin color, classification biases vary by both age and education.[15]

The politics of classification over the last two decades is especially interesting. Affirmative action was first introduced in two public universities in Rio de Janeiro in 2001 and then adopted in many others over the next decade. The legislation did not, however, use census categories but instead used a dichotomous white-black distinction and the term *negro*, clarifying that this included the *pardo* (brown) and *preto* (black) categories of the census.

Francis and Tannuri-Pianto (2013) examine the effect of quotas on racial self-classification by surveying students in the University of Brasilia before and after the introduction of quotas in 2004. They use photographs of students from their secondary school identity cards to classify them by color and then ask them to self-classify during an online interview. They find that the introduction of affirmative action has polarized responses. After the introduction of quotas, higher fractions of lighter skin tone quintiles (based on the photographs) classify themselves as White, and the darker quintiles classify themselves as Black. Bailey (2008) uses data from a national public opinion survey and also finds that the mention of quotas for *negros* doubles the number of respondents who claim that category in an open-format question.

As my final illustration of identity mismeasurement, I consider the recent challenges to the category of Backward Classes in India. As explained in section 2, in the 1950s the Indian state created a fourfold overlay of official identities consisting of the Scheduled Castes, the Scheduled Tribes, the Other Backward Classes (OBCs), and a fourth residual category, often labeled General or Unreserved. The first three groups are collectively called the Backward Classes. The census estimates only the first two scheduled categories, which together form 23 percent of the population. The OBCs are estimated at somewhere between 50 and 70 percent. The SCs, STs, and OBCs each have separate education and employment quotas under India's affirmative action program.

At the time of the original classification, there was very limited data on the economic standing of the many hundreds of caste groups in India. The lines separating large landowning classes such as the Brahmans and the Rajputs were clear, but differences among the rest were hard to measure. The list of Scheduled Castes was drawn up to include groups that had experienced untouchability, and the Scheduled Tribes were those who were isolated in remote villages. The colonial census documented literacy rates by caste but little else, and since access to schooling was very limited in the colonial period, the castes and tribes in these schedules looked similar.

Since 1961, the census has tracked educational attainment for these groups. Figure 10.1 shows school completion rates in 1961 and 2001 for the fifteen largest groups in the SC and ST categories. In 1961 none of the SCs and only one ST group had more than 1 percent of its population graduating from high school. In 2001 graduation rates were still below 1 percent for the Musahars among the SCs, while they were close to 20 percent among the more successful groups. Inequalities among the STs were more muted but still substantial. The policies that were designed to promote equal opportunity now have very unequal impact, benefiting the relatively prosperous among the scheduled groups who have enough schooling to take advantage of quotas in higher education and employment. The category of Scheduled Castes, which was once relatively homogeneous in terms of educational attainment, is no longer so. There appear to be not one but many operational identities within this broad group. While there is broad agreement that affirmative action has been accompanied by some convergence between the scheduled and nonscheduled groups, there has also been considerable divergence within the scheduled categories.

The gains experienced by selected castes have led to fierce battles for reclassification. I have previously referred to this phenomenon as the Demand for Disadvantage (Somanathan 2010 and 2017). Associations for powerful groups such as the Gujars of North India have mobilized to lobby for inclusion in ST lists. In 2008, quotas for university seats were extended to the Other Backward Classes (OBCs). In that year 147 groups petitioned for inclusion in OBC list, and 67 of these succeeded. Each year there are a few more. The basis for the appeal is either that the caste in question is simply a synonym or a subcaste of one already on the schedules or that they live in similar conditions or share the same culture.[16] Committees are formed to consider these cases; they hold public hearings and collect information. With no workable definition of backwardness, it is impossible to engage in its systematic measurement. Political exigency often leads to acquiescence.

Matriculation Rates among Scheduled Castes

Caste

Caste	1961	2001
Adi Dravida	0.8%	21%
Mala	0.6%	19.8%
Adi Karnataka	0.6%	19.3%
Paraiyan	0.5%	19%
Dhobi	0.5%	13.7%
Chamar	0.5%	12.1%
Madiga	0.2%	11.9%
Kori	0.4%	11.6%
Balmiki	0.3%	8.7%
Dusadh	0.2%	8.7%
Rajbanshi	0.4%	7.5%
Pan	0.1%	7.4%
Pasi	0.3%	7%
Bagdi	0.2%	3.2%
Musahar	0%	0.7%

Matriculation Rate

Matriculation Rates among Scheduled Tribes

Tribe

Tribe	1961	2001
Naga	0.2%	24.4%
Boro	0.3%	19.4%
Khasi	1.5%	14.3%
Oraon	0.5%	14%
Ho	0.4%	10.7%
Munda	0.3%	9.3%
Miria	0.1%	9.5%
Shabar	0.2%	7.8%
Gond	0%	6.7%
Santal	0.1%	5.8%
Bhil	0%	5.7%
Dubia	0%	4.9%
Kol	0%	3.3%
Khond	0%	3.2%
Varli	0%	3.2%

Matriculation Rate

Year
1961
2001

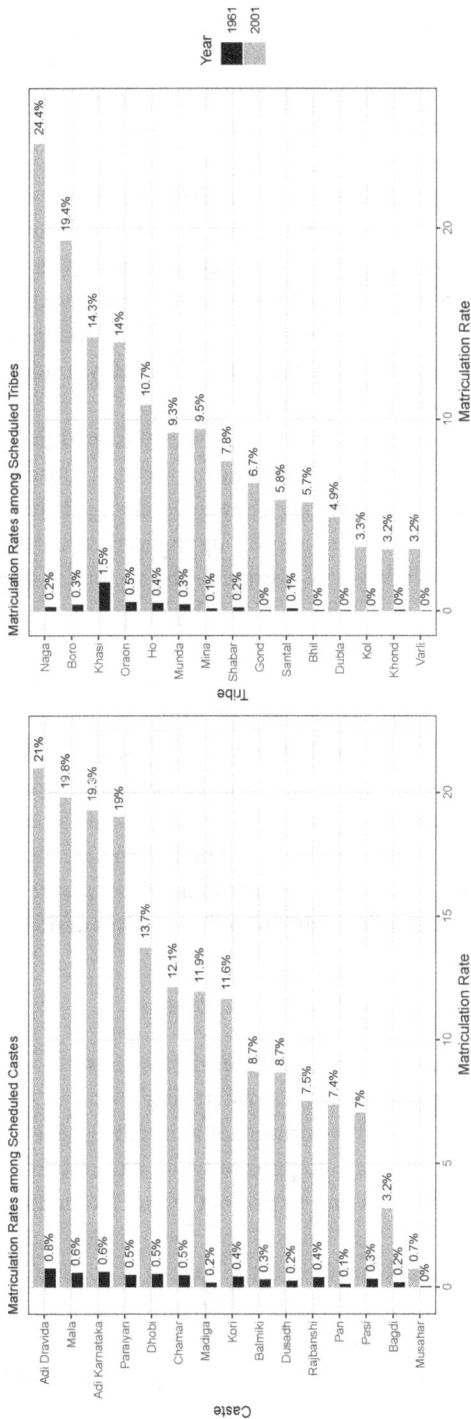

FIGURE 10.1. School completion rates for 1961 and 2001 for the fifteen Scheduled Castes and Scheduled Tribes in 1961 with the largest populations in 1961.

The powerful Jat community of North India, led by its rich farmers, has been petitioning for about a decade for access to affirmative action quotas in universities and government jobs. An agitation by them in 2016 left thirty dead and two hundred injured. Travel was crippled and property worth millions destroyed. On March 20, 2017, the Jat planned an agitation in the capital, Delhi, that was expected to draw a million protestors. Borders to Delhi were thick with police, and families of children taking their school-leaving exams were reported as moving closer to exam locations to ensure they reached them in time. After assurances of compromise by state officials at the last minute, the agitation was called off, and the city started to breathe again after several days under the threat of chaos and riots. Until the next time.[17]

The latest large-scale agitation is by the Patels, a large and important community in Gujarat who are also known for their motel chains on the East Coast of the United States. They have changed the discourse on identity and affirmative action in India by suggesting that one way out of the classification dilemma is to dismantle the system of quotas entirely. The Indian experience has shown us the highly political nature of social data in a high-stakes environment.

Each of these countries has a different lesson to offer on classification. The case of the US census shows us that significant numbers of individuals, particularly those of mixed race, are ambiguous about their identity even when there are no stakes involved. The case of Brazil shows us that policies alter incentives to classify and can dichotomize race even in a society that has celebrated racial mixing. The Indian case illustrates the politicization of classification debates and their interactions with inequality.

I now turn, more briefly, to the two other sources of mismeasurement.

b. Problematic Proxies

The Fractionalization and Polarization indices described in section 4, and other measures of heterogeneity, treat groups as symmetric and equidistant. Neither social proximity nor hierarchy is taken into account. Consider two US cities: one 90 percent white and 10 percent black, and the other 90 percent black and 10 percent white. Our indices would take the same value in these two cases. Those even slightly familiar with the urban landscape in the United States will know how different the poverty levels and the urban environments are likely to be in these cities.

New longitudinal datasets and evidence on policy experiments that have moved households out of very poor neighborhoods suggest strong negative effects of racial segregation among the poor. Akee, Jones, and Porter (2017) match tax returns for all filers between 2000 and 2014 with census data on where they live. They find that racially segregated communities found their incomes declining in relative terms over this period and that starting an employment career in a segregated community is particularly detrimental for blacks, Hispanics, and American Indians. They also find that black workers experience the highest rates of immobility in the poorest earnings quintile and the highest rates of sliding out of the richest quintile when they happen to be there.[18]

Studies based on the Moving to Opportunity (MTO) experiment of the US Department of Housing in the 1990s examine benefits of moving out of segregated high-poverty neighborhoods. Over four thousand families with children in five major cities were part of the experiment. All of them lived in "extreme poverty" neighborhoods defined as those in which at least 40 percent of residents have incomes below the federal poverty threshold. One treatment arm was provided with vouchers to move out to a neighborhood with a poverty rate of lower than 10 percent. Chetty, Hendren, and Katz (2016) find positive long-term effects on college attendance and earnings for those with the MTO vouchers and children under the age of thirteen and disruptive negative effects for adolescents. Ludwig et al. find improvements in subjective well-being and a decline in chronic health disorders. Baseline surveys asked all MTO adults their reasons for signing up for the program. Three-quarters listed getting away from gangs and drugs as one of their top two reasons for wanting to move (Ludwig et al. 2012, 1506). Evidence on the MTO program is relevant for our debate on heterogeneity because many households willingly moved to areas with fewer neighbors of their own race in order to improve other aspects of their social environment.

These findings are consistent with surveys by sociologists who find that while white households prefer segregated neighborhoods, black households state preferences for neighborhoods that are racially mixed, with 50:50 black-white often preferred to other compositions. This asymmetry is not surprising given the enormous differences in average wealth and the quality of public services in white and black neighborhoods (Krysan et al. 2009).

Models with racial and ethnic composition as the main determinant of community outcomes without adequate controls for the social environment and the quality of public services are therefore grossly misspecified. The most pressing collective-action problems of families in poor neighborhoods are not centered on how much to contribute for a Christmas party or any other community activity. These families are trying, just like everyone else, to provide safe and productive school environments to their children and equip them for work *outside* the neighborhoods in which they are raised. This requires a broader system of social cooperation. The chapters by Allen, Rogers, and Wingo in this volume focus on the normative apparatus needed to move toward this.

c. Deliberative Democracy

I discuss two experiments that show that decision-making processes rather than just the policies that emerge from them matter for cooperation. The first is a 2006 laboratory experiment involving undergraduates at Brown University. Students are assigned to groups in which they play prisoner's dilemma games. They can modify the game by voting on a fine to encourage cooperation. They can also vote for a zero fine. A computer then either allows the group the fine that was chosen by majority vote or assigns them a fine (which may be the one chosen by them). Results show that levels of cooperation are 40 percent higher when fines are democratically chosen rather than imposed on the group. Participants find the democratic process valuable in addition to any policy benefits that it generates (Dal Bó, Foster, and Putterman 2010).

The second experiment was undertaken in two districts of northern Liberia a couple of years after the end of civil war in 2003. As part of a community-driven reconstruction program, the UK government funded forty-two randomly selected communities out of a total of eighty-three communities. The selected communities received funds for a new infrastructure project. To be eligible, they needed to choose the project and select community representatives to handle the funds. Fearon, Humphreys, and Weinstein (2015) present results from a public goods game played with twenty-four adults in each of the eighty-three communities. In half of these villages, the group playing the game consisted only of women. In the other half, there were mixed groups with equal numbers of men and women. They compare the levels of cooperation in the control villages (those that did not receive the development assistance) with those in the treatment villages. Their most interesting finding is that the treatment-control difference in the level of measured cooperation is greatest in the mixed groups. In the absence of any possibility of funds coming into the village, they have much lower levels of cooperation than the women's groups. However, when they need to cooperate for the benefit of the village, they are very successful. The authors argue that a community's capacity to cooperate can be changed over a relatively short period of time and with a relatively modest intervention. Leaders in the mixed communities were more active in building consensus and sharing information on the benefits of cooperation.

Both experiments highlight the importance of fostering deliberation in collective decision-making.

6. Final Thoughts

Given the multifaceted nature of identity and the various historical, political, and ideological influences on its classification by the state, it seems inevitable that social differences will be mismeasured. Social statistics, however, also allow us to detect and document systematic differences in outcomes across groups and help us assess whether a democracy is serving all of its people. How do we trade off costs and benefits? Should we collect social data through comprehensive enumeration projects such as national censuses? If so, what types of state policies should be based on these data?

Social data can be effectively used to equalize opportunity only if official classifications of groups are socially relevant and when policies that aim to equalize do not themselves create perverse incentives for identity manipulation.

Recent reforms by some nations that remove identity questions from the mandatory census forms and allow open-ended responses to questions on social background seem steps in the right direction.

In addition, researchers using these data could benefit from greater attention to the processes by which these data are gathered and from broadening their hypotheses to include collaborative rather than just competitive interactions between individuals and groups. The few experiments that have been conducted on strengthening democratic process give us reason to be optimistic. Differences in origin and ancestry need not translate into social distances. In a world where firms and universities are becoming increasingly international and actively seeking out talent from various cultural backgrounds, social scientists should also go beyond modeling communities as spaces where ethnicities have to negotiate what are presumed to be their inherent differences.

In his memoir, Benedict Anderson describes discovering his Irish ancestry only in his thirties. Until then, "identity was mainly connected with mathematics or the forensic investigation of a corpse" (Anderson 2016, 6). Perhaps true justice in diverse democracies would allow us to ignore and acknowledge identity with equal ease.

Notes

1. See, for example, Easterly and Levine 1997, 1204: "In the case of Sub-Saharan Africa, economic growth is associated with low schooling, political instability, underdeveloped financial systems, distorted foreign exchange markets, high government deficits, and insufficient infrastructure. Africa's high ethnic fragmentation explains a significant part of most of these characteristics."

2. Banerjee, Iyer, and Somanathan 2008 and Alesina and La Ferrara 2005 summarize major contributions in this literature.

3. Nobles 2000 quotes from the instructions given to enumerators of the 1870 census: "It must be assumed that, where nothing is written in this column, 'White' is to be understood. The column is always to be filled. Be particularly careful in reporting the class *Mulatto*. The word here is generic, and includes quadroons, octoroons, and all persons having any perceptible trace of African blood. Important scientific results depend upon the correct determination of this class in schedules 1 and 2."

4. Yanow 2015, chaps. 2–4.

5. Stevens, Ishizawa, and Grbic 2015 summarizes changes in US and Canadian censuses over time. The editorial opinion in the July 29, 2010, issue of *Nature*, which appeared just before the 2011 census, criticizes the move from mandatory to voluntary reporting of ethnicity in Canada.

6. Simon 2012 provides a useful tabulation of the data collected by statistical agencies in European countries in the census closest to the year 2000 (table 1, 1369–75).

7. See Loveman 2014, tables 6.1 and 7.1a, for a list of censuses and countries that have recorded race since the early nineteenth century, and figure 5.1 for the changes in tabulation in Mexico.

8. Goldscheider 2002 compares Israel, Canada, and the United States. For Rwanda, see Wimmer 2013, 53–54, for ethnic distinctions under colonial rule, and Eramian 2014 for changes after 1994.

9. Some regions did enumerate populations before the British Crown took over from the East India Company in 1858. For example, there are counts available for districts in Western India from 1826.

10. Guha 2003, 153, notes that "dominant communities often won exemption from taxes, while special levies existed on subordinate ones.... Grocers, grain dealers, tobacco vendors, sellers of colored powder, lac dealers, low-caste weavers, other weavers, etcetera, all were enumerated and taxed at different rates."

11. All figures and quotes have been taken from the General Report for the relevant census year.

12. Arriving at the total number of castes is not straightforward, because lists are published separately for each of the twenty-nine Indian states, and these change from one census year to the next. See Kumar and Somanathan 2016 for one method of combining them to arrive at the above number.

13. See for example Tilly 2003; Brubaker 2009; and Wimmer 2013.

14. The ordering of questions on ethnicity has also been shown to alter the distribution of responses. In 1987 the US Census Bureau conducted a randomized experiment in which the order of the race and Hispanic-origin questions was reversed for about half of a sample of 515 respondents. Putting the Hispanic-origin question before race increased the numbers responding to this question and also reduced the numbers checking Other in the race question: Anderson and Fienberg 2000.

15. See Bailey and Telles 2006 and Powell and Silva 2018 for a comparison of responses in alternative formats. Monk 2016 shows that inequality in education by color is much greater than by census category.

16. These numbers are from the annual reports of the National Commission for Backward Classes.

17. From reports in the *Hindu Daily* on March 19 and 20, 2017.

18. Akee, Jones, and Porter 2017: mobility matrices are on p. 23, and results on racial segregation on pp. 27–29.

Works Cited

Adida, C. L., D. D. Laitin, and M. Valfort. 2016. "'One Muslim Is Enough!' Evidence from a Field Experiment in France." *Annals of Economics and Statistics* 121/122 (June): 121–60.

Akee, R., M. Jones, and S. Porter. 2017. "Adding Insult to Injury: Racial Disparity in an Era of Increasing Income Inequality." Working Paper 2017–01. Center for Administrative Records Research and Applications, US Census Bureau.

Alesina, A., R. Baqir, and W. Easterly. 1999. "Public Goods and Ethnic Divisions." *Quarterly Journal of Economics* 114, no. 4 (November): 1243–84.

Alesina, A., A. Devleeschauwer, W. Easterly, S. Kurlat, and R. Wacziarg. 2003. "Fractionalization." *Journal of Economic Growth* 8, no. 2 (June): 155–94.

Alesina, A., and E. La Ferrara. 2005. "Ethnic Diversity and Economic Performance." *Journal of Economic Literature* 43, no. 3 (September): 762–800.

Anderson, B. 2016. *A Life beyond Boundaries: A Memoir.* New York: Verso Books.

Anderson, M., and S. E. Fienberg. 2000. "Race and Ethnicity and the Controversy over the US Census." *Current Sociology* 48, no. 3 (July): 87–110.

Bailey, S. 2008. "Unmixing for Race Making in Brazil." *American Journal of Sociology* 114, no. 3 (November): 577–614.

Bailey, S., and E. Telles. 2006. "Multiracial versus Collective Black Categories: Examining Census Classification Debates in Brazil." *Ethnicities* 6, no. 1 (March): 74–101.

Banerjee, A., L. Iyer, and R. Somanathan. 2008. "Public Action for Public Goods." In *Handbook of Development Economics*, edited by T. P. Schultz and J. Strauss, 4:3117–54. Amsterdam: North-Holland/Elsevier.

Boyd, M. 1999. "Canadian Eh? Ethnic Origin Shifts in the Canadian Census." *Canadian Ethnic Studies* 31, no. 3 (Fall): 1–19.

Brubaker, R. 2009. "Ethnicity, Race, and Nationalism." *Annual Review of Sociology* 35 (August): 21–42.

Caselli, F., and W. J. Coleman. 2013. "On the Theory of Ethnic Conflict." *Journal of the European Economic Association* 11, no. 1 (January): 161–192.

Census of India. 1931. Vol. 1, pt. I: Report. Compiled by J. H. Hutton, census commissioner.

Chetty, R., N. Hendren, and L. Katz. 2016. "The Effects of Exposure to Better Neighborhoods on Children: New Evidence from the Moving to Opportunity Experiment." *American Economic Review* 106, no. 4 (April): 855–902.

Chetty, R., N. Hendren, M. Jones, and S. Porter. 2018. "Race and Economic Opportunity in the United States: An Intergenerational Perspective." NBER Working Paper Series, 24441. Cambridge, MA: National Bureau of Economic Research.

Dal Bó, P., A. Foster, and L. Putterman. 2010. "Institutions and Behavior: Experimental Evidence on the Effects of Democracy." *American Economic Review* 100, no. 5 (December): 2205–29.

Dirks, N. 2001. *Castes of Mind: Colonialism and the Making of Modern India.* Princeton, NJ: Princeton University Press.

Easterly, W., and R. Levine. 1997. "Africa's Growth Tragedy: Policies and Ethnic Divisions." *Quarterly Journal of Economics* 112, no. 4 (November): 1203–50.

Eramian, L. 2014. "Ethnicity without Labels? Ambiguity and Excess in 'Postethnic' Rwanda." *Focaal: European Journal of Anthropology* 70 (December): 96–109.

Esteban, J., and D. Ray. 2008. "On the Salience of Ethnic Conflict." *American Economic Review* 98, no. 5 (December): 2185–2202.

Esteban, J., and D. Ray. 2011. "Linking Conflict to Inequality and Polarization." *American Economic Review* 101, no. 4 (June): 1345–74.

Farkas, L. 2017. *Data Collection in the Field of Ethnicity: Analysis and Comparative Review of Data Collection Practices in the European Union.* Luxembourg: Directorate-General for Justice and Consumers, European Commission.

Fearon, J. 2003. "Ethnic and Cultural Diversity by Country." *Journal of Economic Growth* 8, no. 2 (June): 195–222.

Fearon, J., M. Humphreys, and J. M. Weinstein. 2015. "How Does Development Assistance Affect Collective Action Capacity? Results from a Field Experiment in Post-conflict Liberia." *American Political Science Review* 109, no. 3 (August): 450–69.

Francis, A., and M. Tannuri-Pianto. 2013. "Endogenous Race in Brazil: Affirmative Action and the Construction of Racial Identity among Young Adults." *Economic Development and Cultural Change* 61, no. 4 (July): 731–53.

Goldscheider, C. 2002. "Ethnic Categorizations in Censuses: Comparative Observations from Israel, Canada, and the United States." In *Census and Identity: The Politics of Race, Ethnicity, and Language in National Censuses,* edited by D. I. Kertzer and D. Arel, 71–91. Cambridge: Cambridge University Press.

Guha, S. 2003. "The Politics of Identity and Enumeration in India c. 1600–1990." *Comparative Studies in Society and History* 45, no. 1 (January): 148–67.

Jones, N. A., and J. J. Bullock. 2013. "Understanding Who Reported Multiple Races in the US Decennial Census: Results from Census 2000 and the 2010 Census." *Family Relations* 62, no. 1 (January): 5–16.

Kitts, E. 1885. *A Compendium of the Castes and Tribes Found in India.* Bombay: Education Society's Press.

Krysan, M., M. P. Couper, R. Farley, and T. Forman. 2009. "Does Race Matter in Neighborhood Preferences? Results from a Video Experiment." *American Journal of Sociology* 115, no. 2 (September): 527–59.

Kukutai, T., V. Thompson, and R. McMillan. 2015. "Whither the Census? Continuity and Change in Census Methodologies Worldwide, 1985–2014." *Journal of Population Research* 32, no. 1 (March): 3–22.

Kumar, H., and R. Somanathan. 2016. "Affirmative Action and Long-Run Changes in Group Inequality in India." World Institute for Development Economics (UNU-WIDER) Working Paper 2016/85, June 2016.

Lieberman, E. S., and P. Singh. 2017. "Census Enumeration and Group Conflict: A Global Analysis of the Consequences of Counting." *World Politics* 69, no. 1 (January): 1–53.

Liebler, C., A. Porter, S. Fernandez, R. Noon, and L. Ennis. 2017. "America's Churning

Races: Race and Ethnicity Response Changes between Census 2000 and the 2010 Census." *Demography* 54, no. 1 (January): 259–84.

Loveman, M. 2014. *National Colors: Racial Classification and the State in Latin America.* Oxford: Oxford University Press.

Ludwig, J., et al. 2012. "Neighborhood Effects on the Long-Term Well-Being of Low-Income Adults." *Science* 337, no. 6101 (September 21): 1505–10.

Miguel, E., and M. K. Gugerty. 2005. "Ethnic Diversity, Social Sanctions, and Public Goods in Kenya." *Journal of Public Economics* 89, no. 11–12 (December): 2325–68.

Monk, E. 2016. "The Consequences of 'Race and Color' in Brazil." *Social Problems* 63, no. 3 (August): 413–30.

Montalvo, J. G., and M. Reynal-Querol. 2005. "Ethnic Polarization, Potential Conflict, and Civil Wars." *American Economic Review* 95, no. 3 (June): 796–816.

Morning, A. 2008. "Ethnic Classification in Global Perspective: A Cross-National Survey of the 2000 Census Round." *Population Research and Policy Review* 2, no. 2 (April): 239–72.

National Commission on Backward Classes. 2008. *Annual Report, 2007–2008.* New Delhi, July 9, 2008.

National Commission on Backward Classes. 2009. *Annual Report, 2008–2009.* New Delhi, July 2009.

National Commission on Backward Classes. 2010. *Annual Report, 2009–2010.* New Delhi, July 2010.

National Commission on Backward Classes. 2011. *Annual Report, 2010–2011.* New Delhi, July 9, 2011.

National Commission on Backward Classes. 2012. *Annual Report, 2011–2012.* New Delhi, July 2012.

National Commission on Backward Classes. 2013. *Annual Report, 2012–2013.* New Delhi, July 2013.

National Commission on Backward Classes. 2014. *Annual Report, 2013–2014.* New Delhi, July 2014.

National Commission on Backward Classes. 2015. *Annual Report, 2014–2015.* New Delhi, July 2015.

Nature. 2010. "Save the Census." Editorial. *Nature* 466 (July 29): 532.

Nobles, M. 2000. "History Counts: A Comparative Analysis of Racial/Color Categorization in US and Brazilian Censuses." *American Journal of Public Health* 90, no. 11 (November): 1738–45.

Putnam, R. D. 2007. "E Pluribus Unum: Diversity and Community in the Twenty-First Century." *Scandinavian Political Studies* 30, no. 2 (June): 137–74.

Powell, B., and G. Silva. 2018. "Technocrats' Compromises: Defining Race and the Struggle for Equality in Brazil, 1970–2010." *Journal of Latin American Studies* 50, no. 1 (February): 87–115.

Shelby, T. 2016. *Dark Ghettos: Injustice, Dissent, and Reform.* Cambridge, MA: Harvard University Press.

Simon, P. 2012. "Collecting Ethnic Statistics in Europe: A Review." *Ethnic and Racial Studies* 35, no. 8 (August): 1366–91.

Somanathan, R. 2010. "The Demand for Disadvantage." In *Culture, Institutions, and Development: New Insights into an Old Debate*, edited by Jean-Philippe Platteau and Robert Peccoud, 125–40. New York: Routledge.

Somanathan, R. 2017. "How India's Caste Politics Is Mostly Scramble for Privilege or Catalyst for Communalism." *India Today*, January 16, 2017.

Stevens, G., H. Ishizawa, and D. Grbic. 2015. "Measuring Race and Ethnicity in the Censuses of Australia, Canada, and the United States: Parallels and Paradoxes." *Canadian Studies in Population* 42, nos. 1–2 (March): 13–34.

Tilly, C. 2003. "Political Identities in Changing Polities." *Social Research* 70, no. 2 (Summer): 605–20.

Wimmer, A. 2013. *Ethnic Boundary Making: Institutions, Power, Networks*. New York: Oxford University Press.

Yanow, D. 2015. *Constructing "Race" and "Ethnicity" in America: Category-Making in Public Policy and Administration*. London: Routledge.

11

Immigration, Membership, and Justice

ON THE RIGHT TO BRING OTHERS INTO THE POLITY

Claudio López-Guerra

Up until this point in the volume, all the chapters have assumed an un-problematic definition of membership in the political community for which we seek to establish democratic justice. Yet the issue of member-ship is not unproblematic, as controversies over immigration make clear. More significantly, the kinds of diversity any democracy finds itself nego-tiating, perhaps in pursuit of difference without domination, inevitably flows directly from the nature of its membership policies. In order to bring into view the contingent nature of who is in the polity and the de-gree to which we have naturalized familial-based models of membership, I offer in this chapter an alternative model based on an individual right to bring others into the polity. This argument generates a different pic-ture of the requirements flowing from the right of association from what has been presumed about that right in the earlier chapters of the volume.

It is already the case that the lawful members of a polity, acting *indi-vidually*, can endow others with immigration rights. Not everyone has the authority to do this, however. Only family members can extend this endowment. There are two main routes. First, most countries permit citizens and permanent residents to sponsor the admission of certain relatives, such as spouses. Second, citizens of virtually all countries can pass on their nationality to their children and hence endow them with the right to inhabit the polity in question. In addition, current members can sometimes endow outsiders with entry rights by acting *collectively* — although not through the state. For instance, companies can sponsor the

I am very grateful to all the contributors to this volume for their generous comments, especially the editors, Danielle Allen and Rohini Somanathan, who very carefully read the chapter on multiple occasions. I also want to thank Enrique Camacho, Matthew Lin-dauer, Matthew Lister, Paulina Ochoa-Espejo, Thomas Pogge, and audiences at Univer-sidad Nacional Autónoma de México (UNAM), Universidad Panamericana, and Yale University for their helpful criticisms.

admission of prospective employees. I shall refer to this system as the conservative or kinship model of membership endowment.

Against this model, I defend a liberal model that proposes the following:

1. Individual members of the polity should be allowed to sponsor the admission of nonrelatives; limiting eligibility to (close) family members is unjust.
2. If organizations are given sponsorship prerogatives, eligibility should not be limited to potential employees; allowing companies and universities to sponsor the admission of valuable assets while preventing other associations from doing the same requires justification.
3. At least presumptively, the requirements for sponsoring nonrelatives and nonemployees should be no stricter than those for relatives and prospective employees.
4. Sponsorship requirements should ultimately approximate the undemanding conditions that currently allow individual citizens to endow others with membership rights via *ius sanguinis*.

In an insightful article, Luara Ferracioli has argued that allowing members to invite only outsiders who have a certain kind of relationship with us, specifically family members, violates important liberal principles.[1] The state has no business telling us which types of relationships are valuable and which are not. Hence, Ferracioli claims, a liberal state should either curtail sponsorship rights for relatives or expand them to include nonrelatives. This is a step in the right direction. But it is not enough. Ferracioli fails to acknowledge that current members of all polities are allowed to endow certain others with immigration rights. They do this not by inviting them from another polity but by *creating* them from within. For in giving birth to a child we bring a new person in the polity. Through *ius sanguinis*, our offspring become nationals. Once we realize this, Ferracioli's dilemma—the idea that we must choose between curtailing sponsorship rights and extending them to nonrelatives—disappears. This is because no one would deny that people have a right of some kind to procreate and endow their children with residency rights. The first prong of Ferracioli's dilemma is actually a nonchoice, already off limits. Now this unlimited right to procreate is largely grounded on the interest of potential parents to establish an association that *they* value. In other words, the *legal* right to have and raise children is at least in part justified on the basis of a *moral* right to associate with others. Yet other members of the polity who do not value that specific kind of relationship—or who equally value other kinds—nevertheless have exactly the same associational interest. Thus, absent a good reason to the contrary, people should be able to do via immigration what others do via procreation. The liberal membership model that I outline here rests on this insight.

It is important to emphasize that on this view, the right to bring new members in the polity—either through procreation or through immigration—is merely a formal institution: a *legal* right. The justification of this right, I shall argue, rests on the fundamental and underlying moral right to freedom of association.[2] We have a basic interest in being free, within limits, to establish and cultivate relationships with others. This is not simply about being able to choose with whom we wish to associate under certain preestablished terms but also to choose the terms of the association. For instance, it is not simply about being able to marry whomever we choose but also about determining the precise nature of the relationship: the properties that the interaction ought to have for it to be valuable to the parties. This is important, for some have argued that a marital relationship, for instance, requires long-term continuous physical proximity, whereas a relationship of friendship does not, which explains why sponsorship rights are justified to endow spouses with immigration rights but not friends. I shall argue that this is problematic. In short, I shall defend the legal right to universal sponsorship on the basis of a robust moral right to freedom of association.

My proposal, then, is to think critically about current immigration practices and institutions—specifically, immigration sponsorship prerogatives—in the light of a larger problem that has received scant attention in political theory: the nature and extent of the right of citizens to replace themselves and renovate the composition of the state to guarantee its continuity. If individual citizens were equally free, within reasonable limits, to bring new members in the polity by either method—procreation or immigration—the demographic composition of the state would be established in a far more just way than under the current system.

To be sure, the immigration practices in some regions of the world, most notably within the European Union, are in no need of reform along the lines that I defend here. Since EU citizens can move freely across the borders of member states, there is no need to establish sponsorship rights to realize the right to freedom of association in the case of relationships between citizens of these states. However, virtually everywhere else, and also with respect to relationships between EU citizens and non-EU citizens, sponsorship rights would be needed in the absence of further EU-like integration.

This chapter represents a fresh approach to the morality of immigration restrictions. It is based on the perspective of insiders—members who reasonably want to associate with outsiders without being forced to leave the country. Political philosophers studying global justice have focused almost exclusively on what prosperous states with closed borders owe to outsiders who want to immigrate in search of better standards of living.[3] There is nothing wrong with this line of inquiry, of course. But there is more to the morality of immigration than it conveys. The mainstream outsider-global stance ignores the interests of *insiders* who desire more open borders. Consequently, it downplays the relevance of immigration as a problem of *domestic* or national justice. The insider-domestic approach turns the current debate on its head: What do we owe to insiders who would like to bring new members into the polity? In a just society, what are fair limits on the freedom of its members to associate with outsiders? Specifically, is the current kinship model just? Can a less restrictive model be defended?[4]

This paper has four sections. The first identifies the normatively relevant factors for a proper defense of my claims and clarifies some important aspects of my thesis. The second section argues that the establishment of universal sponsorship is prima facie required by a liberal conception of justice. The third section addresses four relevant demographic-consequentialist arguments against universal sponsorship. A brief conclusion follows.

1. The Ethics of Membership Endowment

To fix ideas, consider two hypothetical but entirely realistic cases:

Case A. Linnea, a Norwegian, marries a foreigner. The couple wants to live in Norway, but Linnea's partner lacks a residence permit. She also wants to look after her recently widowed mother, a sexagenarian Canadian who lives in Toronto and is now without relatives in Canada. Fortunately, Norwegian law allows Linnea to endow her family members with permanent residency rights. The process is not automatic, however. In addition to proving her ties to these persons, Linnea has to show that she has earned an income before and that she is likely to earn one in the future. She also has to demonstrate her status as a non-recipient of financial social support. Finally, she must be able to provide housing for the newcomers. But once these conditions are met, admission is relatively certain.

Case B. Emma is a graphic designer who wants to open an advertising agency in Norway, her home country. As is standard in her profession, she plans to team up with a partner to form a creative duo. Emma met her professional other half in graduate school, a Colombian woman who is now her best friend. Emma is also a person with a particular sense of empathy. She was seriously affected by the recent divisive case of Maria Amelie, a girl who was smuggled into Norway by her parents as a teenager and who was deported in 2011 at the age of twenty-five years, despite her deep roots in Norway. If she could, Emma would sponsor both her best friend and Maria Amelie. But the law does not allow her to endow nonrelatives with immigration rights.

Are Norwegian institutions—which exemplify the kinship-based conservative model—compatible with justice? Since I am approaching the morality of immigration restrictions only from the perspective of insiders, as I explained above, the relevant considerations to address this question are fundamentally two. The first refers to the interests of those who would like to invite outsiders. In other words, it concerns how potential sponsors would be affected by a denial of invitation rights. Would those who desire to sponsor family members be more seriously hurt than those who wish to invite other people? Do we have a stronger interest in associating with our relatives than with persons outside our family? The second consideration refers to the interests of all other members of the polity, since they may be affected by the actions of those who sponsor the immigration of outsiders. Would universal sponsorship produce objectionable demographic consequences? Are there good reasons of public interest to allow only the sponsorship of relatives?

Imagine that those in a position like Emma's complain as follows. We simply demand to be allowed to sponsor nonrelatives on the same terms on which others currently sponsor their relatives. We are not asking for privileged treatment. The fact that family relations do not figure quite as prominently in our plans of life as they do in the plans of life of most other people is not a good reason to place us at a disadvantage. It may be atypical for a person to value a successful career or philanthropy more than having multiple and strong family bonds. But it is not an unreasonable worldview, or a less reasonable one, so that the state would be justified in restricting it. Our interest in being allowed to associate with nonrelatives is as important as the interest of others in joining their relatives. From our point of view, the blanket ineligibility of nonrelatives for sponsorship is simply unfair.

In response, the skeptic could first claim that there is something plainly wrong with the idea that a person who wants to look after her elder mother would be similarly affected by a denial of sponsorship rights as someone who just wants to join with her business partner. In this view, keeping two relatives apart is by far a more serious hurt than severing other types of human relationships. Linnea wants to look after a person toward whom she believes herself to have special obligations. Emma, by contrast, just feels sorry for a deported girl she has never met. It seems obvious that the state has stronger reasons not to frustrate Linnea's plans. As one of the few authors who have entertained the general idea of universal sponsorship has suggested, "family members and romantic partners who want to (re)unite with one another" are special cases.[5]

Moreover, in accordance with the second morally relevant consideration mentioned above, the skeptic could argue that the kinship requirement is just another sensible measure to ensure a good fit between newcomers and society, since relatives are presumably more likely than nonrelatives to have a similar background. And it is not only a problem about types. It is also about numbers. While not everyone has relatives abroad who could be sponsored, in a system with universal sponsorship all adult members would be able to invite any outsider. Suppose that, on average, individuals would sponsor the immigration of two persons and have two children in their lifetime. In this scenario, the state's population would multiply several times in a generation, arguably risking the polity's viability.

But the skeptic can be answered. Before we turn to the argument, it is important to clarify a number of points in the remainder of this section. The first concerns the idea of universal sponsorship. It has two features that need emphasizing. To understand the first, consider by way of contrast how Christopher Heath Wellman imagines the right to invite outsiders: as the right "unilaterally to invite in as many foreigners as she would like."[6] This is *not* what I propose. Given that the number of people a state can host is not infinite, and given the interests of future generations, current members of a polity should be allowed to bring in only a certain number of new members. The relevant question is whether there are good reasons to prohibit people from filling their quota in any way they want: by sponsoring the admission of outsiders (relatives or nonrelatives) or by creating new people who inherit the right to stay. I shall not try to determine here what the quota should be. For argument's sake, suppose that no one should be allowed to introduce more than two new members. My position is that the state should not discriminate against persons who, like Emma, would use their quota to develop ethical or professional associations rather than to nurture relationships of kin.

The other important aspect of my account of universal sponsorship is that potential sponsors would not have an unconditional right to bring in whomever they want. Asking the potential newcomer to meet certain conditions is perfectly justifiable. For instance, it makes sense to ask that the sponsored be free of deadly contagious diseases. Indeed for purposes of defending *only* the first part of my thesis — that a general ban on the sponsorship of nonrelatives is unjustifiable — we could imagine a system with the same kind of requirements that countries currently impose for the sponsorship of relatives, or for the admission of the many random (i.e., nonsponsored) foreign nationals who directly apply for a residency permit. If these requirements are currently deemed sufficient to protect the polity from the admission of undesirable types, they would presumably be effective as well under a universal sponsorship scheme. The general point is that universal sponsorship is not tantamount to indiscriminate immigration at the will of insiders.

The second part of my thesis, however, states that the requirements for sponsoring outsiders, in addition to not being stricter for nonrelatives compared to relatives, should ideally be as lenient as the current conditions for conferring immigration rights through *ius sanguinis*. The more general problem that motivates this study, indeed, is that of identifying what justice requires regarding the process of renewing the membership of the polity. This is a significant matter that has been neglected in political philosophy. A state, to subsist, needs to replace its dying members. And that task is everywhere assigned to current members in one way or another. But what is a just arrangement? My overall claim, as I suggested above, is that every member of the polity should presumptively have an equal right to bring a certain number of new members during her lifetime and that she should be free to choose the path: by sponsoring the immigration of outsiders (broadly understood as persons who are physically abroad or persons who are residing in the polity illegally) or by endowing their offspring with the right to stay.

To appreciate what is at stake, consider now a third case:

Case C. Thea, also a Norwegian citizen, gives birth to twins. The boys automatically acquire access to their mother's nationality and therefore to the right to inhabit Norway. There are no further conditions. As in any other country with *ius sanguinis*, Thea's motherhood is sufficient to endow her children with this advantage, among others. Indeed, even if she were likely to place heavy demands on social welfare benefits to raise the boys, Norway would still welcome the new family members. However, to remain together, Thea does have to meet important requirements. For instance, if she failed to take proper care of her children, she would lose custody rights.

Can persons like Emma and Linnea reasonably complain about how the state treats them compared to persons like Thea? Why should the *ius sanguinis* path be easier than the sponsorship path? Here the relevant moral factors are the same as above. Many will claim that the parent-child bond is unlike any other. The value of this relationship permits and even compels the state to protect it more forcefully than any other kind of association, kin-based or otherwise. Moreover, from the perspective of how an institution such as endowment via *ius sanguinis* may affect society at large, one can say that it is the safest way of replacing the state's population. Thea's twins are not only new persons *in the polity* but also *new persons* in the polity: that is, individuals presumably more likely than fully grown adults educated in a different country to acquire the necessary traits and values to function properly as members. Also, they have no criminal record and cannot introduce new deadly contagious diseases, for instance.

This is all very plausible. But I shall contest it in the following sections. I shall argue that appealing to the special status of the parent-child relationship is incompatible with any liberal conception of justice. I shall further discard the possible claim that the values behind an adequate theory of justice, even without relying on a comprehensive notion of worthy relationships, allow us to rank the significance of rights and liberties in such a way that it would be clear that restricting the opportunity to endow nonmembers with admission rights via *ius sanguinis* would hurt members more severely than restricting their opportunity to sponsor outsiders (relatives or nonrelatives). Finally, I shall argue that demographic considerations do not defeat the case for making nonrelatives eligible to be sponsored, and that sponsorship requirements in general should be roughly as lenient as the current requirements for residency endowment by *ius sanguinis*.

There are mainly two strategies that might be used to construct the argument. The first is incremental and involves two steps: one would first make the case that those who want to sponsor nonrelatives are being treated unjustly compared to those who want to invite family members, and then argue that both classes of persons suffer an unfair disadvantage compared to those who merely want to develop a parent-child relationship. Instead of this, I shall follow a one-step nonincremental strategy: to put it in terms of our cases, I will argue directly that persons like Emma, who demand to be allowed to sponsor the immigration of nonrelatives, have a reasonable complaint about how they are treated compared to persons like Thea, who mainly care about the parent-child bond. This is a more efficient strategy because, if successful, it will defend the two parts of my thesis at once.

To conclude this section, I want to clarify one more aspect of universal sponsorship. In my theory, the right to invite outsiders is just a legal right. I am not interested here in the further question of whether people have a basic moral right to give admission rights to others. This is important to avoid spurious debates. David Miller, who is another exception to the silence on the subject, has argued against the idea that citizens have a basic human right to invite outsiders, because the right of free association is not "absolute and unconditional."[7] Miller might well be right about this. But to show that we do not have a basic human right to invitation is not to show that states should not confer it, just as showing that the right to vote is not a basic human right is not to show that universal suffrage is not typically justified. That said, some reasons advanced by Miller, which I shall take on in due course, do seem to undermine the case for universal sponsorship.

2. Freedom of Association and Membership Endowment

From the perspective of insiders, *ius sanguinis* ensures that prospective parents will not be separated from their offspring for lacking a place where they all enjoy immigration rights. In this sense, it is an institution that protects the freedom to establish and maintain a parent-child relationship. Similarly, universal sponsorship rights would protect the freedom of insiders to establish and maintain relationships of other sorts with outsiders. In this section I argue that there are no good reasons, based on a liberal idea of justice, to claim that the first of these instances of freedom of association is more important and deserves greater protection than the other. The implication is that, at least prima facie, there is not a stronger case to let insiders inherit admission rights via *ius sanguinis* than to let them do so through (universal) sponsorship.

There are two ways to argue, contrary to my view, that the liberty to endow our offspring with residency rights (call it "parental endowment") is more significant than the liberty to endow any outsider with such rights (what I have called "universal sponsorship"). The first possible argument is that the greater significance of parental endowment mirrors the greater significance of the relationship that it protects: on this account, the parent-child relationship appears as perhaps the most valuable type of human affiliation. In the first part of this section I contend that this line of thought is contrary to a liberal understanding of justice. The second argument avoids passing judgment on the value of the relationships that these institutions protect. Instead it establishes that the very values behind an adequate theory of liberal justice allow us to assess the significance of rights and liberties such that parental endowment would clearly be ranked higher than universal sponsorship. I reject this alternative in the second part of the section.

a. Impartiality and the Value of Associations

There is one idea at the core of most conceptions of liberal justice that suffices for the point I want to make. It was clearly and succinctly articulated by Brian Barry in the context of analyzing the sense in which justice requires impartiality: "Nobody should be able to claim a privileged position for any conception of the good on the basis of its correctness or its superiority to others."[8] In other words, a paradigmatic form of injustice is to restrict a person's rights and opportunities on the grounds that her life project is allegedly unworthy in the light of some comprehensive worldview. Instead social goods should be distributed independently of the goals that people want to pursue, as long as they are reasonable. Justice is precisely the necessary moral response to the fact that we do not have a satisfactory way to pass judgment on the merits of alternative comprehensive conceptions of the good life.[9]

According to this broad notion of impartiality, it is impermissible to invoke a certain doctrine of valuable relationships in order to limit the freedom of consenting adults to associate with each other. For instance, a state that permits only sexual intercourse aimed at procreation—because this allegedly is the only valuable or acceptable use of our sexual faculties—would infringe the principle of impartiality. The same goes for relationships of other kinds. In the present case, my point is that we cannot justifiably appeal to a particular conception of valuable relationships in order to give some members of the polity, but not others, the opportunity to endow people with immigration rights. Those who want to pursue a parent-child relationship are not more entitled to a greater share of liberties than those who want to pursue other kinds of associations.

It has been said that raising children is "one of life's deepest, most joyous, and most fulfilling kinds of nurturing roles and social affiliation."[10] This is a reasonable belief. But some people will think that other types of roles and relationships are equally or even more valuable. In fact some might believe, to the contrary, that one of life's deepest, most joyous, and most fulfilling kinds of social affiliation actually involves giving up on the previous idea of parenting. From this perspective, the ties that we can develop with our offspring are nothing compared to the greater, more profound ties that we can develop with other citizens in pursuit of the common good. The case for clerical celibacy often rests on a similar basis: to serve one's kin is mundane, to serve all the children of God is next to heavenly. How are we to settle these competing claims? A tenet of liberal justice is that we cannot hope to do so.

It is important to emphasize that forbidding the invitation of outsiders who are not related by kin to the sponsor is not a matter of failing to subsidize something like an expensive taste. Instead it is a matter of the state actually denying many people a degree of freedom that is necessary to pursue a reasonable conception of the good life. Consider an example that is directly related to our topic. Just as many Christian groups regard peace or solidarity with the poor as one of their their fundamental values, others build an identity around the principle of providing a home for undocumented immigrants.[11] This is the case of many churches around the world, some of which are willing to engage in civil disobedience. The ecumenical New Sanctuary Movement across the United States, for instance, is arguably one of the most important social crusades since the civil rights era. The United Methodist Church goes by the motto "Open hearts. Open minds. Open doors" and explicitly encourages its members to welcome the undocumented immigrant and to actively oppose laws that seek to track them down.[12] An affiliate of this organization, the Arch Street United Methodist Church, belongs to the New Sanctuary Movement of Philadelphia. The latter's mission statement calls for "radical hospitality," even if this involves breaking the law, since they believe that "God's law surpasses human law."[13]

In the previous cases, opening the doors to foreigners is valued intrinsically—it is the content of various doctrines. But receiving outsiders can also be instrumentally vital for the realization of some worldviews. Consider the case of those who think that a good life consists of making a permanent commitment to a romantic partner. Persons in that situation sometimes see their plans of life frustrated simply because they lack a common nationality and a sponsorship program is either unavailable to them or dysfunctional. Of course, as I have noted, my opponent will say that "family members and romantic partners" are indeed special cases, and invitation rights could be acceptable with respect to them.[14] But the point I have been making is that this case cannot be made by appeal to the alleged superiority of these types of relationships. Friendship and professional development are of the utmost importance to many people. Figure skaters in a duo could believe that they are made for each other and thus consider their separation by national borders as dramatic as, or even worse than, the separation of two lovers. To say that romantic love is more valuable than figure skating is to make an invalid appeal to the truth of a conception of the good.

Let me address two likely objections at this point. It could be said that the right to invite outsiders cannot be justified as long as people remain, within their country, "able to consort with a sufficiently large number of people to generate a wide choice of friends, marriage, partners, work colleagues, fellow sports enthusiasts, and so forth."[15] David Miller makes this point against the idea that there is a *human right* to *unlimited* freedom of association. As I have explained, I am not arguing for a right to unlimited freedom of association. Instead I argue for equally allocated rights to freedom of association. Yet someone might wonder how this point (about the availability domestically of a rich pool of prospects for association) affects the case for universal sponsorship. The question is whether, all else being equal, the existence of a large range of options within one's country defeats by itself the case for invitation rights. For this to be the case, the availability of those options would have to nullify or seriously undermine the interest that people have in being free to invite outsiders.

Consider Miller's example of a person who dreams of becoming an opera singer yet lives "in a society that provides for various forms of musical expression but not for opera."[16] Let us understand this as a ban on opera, just as there is a ban on inviting any outsider. Perhaps the vetoing of Wagner would still allow this person to be who she wants to be, but the possibility of singing other genres might be no consolation if opera were not available. She might rather do political philosophy. Her plan of life would be frustrated, and she would be harmed as a result. Similarly, you cannot tell someone, "So national borders separate you from your would-be spouse? No biggie. Look at the current national stats on single people!" A person whose plan of life includes marrying a specific person may or may not care about marriage in general: she might not be willing to marry others. To point out the availability of other prospects in this case would be as insulting as in the case of someone whose spouse has passed away.

The second objection is that family relationships are special not because they are more valuable but because they cannot be properly developed, in cases of international separation, unless a system of sponsorship rights is in place. By contrast, all other types of relationship allegedly require less. For instance, a system of temporary invitations would suffice for transnational friendships to flourish but not for marriages.[17] According to Matthew Lister, our bonds with nonrelatives are significantly different in the sense that they "do not, *by their nature*, require close and intimate contact in perpetuity. . . . It follows that freedom of association in these cases does not impose strong limits on the rights of majorities to limit immigration as does the case of the family."[18] Lister's argument, in a nutshell, is that long-term physical proximity is not "an important, even essential, aspect" of relationships outside the family, so that sponsorship rights are not called for in these cases. The hidden assumption is that long-term proximity must be an *essential* attribute, as opposed to a chosen or constructed one, for a relationship to merit protection via sponsorship rights. In other words, not only must a certain relationship be understood by the parties as requiring long-term proximity; in addition, the *nature* of the relationship must be such that it involves long-term proximity. But why should we accept this questionable premise?

Imagine two persons, unrelated by kinship, who regard each other as friends. Further, suppose that to them their relationship is unimaginable without long-term proximity. If they are separated, we might be able tell them, following Lister, that they should not worry, because long-term proximity is not an essential feature of friendship; they can still be regarded as friends. Naturally, the response would be that they do not care about how their relationship can be classified; what they care about is being together. And they want to know why others who have a similar relationship, substantively speaking, but are further connected by genes (or worse: others who are connected *merely* by genes) would have sponsorship rights but not them. Indeed whether long-term proximity is an essential or constructed feature of a given relationship; whether we classify a relationship as this or that; and whether persons are genetically related or not—all of this is irrelevant and arbitrary for purposes of morally assessing the scope of sponsorship rights. What matters is how the lives of persons would be affected if we frustrate their (actual or projected) associational goals by denying them sponsorship rights.

b. Justice and the Significance of Liberties

I have argued that a system featuring parental endowment of residency rights (as well as the invitation of relatives) but forbidding the sponsorship of nonrelatives cannot be justified in terms of the allegedly superior value of family relationships. Justice requires, prima facie, that individuals be allowed to pursue their own conception of valuable relationships by extending sponsorship eligibility to nonrelatives and by making the sponsorship procedure in general as simple as that of parental endowment. A complete, all-things-considered case requires an assessment of the expected demographic consequences, which is the subject of the next section. But first, in this segment I address the idea that it may be possible, *from within* a liberal account of justice, to consider that the freedom to create and maintain a parenting relationship is more significant than the freedom to create and maintain other kinds of relationships, which could undermine my thesis.

Rights and liberties are rarely, if ever, thought to be equally important. We typically identify some of them as "basic" or "fundamental," and indeed we often treat a subset of these as more basic than the rest. John Rawls, for instance, included political liberties in his first principle of justice, but he ranked them lower than the other basic freedoms. (This point is at the center of Danielle Allen's chapter in this volume; she argues against Rawls's ranking.) What is the appropriate criterion to determine the relative importance of different liberties? This is a difficult question.[19] For present purposes I shall rely on a broad notion of significance. As a first approximation, consider the formula advanced by some influential authors: "the more central and far-reaching the impact of a particular decision on an individual's life, the more substantial a person's self-determination interest in making it."[20] From this perspective, the main question is this: how much does the deprivation of a certain liberty impact a person's life?

To answer this question, we need to clarify the idea of being deprived of a liberty. What exactly does it mean to lack the liberty to do something? It is easy to miss the full picture. Of course, in general it simply means that we cannot decide on the matter at stake. But this is ambiguous. Individuals can be unfree by means of a universal proscription or a universal prescription. Consider the freedom to have a certain sexual experience. This liberty can be violated by forbidding everyone to have the experience in question, or by requiring everyone to do so. The freedom to P comprises both the freedom to do P and the freedom not to do P. To fully appreciate the significance of a given liberty, we have to consider these two aspects of its deprivation.

The next step in explaining the idea of significance as impact of deprivation is to provide an adequate understanding of "impact." This has to be an objective notion in two ways. First, to say that the impact of a certain practice is objective is to say that it affects persons in the same way regardless of *their* conception of the good. If we took the impact of a given issue to depend on people's conceptions of the good, there would be no way to settle competing claims for purposes of making collective institutional choices. We need an independent notion precisely because people disagree on the basis of their worldviews. The second sense of objectivity is simply that our understanding of impact, as I have mentioned already, cannot be grounded on one particular conception of the good.

In what way does the deprivation of a certain freedom relevantly and objectively affect people's lives more (or less) than the deprivation of another? What, in other words, is the substance of *impact*? I propose to make sense of it in the light of two main ideas: harm and opportunity cost. The greater any of these factors, the greater the impact of depriving a person of a liberty. Let me discuss them in that order. Certain experiences are universally regarded as harmful. Persons cannot live a decent human life if they are seriously ill, malnourished, subjected to physical or mental torture, or, in the extreme, moribund.[21] It is precisely because certain things are universally regarded as evils that they have been used everywhere as forms of punishment. Regardless of their conceptions of the good life, people everywhere strive to avoid bodily mutilation, fear, abduction, grief, disease, involuntary confinement, domination, humiliation, and so on. The more a deprivation of a liberty harms people in these ways, the greater its impact.

As employed by economists, the opportunity cost of something is what has been sacrificed to obtain it, specifically in terms of the value of the best unchosen alternative. This value can be measured in different units—for instance, utility or money. A rather compelling metric for our purposes is "discretionary time."[22] According to economists who speak of opportunity costs, we all have to devote some part of our lives to satisfy three types of necessities: economic (obtaining the means for a minimally decent life), biological (sleeping, feeding, recovering from illness), and domestic (taking care of the household, which often includes nurturing and raising children). Whatever remains is our discretionary time. Of course, money can buy us time, since the third kind of necessity can be outsourced to some extent. But the net effect is unclear, since most people can obtain the money to purchase time via outsourcing only by devoting more time to economic activity.

A practice or undertaking can eat up our discretionary time in two ways. One is by broadening our realm of necessities. Parenting is a clear case in point. The other way is by reducing discretionary time directly. Having to attend military training several hours a week cannot be considered a necessity, and yet it is not optional. It strictly diminishes our discretionary time. The conclusion is that the significance of an activity, and hence of the liberty to undertake it, is positively correlated with its worth in terms of discretionary time. In other words, the greater the opportunity cost thus understood of being forced to pursue a certain practice, the greater the relevance of the liberty to decide whether to perform it.

On these bases, let me now compare the significance of the freedom to establish a parenting relationship (which would be undermined without parental endowment of immigration rights) and the freedom to establish other types of relationship (which would be undermined without universal sponsorship). As I mentioned above, unfreedom can take the form of a universal proscription (nobody can do it) or a universal prescription (everyone ought to do it). Regarding the former, the point here is straightforward. The liberal presumption in favor of freedom is grounded in the idea that people are harmed when they are prevented from carrying out their plans of life. Not being allowed to (try to) live the life one values is a serious deprivation. If one's idea of the good life includes raising one's own children or being with a certain outsider in one's country, the denial of these possibilities is, as such, harmful. The general point holds even when the plan of life at stake is morally unacceptable and ought to be outlawed. A bullfighter, for instance, might honestly come to think that his life is not worth living without bullfighting. The fact that bullfighting should be prohibited does not change the fact that bullfighters would be injured as a result of the ban, just as the fact that a certain punishment is deserved does not change the fact that it is a harmful experience.

In this sense, frustrating a certain relationship is equally harmful. That many more people include family relationships in their conceptions of the good life is not a sound reason to conclude that the freedom to establish such relationships is more important than the freedom to establish other kinds of relationship. This might strike some as clear enough, but the point is worth insisting on given that some influential liberal authors have suggested the opposite. Consider Rawls. After pointing out that political participation is no longer valued as such under the comprehensive doctrines of "most citizens" in modern societies, Rawls argues that "the political liberties *can still* be counted as basic even if they are only essential institutional means to protect and preserve other basic liberties."[23] This entails that being a common denominator in the conceptions of the good of "most citizens" is sufficient to count a liberty as basic. This thought contradicts Rawls's own statement that the case for primary goods is independent of the given distribution of comprehensive doctrines in a society and creates a bias against minoritarian conceptions of the good.[24] Notice that my point is not the familiar one that the very idea of primary goods, including the individual liberties, is unfair to non-individualistic doctrines.[25] My point here is that a liberty should not be downplayed simply because it figures only in conceptions of the good that have few adherents.

Consider now the second form of unfreedom mentioned above: general prescription (everyone ought to become a parent). Here, too, the greater relevance of the freedom of parental association is questionable. To be sure, being forced to engage in a parental relationship—or, more general, a family relationship of any sort—would have a serious impact in a person's life. This is because of both the normal understanding of the informal duties related to these relationships and the legal obligations attached to them. Indeed one of the reasons parenting is quite a serious matter is that people cannot simply walk away from its responsibilities. Consider the standard case of divorced or separated parents where the mother keeps custody of the children. If the father has an income or estate, he is legally compelled to provide child support.

However, other relationships not based on kin, such as friendship, also have special duties attached to them. And, more importantly, sponsorship rights can and should also be linked to legally enforceable obligations—indeed, obligations comparable to those that apply to parenting. Just as a child needs help to function properly in the world, newly arrived immigrants often need help to get around in the new country. Like everyone else, immigrants need shelter, food, access to health care, and an income, among other things. Before they are able to satisfy these needs by themselves, they normally have to learn the national language (or one of the official languages). It normally takes time to become a fully functioning member of society—for children and immigrants alike. For the duration of that process, those who are responsible for bringing new members in the polity should bear some part of the burden. Thus sponsoring an outsider is not a trivial matter. The opportunity costs for most people would be significant. This would have a positive effect: it would establish strong incentives not to make a sponsorship invitation lightly.

On the basis of these considerations, we can conclude that there are no liberal bases for thinking that the freedom to establish a parenting relationship is more significant than the freedom to establish other kinds of relationships. Had the opposite been true, it would have been a problem for my overall argument.

3. Demographic Considerations

I now turn to consider the potential demographic consequences of establishing universal sponsorship. The reader should recall that the right to sponsor outsiders (relatives or nonrelatives) is not a right to invite as many outsiders as one wants. Assuming then that people would be allowed to bring only a certain number of new members into the state, the question now is whether there are any good consequentialist reasons to forbid people to fill their quota—whatever the number might be—via universal sponsorship. I shall proceed by addressing the most plausible arguments against my position.

a. Cultural Discontinuity

The first objection I shall consider is based on the potential consequences of sponsorship immigration on the public political culture of society. This is one of the most common arguments by opponents of open borders. Specifically, the argument is that citizens have good reasons "for wanting to stay in control of the process" of cultural change.[26] Although cultural transformations are inevitable, and a wide variety of cultures are compatible with the values of liberal democracy, the current members of a polity have a legitimate interest in securing some cultural continuity (as opposed to rigidity). Imagine that the language, landscape, and day-to-day social norms of one's country were to change drastically, say, twice during our lives. It would be difficult to feel at home in such a place. Uncontrolled immigration is a problem precisely because it compromises controlled cultural change.

Let us assume that all the empirical and philosophical aspects of this argument are sound. While it might then undercut the standard case for open borders to some extent, it has no bite against universal sponsorship. In fact, exactly the opposite is the case. If citizens were allowed to invite foreigners, they would *gain* control of the process of cultural change compared to the current system of centralized immigration policymaking. The control that citizens currently exert on immigration decisions through the exercise of their political rights is indirect and weak at best. There is no guarantee that immigration officials will interpret correctly citizens' preferences on how much cultural change via immigration is acceptable to them. Moreover, in a diverse society it seems wrong to subject the question of acceptable cultural change via immigration to a majoritarian decision-making process. Cultural continuity in such a society means preserving the specific cultural mix that exists as a result of pluralism, and this is more likely to occur through a decentralized system of immigration decisions, which is what the right to invitation is all about. My argument, in other words, aligns with Gerken's argument that decentralization endows people, and especially minorities, with control.

Let me address two potential objections to these points. First, it could be argued that the case for *equal* sponsorship rights (both kin-based and non–kin-based sponsorship) is compelling only under the empirical assumption that these rights would be exercised similarly by all groups in society. If, to the contrary, some cultural minorities tended to invite many more outsiders than other groups, cultural continuity may be threatened. Assuming further that it would not be acceptable to compel the members of all other groups similarly to exercise their invitation rights, the solution would be to assign fewer invitation rights to some citizens. The objection, however, refutes itself. The problem is that this point really makes a case for reducing the quota of new members that these groups can bring in, whether through invitation or procreation. Indeed an implication of this argument for unequal invitation rights is that in a context where no such rights exist, it would be acceptable to limit the procreative freedom of groups that tended to reproduce more than others. In rejecting this implication, we reject the objection.

The other possible objection is that decentralized immigration decisions could produce a collective action problem. Suppose that most citizens exercise their sponsorship rights to the same extent. However, if they happen to invite outsiders whose cultural background is very different from that of the country, on the assumption that *their* doing so makes no difference, the collective result is cultural discontinuity. But this is a big "if." Individual citizens do not have any special incentives here (as they do in typical cases of collective action problems) to act in ways that are harmless in isolation but hurtful in the aggregate. It is true that those who choose to exercise their invitation rights to help people escaping the economic or political conditions of another country might be inviting people with a "discontinuous" culture. However, since exercising the right to invite an outsider would carry significant costs, we should not expect a culture-changing inflow from philanthropic invitations. In any case, here again the interest in cultural continuity would have to be weighed against the interest in being able to help those in need.

b. Demographic Explosion

Let us consider now what could be called the "snowball-effect" objection. The point of limiting the number of new members that a person can bring into the polity—via parental endowment or open sponsorship—is to curb any potentially harmful effects of a sudden and significant influx of people. However, one might worry that endowing newcomers with sponsorship rights will set off a chain reaction that would actually produce an effect akin to the one we would expect from fully open borders.

If we exhaust our right to invite, say, up to five persons, and those persons do the same, and so on, soon the situation will be out of control. This is not a problem with parenting, because that process takes much longer. For instance, if we assume reproductive intervals of thirty years, it takes someone her entire life—if she is lucky to live ninety years—to see her grandchildren give birth to new citizens. With invitation rights, these three cycles could be completed in a few years, or even months.

This certainly would be a serious problem, but we should not overestimate the risk. There is, first of all, the fact that people would not make these decisions frivolously given the important responsibilities that they would acquire when inviting someone. Moreover, newcomers would not acquire the right to sponsor other outsiders automatically upon arrival. As is the case with other rights—for instance, the right to vote—there are good reasons to limit this right to those who can be regarded as long-term participants in the political association. Hence the sponsored newcomer could become a sponsor only after a significant number of years. This would slow down a potential snowball effect, giving us time to spot it and respond.

In any case, there are ways to avert the problem. One is to begin with a very limited system of sponsorship rights (say, a right to sponsor only one or two persons) in order to get a sense of the rate at which people would invite outsiders, and on that basis to make adjustments to the number of allowed invitations per person (within their general quota of new memberships). Alternatively, we could artificially slow down the rate of sponsorship petitions from the outset by not allowing people to exhaust their quota in a short period. Instead they would be required to spread their invitations throughout their (adult) life. In this way, in addition to having to wait several years in order to become entitled to invite others, the sponsored, just like everyone else, would be allowed to issue only a limited number of invitations at their first opportunity. A combination of these and other possible devices would successfully address a potential snowball-effect problem.

One way to avert the problem that does not seem acceptable, however, is to make the invitation rights of the sponsored more limited than the rights of both their sponsors and those who join the polity during the same period through parental endowment. Such an inequality of rights seems hard to justify. For present purposes, at any rate, I shall assume that it cannot be justified. Notice that this assumption is to the advantage of my opponent, since I am thereby canceling a way of mitigating the snowball-effect objection.

Admittedly, the previous remarks presuppose full compliance with the rules. In practice, however, this will certainly not happen. Consider two cases. Imagine first someone who, after having filled her quota of new members, involuntarily gets pregnant, not once but twice. Or imagine a person who exhausts her quota by sponsoring immigrants but later regrets her decision to not have kids. Defying the state, she gets pregnant. How should we deal with these cases? What kind of sanctions would be effective and acceptable, assuming that forcing people to have an abortion or to become sterile would be an abhorrent, impermissible policy? These are difficult practical problems. If many failed to comply with the limits of the scheme, it would have to be dismantled. But presumably there are economic sanctions for noncompliance that could keep the system functional. Addressing this issue properly, however, is beyond the scope of this essay.

More generally, it is possible that a scheme of sponsorship rights of the sort proposed here is viable only under certain conditions. In contexts where the state lacks the capacity to enforce the rules of the sponsorship scheme, such as to impose sanctions for violations, it could lead to dire results and few benefits. In nonideal settings, the suitability of an arrangement of universal sponsorship rights has to be determined on a case-by-case basis.

c. Public Dangers

It could be argued that despite the previous argument, allowing a person to sponsor any outsider directly poses a major, unacceptable danger to others—and to herself. The argument runs as follows. Even if public ills such as unwanted cultural change and environmental impact would not occur or could be averted, and even if the individual responsibilities of the sponsors would mitigate the impact on welfare provisions, the admission of certain individuals could seriously affect two important public goods: safety and health. The threat does not come from the number of expected newcomers but from the kind of persons they might be—for instance, contagious disease carriers or dangerous criminals. If only a few of those types made it in the polity, the consequences could be very serious. The possibility is not far-fetched. Terrorism is the obvious problem that comes to mind. Local terrorists and their supporters could use their right to invitation to increase their ranks. Even well-intentioned citizens could end up helping out these criminal organizations. For surely the existence of universal sponsorship rights would motivate many outsiders to misrepresent their identities, hoping to prey on the goodwill of current members. This is already happening in other contexts. For instance, some people are lured into dangerous situations by online predators who pretend to be someone else.

Here again it is important not to overestimate the dangers. Regarding the public health issue, it is worth recalling that thousands of citizens who have been traveling all over the world return every day to countries such as the United States without undergoing a medical examination, not to mention the thousands of tourists who are similarly admitted. If health threats were really that serious, a different system would already be in place. In the end, the simple solution would be to have all invitees undergo an examination upon their arrival. As for the terrorism threat, it seems to already be fairly easy for terrorists to come in if they want to. For instance, it has been estimated that "in the United States, unauthorized immigration accounts for one-third to one-half of new immigrant inflows."[27] This means that more than one thousand undocumented persons enter that country every day. It would be foolish to think that this is an option for a poor Mexican peasant and not for a well-funded global terrorist.

In any case, universal sponsorship need not be understood as a completely unilateral process. There would be a strong presumption for letting all invitations run their course, but state officials could block a particular sponsorship petition if they can provide compelling evidence of a person's unfit status. I shall not discuss here which attributes may disqualify outsiders (e.g., should someone be disqualified for having committed a minor crime at some point in her life?). But it is clear that some persons should not be admitted.

d. Corruption

I have argued that the legally enforceable obligations associated with sponsorship rights would prevent people from making reckless invitations. But there may be a way around these obligations. Since they would be mostly economic, they could be transferred to a potential newcomer who is willing and capable to pay for them—with an additional fee for the sponsor. In other words, many people would be willing to sell their sponsorship rights. Given what is at stake, in many countries it would be a quite lucrative operation—or set of operations, if the person is not interested in using her invitation rights for a valid purpose at all. Imagine a large-scale version of the current problem of fraudulent marriages. As is well known, some citizens marry foreigners for the money, but not in the classical sense; they marry literally for a fee. In exchange, the foreigner gets a resident visa. According to some reports, the rate in the

United States is between \$10,000 and \$35,000.[28] To get away with this, people are willing to make significant sacrifices, such as sharing a home with a stranger for some time. Presumably, since the supply of visas would be greater in the case of invitation rights, their price would be lower. But the costs would also be significantly lower. Indeed since there would be many legitimate grounds for sponsoring people, it would be difficult to detect fraud by examining the relationship between the inviter and the invitee. Prosecutors would need evidence of the monetary transaction. To use another example, the comparison with parenting is again fitting. As we know, there is a big market for surrogate motherhood. The market for sponsorship rights would be much larger in many countries, given both the greater demand and the lower costs. Unlike pregnancy, sponsoring an outsider would be a relatively simple matter.

In response, one could argue that the state should not interfere with surrogacy contracts, interested marriages, or even utilitarian births— decisions to have (more) children in order to improve the family economy in the long run. Take the latter example. Assuming that the children would be loved despite their parents' economic motivation to have them, why should society forbid procreation in those cases (setting aside the fact that this prohibition would be impossible to enforce)? Similarly, if the inviter would assume the responsibilities of invitation cited above (whether directly or via resources provided by the invitee herself), why is it a problem that money might be exchanged in the process? These are controversial questions, and I cannot hope to answer them here. I pose them, and stress their contentious character, just to suggest that the case against a market for sponsorship rights is not clear-cut.

However, let us just assume that it would be wrong to receive a fee for sponsoring someone and that the state should prohibit those transactions. This does not amount to a case against universal sponsorship rights. The conclusion should be that states ought to investigate and prosecute these actions. Surely this cannot be done perfectly and many will get away with the outlawed behavior—as is the case with virtually every other outlawed behavior. It does not follow from the existence of fraudulent marriages that people should not be allowed to marry foreigners, or from the existence of economic births that people should not be allowed to have children. Similarly, the possibility of fraudulent sponsorship petitions does not defeat the case for sponsorship rights. Moreover, notice that the prohibition in this case would be grounded on an invalid use of universal sponsorship, not on any expected harm. No one would be hurt provided that (1) the personal quota of new memberships has been properly estimated, (2) adequate responsibilities are attached to sponsorship rights, and (3) institutions are in place to detect and block the admission of potentially dangerous types.

e. Inequality

The final worry I shall consider is that a scheme of universal sponsorship rights would only—or mostly—benefit the wealthy. Those who lack resources to afford the costs of bringing new members from other countries would be prevented from making any invitations. This seems unjust. For the scheme to be acceptable, the state would have to provide low-income citizens with additional resources. But then the problem would be that this could have very serious consequences for the viability of the welfare state.

In response, notice that the permission to procreate suffers from exactly the same problem. Some people want to have more children, but they cannot afford it. And yet few claim on that basis that nobody should be allowed to have children, or that nobody should be allowed to have more children than those that the poorest citizens can afford. If there are good reasons for this, as I assume there are, then the same holds for sponsorship rights. For my argument in this paper has been that procreation and sponsorship are simply different ways of doing the same thing: bringing new members into the polity. If my case is compelling, it is unjust to allow one but not the other. This form of injustice has to be distinguished from the more general form of injustice that lurks behind the objection under consideration. One thing is to be unjustly deprived of a formal liberty—the kind of claim I am making here—and another is to be unjustly deprived of a fair share of resources to make the most of the formal liberty in question.

4. Conclusion

As I write, some of the countries that once hoped to lead the global community in the promotion of human rights are turning their backs on desperate refugees, using immigrants as scapegoats for everything that is wrong in their territory, breaking apart families through callous deportations, and building walls at the border with peaceful and cooperating neighbors. It is hard to imagine a bleaker scenario for a radical proposal of the sort I have defended here. But it is also a scenario that highlights the value of such a scheme. If individual citizens were allowed to sponsor the admission of a certain number of outsiders—regardless of family ties, and under conditions no stricter than those for bringing new members into the polity through procreation—some people in the countries alluded to would presumably step up and help many immigrants and refugees in need. If the argument I have offered above is compelling, this would be valuable from the perspective of not only those outsiders but also those citizens who would like to establish these types of associations.

Notes

1. Ferracioli, "Family Migration Schemes and Liberal Neutrality."

2. Matthew Lindauer offers an alternative line of argument for the basic right to invite outsiders in "Entry by Birth Alone? Rawlsian Egalitarianism and the Basic Right to Invite."

3. There is a rich and growing literature on this subject. See, for instance, Arash, "Democratic Theory and Border Coercion"; Bader, "Ethics of Immigration"; Barry and Goodin, *Free Movement*; Carens, "Aliens and Citizens"; Cole, *Philosophies of Exclusion*; Higgins, "Immigration Justice"; Joppke, *Citizenship and Immigration*; Miller, "Immigration: The Case for Limits"; Pevnick, *Immigration and the Constraints of Justice*; Risse, "On the Morality of Immigration"; Schwartz, *Justice in Immigration*; Shachar, *Birthright Lottery*; Seglow, "Ethics of Immigration"; Swain, *Debating Immigration*; Wellman, "Immigration and Freedom of Association"; Ypi, "Justice in Migration."

4. The insider-domestic perspective has been acknowledged by some theorists, but it has not been systematically examined. To my knowledge, in addition to the piece by Ferracioli cited above, the only other exception is Lister, "Immigration, Association, and the Family." For partial treatments, see Kukathas, "Case for Open Immigration"; Miller, *National Responsibility and Global Justice*, 209–13; Steiner, "Hard Borders, Compensation, and Classical Liberalism"; and Wellman, "Freedom of Association and the Right to Exclude."

5. Wellman, *Debating the Ethics of Immigration*, 92. This is also the thesis defended by Matthew Lister (see "Immigration, Association and the Family").

6. Wellman, "Immigration and Freedom of Association," 134.

7. Miller, *National Responsibility and Global Justice*, 212.

8. Barry, *Justice as Impartiality*, 142.

9. It is not possible to provide a justification of these ideas here. I merely acknowledge them as premises for my argument.

10. Weinberg, "Procreative Justice: A Contractualist Account," 417.

11. On Christianity and immigration, see the essays by Richard Miller and Nigel Biggar in Miller and Hashmi, *Boundaries and Justice*.

12. United Methodist Church, *Book of Resolutions* (2004).

13. New Sanctuary Movement, "Who We Are."

14. Wellman, *Debating the Ethics of Immigration*.

15. Miller, *National Responsibility and Global Justice*, 213.

16. Miller, *National Responsibility and Global Justice*, 207.

17. As I explained in the introductory section, a sponsorship system for my purposes refers to the conferral of permanent residency rights.

18. Lister, "Immigration, Association, and the Family," 736 (my emphasis).

19. Rawls, *Justice as Fairness*, 42n2.

20. Buchanan et. al., *From Chance to Choice*, 216.

21. See Barry, *Culture and Equality*, 284–86.

22. Goodin et al., *Discretionary Time*. See also Rose, *Free Time*.

23. Rawls, *Justice as Fairness*, 143.

24. Rawls explains that in his theory the basic liberties and other primary goods are derived independently of "comprehensive doctrines that now exist, or that have existed, or that might exist": *Political Liberalism*, 40.

25. See Nagel, "Rawls on Justice."

26. Miller, "Immigration: The Case for Limits," 201.

27. Hanson, "Illegal Migration from Mexico to the United States," 918.

28. Amrhein, "Telling True Love from Immigrant Scam," *Tampa Bay Times*, July 14, 2007.

Works Cited

Amrhein, Saundra. "Telling True Love from Immigrant Scam." *Tampa Bay Times*, July 14, 2007.

Arash, Abizadeh. "Democratic Theory and Border Coercion." *Political Theory* 36, no. 1 (2008): 37–65.

Bader, Veit. "The Ethics of Immigration." *Constellations* 12, no. 3 (2005): 331–65.

Barry, Brian. *Culture and Equality*. Cambridge, MA: Harvard University Press, 2002.

Barry, Brian. *Justice as Impartiality*. Oxford: Clarendon, 1995.

Barry, Brian, and Robert Goodin, eds. *Free Movement: Ethical Issues in the Transnational Migration of People and of Money*. London: Routledge, 1992.

Buchanan, Allen, et al. *From Chance to Choice: Genetics and Justice*. Cambridge: Cambridge University Press, 2000.

Carens, Joseph H. "Aliens and Citizens: The Case for Open Borders." *Review of Politics* 49, no. 4 (1987): 251–73.

Cole, Phillip. *Philosophies of Exclusion*. Edinburgh: Edinburgh University Press, 2000.

Ferracioli, Luara. "Family Migration Schemes and Liberal Neutrality: A Dilemma." *Journal of Moral Philosophy* 13, no. 5 (2016): 553–75.

Goodin, Robert E., James Mahmud Rice, Antti Parpo, and Lina Eriksson. *Discretionary Time: A New Measure of Freedom*. Cambridge: Cambridge University Press, 2008.

Hanson, Gordon H. "Illegal Migration from Mexico to the United States." *Journal of Economic Literature* 44, no. 4 (2006): 869–924.

Higgins, Peter W. "Immigration Justice: A Principle for Constructing Admissions Policies." *Social Philosophy Today* 25 (2009): 149–62.

Joppke, Christian. *Citizenship and Immigration*. Cambridge: Polity, 2010.

Kukathas, Chandran. "The Case for Open Immigration." In *Contemporary Debates in Applied Ethics*, edited by Andrew I. Cohen and Christopher Heath Wellman, 207–20. Malden, MA: Wiley-Blackwell, 2005.

Lindauer, Matthew. "Entry by Birth Alone? Rawlsian Egalitarianism and the Basic Right to Invite." *Social Theory and Practice* (forthcoming).

Lister, Matthew. "Immigration, Association, and the Family." *Law and Philosophy* 29, no. 6 (2010): 717–45.

Miller, David. "Immigration: The Case for Limits." In *Contemporary Debates in Applied*

Ethics, edited by Andrew I. Cohen and Christopher Heath Wellman, 193–206. Malden, MA: Wiley-Blackwell, 2005.

Miller, David. *National Responsibility and Social Justice, National Responsibility and Global Justice*. Oxford: Oxford University Press, 2007.

Miller, David, and Sohail H. Hashmi, eds. *Boundaries and Justice*. Princeton, NJ: Princeton University Press, 2001.

Nagel, Thomas. "Rawls on Justice." *Philosophical Review* 82, no. 2 (April 1973): 220–34.

New Sanctuary Movement of Philadelphia. "Who We Are." https://www.sanctuary philadelphia.org/who-we-are-new-sanctuary/.

Pevnick, Ryan. *Immigration and the Constraints of Justice*. Cambridge: Cambridge University Press, 2011.

Rawls, John. *Justice as Fairness: A Restatement*. Cambridge, MA: Belknap / Harvard University Press, 2001.

Rawls, John. *Political Liberalism*. Exp. ed. New York: Columbia University Press, 2005.

Risse, Mathias. "On the Morality of Immigration." *Ethics & International Affairs* 22, no. 1 (2008): 25–33.

Rose, Julie. *Free Time*. Princeton, NJ: Princeton University Press, 2016.

Schwartz, Warren F., ed. *Justice in Immigration*. New York: Cambridge University Press, 2007.

Seglow, Jonathan. "The Ethics of Immigration." *Political Studies Review* 3, no. 3 (2005): 317–34.

Shachar, Ayelet. *The Birthright Lottery*. Cambridge, MA: Harvard University Press, 2009.

Steiner, Hillel. "Hard Borders, Compensation, and Classical Liberalism." In *Boundaries and Justice*, edited by David Miller and Sohail H. Hashmi, 79–88. Princeton, NJ: Princeton University Press, 2001.

Swain, Carol M. *Debating Immigration*. New York: Cambridge University Press, 2007.

United Methodist Church. "Immigrants in the United States: Ministries of Hospitality, Advocacy, and Justice." In *The Book of Resolutions of the United Methodist Church*. Revised 2004. http://archives.umc.org/interior.asp?ptid=4&mid=1064.

Weinberg, Rivka M. "Procreative Justice: A Contractualist Account." *Public Affairs Quarterly* 16, no. 2 (2002): 405–25.

Wellman, Christopher Heath. *Debating the Ethics of Immigration*. New York: Oxford University Press, 2011.

Wellman, Christopher Heath. "Freedom of Association and the Right to Exclude." In *Debating the Ethics of Immigration*, by Christopher Heath Wellman and Phillip Cole, 13–155. New York: Oxford University Press, 2011.

Wellman, Christopher Heath "Immigration and Freedom of Association." *Ethics* 119, no. 1 (October 2008): 109–41.

Ypi, Lea. "Justice in Migration." *Journal of Political Philosophy* 16, no. 4 (2008): 391–418.

Conclusion

REDEFINING INTEGRATION

Danielle Allen and Rohini Somanathan

Roughly half a century ago, in 1962, Martin Luther King Jr. gave a speech called "The Ethical Demands for Integration." In this speech he argued that American democracy still needed to "complete a process of democratization." Democratization, this suggests, comes in pieces and parts. The specific work facing American democracy, he argued, was to solve "the problem of race and color prejudice." King argued that the solution involved not merely desegregation—legal opening of public spaces and opportunities to all—but also integration. Calling "integration" the ultimate goal, he defined integration thus: "the welcomed participation of Negroes into the total range of human activities. Integration is genuine intergroup, interpersonal doing." He wrote that a society that achieved desegregation or nondiscrimination without also achieving integration would be a society that "leads to 'physical proximity without spiritual affinity,' . . . a society where elbows are together and hearts are apart." He added, "It leaves us with a stagnant equality of sameness rather than a constructive equality of oneness." With his moving rhetoric, personal commitment, and self-sacrifice as an activist, he captured the imagination of the citizenry of the United States, shifting its culture and its understanding of its most salient values. He thereby drove change in the political agenda.

In King's most famous speech, he conjured up his dream with an evocative image that is important for our work in this volume. "I have a dream," he declared, "that one day on the red hills of Georgia, the sons of former slaves and the sons of former slave owners will be able to sit down together at the table of brotherhood." We should pause to ask specifically what picture is conjured by this rhetoric. If we do ask that, we will discover the reigning paradigms that have governed the project of integration for the last half century. What picture does King's image bring to mind for you? Do you imagine a table of eight people where seven are

FIGURE C.1. Elizabeth Eckford, one of the Little Rock Nine.

white and one is black? Or do you imagine a table split 50–50? Do you imagine a table where the sons of former enslavers cluster at one end and the sons of the formerly enslaved cluster at the other, yet still, in a sense, they all sit together? Or do you imagine a dinner table around which are seated, say, six, or eight, or ten, or even fifty or a hundred people, with seats alternating between black and white?

The latter images—of a table split 50–50, with black and white inter-mingling, and with maximal dispersal of the representatives of each group—is, we contend, probably the more common picture that comes to mind when people hear King's rhetoric. The symbolism of integration has often involved the idea that in an integrated world people of different colors will be distributed evenly throughout a population, or an organiza-tion, or an institution, as if on a checkerboard. When Elizabeth Eckford, one of the Little Rock Nine who integrated Central High School in Little Rock, Arkansas, in 1957, prepared for her first day of school, she sewed herself a dress with a border consisting of black and white checks. Dur-ing the fiftieth-anniversary celebrations of the events in Little Rock, this dress became a museum piece, included in a traveling exhibit. Its symbol-ism is impossible to miss.

Strikingly, King's imagined table of brotherhood, Eckford's vision as expressed through her dress, and popular ways of imagining integration too always exceeded mathematical reality. In 1960, African Americans, then still the largest ethnic minority, constituted just under 10 percent of the American population. It was never possible for black and white to be, as in King's metaphor, elbow to elbow, in the sense of evenly distributed throughout the population. To whatever degree the symbolism of integration inspired this mental image, it oriented people toward a mathematical fantasy. Demographic realities would have dictated that on the checkerboard of integration, there would have been one black square for every nine white squares.[1] For mathematical reasons, there has historically never been any realistic chance of Americans of different races or ethnicities being genuinely elbow to elbow throughout the entire social fabric of the nation, yet the goal laid out for us was nonetheless spiritual affinity. The gap between reality and the imagined utopia has strained the project of integration.

This volume affirms the goals of nondiscrimination, desegregation of opportunity and mobility, and, yes, even integration, but we offer a more modest definition of integration, a more mathematically realistic vision of what life would be like in a genuinely integrated world. Rather than suggesting that integration requires full spiritual affinity, we argue herein that it requires merely an ethos of nondomination, that is, of social equality. Rather than arguing that it requires statistical mirroring, we argue that it requires social patterning that flows from institutions and practices of nondomination. We focus on social norms—on the tacit understandings developed in a society about how members of that society should treat one another in their actions. In this regard, our focus is on relationality—how people interact with each other and the implicit rules that structure those interactions—not on the emotional bonds among them.[2] The papers in this volume have treated social difference and even social distance as a necessary feature of human societies; we think a certain lumpiness in the distribution of people from different backgrounds across organizations is inevitable. We also think, though, that the goal should be to ensure that any group-based social patterning is disconnected from injustice. This is a very great challenge indeed. How to achieve it?

That disconnection of social difference from injustice depends on finding a path toward difference without domination, a way of decoupling emergent forms of social differentiation from the mechanisms that result in oppression. The chapters in the volume have spelled out in great detail a diversity of visions for what is required of social relations stripped of habits, practices, and patterns of domination. The authors in this volume join the swelling ranks of scholars exploring relationality and social equality, first among them Axel Honneth, Elizabeth Anderson, Pierre Rosanvallon, Carol Gould, and Niko Kolodny.[3]

In human life, social, political, and economic realms are integrally related to one another. We might think of the social realm as equivalent,
roughly, to civil society—the domain of the family, of churches and universities and other associational organizations and institutions, of the
media and producers of culture. We might think of the political realm
as comprising the formal institutions of the state, from its highest level
of national legislatures and executive bodies to city councils and school
boards and local water districts. We can think of the economic realm as
consisting, of course, of firms and profit-seeking entities but also of the
various mechanisms of distribution, including the family and the state
but also public services and infrastructure like transportation systems. In
other words, although in this volume we often use the categories of the
social, political, and economic as if they were separable, they are instead
thickly intertwining.[4] The analytical distinction can nonetheless be helpful. Very often in the scholarship of the disciplines represented in this volume—economics, psychology, political science, law, sociology, history,
and philosophy—the starting-point assumption is that economic relations govern all else. In this volume we flipped that paradigm on its head.
Consistently these papers argue for the importance of the relational, the
social, the associational to the emergence of structural facts about modern societies. All the contributors to this volume hope to nudge practi-
tioners of their home disciplines toward a strengthened focus on relationality and the social realm.

As we sought both to redefine and to reimagine integration, then, we
also sought to drive a paradigm change within our disciplines. The key
concepts that have shifted over the course of our work together are ideas
of justice, statistical mirroring, identity, and groups as the building blocks
of social organization.

Martin Luther King suggested that America might imagine itself able
to complete the project of democracy. We make a slightly different and
less lofty suggestion. Group-based social patterning is, we think, a permanent feature of human experience. The goal is to disconnect that
patterning from injustice and domination. Doing so, however, requires
understanding the hydraulics of inequality. This in turn requires being
constantly at the ready to see new forms of inequality as they begin to
emerge and to identify the mechanisms for undoing them. Completing
democracy, we think, is not about achieving spiritual affinity across all
lines of difference but of establishing a baseline expectation that respect
for human dignity and practices of nondomination govern all social relations. It is also about being repeatedly ready to repair social relationships
as impairments from domination continuously emerge. Democracy and

justice, then, are not to be completed but must be constantly repaired and renewed.

Notes

1. For a good overview of the mathematical realities, see Ingraham, "Three Quarters of Whites Don't Have Any Non-white Friends."

2. On relationality in sociology, key texts include Bourdieu, *Outline of a Theory of Practice*; Small, *Unanticipated Gain*; Tilly and Tarrow, *Contentious Politics*; and Honneth, *Struggle for Recognition*.

In political philosophy, see Pettit, *Just Freedom*; Kolodny, "Rule over None I: What Justifies Democracy?"; Kolodny, "Rule over None II: Social Equality and the Justification of Democracy"; Rosanvallon, *Society of Equals*; Allen, *Talking to Strangers*; Allen, *Our Declaration*; Viehoff, "Democratic Equality and Political Authority"; Ferguson, *Sharing Democracy*; Anderson, *Imperative of Integration*; Anderson, "What Is the Point of Equality?"

3. See previous note.

4. For an account of how social, political, and economic domains intersect to structure the public sphere, see Allen, "Reconceiving Public Spheres." See also Habermas, *Between Facts and Norms*.

Works Cited

Allen, Danielle. *Our Declaration: A Reading of the Declaration of Independence in Defense of Equality*. New York: W. W. Norton, 2014.

Allen, Danielle. "Reconceiving Public Spheres: The Flow Dynamics Model." In *From Voice to Influence: Understanding Citizenship in a Digital Age*, edited by Danielle Allen and Jennifer Light, 178–209. Chicago: University of Chicago Press, 2015.

Allen, Danielle. *Talking to Strangers*. Chicago: University of Chicago Press, 2004.

Anderson, Elizabeth. *The Imperative of Integration*. Princeton, NJ: Princeton University Press, 2010.

Anderson, Elizabeth. "What Is the Point of Equality?" *Ethics* 109, no. 2 (January 1999): 287–337.

Bourdieu, Pierre. *Outline of a Theory of Practice*. Translated by R. Nice. Cambridge: Cambridge University Press, 1977.

Ferguson, Michaele. *Sharing Democracy*. New York: Oxford University Press, 2012.

Habermas, Jürgen. *Between Facts and Norms: Contributions to a Discourse Theory of Law and Democracy*. Translated by William Rehg. Cambridge, MA: MIT Press, 1996.

Honneth, Axel. *The Struggle for Recognition: The Moral Grammar of Social Conflicts*. Translated by Joel Anderson. Cambridge, MA: MIT Press, 1996.

Ingraham, Christopher. "Three Quarters of Whites Don't Have Any Non-white Friends." *Washington Post*, August 25, 2014.

Kolodny, Niko. "Rule over None I: What Justifies Democracy?" *Philosophy and Public Affairs* 42, no. 3 (2014): 195–229.

Kolodny, Niko. "Rule over None II: Social Equality and the Justification of Democracy." *Philosophy and Public Affairs* 42, no. 4 (2014): 287–336.

Pettit, Philip. *Just Freedom: A Moral Compass for a Complex World*. New York: W. W. Norton, 2014.

Rosanvallon, Pierre. *The Society of Equals*. Cambridge, MA: Harvard University Press, 2014.

Small, Mario. *Unanticipated Gains: Origins of Network Inequality in Everyday Life*. New York: Oxford University Press, 2010.

Tilly, Charles, and Sidney Tarrow. *Contentious Politics*. New York: Oxford University Press, 2006.

Viehoff, Daniel. "Democratic Equality and Political Authority." *Philosophy and Public Affairs* 42, no. 4 (2014): 337–75.

Index

on the Intellectual Character, and Civic and Political Condition of the Colored People of the United States, 65, 72
Eckford, Elizabeth, 340
economic theory, inadequate for explaining racial inequality, 18, 171–84
Educational Goods (Swift et al.), 3
18MR ("18 Million Rising"), 208
80-20 Educational Foundation, 209, 211
Eizenstat, Stu, 198
Ely, John Hart, 248
Encyclopaedia Britannica, 297
equality: affirmative action and, 266–71, 274–79; decentralization's roles concerning, 228–31, 238–43; in democracies, 148–49; federalism and, 231; of liberties, 43–52; national norms of, 228–29, 233–43; politics vs. law as means of assuring, 234–35, 238–43; universality of, 149–50, 168n16, 168n17. See also inequalities; moral equality; political equality (public autonomy)
essentialist theories, 96, 98, 99, 105–6, 181–82, 273, 280n8
Esteban, Joan, 296–97
Ethnolinguistic Fractionalization Index (ELF), 287, 296–97, 302
Europe, census administration in, 292
European Union, freedom of association within, 313

Fazio, R. H., 131
Fearon, J., 297, 304
Federal Bureau of Investigation (FBI), 194
federalism: disaggregated character of, 231–32, 238; and equality, 231; misconceptions of, 228; national power in relation to, 233, 234; objections to, 228–29, 233; state and local impacts on, 232; uses of, 229, 238–39. See also decentralization
Ferguson, Missouri, police-involved shooting in, 164, 189, 213, 230, 249–50
Ferracioli, Luara, 312
Filipino American Democratic Club, 200

First Amendment, 238, 241
Fish, Stanley, 281n25
Fisher, Abigail, 206
Fisher v. University of Texas, 206, 208
Flint, Michigan, 250
Ford, Richard T., 255n89
Forman, James, Jr., 245; Locking Up Our Own, 93
Foucault, Michel, 281n20
Fourteenth Amendment, 207, 248
framing effects, 129
Francis, A., 299
Frankfurt, Harry, 268
Fraser, Nancy, 263, 280n1
Frederick Douglass' Papers (newspaper), 73
freedom. See liberties/freedom
freedom of association, 35–36, 43–45, 313, 319–27
Freedom's Journal (newspaper), 64, 68
French Revolution, 12, 13, 68, 149, 151
Freud, Sigmund, 171
Fryer, Roland, 103
Fugitive Slave Law, 72–74
Fuller, Lon, 162

Gadhafi, Muammar, 160
Gardner, David, 204
Gates, Henry Louis, Jr., 103
Gerken, Heather, 6, 18, 70, 94, 107
Germany: affirmative action in, 19, 265, 280n4; Federal Anti-Discrimination Agency, 127
Gibson, J. J., 125
Glaude, Eddie, 70
Glazer, Nathan, 213n11
good. See human good
Gould, Carol, 341
Granovetter, Mark, 10
Gratz v. Bollinger, 116
Griggs v. Duke Power Co., 96
Groubert, Sean, 102
groups: formation of, 10–11; heterogeneous, 287–90, 304–5; identity of, 254n76, 255n93; implicit bias related to membership in, 121–23; statistical mirroring of, 10
Grutter v. Bollinger, 116

opportunity costs, 325–26

opportunity hoarding, 45, 47, 273–74, 276, 278, 281n24

oppositional identities, 180, 185n7

Other Backward Classes (OBCs), 280n3, 296, 299–300

Padgett, John, 10

parental leave and allowance, 266, 277, 279

Patel community, 302

Patterson, Orlando, 83n9

personal autonomy: intrinsic value of, 28–29; moral equality and, 36–37; negative liberties linked to, 30; political equality in relation to, 31–37, 43–44, 50–52; Rawls and, 28–34, 37, 44

Pettit, Philip, 5, 38, 60, 61, 76–79, 81–82, 86n62, 251n21

Pfaff, John, 107

Phillips, Anne, 256n99

Piketty, Thomas, 2

Polarization Index, 287, 296–97, 302

police-involved shootings, 97, 102–4, 124, 164, 169n39, 189, 212

political equality (public autonomy): access to decision-making as component of, 39; ancients vs. moderns on, 30–32; components of, 37–43; co-ownership of political institutions as component of, 42; decentralization as means of, 244–47; economic realm's effect on, 49–50; epistemic egalitarianism as component of, 39–40; as human good, 28–31; intrinsic value of, 28–29, 33–34, 36, 52; justice grounded in, 28–31, 46, 48–49, 53n5; moral equality in relation to, 36–37, 52; as multivalent good, 29, 32; non-domination as component of, 38; personal autonomy in relation to, 30–37, 43–44, 50–52; positive liberties linked to, 30; reciprocity as component of, 41–42. See also democracy; dignity

Porter, S., 303

positive liberties, 5, 30–32, 36–37, 43–44

Powell, Lewis, 201–2

Princeton Trilogy, 117

Princeton University, 208

Project on Fair Representation, 189, 206

proportional representation. See statistical mirroring/proportional representation

Proposition 209 (California), 209

Purna Swaraj (India), 14

Putnam, Robert, 177

quotas, 265

race: attitudes about, 116–18; classification by, 69–71, 74, 80, 173–75; collection of data on, 288, 291–93, 298–99; concept of, 173–75, 255n89; crime in relation to, 95–110; domination as productive of, 173, 179, 181; implicit bias concerning, 119–39; incarceration rates by, 1, 2, 8, 93, 95–96, 105–8, 193; inequalities associated with, 173, 175–84, 192–93; and marriage, 182–83; relationality and, 171–84; scholarship on, 2; social construction of, 173–75, 179, 255n89; statistical mirroring applied to issues of, 192–93; stereotypes based on, 98–110; stigma associated with, 173, 175–84, 281n25

racial classification, 69–71, 74, 80, 173–75

racial domination: African American intellectual responses to, 59–76; African American solidarity as weapon against, 70–71; civic virtue under, 62, 64–76; cultural extension of slavery as, 62–63, 79–83, 105–6, 110; non-domination in context of, 63

racial stigma, 173, 175–84, 281n25

racism, entrenchment of, in United States, 233–35

Rawls, John, 4, 28–37, 43–44, 48–51, 53n11, 53n12, 54n22, 55n27, 268–69, 272, 275, 324, 326, 336n24

Ray, Debraj, 297

reciprocity, 41–42

Reconstruction Amendments, 234, 235

redistricting, 42

Author Bios

DANIELLE ALLEN

Danielle Allen, James Bryant Conant University Professor at Harvard University, and director of Harvard's Edmond J. Safra Center for Ethics, is a political theorist who has published broadly in democratic theory, political sociology, and the history of political thought. She is the author of many books, including *Our Declaration: A Reading of the Declaration of Independence in Defense of Equality* (2014), *Education and Equality* (2016), and *Cuz: The Life and Times of Michael A.* (2017).

ROHINI SOMANATHAN

Rohini Somanathan is professor of economics at the Delhi School of Economics. Her research focuses on the evolution of group identities, inequality, and public goods.

MELVIN ROGERS

Melvin Rogers is associate professor of political science at Brown University. He is the author of *The Undiscovered Dewey: Religion, Morality, and the Ethos of Democracy*, editor of John Dewey, *The Public and Its Problems*, and coeditor of *African American Political Thought: A Collected History*.

RAJIV SETHI

Rajiv Sethi is professor of economics at Barnard College, Columbia University, and an external professor at the Santa Fe Institute. His research examines the manner in which stereotypes affect interactions among strangers, especially in relation to crime and the criminal justice system. In collaboration with Brendan O'Flaherty, he is an author of *Shadows of Doubt: Stereotypes, Crime, and the Pursuit of Justice* (Harvard University Press, 2019).

CALVIN LAI

Calvin Lai is an assistant professor of psychological and brain sciences at Washington University in St. Louis. He studies how people create, interpret, and maintain social group distinctions. He is particularly interested in implicit biases: automatic or unconscious mental processes that create a gap between what people value (e.g., racial equality) and what people do (e.g., racial discrimination). His research focuses on (1) learning how implicit biases change, (2) understanding the consequences of implicit bias for behavior, and (3) developing interventions to reduce the impact of implicit biases on behavior.

MAHZARIN R. BANAJI

Mahzarin Banaji is Richard Clarke Cabot Professor of Social Ethics in the Department of Psychology at Harvard University. Banaji studies the disparities between values and action, and she has explored the implications of her research for questions of individual responsibility and just treatment in democratic societies. Her current research interests focus on how to use scientific knowledge about human minds to improve organizational practices (www.outsmartinghumanminds). Her book with Anthony Greenwald, *Blindspot: Hidden Biases of Good People*, was published by Delacorte.

AJUME WINGO

Ajume Wingo is an associate professor of philosophy, associate director of the Center for Values and Social Policy, and director of the Law and Philosophy Program at the University of Colorado at Boulder and senior fellow at the Duke University's Center for WaSt+Aid.

His book *Veil Politics in Liberal Democratic States* was published by Cambridge University Press. He is the author of numerous published journal articles on democratic politics, election, civic immortality, and civic education.

GLENN C. LOURY

Glenn C. Loury is Merton P. Stoltz Professor of Economics at Brown University. He holds the BA in mathematics (Northwestern) and the PhD in economics (MIT). He is among America's leading critics writing on racial inequality.

ELLEN WU

Ellen D. Wu is associate professor of history and director of the Asian American Studies program at Indiana University Bloomington. As a specialist in twentieth-century US history, she focuses her research and teaching interests on race, migration, and the Pacific World. She is the author of *The Color of Success: Asian Americans and the Origins of the Model Minority* (Princeton, 2014).

HEATHER GERKEN

Heather Gerken is the dean and Sol & Lillian Goldman Professor of Law at Yale Law School. A founder of the "nationalist school" of federalism, she focuses particularly on federalism, diversity, and dissent. She has published in the *Harvard Law Review*, the *Yale Law Journal*, the *Stanford Law Review* as well as numerous popular publications. In 2013 her proposal for creating a "Democracy Index"—a national ranking of election systems—was adopted by the Pew Charitable Trusts, which created the nation's first Election Performance Index.

URS LINDNER

Urs Lindner is assistant professor at the Max-Weber-Center of the University of Erfurt, Germany. He is the author of *Marx und die Philosophie*.

CLAUDIO LÓPEZ-GUERRA

Claudio López-Guerra is associate professor of political science and PPEL (Program in Philosophy, Politics, Economics, and Law) at the University of Richmond. He is particularly interested in the design of democratic institutions, the justification of political rights, and evaluation of public policies for the advancement of social justice. His work has appeared in such journals as the *Journal of Political Philosophy*; *Politics, Philosophy & Economics*; and *Social Theory and Practice*.

www.ingramcontent.com/pod-product-compliance
Lightning Source LLC
Chambersburg PA
CBHW060023030426
42334CB00019B/2153